THE HERALD BOOK OF
OLD FIRM GAMES

THE HERALD BOOK OF

Old Firm

Games

A COMPLETE RECORD OF ALL THE OLD FIRM MATCHES FOUGHT SINCE THE SECOND WORLD WAR

FOREWORDS BY

John Greig and Billy McNeill

Canongate

FIRST PUBLISHED IN GREAT BRITAIN IN 1995 BY CANONGATE BOOKS LTD 14 HIGH STREET
EDINBURGH

PUBLISHER'S NOTE : DUE TO SHORTAGE OF SPACE IN THE BOOK, SOME OF THE MATCH REPORTS
HAVE BEEN ABRIDGED.

COPIES OF MOST PICTURES IN THIS BOOK ARE AVAILABLE FOR PERSONAL OR COMMERCIAL USE.
CONTACT PHOTO SALES DEPARTMENT, CALEDONIAN NEWSPAPERS,
195 ALBION STREET, GLASGOW, G1 1QP

ISBN 0 86241 597 7 cased
ISBN 0 86241 543 8 paper

BRITISH LIBRARY CATALOGUING-IN-PUBLICATION DATA
A CATALOGUE RECORD IS AVAILABLE ON REQUEST FROM THE BRITISH LIBRARY

DESIGNED BY JAMES HUTCHESON
TYPESET BY CORDFALL LTD, 26 CIVIC STREET, GLASGOW
PRINTED IN GREAT BRITAIN BY BPC WHEATONS LTD, EXETER

Contents

Foreword by Billy McNeill   vii

Foreword by John Greig   ix

List of Subscribers   x

The Post War Years   1

The Fifties   17

The Sixties   55

The Seventies   101

The Eighties   153

The Nineties   203

Tables   239

Foreword

Old Firm games are an institution and Scottish football, maybe even the country, would be poorer without them. Although they decorate the fixtures list, perfection is too much to ask for in such heated and defiantly partisan fixtures. Bigotry is the least attractive of the many side issues but it's also difficult to achieve composure and style. Good sense is challenged head on. Happily, more often than not sanity emerges the winner. My opinion is that the standard was better and more relaxed in my day and this is not a blinkered old fogey speaking

In spite of the minefields, many of the games with Rangers in which I played or managed are indelibly printed in my mind. Fans will recall them too. It always riled me that the media previews very nearly put us on a war footing. I always tried to play down enmity and do my best to protect the most important games in our domestic calendar. Of course, there will always be hostility. We felt it before the bus even arrived at Ibrox. I'm sure Rangers felt the same at Celtic Park but I've always counted men like Jim Baxter, John Greig, Davie Wilson and others among genuine friends. In my day there was an understanding of each other's problems and respect for each other's ability. However, the traditions of both clubs encourage bias which people outside Scotland can't understand. I was brought up to believe that religion is a private matter and my dad would have cuffed my ear as a boy if I'd regarded it as a reason for judging people. However, a serious Old Firm flaw is that matches open up the divide, particularly in the West of Scotland, and not enough effort is put into stopping this. The more that can be done to defuse hatred the better. There will never be resistance from players or the clubs. It's silly even to think of abandoning these matches – without them Scottish football would be very ordinary and I mean no disrespect to the 38 other clubs.

At Celtic Park or Ibrox, the air always seems to be charged with electricity before games. We could feel it. The stadiums talked. I enjoyed and absorbed it all. On the pitch we were aware only of incredible noise. It inspired and motivated. Managers could save their breath before the kick-off. When I managed Manchester City, our clashes with United were teethy and combative but were picnics by comparison. The biggest thing was always to go to Ibrox and win, but a point was almost as acceptable. Form goes out the window. Hugh Taylor, a smashing sports-writer in my day, underlined the tightness of Old Firm matches by saying jokingly in a preview: "Only a fool would predict the outcome, but I think it'll be a draw!"

One of the most significant Old Firm games I played in was on October 23, 1965, because not only did we beat Rangers 2-1 in the League Cup Final, but it was only few months after a 3-2 Scottish Cup Final victory over Dunfermline in which I headed the winner from a Charlie Gallagher corner with nine minutes to go. The League Cup win confirmed our success. The 1969 Cup Final was another I recall vividly and not just because I headed a goal in the second minute and Celtic won 4-0. George Connnelly, who was a marvellous youngster, wandered round John Greig and 'keeper Martin to stick the ball in the net for no 3. It became a coasting case which doesn't happen often in Celtic-Rangers collisions. Generally, they taught us never to take anything for granted.

In season 1971-72 we beat Rangers twice in the League Cup - and then lost 4-1 to Partick Thistle in the final. We beat Rangers 2-0 and 3-0 even though both matches were at Ibrox. I recall in the first telling Kenny Dalglish to take a penalty in his Old Firm debut. I wanted to get a goal against his name for posterity but I certainly had no worries about him being too nervous. Kenny even took time to tighten his bootlace before driving the ball away from Peter McCloy.

There was always drama. None more than in our 1987 Ibrox League game with Rangers in which referee Jim Duncan ordered off Frank McAvennie, 'keeper Chris Woods and central defender Terry Butcher. This led to court proceedings involving these three and Graham Roberts. Frank was 'not guilty', Roberts 'not proven', but Woods was fined £500 and Butcher £250. Old Firm games are placed under a special microscope and these events underlined this. Other players are never under the same scrutiny and the incidents would have been left to the SFA to handle. The Crown Office action, in my opinion, was over-zealous. It was a sad day football.

Another very significant game was in the 1980 Cup Final when we beat Rangers 1-0 in extra time. Danny McGrain hit a shot and George McLuskey got in the way to deflect the ball into goal. Mike Conroy was drafted in at centre half and was the Man of the Match. But a great performance by Mike and Celtic was overshadowed by crowd riots which needed mounted police to quell. I hated anything to tarnish Celtic or indeed the Old Firm. We were always warned that our actions could cause an awful lot of distress and problems off the field. As a manager I always reminded teams to keep the head. Despite everything I wouldn't have missed a single Old Firm game as player or manager. Not for anything.

Billy McNeill

Foreword

Many people who watch and have played in Old Firm matches will say that it's the best club match in the world. Obviously this could be questioned by people from Liverpool, London, Milan or Turin. But having had the opportunity of participating in Old Firm games over a long number of years, more than most, it was always a fascinating environment to play in.

Because of the great pride and passion in each club, I'm quite sure that the majority of supporters leave for the game thinking that as long as they didn't lose the game, they'd be 50% happy. It's one of the few occasions that supporters of both Rangers and Celtic would settle for a draw. The reason for this is that so much attention is paid to these games, irrespective of whether it was a cup game, league match or whatever.

The thing is, each set of supporters dreads going into their local pub that night, or their work on the Monday morning, after a defeat by the old enemy. Sometimes that is even the first thought which crosses the fan's mind when the final whistle blows for the end of 90 minutes' play. This is a game where you either have to be a very brave man, or completely stupid, to forecast the result beforehand – that's how unpredictable Old Firm games are.

The hardest question I get asked is how the next one is going to go, because they are so hard to analyse. This stems from the players on the park because their great determination and passion for the club to beat their biggest rivals makes all Old Firm games, no matter the occasion, like cup finals.

Many players have made their reputations in Old Firm games. These matches have a habit of throwing up personalities from both clubs over a number of years. However, they have also signalled the end of players' careers because if you made a mistake in an Old Firm game and the match was lost as a result, the supporters took a long time to forget about it.

Rangers and Celtic obviously try their utmost to beat each other. But contrary to what many people think, or have thought in the past, and irrespective of the competition on the field, many of the two sets of players were very friendly. Much of that came from our international trips together.

There have been some marvellous individual confrontations over the years with players of each side and that will continue. It was always a very tension-filled atmosphere, but I think that has been lessened by the League reconstruction which forces the two clubs to face each other four times a season at least.

The introduction of English, Irish and foreign players has added a new dimension to these games. But testimony to the point I made right at the start, is that those foreigners who come into the Old Firm environment are usually in awe of the occasion. They can't believe the atmosphere and the pace at which the game is played at.

Having played in so many of these matches, obviously there were plenty of memorable incidents in my favour and against me. But the one that remains my favourite is the sight of Tam Forsyth scoring the winner in the 1973 Scottish Cup Final against Celtic from six inches with the studs of his boots. Tam never scored goals and it was nice to see a guy like him score such an important goal in such an important cup final.

The supremacy of Rangers and Celtic has been questioned and challenged over the years, but the Old Firm always come out of any slump to answer their critics. You only have to look at the number of times the two clubs have won League Championships, League Cups and Scottish Cups.

From a Rangers point of view, I've seen many great players grace the Old Firm stage. From Jim Baxter, Ralph Brand, Davie Wilson, Jimmy Millar to Colin Stein, Willie Johnston and Alex MacDonald right through to Ally McCoist, Terry Butcher, Ray Wilkins and Graeme Souness. Now, like Celtic we have a new era to look forward to with the likes of Brian Laudrup and Paul Gascoigne. Having players of that stature can only add to the magic of the Old Firm encounters which I relished so much and still look forward to every month of every season.

John Greig

Rangers Supporters Subscribers List

F.J. Addison
Gordon Addison
Alexander P. Agnew
W. B. Ainslie
A. F. Allan
David B. Allison
Robert Allison
Ivan Andonovic
Bill Arbuckle
Lesley Arbuckle
Brian E. Armstrong
William Arnott
Jim and Gary Baillie
A.J. Barclay
Graham Barclay
Tom Barrie
James S. Beedie
Ralph Bell
Gordon Bennett
Alistair Berry
Iain Bisset
James A. Black
James Martin Boult
James Boyce
Alan Boyd
George Douglas Boyd
Stewart Boyd
William Boyd
Graham W. Brannigan
Alex Brown
R.G. Browne
William H. M. Brown
Alan Bruce
James Bruce
Richard F. Bruce
Mark Bryce
Douglas W. Buchanan
Alan Buick
Ernest Burtt
Margaret Bux
Derek Calikes
John T. Cameron
David Campbell
Douglas W. Campbell
Graham M.M. Campbell
Hugh Campbell
Duncan Chalmers
George Chalmers
William Chapman
Angus Chisholm
James D. Chisholm
Scott J. Christian
Jamie Clark
James Clements
David Collins
Christopher Colquhoun

J.B. Colquoun
Bill Condie
David T. Cook
Kenneth G. Cook
John Coyne
Robert Craig
William J. Crompton
Richard J. H. Davidson
Campbell Davie
David Davies
Graham Davies
Robert Deans
David C.M. Dearie
Ian M. Dempster
George Dey
Robert Dodds
Allan Downie
John Drake
Thomas Rogers Duff
Ronnie Dunachie
David Dunn
George Easton
Alan Elliott
Philip Ewing
David Falconer
Nick R. Fannin
Andrew Farrell
Mark Faulds
Alexander Fawcett
Peter A. Fernie
Louise Findlay
Alex Flockhart
Iain M. Forbes
Tom Forrester
Jim Forrest
Alan C. Fotheringham
Alan W. Frame
Raymond Francis
Craig Fraser
Peter Munro Fraser
John S. Fulton
Robert Fulton
Jim Geddes
Kenneth W. Gillespie
David Gillon
Norman Gordon
Robert C. Gorman
David Alexander Grant
R.L. Grant
Archie Gray
William MacLean Gray
Ralston J. Green
George Gruber
Agnes Haining
David Hale
Kenneth Hall

Kevin G. Hall
Malcolm Hall
John William Hamilton
Douglas Hannan
Alex Harris
Derek Harrison
Barry Hastie
R.G. Hattle
Archie Hayes
David Henderson
Jim Henderson
John Henderson
Ian Hendrie
Les Hetherington
Charles Heyburn
James Hill
Samuel Ferguson Hood
Craig Alan Hosie
Jim Hosie
Archie Houston
Harry Houston
Billy Howard
Ian Howatson
Douglas R. Hume
Ian Hunter
Derek John Hyndman
Dean Inglis
Colin Jack
Daniel Johnston
Carl N. Jones
David Kearney
Stewart Keddie
David Kermack
Alan Kerr
Archibald McV. Kerr
E. M. Kerr
Joseph Prior Kyle Kilpatrick
Margaret Kilpatrick
John H. King
Gordon Kirker
Alan Kirkwood, Jnr.
Harry Allan Laidlaw
Stewart Lang
Tom Laughland
Christopher Lawn
Gavin Lawson
John Leishman
Gordon Liddell
William Linton
Danny Litster
Alan Livie
Douglas Livie
Gordon Lowe
Ben MacCorquodale
Angus MacDonald
Calum MacDonald

John William Macdonald
Neil A. MacDonald
D. J. MacFadyen
W. Macfarlane
Allan M. MacIntyre
Iain Mackay
Rhuaridh MacKay
William J. MacKenzie
Frank Maclachlan
Rev. Dr. David W. Maclagan
Andrew MacLaren
Calum Maclean
Iain Macleod
Iain William MacLeod
Neil MacLeod
Rod MacLeod
Douglas MacNeilage
Gordon S. Macpherson
Alistair W. Malloch
Alexander Mann
Alistair I. Martin
Campbell Martin
Robert Martin
Donald D.M. Masterton
Alister Mathers
Sheila A. McAinsh
Iain W. McArthur
Jas T. McCabe
John Donald McCallum
Geoff McCartney
David McCaughie
Scott James McColl
Thomas Ronald McCormick
James N. McCosh
William A.M. McCracken
Gordon McCreath
Paul McCulloch
Alan McDermott
Colin McDonald
D.A. McDowall
Iain McEwan
Nancy McEwan
John George McFadyen
William McFaull
Graham McIntyre
Colin A. McKellar
Sandy McKenzie
Joyce McKerley
Donald P. McLarty
Kenneth F. McLean
Ford McLeod
William McLeod
A. McLerie
Kenneth McMaster
Bernard McMillan
Angus A. McMurchy
John McNicol
W.A. McNicol
William A. McNicol

Colin McPhail
Donald McPhee
Douglas McPherson
Bill McPhie
Colin McQueen
David McQueen
Stephen McRae
Eric Merrall
Graham Miller
Harry Miller
Andrew W. Milligan
Wallace Milligan
George C. Mills
Alexander F. Mitchell
David Mitchell
Neil Mitchell
Ross Mitchell
James F. F. Moffat
Neville E. Moir
Alistair C. Morrison
William D. Morrison
Alistair Moyes
Jim Moyes
J. Muir
Craig Mundy
Kenneth Munro
Grant Murchie
Dr. D.L. Murdoch
James K.W. Murphy
Fiona Murray
Kenneth Murray
Stewart Gray Murray
John Neill
Jensen Newton
Alan B. Niblett
Angus Nicholson
David Nimmo
Andy Noble
Ewan R. Ogilvie
A. O'Pray
Alasdair Paterson
Ian Payne
W. A. Pearson
William Peden
David Plews
David Pollock
Steven McEwan Porter
Robert Rae
Julie Rachael Ralston
David M. Ramsay
Ian Ramsey
James George Rankine
Angus Macdonald Reid
John Reid
David Rennie
Robert J. Richardson
Margaret Ridland
Iain Ritchie
William Rodney

Andrew Russell
Alexander Scott
Douglas Scott
James L. Scott
Thomas A. Scott
William J. Scott
Colin Sellars
Gordon D. Shand
William F. Shannon
Robert Shaw
Jack Shepherd
Robert Shepherd
Gordon Shiels
Iain Sinclair
Angus L. Skilling
Craig Smillie
David George Smith
Ian A. Smith
James M. Smith
T. R. Smith
William Smith
David Smollett
George Sneddon
George Stevenson
George M. Stewart
Hugh Stewart
Ian Stewart
Neil R. Stobie
Jean M. Strachan
R. Jody Struthers
Stanley Fletcher Summerfield
Craig R. Sutherland
Dr. Ian A. Sutherland
Robert Taylor
David G. Terris
Tommy Thompson
Greg John Thomson
Ian F. Thomson
Gary Tighe
Alan Topping
Andrew Torrance
A.W. Truman
Andrew I. W. Turnbull
Karen Turnbull
Douglas Walker
Joseph M. Walker
Michael D. Wallis
Robert Ward
Gordon M. Watson
Ian F. White
John C. F. White
W. J. White
James Wilson
Douglas Wilson, Jnr.
L. J. Wilson
Douglas J. Woodhouse
Sandy Workman
Russell L. Yeamans
George Young, Jnr.

Celtic Supporters Subscribers List

Stuart Allan
Andrewina Ball
Samuel J. Ball
Jason Barrie
M.J. Barrie
Charles Barton
Paul Charles Baxter
Peter Bell
William Beresford
David Berry
Stephen Biagioni
Aldo Bove
John Patrick Boyd
Graeme Boyle
James Harkin Boyle
Kevin A. Boyle
Pauline Bradley
Peter Brawley
M.C. Brayford
Hugh Breen
John J. Brolly
Mark Stephen Burke
Michael Burke
John S. Burnett
Andrew Burns
Gary Burns
Kenneth Burns
Peter Burns
Bryan Butler
Jackie Butler
Jamie Byng
John Byrne
Joseph P. Byrnes
John Patrick Cameron
Donald Campbell
Eddie Campbell
Mark W. Campbell
Tom Campbell
Jim Cannovan
Francis Carrigan
Patrick Carr
Gary J. Caulfield
Tracy A. Caulfield
John Charles
Stephen Church
Nicholas P. Ciarella
James R. Clark
Peter S. Clark
Eddie Cocozza
Graeme Christopher Coleman
Tony Conaghan
Mark Condron

Peter Connolly
Tam Conroy
Brendan Corish
Christopher Cowan
John Coyle
Jonathan S. Craig
Gerard P. Crampsie
David M. Crotty
Patricia Cunningham
Richard A. Cunningham
Sean B. Curran
Fraser Currie
John Dallas
Hugh Dempster
Kevin Devine
Lawrence Peter Devlin
Gordon Dickson
Christopher Dixon
Bernard G. Docherty
Kevin Docherty
Neil Docherty
Peter Docherty
Nick Doherty
Jim Donaldson
Paul Donnelly
Steven Donnelly
John Doogan
John Michael Dorrian
Edward Doyle
James T. Doyle
Martin Doyle
Frank Duffy
James Dunn
Kenneth Eadie
Graham S. Farquhar
Tony Farrell
Mark Ferguson
Calum Ferris
B. Finnell
Jimmy Finn
Andrew Fitzpatrick
John H. Fitzsimmons
Mick Forbes
John Forrester
John Fulton
Charles Gallacher
Francis Joseph Gallacher
Gerald Gallacher
Daniel P. Gallagher
Manus Gallagher
Pat Gallen
A.C. Galloway

Gerald Gara
Bill Gaughan
Gordon Gerrard
James Gibb
John Giffen
John Corbett Gillespie
Andrew Gillon
Stewart Glencross
Danny Goldie
Paul Grace
Ian Grant
Harry Gray
Thomas Gray
Stephen Gribben
Robert Grome
George Gruber
David Hand
Martin Hania
Philip Hugh Harkins
Charles Harold
Philip Harris
Hugh Healy
William P. Hendry
John Heron
Tommy Hill
Brian James Hogg
V. Hollywood
Nicky Hood
John Hudson
James Hughes
David Hutchison
Colin Jardine
Andrew Jarvie
Brian John Jones
Kevin Jones
Martin Joyce
James G. Kane
Frank Kelly
Gerard A. Kelly
John Kelly
John Michael Kelly
Liam Kelly
Ruari Kelly
Thomas Kelly
David Kennedy
Paul Kernohan
Gerald Lang
Stephen Lang
Paul D. Leeson
Bobby Lennox
David Lewis
David S. Links

John Lynch
Geo MacAskill, Snr.
Paul MacColl
Alistair A. MacIver
Kenneth Mackintosh
Stephen Mallon
Sheila McAinsh
Jamie McArdle
Kevin McBride
Stephen McBrinn
Colin McCaffery
Francis P. McCaffrey
Michael McCahill
Paul McCallum
Liam McCarron
John McColl
Alice Conlin McCormack
Michael McCready
Edward McDaid
Paul A. McDaid
Stuart McDougall
James F. McEwan
Alistair P.T. McGeough
George McGhee
S. McGinness
S. M. McGinness
Gerard McGlinchey
H.J. McGoldrick
Duncan McGonagle
John McGrady
John McGrevey
Francis McGuigan
Charles McGuire
James McGuire
Joseph McGuire
Ronald McIlwraith
James McIntyre
Joe McIntyre
Mary McIvor
Neil McKay
Joseph McKenna
Hugh McLaughlin
J.C. McLaughlin
Pat McLaughlin
James McLuskey
Brendan McMahon
Mark McManus
Patrick McManus
Thomas McManus
John Ryan McMulkin
Paul James McNamee
Stan McNicol
Peter E. McNiven
Vincent McSherry

James McVeigh
Kevin F. Meledy
Martin Mellon
Douglas Milton
Paul Moodie
Samuel Mooney
Wayne Morrison
Luke Muir
Arthur Mulgrew
James Gerard Mulgrew
Owen Mullan
Robert Mulvey
Andrew Bruce Murdoch
Adrian J. Murphy
Frank M. Murphy
Karie Murphy
Patrick K. Murphy
Peter John Murphy
Alan D. Murray
Allan Murray
James Murray
John W.M. Murray
Laurence Murray
Stephen Murray
Stephen Bernard Murray
Ian Neilson
Frank O'Brien
James O'Brien
John O'Donnell
Diarmid C. O'Hara
John Gerard O'Hare
Hugh O'Neil
Paul O'Reilly
Liam Paterson
William Peden
Vincent Pinterich
Paul Pisacane
David A. Pitt
Gordon Pittendrigh
James Anderson Porter
Tommy Porter
Lesley Provan
Gerry Quinn
John L. Quinn
Colin Rafferty
James Rafferty
John R. Rankin
Michael Redwood
Eric Reid
Stewart Reid
Neil Rocks
Gordon M. Rose
James Peter Ross
James Rush

Ian Rutherford
James Savage
John Scally
Victor T. Schenk
Jer Scollin
Stephen Scott
John Sharpe
Gordon R. Sharp
Pat Shearer
James Sheridan
Adam Shiels
Alex Simonini
David Simpson
April Smith
Elizabeth Smith
Gordon Smith
Kenneth Raymond Smith
Mark Smith
Martin Smith
Peter Smith
Sean Smith
Thomas G. Smith
John Sneddon
Andy Spence
Iain Spicer
John Pennycook Stewart
Michael Strang
Chris Strickland
Gavin Stronach
Gerard Sundstrem
Brendan Taheny
Damian Paul Taylor
Derek Taylor
Ian Taylor
John Taylor
Peron Thierry
Campbell W. Thomson
Douglas Thomson
Ralph Togneri
Paul Trevisan
Paul Truss
Peter F. Tulips
Jonathan D. Viney
Colynn Walker
Jim Walker
John R. Walker
Kenny Walker
John James Walsh
William Watson
Douglas Wilson
Robert Wilson
Robert D. Wilson
Slat Wilson
Bob Winter
Patrick Woods

The Post War Years

By Jim Reynolds

The Post-war Years, immediately after the war, Rangers dominated Scottish football just as they had done when the government appreciated the need for recreation to continue as normal as possible during the fighting. As well as helping maintain physical fitness, it was seen as a stimulus to morale among the people.

On the declaration of war, football was immediately banned, but when that was lifted things fell quickly into place and the game continued right through until the end of the war, albeit in an unofficial capacity.

In the six seasons of "unofficial" football, Rangers, under the guidance of the legendary Bill Struth, had an impressive haul of trophies - War Cups (2), West League (1), Southern League (5), Summer Cup (1) and League Cup (three).

Struth's forward thinking was the base on which Rangers built their domination of Scottish football after the war. Guest players such as Torry Gillick and Jimmy Caskie, of Everton, were happy to join the club on a full-time basis, joining such stalwarts as Jock Shaw, Willie Woodburn, George Young, Willie Waddell and Willie Thornton.

Celtic, on the other hand, had not enjoyed success during the "unofficial" seasons and their record in the Old Firm meetings was abysmal. Celtic's only trophies during the war years were the Glasgow Cup in season 1940-41, when they beat Rangers 1-0 in the final, and the Charity Cup two seasons later.

The first Old Firm league match in season 1946-47 - played in the old A Division - was a classic at Celtic Park which Rangers won 3-2, and in the return at Ibrox on New Year's Day a crowd of 85,000 saw the two sides draw 1-1. Rangers went on to win the Championship, having already beaten Aberdeen 4-0 to take the League Cup, too.

Celtic had to wait until September 1, 1947 to gain their first post war victory over their old rivals. That was in a League Cup match at Celtic Park. In those days the early stages of the League Cup was made up of sections of four clubs. Despite that 2-0 Old Firm win, Celtic failed to qualify from their section, having lost 2-0 at Ibrox and also having been beaten by Dundee and Third Lanark.

Rangers finished second in the championship to Hibernian, but won the Scottish Cup, beating Morton in the final.

The decade closed with Rangers maintaining the upper hand in Old Firm clashes, but Celtic, with players such as Bobby Evans, Bobby Collins, John McPhail and Charlie Tully, were looking to a brighter future.

Rangers 3, Celtic 1 – Saturday, 25th August, 1945

Play Difficult in High Wind

WELL-BALANCED RANGERS

The standard of play was not high in Saturday's games, when ball control was made especially difficult by the prevailing high wind.

In these circumstances winning the toss was of considerable importance, and in the major event of the day – the Glasgow Cup first-round tie between Rangers and Celtic at Ibrox – Rangers, with the wind behind them, had an interval lead of 3-0.

Paton scored for Celtic when 26 minutes of the second half had gone but Rangers held their two-goal lead to win by 3-1.

Rangers with Dawson and Gray again in the team and Young at centre half, were the better-balanced side throughout a game which fell short of past encounters between the rivals.

Celtic disputed Rangers' opening goal, claiming that Williamson used his arm to control the ball. Young scored Rangers third goal from a penalty and the referee disallowed a well-taken goal by Gillick who went on to score after being injured.

Glasgow Cup, 1st round

Rangers (3) 3	Celtic (0) 1
Williamson	Paton
Gillick	
Young (pen.)	

Rangers 5, Celtic 3 – Saturday, 8th September, 1945

Celtic Still to Win

SUPERIOR IBROX ATTACK

Over 40,000 saw Rangers defeat Celtic at Ibrox for the second time within a fortnight. Celtic played with more spirit than in the recent cup-tie but Rangers were superior at centre-half and at all the forward positions.

The Ibrox team scored twice in the first half with well taken goals by Duncanson and Johnstone and continued to dominate play at the beginning of the second half. In the 17th minute after the restart, however, Delaney scored for Celtic and two minutes later McGinley made the score level.

Rangers reasserted themselves and added quick goals by Venters and Williamson. Ten minutes from the end the latter scored a fifth goal and in the closing minutes Delaney got a third goal for Celtic from a penalty.

Rangers (2) 5	Celtic (0) 3
Duncanson	Delaney 2 (1 pen.)
Johnstone	McGinley
Venters	
Willamson 2	
Attendance	over 40,000

The inimitable Charlie Tully who moved to Glasgow from Belfast Celtic in 1948.

Celtic 0, Rangers 1 – Tuesday, 1st January, 1946
Thornton Scores only Goal of Quiet Game

A goal by Thornton 27 minutes after the start carried Rangers though against Celtic at Parkhead and left the Ibrox club with only five points to secure from their remaining eight matches to make another championship secure.

It was one of the quietest "Old Firm" games on record. The frost-bound ground made accurate and sustained play impossible while the crowd seemed frozen into apathy. After all the complaints about the 75,000 limit for the game (all ticket), the attendance did not seem to be more than 50,000.

All through Rangers were the more polished side, and the goal which gave them the points was the outcome of one of the best moves of the game. Gillick and Thornton moved down the right with close passes and the centre lobbed the ball towards the goal as Gillick ran in. Mallon stopped Gillick's shot but Thornton, following up, collected the ball cleverly and speedily shot it into the corner of the net.

In the matter of pressure Celtic were first. But it was storming football. It had no guile to support it, and it was certainly not good enough to beat players like Shaw, the left back, and Woodburn, who played magnificently.

Celtic had a goal disallowed for offside early on, and just before the interval their wingers sent over a series of well-placed corners, from one of which J. Gallacher headed against the crossbar.

In the second half Celtic pursued their storming tactics, but apart from a Kiernan shot which was brilliantly saved by Shaw, they never looked like scoring. Even when Delaney went to centre-forward it made no difference.

In what combined play there was Thornton and Gillick were outstanding with their short, well-placed passes. Celtic had nothing to compare with the work of these two forwards.

Late on Celtic almost got a goal when Gray and Shaw got mixed up and the ball ran out past the empty goal post.

Celtic (0) 0	Rangers (1) 1
	Thornton
Attendance	approx 50,000

CELTIC :– MILLER; HOGG AND MILNE; LYNCH, MALLON AND MACAULAY; DELANEY AND KIERNAN; J. GALLACHER; W. GALLAGHER AND PATON.

RANGERS :– SHAW; GRAY AND SHAW; WATKINS, WOODBURN AND SYMON; WADDELL AND GILLICK; THORNTON AND CASKIE.

Celtic 1, Rangers 3 – Tuesday, 14th May, 1946
"New" Rangers Success

By defeating Celtic at Celtic Park last night Rangers qualified to meet Third Lanark in the Charity Cup final at Hampden Park on June 8th.

In the first half – a goalless one – the best shot came from Rangers right back, Cox – an indication of the lack of penetrative power of both forwards.

Rangers pressure in the second half culminated in Duncanson shooting past Miller, and then came a burst of scoring with three goals in four and a half minutes, Thornton and Duncanson counting for Rangers and Rae for Celtic.

Celtic scored before Rangers second goal, but the referee's whistle had already gone for a foul against Woodburn, and in an all-in raid on the Ibrox goal the ball came off the crossbar and was kicked clear by a defender attending on the goal line.

During the first half the ball burst, and the second one went soft and had to be replaced.

Duncanson showed to advantage for the Rangers who had nine positional changes – and seven in personnel – from the team which lost to Aberdeen on Saturday.

Charity Cup semi-final

Celtic (0) 1	Rangers (0) 3
Rae	Duncanson 2
	Thornton

CELTIC :– MILLER; HOGG AND MILNE; MCPHAIL, MALLON AND PETERSON; HAZLETT AND KIERNAN; RAE; SIRRELL AND O'SULLIVAN.

RANGERS :– BROWN; COX AND LINDSAY; WATKINS, WOODBURN AND RAE; WADDELL AND DUNCANSON; THORNTON; WILLIAMSON AND MCNEE.

Celtic 0, Rangers 0 – Saturday, 1st June, 1946

Goalkeeping at its Best

It is a football maxim that a goalkeeper thrives on work. The more he gets, the better eventually is his performance. That was certainly true in the case of Miller of Celtic in this Victory cup semi-final at Hampden Park on Saturday. The match had no sooner begun than he made a breathtaking save at the feet of Thornton, Rangers' centre-forward, and from that moment the goalkeeper defied the Ibrox attacker.

Miller's uncanny anticipation of the flight of the ball, whether on the ground or in the air, had to be seen to be believed.

Thornton, Waddell and Duncanson in turn had efforts to score that would have beaten most goalkeepers. Thornton's is worthy of description. It was a bullet-like drive that was going away from Miller and making for the top left-hand corner of the net. Miller, almost at the opposite post, rose to it in a manner reminiscent of the great John Thomson and touched the ball over the bar for a corner.

Celtic can thank Miller for earning them a replay although it would be unfair not to mention the splendid defensive work of his colleagues, especially of Hogg, Mallon and MacAuley. The last two players were not perhaps always scientific in the method of their approach, but they were effective and kept their eye on the ball, a specially important point when opposed as they were by Miller and Thornton. Macauley kept the inside-right fairly quiet and the result was that Waddell had to do a bit of roaming for the ball on his own account.

Corbett, the Celtic centre-half, had perhaps the most difficult job trying to quell Thornton and if he started shakily he finished up well in the picture.

Rangers, better together than Celtic, again had that uncertainty in defence which has been with them more or less for the past few weeks. If the Celtic forwards had been worth their salt they would have turned quite a few openings to account. But only Kiernan at inside-right made his presence felt; the others lacked the punch and spirit of adventure which characterised Celtic teams of the past.

Waddell and Thornton were happy warriors for Rangers who still have a left-wing problem.

Victory Cup semi-final

Celtic (0) 0   Rangers (0) 0

Rangers 2, Celtic 0 – Wednesday, 5th June, 1946

Rangers in Victory Cup Final

By defeating Celtic in the semi-final replay of the Scottish Victory Cup competition at Hampden Park, Glasgow last night, Rangers qualified to meet Hibernian in the final on the same ground on June 15.

A scene remarkable in Scottish senior football occurred in the second half and completely spoiled what had previously been a hard and sporting game.

About 20 minutes from the end Rangers were awarded a penalty kick when Thornton, their centre-forward, was tackled and fell. After a protest by the entire Celtic team the referee ordered off Paterson, the Celtic inside-left, who had been playing centre-forward at the time of the incident and who had been warned in the first half about appealing against a decision.

Celtic continued to protest, and after the ball had been replaced for Young to take the spot-kick Mallan kicked it away. The left back was immediately ordered off in turn.

POLICE ARRESTS

Then when Young, Rangers' centre-half, had converted the penalty, one of the 43,000 supporters broke on to the field. Play was stopped until he had been arrested by the police, who made three further arrests.

Later, an obvious penalty-kick was denied Rangers – as obvious as the one they failed to get in the first five minutes of the match when Miller, the Celtic goalkeeper, in desperation gripped Gillick's ankles when the inside-right had side-stepped his attempted dive to save.

Celtic, with a most unusual assortment of forwards, used the ball to extremely good advantage in the early minutes, Kiernan and Paterson being specially useful in contriving to keep the ball on the ground when they made the pass. But with the wind against them, the Celtic defence found many of their clearances ballooning back on them and, as on Saturday, Miller had hardly an idle minute.

Rangers, more dangerous near goal, were however clearly superior. After Waddell had shot a most deliberate goal from Gillick's speediest service, the crossbar kept out a mashing drive from the inside-right.

The gallantry of Celtic's defence let their team turn round only one goal down – a slender enough lead for Rangers, who then faced the wind. But after only a minute Gallacher was injured for the second time in the match and had to go outside-left. Soon afterwards he came down again, and had latterly to be carried off on a stretcher. With Sirrell limping on the right wing and then the ordering-off of the two others, Celtic were left with seven men and a cripple. Rangers, one felt, were not unsympathetic towards their opponents' plight and made no attempts to press home unduly their advantage.

Victory Cup semi-final replay

Rangers (1) 2	Celtic (0) 0
Waddell	
Young (pen.)	
Attendance	43,000

Celtic 2, Rangers 3 – Saturday, 9th September, 1946

Celtic's Failing

Playing with something like the fighting spirit of the teams of the past, Celtic came near to achieving a success that, more than any other, which would have re-established them in the good graces of their sorely tried following.

It takes more than sheer enthusiasm to beat Rangers, however, and there was not a sufficient leavening of skill in Celtic's effort to transform them into a winning side. In Kiernan they had the cleverest individual player on the field, and in the first half particularly he had Symon running round in circles.

But Kiernan was afflicted, as all his team-mates were, with the most troublesome weakness of the footballer – failing in the art of making the pass. Rangers were overwhelmingly superior in this phase of the game. Cox, Stead, Gillick, Duncanson, Caskie and Symon could – and did – find their man with great accuracy, and despite all the feinting and swerving of Kiernan, Symon, when he did succeed in the tackle gave his tormentor an object lesson on how to part with the ball.

Rangers must have been well satisfied with the play of Stead, deputy for Waddell. Although obviously more left-footed than right, the outside right struck a happy partnership with Gillick and their understanding led to the best combined football of the game. One splendid run from midfield in which Stead and Gillick twice interchanged positions, before Stead's final pass was whipped against the post by his partner, was the highlight.

Parlane, like Stead, playing his first game for Rangers' first eleven this season, was generally mastered by Corbett and the other newcomer to First League football this season, McMillan of Celtic, though he defended stubbornly and well, was unable to supply the urge from wing half that Celtic's forwards needed so much.

There were far too many free kicks in this match. Each side was penalised 17 times and Kiernan, Gallagher and Macaulay each had a word from the referee, the first-named presumably for questioning a decision.

Celtic thrice claimed penalty kicks for handling and seemed unlucky not to be awarded one when late in the game Young's arms stopped Brogan's cross-shot. Against that, both Gillick and Stead both came down in tackles in the Celtic penalty area which might well have called for the full punishment. The referee was always well up with the play, however, and his handling of the entire match must be commended.

Celtic (1) 2	Rangers (2) 3
Keiran	Duncanson 2
Bogan	Parlane

Rangers 1, Celtic 1 – Wednesday, 1st January, 1947

Fifty Free-Kicks in Ibrox Game

A record crowd for a club game in Britain this season – over 80,000 - attended what was advertised as a football match at Ibrox stadium yesterday. The majority of them must have been sadly disappointed; rarely has a greater travesty of a sporting function been perpetrated on a football public that is by no means unused to seeing Rangers and Celtic in opposition destroying the good name of the game.

It would almost be possible to dismiss this latest exhibition by reporting that 50 free-kicks were given during the 90 minutes allocated for play. Celtic conceded no fewer than 34 of these – 16 in the first half and 18 in the second.

One cannot however refrain from suggestion to the authorities of football that yesterday's match should be the subject of an inquiry. The behaviour of at least two Celtic payers was such that the club itself should hold one: certainly, the culprit's own clubmates on the field were most concerned at the number of occasions on which one of them seemed on the point of being ordered off. That there was not even a warning administered by the referee, so far as could be seen from the press-box, was as astonishing as the foul play itself.

One Celtic defender committed almost every known type of offence; he obstructed, pushed, pulled, tripped and kicked his immediate opponent who, for his part, is not himself the soul of discretion and by the manner of his retaliation placed himself in the same class as the Celtic player. But at the same time the player who is being intimidated does expect to get protection from the referee.

Celtic's bustling tactics certainly succeeded in upsetting Rangers, and though their goal had some remarkable escapes and was saved time and time again by superb play by Miller, who had ten times the work of Brown, a draw was not an unfair result. If only the many bearing of such as Hogg, who, while he shirked nothing, was scrupulously fair in all his tackles, had been copied, Celtic would have taken much more credit than they did.

Hazlett scored for Celtic in the first half – his first goal of the season, by the way – and Gillick for Rangers in the second half.

Rangers (0) 1	Celtic (1) 1
Gillick	Hazlett

RANGERS:- BROWN; YOUNG AND SHAW; MCCOLL, WOODBURN AND RAE; WADDELL AND GILLICK; DUNCANSON AND MCLEOD.

CELTIC:- MILLER; HOGG AND MALLAN; LYNCH, MCMILLAN AND MILNE; EVANS AND MCALOON; AIRLIE, GALLAGHER (W.) AND HAZLETT.

Rangers 2, Celtic 0 – Saturday, 9th August, 1947

Firm Control at Ibrox

The outstanding and the most pleasing feature of the match at Ibrox was the sportsmanlike manner in which it was contested and both Rangers and Celtic have to be congratulated on their demeanour on a day more suited to the leisure of cricket than the hurly-burly of "Old Firm" football rivalry.

Unfortunately, the standard of play did not make so good an impression as the players' behaviour. The feet of the opponents seemed to hold a magnetic attraction for the passes of both sides.

Rangers survived an uncomfortable first half in which Celtic's wing-halves dictated the run of play and quite outshone their opposite numbers. But apart from a 21-yard drive from Sirrell that bounced from the post, with Brown helpless, Celtic's forwards never looked like scoring. Rangers had the easier chances, most of them in fact from a quarter that Celtic could have been pardoned for thinking would have been the least of their worries.

DUNCANSON'S MATCH

Duncanson has been considered a more or less stop-gap outside-left, more notable for his thrust than his subtlety, but on Saturday he was far more puzzling to Hogg than Waddell was to Mallon. It was late in the game when Waddell, impatient at the lack of service from his mercurial partner, went in search of his own supplies and played football of international class.

Both Rangers' goals, within seven minutes of each other in the second half, were made by Duncanson and finished off by Williamson. On each occasion the winger manoeuvred for a corner kick and took it quickly but accurately, and Williamson, not satisfactorily marked, headed a goal.

At the end of the day Celtic were down and out. Their defence, particularly Mallon and Corbett, played splendidly and the wing-halves deserved better treatment from their own forwards, none of whom was in the old Celtic class. Shaw and Woodburn were, like the opposing left-back and centre-half, magnificent defenders, and one felt that Duncanson and Waddell could have won the game even if they had been burdened with the Celtic inside men.

Rangers (0) 2	Celtic (0) 0
Williamson 2	

RANGERS:- BROWN; COX AND SHAW; MCCOLL, WOODBURN AND RAE; WADDELL AND GILLICK; WILLIAMSON; THORNTON AND DUNCANSON.

CELTIC:- MILLER; HOGG AND MALLAN; MCPHAIL, CORBETT AND MACAULEY; F. QUINN AND MACALOON; KIERNAN; SIRRELL AND PATON.

Celtic 2, Rangers 0 – Saturday, 29th August, 1947

Wing Halves Inspire Celtic

Rangers' cloak of invincibility was torn to shreds by Celtic at Parkhead on Saturday and it may be extremely difficult to repair. There have been threadbare patches in it since the start of the season and these were eagerly seized by the Celtic team that did much to reinstate themselves in the good graces of their followers.

This was the best Celtic eleven I have seen for several years – strong and skilful from goal out to left-half, and with such speed and thrust amongst the forwards that the niceties of former famous lines were hardly missed.

Instead of the usual harmony in the Ibrox ranks, we had the extraordinary sight of Brown and Shaw muddling an easy clearance, conceding a corner between them and showing the 70,000 crowd that each thought the other to blame. And when Cox was injured midway through the second half there was a most unorthodox chopping and changing. I could not but think, judging from the looks exchanged, that the reorganisation was haphazard and largely dictated by individual wishes.

EXCELLENT HALF-BACKS

Once again it has to be recorded that the keystone of Celtic's victory was the excellent play of their half-back line. The Scottish selectors present would be further impressed by McPhail and McAulay whose zeal and cleverness made Gillick and Thornton look jaded. Corbett was a dominating centre-half, only just short of the standard set by Woodburn who was his imperturbable self.

Miller's goalkeeping was outstanding, and Brown's almost so. In a match of many powerful and well-directed shots, each had to be constantly alert. But the Rangers' goalkeeper might have prevented Celtic's first goal. Seven minutes after the restart the lively Evans bustled and dispossessed Gillick, veered to the wing, and, when everyone expected him to cross, shrewdly cut the ball back to McAulay, who sent an inch-perfect pass wide of Woodburn to Gallacher. Brown saw the danger but hesitated for a second before advancing and was unable to stop Gallacher's carefully-placed shot. Six minutes later Paton, by sheer persistence, beat Cox and from 26 yards almost burst the net behind.

Celtic (0) 2	Rangers (0) 0
Gallacher	
Paton	
Attendance	70,000

CELTIC:- MILLER; HOGG AND MALLAN; MCPHAIL, CORBETT AND MCAULEY; BOGAN AND R. QUINN; J. GALLACHER; EVANS, PATON.

RANGERS:- BROWN; COX AND SHAW; WATKINS, WOODBURN AND RAE; WADDELL AND GILLICK; WILLIAMSON; THORNTON AND DUNCANSON.

Willie Miller

Undoubtedly one of the best goalkeepers ever to play for Celtic, although he was unfortunate in that his reign as the No.1 at Parkhead coincided with perhaps the most barren period ever in the club's history. He must be one of the few regular first team players never to have picked up a winner's medal with the club.

Miller was born in Glasgow in 1924 and joined the club from the junior side Maryhill Harp, making his first team debut in a 2-1 defeat by Morton at the start of the 1946-47 season. He was a brave and agile keeper and often saved Celtic from a "drubbing". Played in only two winning sides in Old Firm matches, but gained six full caps for Scotland and played in seven League internationals.

Miller was transferred to Clyde in 1950 and, ironically, after his barren years at Parkhead, he won Glasgow and Charity Cup medals with the then Shawfield side, and also a Second Division Championship medal. He moved on to Hibs in January, 1954, but could not displace Tommy Younger and eventually retired from the game a year later.

Bobby Hogg

A Larkhall man, born in the Lanarkshire town in 1914. When he signed for Celtic from Royal Albert Juniors in 1931, he became the youngest ever player to sign professional forms in Scotland. Hogg was a tough tackling right back with a fine football brain and went on to make almost 400 appearances for the club between 1932 and 1948. His last match for Celtic was in a 2-0 defeat by Rangers in the Glasgow Cup Final in May, 1948.

He was one of many players who was never allowed to fulfill his potential because of the Second World War, and, to many older Celtic fans, it will remain a mystery why he won only one official international cap, against Czechoslovakia. He also played in six League internationals.

Hogg's final season with Celtic was almost a disastrous one for the club. Indeed on the final day of the season they had to travel to Dens Park to meet Dundee with the threat of relegation still hanging over them. Hogg had earlier been replaced by Jimmy Mallen, but Celtic recalled him for the Dundee match and his experience helped the club to a 3-2 win, thus keeping their place in the top division.

Charlie Tully

If Len Shackleton was the "Clown Prince of Soccer" in England, then Charles Patrick Tully, born in Belfast on July 11, 1924, had a just claim for that title in Scotland. A brilliant inside left, he joined the club from Belfast Celtic for £8,000 in 1948 and showed a marvellous enthusiasm for the game, both on and off the field, although he was never too fond of the rigid training involved.

With Celtic, Charlie won one Championship medal, two Scottish Cups and two League Cups, including the 1957 7-1 defeat of Rangers at Hampden. He was a member of the 1953-54 Double-winning side and gained ten caps for Northern Ireland, although a man of his talent deserved many more.

Many of the older generation of Celtic fans will remember "Cheeky" Charlie for an incident during a Scottish Cup tie against Falkirk at Brockville in 1953. Tully scored direct from a corner, and after being ordered to re-take it, he scored again.

Tully was one of the greatest personalities to grace Scottish football and his sense of humour was a bit special. In 1967 he was asked if he could have got a game in the Lisbon Lions team and said that he could, perhaps, have taken corners for them.

Bobby Evans

Must be included in any list of Celtic all-time greats. His flaming red hair made him instantly recognisable, but his tremendous ability did so anyway. Joined the club as an inside forward during the War from St. Anthony's Juniors, but was switched to a more defensive role for the vital relegation clash with Dundee in 1948, and that is where his future lay.

Despite his lack of height, he had great ability in the air and, in fact, played at centre half for Scotland before moving into that slot for Celtic. He deputised for injured Ranger George Young against Austria and Hungary in 1955, and later captained Scotland twice against England. He was also club captain.

With Celtic he won a Championship and made four Scottish Cup Final appearances, winning two. He also played in the 7-1 League Cup triumph against Rangers, and was outstanding in the Celtic side which won the Coronation Cup in 1953. Left for Chelsea in 1960 and had spells with Newport, Morton, Third Lanark and Raith Rovers before retiring at the age of 40 in 1968.

Rangers 2, Celtic 0 – Saturday, 20th Sept, 1947
Unimpressive Internationalists

When such a haphazard forward line as Celtic had on Saturday can cause such uncertainty and even panic in Scotland's back division there may be something unpleasant in store for our International team at Windsor Park, Belfast, on October 4. One can imagine what Peter Doherty and Stevenson would do with the chances that McAloon squandered.

Young and Shaw were, surprisingly, the weakest part of Rangers' team, and for a period in the second half it seemed as if the energy displayed by Gallacher and Evans, coupled with the skilful touches of the Pole, Kapler, would earn Celtic a draw. Even Woodburn was not his normal masterly self, although it was the centre-half's penchant for dribbling before clearing that frequently brought danger to Brown's goal, rather than the efforts of Celtic's forwards.

Fortunately for Rangers, their forwards were man for man superior to their opposite numbers. Waddell had something of a field day against Milne, and it was only splendid goalkeeping by Miller and a magnificent display by Corbett that prevented a goal revel.

Celtic were, of course, much under strength with Hogg, Mallon, McPhail and Paton absent. Only McAulay could match his opponents in constructive skill; what a brilliant player this wing half would be if he could learn the art of passing.

There was much to admire in the pluck of Evans for Celtic. I saw him take corner kicks on both sides of the field in addition to throw-ins, and he was frequently back in defence, helping his backs. That such ubiquitousness was necessary was indicative of Celtic's troubles.

Williamson's goal in 17 minutes led to a protest from Miller, and it did look as if the centre-forward was offside when, standing on the goal-line, he breasted Duncanson's header through. But five minutes later when Williamson again scored the offside decision against him was hard to understand. Findlay took the second goal coolly 11 minutes from the end when Thornton's header rebounded from the bar.

Rangers (1) 2	Celtic (0) 0
Williamson	
Findlay	

RANGERS:- BROWN; YOUNG AND SHAW; MCCOLL, WOODBURN AND COX; WADDELL AND FINDLAY; WILLIAMSON; THORNTON AND DUNCANSON.

CELTIC:- MILLER; FERGUSON AND MILNE; R. QUINN, CORBETT AND MCAULEY; BROGAN AND MCALOON; J. GALLACHER AND KAPLER.

Celtic 0, Rangers 4 – Friday, 2nd January, 1948
Sixty Thousand Spectators see Celtic Outclassed

Rangers meandered back to the top of the "A" Division of the Scottish League yesterday. In beating Celtic at Parkhead in the match postponed from New Year's Day they were able to play with one eye on today's fixture with Dundee, so feeble was the opposition.

The bravest man I saw in the vicinity of Celtic Park as the multitude left the ground was a vendor of "Souvenir of the Celtic team in colour – price one shilling" – not just the best of bargains in the circumstances.

Once they survived Celtic's opening burst, during which Bogan, dummying and back-heeling his way past Shaw, promised much, the Ibrox team played magnificent football. They were not, however, into their stride when the first goal was scored. In nine minutes Miller had not made a save. Then Milne was somewhat harshly penalised for tackling Rutherford in midfield and, when Cox's free-kick was only partially cleared, McColl's shot from the edge of the penalty went in low off the post, with Miller probably blinded by the ruck of players in front of him.

The longer the first half progressed, the more apparent did it become that Celtic's forwards were quite incapable of beating Rangers' defence. A cracking first-time shot by Thornton, taken on the half-turn after 26 minutes following Rutherford's corner kick, ended the match as a contest.

Thornton's was a most spectacular goal; Rutherford's, seven minutes from the interval, was a football gem typical of the way in which the Rangers players could find their man with the pass, in contrast to the flurried attempts of their opponents.

Celtic's day of misery was almost complete when Bogan was injured in a tackle with Shaw and had to be assisted off with 23 minutes left for play. His return 10 minutes from the end, after Rangers' fourth goal, was plucky but ill-advised, for two minutes later he again limped off, this time for good. The fourth goal was almost a replica of the third. On this occasion it was Thornton and Duncanson who weaved their way through the defence, for the latter to score at his leisure.

Rangers' victory had but one flaw; with the score 4-0 and the ball out of play Cox fouled Paton without apparent provocation, and was spoken to by the referee. The back's fall from grace was surprising as he had completely mastered his opponent in every phase of the game.

Celtic (0) 0	Rangers (3) 4
	McColl
	Thornton
	Rutherford
	Duncanson
Attendance	60,000

CELTIC :- MILLER; MALLAN AND MILNE; MCPHAIL, CORBETT AND MCAULAY; BOGAN AND MCDONALD; WALSH; EVANS AND PATON.

RANGERS :- BROWN; COX AND SHAW; MCCOLL, YOUNG AND RAE; RUTHERFORD AND GILLICK; THORNTON; DUNCANSON AND CASKIE.

Ranger, 2, Celtic 0 – Saturday, 8th May, 1948

Record Crowd for Charity

If some of the football giants of the past had trodden Hampden turf on Saturday they might have been inspired by the record Charity Cup Final crowd to make the occasion memorable. The fact is, however, that the crowd of 69,000, representing a "gate" of over £5718 was the day's outstanding feature.

Neither Rangers nor Celtic were capable of mastering the almost oppressive heat that seemed concentrated in the bowl of the ground. In fairness to the players it must be said that the thousands of spectators found it irksome to watch the match fully clad and the atmosphere was akin to what one imagined prevailed at the Oval where Bradman and Barnes were much more pleasantly occupied.

Rangers won the trophy for the twenty-eighth time – their fifth victory in successive years – easily enough in the end. In the first half, and particularly before McMillan had to retire through a sciatic nerve injury, they were far from impressive and their most successful players were, as has been the writer's duty to record all season, defenders.

Duncanson, the best attacker on the field, won the match with his enviable faculty of purposeful approach.

Eleven minutes from the interval he beat Hogg without deviating from the direct path to goal, and when Miller intelligently narrowed the angle of the probable shot, the outside left lifted the ball over the goalkeeper's head to Williamson, who headed a goal similar in type to that which won the Scottish Cup, the header being made from almost the same spot. Four minutes later Duncanson gave Miller as little chance with a powerful hook from Findlay's pass.

Young, Lindsay (a capable deputy for Shaw), Woodburn, Rutherford and Duncanson were Rangers' best players. Miller, who several times effected thrilling saves, Hogg who is still a fine back, McPhail and Baillie shone for Celtic. If the others on both sides did not provide more than average entertainment, they did at least show with their colleagues that Rangers-Celtic matches can be contested in a thoroughly sporting spirit.

Charity Cup Final

Rangers (2) 2   Celtic (0) 0
Williamson
Dunchanson

Celtic 0, Rangers 1 – Saturday, 21st August, 1948

Celtic's Tale of Woe

The wearin' o' the green (and white) is still a tale of toil and tribulation. Some of these days the legions of Celtic supporters will be struck as with a lightning-shaft, for one of their players will score a goal and it will be all that the sanest man can do to keep his reason.

Against Rangers at Parkhead on Saturday, Celtic plumbed the depth of inefficiency when the chance to score presented itself – even the opportunity of converting a penalty kick was squandered. It is more correct to say that Celtic lost the two League points at stake than that Rangers won them.

Two of the home players will receive most of the blame for their side's defeat – Miller who conceded the only goal of the match, and Mallan, who failed to score from the penalty award. Miller's lapse was astonishing. An apologetic effort of a shot by Findlay from fully 30 yards seemed to be dropping outside Miller's right-hand post when the keeper casually attempted to pull it in, no doubt with his mind on the goal kick that should have followed. The ball, however, spun inward off his arm and into the net, to the accompaniment of a mere whisper of acclamation from the bewildered crowd. That freak goal was recorded in six minutes. With half an hour played Mallan, taking the penalty kick given for Woodburn's handling offence, gently trundled the ball straight at Brown in a manner at variance with the left-back's usual aggressive style.

If Miller had been crestfallen at his blunder, Mallan bore all the signs of agony at his. Yet dreadful mistakes as they were, they were only incidents in a day of Celtic errors. They were the only flaws in the display of either defender and were, in the long run, pardonable when compared with the countless blemishes in the forwards' performance. Evans and McAulay were on top of Rangers' inside men throughout and were able to give their own attack a supply of the ball that is rarely forthcoming to them in an "Old Firm" game. But the Celtic wingers were inept, Docherty probably on account of inexperience and the fact that he was playing out of position, Paton because he was obsessed with the notion that he could beat Young, and the inside trio fluffed their shots and over-elaborated when within shooting range. Tully, from Belfast, was the most attractive ball player on the field but I cannot recall his delivering a single shot. Weir expended enough energy to have won a dozen matches without showing even a smattering of skill at the vital stage.

Celtic (0) 0   Rangers (1) 1
                      Findlay

CELTIC:- MILLER; MILNE AND MALLAN; EVANS, BODEN AND MCAULEY; DOCHERTY AND MCPHAIL; WEIR; TULLY AND PATON

RANGERS:- BROWN; YOUNG AND SHAW; MCCOLL, WOODBURN AND COX; RUTHERFORD AND GILLICK; THORNTON; FINDLAY AND DUNCANSON.

Celtic 3: Rangers 1 – Saturday, 25th September, 1948
Tully Bewilders Rangers

The oddest explanation of Rangers' defeat at Parkhead was that offered by a former Ibrox player who thought Young's positional play at centre half was faulty and responsible for Celtic's first and second goals. My informant was, I think, still in a state of bewilderment at the sight of one Celtic player so repeatedly outwitting so many of his opponents. Young, in my opinion, was easily the best Ranger and in no way responsible for the defeat. The person who must take most of the blame or credit for that is Tully, undoubtedly the cleverest forward in the last 10 years of Scottish football.

There were occasions on Saturday when the Irishman beat three would-be tacklers in the space of as many yards – and each time by a different manoeuvre.

The other Celtic forwards grew in confidence as they watched Rangers' defence torn to shreds and in the second half even J. Gallacher was indulging in feats of ball manipulation. The switch of Gillick from outside left to inside right was the best indication of the poverty of the Ibrox side's forward display. The change had little effect.

Rangers had the advantage of the opening goal when Miller, in 10 minutes, made his one contribution in dropping the ball at Findlay's feet. It was a cheap score and not to be compared with the equalising goal. In 20 minutes Tully, trailing half the Rangers defenders after him,

gesticulated to Paton whither the pass would go and served him perfectly; when Young had to go for the winger, J. Gallacher had an easy task to shoot the cross through. One minute from half-time, and just after Thornton had hit the post, came another splendid goal for Celtic. Weir danced in front of Shaw for almost a minute before sidefooting a most unorthodox pass to Evans. The wing half swerved through and glided the ball to Tully and when the latter's pass continued the operation, W. Gallacher was in the centre forward position to score.

The deciding goal 20 minutes from the end led to heated protests from Rangers. There may have been some justification in their claim that before Weir shot, Brown was impeded by J. Gallacher; but none for their method of trying to prove it; the referee almost parted company with his jacket.

Celtic (2) 3	Rangers (1) 1
J Gallacher	Findlay
W Gallacher	
Weir	

CELTIC:- MILLER; MILNE AND MALLAN; EVANS, BODEN AND MCAULEY; WEIR AND W. GALLACHER; J. GALLACHER; TULLY AND PATON.

RANGERS:- BROWN; LINDSAY AND SHAW; MCCOLL, YOUNG AND COX; WADDELL AND FINDLAY; THORNTON; DUCANSON AND GILLICK.

Rangers 2, Celtic 1 – Saturday, 16th October, 1948
Waddell the Match-Winner

The significance of an incident early in the first half at Ibrox may not have been apparent to many of the crowd. When Tully, on whom Celtic depend so much as the inspiration of their attack, was penalised only five yards from his own goal-line for using his hands, it was an indication that if Celtic's hero had to adopt the role of spoiler he would have few opportunities of repeating the constructive football that demoralised Rangers in the previous League Cup match between the rivals.

Waddell was to Rangers what Celtic hoped Tully would be to them. If ever a player seemed likely to score the decisive goal, it was Waddell. Celtic questioned the validity of the score 17 minutes from the end but I thought Waddell's anticipation of Thornton's pass was timed to the correct fraction of a second and he was onside when the ball left his partner's foot.

Celtic's goal four minutes after half time also was the cause of complaint, Rangers appealing that Woodburn's tackle of Gallacher, which led to a penalty kick, from which McPhail scored, was fair. Gallacher would probably have caught up with Tully's pass but Woodburn's infringement was immediately and correctly penalised by the referee who was in close proximity to the incident.

There was no protest about Rangers' first goal in 28 minutes – rather, there was bewilderment by friend and

foe alike. The goal will be credited to Williamson in the records; one feels that the description "scored" is hardly applicable. The centre forward's back was to the Celtic goal when, 20 yards out, he lunged to block Boden's clearance but fortuitously the ball struck his foot, rose in the air and sailed over Miller's head.

Rangers won on their merits. They had the best full back (Young), the best half-back (Cox) and the best forward (Waddell). In addition Young, Cox, Waddell and Thornton frequently dovetailed into a powerful attacking force which Celtic never emulated. It was perhaps fortuitous for Rangers that the right side of their field was so strong, as the left, apart from the defenders, faded badly after a promising start.

Celtic, deprived of the confidence that Tully's normal brilliance provides were a struggling side fighting stoutly to the last but tactically inferior to their opponents.

Rangers (1) 2	Celtic (0) 1
Williamson	McPhail (pen.)
Waddell	

RANGERS:- BROWN; YOUNG AND SHAW; COX, WOODBURN AND RAE; WADDELL AND THORNTON; WILLIAMSON; MARSHALL AND DUNCANSON.

CELTIC:- MILLER; MILNE AND MALLAN; EVANS, BODEN AND MCAULEY, WEIR AND MCPHAIL; J. GALLACHER; TULLY AND PATON.

Bobby Brown

Brown was born in Stirlingshire in 1923, and spent ten years with Rangers. He will be regarded as one of the club's top goalkeepers since the war, taking over from Jerry Dawson. Joined Queen's Park in 1939 and spent the war years, while serving in the Navy, guesting with English clubs, including Portsmouth and Chelsea. He joined Rangers in May 1946, and while his career at Ibrox was a relatively short one it was also highly successful.

As Rangers dominated Scottish football in the years immediately after the war, Brown, an agile keeper with safe hands, played in the Championship–winning sides of 1947, 1949 and 1950. He also won three Scottish Cup medals and two League Cup badges. He was a great favourite with the crowd.

He was transferred to Falkirk in 1956 for £1,000 and retired two years later. Brown went into management with St. Johnstone in 1958 and although as a player he gained only three full caps, (he also won eight League caps and played in two wartime internationals), he had a successful spell as Scotland team manager from 1967-71. Managed the Scottish side which beat the then World champions England at Wembley in 1967.

Jock Shaw

Born in the little Lanarkshire mining village of Annathill, better known as Bedlay, Shaw was a courageous full-back, who often played down injuries to turn out for Rangers–all of which earned him the nickname of "Tiger".

He was Rangers captain in their dominant years after the war and was, undoubtedly, one of the club's greatest servants of all time. He was the elder brother of Hibs and Scotland full-back Davie and a neighbour and friend of two more stars, Bobby Flavell and Frank Brennan–all internationalists, and all from the same miners' rows in Bedlay.

Jock was transferred from Airdrie to Rangers in 1938 and played on until he was 41 before hanging up his boots in 1953. Even then, he still served the club as a trainer and later as groundsman. Shaw also had a newsagents' business in Glenboig, but he will always be remembered first and foremost as a Ranger.

Shaw had only four full caps for Scotland and two League caps, but he played in two wartime internationals. His club honours included four Championships, three Scottish Cups and two League Cups.

Willie Thornton

Signed in March 1936, from Winchburgh Albion when the great Bill Struth beat Hearts for his signature. He made his debut against Partick Thistle at Firhill when he was just 16. Willie was another of those players whose careers were affected by the war. He served in the Army, took part in the Middle East campaign, and was awarded the Military Medal in Sicily.

Thornton was a marvellous sportsman and a class centre forward who formed an almost telepathic partnership with Willie Waddell. His heading ability alone made him a legend, although he was only 5ft 9in in height. He was a prolific scorer, netting 248 times in 406 matches for Rangers. His best effort came in season 1948-49 when he scored 36 goals.

Thornton won seven full caps for Scotland and had one League cap. With Rangers he collected four Championships, three Scottish Cups and one League Cup. He retired as a player in 1954 and was appointed manager of Dundee. Five years later he moved back to Glasgow to manage Partick Thistle, and returned to Ibrox in 1968 as assistant manager.

Willie Woodburn

Will always hold a place in the history of Scottish football, because of his *sine die* suspension from the game in September 1954, but "Big Ben" was one of the most talented central defenders ever to grace the sport. He had class and style in abundance and was probably, in the football sense, way ahead of his time. The "life" ban was lifted in 1957, but Willie refused to play again, and that was football's loss.

Born in Edinburgh in 1919, he joined Rangers as a professional in 1937. Like men such as Young and Waddell, he played for only one senior club, Rangers. Was later to enter sports journalism, where his habit of kicking every ball from the press box caused colleagues to pull limbs out of the way. It also showed that while he had lost the edge to play, he had lost none of his enthusiasm for the sport itself.

Willie played for Scotland on 24 occasions and gained seven League caps. His club medal haul was four Championships, four Scottish Cups and two League Cups.

Old Firm Hall of Fame

Celtic 3, Rangers 2– Saturday, August 13th, 1949
McAuley's Inspiring Display

Rarely in the long series of Celtic-Rangers matches has an individual display of craftsmanship obtruded as did that of McAuley, the Celtic left half, at Parkhead on Saturday. We remember previous encounters still described as Morton's match, Meiklejohn's match, Gallacher's match, or McGrory's match.

Complete mastery of trapping the ball on the ground or killing it in the air, immaculate control of it in the dribble, accuracy of the pass whether it was square or forward, long or short - McAuley dovetailed all these attributes of the skilful constructive player into the necessary defensive duties of a wing half-back. He sold more "dummies" to Finlay than are usually bought in an entire season, and he prompted and spurred Tully to some of the form that made good business for parody-makers in the early part of last season

TRIBUTE TO COLLINS

Rangers, of course, expected stern opposition from such as McAuley and Tully. I am not so sure that they or many of the 70,000 crowd anticipated the success of Collins and Haughney, two Celtic players making their first appearance in senior football. Collins who was "faur ower wee" to many before the start - he is only 5ft 1in - was paid a delightful tribute by Shaw, his immediate opponent, at the end of a highly entertaining match. The handshake and pat on the back from the Rangers veteran immediately dispelled the impression created by one or two foolish actions by other players in the closing furious minutes.

I cannot recall Shaw being able to tackle Collins on more than half a dozen occasions. The outside right showed fine intelligence in parting with the ball at exactly the correct moment, and to those who recall the feast of crosses that Connolly, Bert, Thomson and Delaney used to send into goal, the service supplied by Collins was particularly heartening.

Haughney, who started at outside left and late in the second half moved to centre forward, was concerned in the scoring of all Celtic goals Baillie, formerly a wing half-back, was another young Celt who pleased his sponsors in his new position of left back - and he had the best Rangers forward, Waddell, to face.

If McAuley had not been such a dominating personality both Evans and Boden would have been acclaimed outstanding in the Celtic half-back line. Evans, who is famed for his great endeavour, can never have played harder, and Boden by concentrating on the ball and not Thornton's wiles, prevented Rangers from having any thrust in the middle.

There was, however, one serious defect in the Celtic display. McGuire rashly conceded a penalty kick (from which Waddell scored the opening goal) after he had been lucky to escape punishment for a more serious offence a few minutes earlier; had his name taken by the referee in the second half, after a succession of crude tackles, and came within an ace of giving Rangers an equalising goal near the finish when they claimed - and justifiably - another penalty kick. McGuire must discipline himself or others will do it for him.

There were occasions on Saturday when Woodburn did Rangers similar disservice. He gave away the penalty kick from which McPhail equalised in the first half, and other incidents of recklessness spoiled his display which was, at other times, full of constructive ideas. Rangers' wing half-backs had far too heavy a burden thrust on them not only by McPhail and Tully but by their own inside forwards. Thornton scored their second goal and McPhail and Haughney had Celtic's others.

Celtic (2) 3	Rangers (1) 2
McPhail 2	Waddell (pen.)
Haughney	Thornton
Attendance 70,000	

CELTIC: MILLER, MCGUIRE AND BAILLIE, EVANS, BODEN AND MCAULEY, COLLINS, MCPHAIL, JOHNSON TULLY AND HAUGHNEY

RANGERS: BROWN, YOUNG AND SHAW, MCCOLL WOODBURN AND COX, WADDELL, FINDLAY, THORNTON, DUNCANSON AND RUTHERFORD.

Rangers 2, Celtic 0 – Saturday, 27th August, 1949

Slow-Motion Second Half

The 95,000 crowd had splendid entertainment in the first half-hour and it did appear as if Rangers would exact revenge for their defeat at Parkhead a fortnight ago. Apart from a magnificent double save by Miller from Findlay in the seventh minute – Rangers' inside right was so close in on goal on the second occasion that three or four goalkeepers should not have been able to prevent his scoring – Celtic looked much more likely to lead.

As it was, Haughey hit the underside of the crossbar when Woodburn blundered in passing back to Brown, and McPhail was clean through after a splendid ground passing movement by the wing half-backs and forwards, but missed the goal with his shot. Evans and McAuley were outstanding in this period of Celtic supremacy and a McGrory type of leader would have revelled in the chances supplied.

In 39 minutes with as many eyes on the trouble centre on the terracing as on the play, Findlay scored for Rangers. Miller, I thought, erred in advancing far from his goal when Waddell centred and when Rutherford shot, the goalkeeper, scrambling back, could only knee the ball out to the scorer.

Ten minutes after half time Rangers were awarded a penalty kick after Waddell had been tackled by Boden. The decision was followed by another outbreak in the area in which the pre-interval and interval disturbance had broken out. The decision, I thought, was correct; Boden's tackle was too late and though Waddell would not have regained control, even unimpeded, a technical offence had been committed. Young hit the crossbar from

the spot and that was almost the final thrill of the match that not surprisingly deteriorated. For one thing, the excessive heat had slowed almost every player to walking pace; most of them seemed to want nothing to do with the ball and those who did accept the responsibility of holding it, performed at a snail's pace. Secondly, even the most seasoned players must have been affected by the sights of the first half and the early part of the second.

Waddell, leading Rangers' attack in place of Thornton, who suffered a broken bone in his foot after a tackle with Boden, raced in on Miller, after the centre half had misheaded a clearance by Cox, and gave the goalkeeper no chance with a left-foot grounder.

Rangers were not the better footballing side, but they did accept the few chances that the opposing defence allowed. Celtic have recovered much of their traditional poise, and in the first half particularly were far superior in passing and running into the open space. But they sorely needed a finisher. The fact that they had once again to switch Haughney, Johnston and Tully midway through the second half was proof.

Rangers (1) 2	Celtic (0) 0
Rutherford	
Waddell	
Attendance	95,000

RANGERS:- BROWN; YOUNG AND SHAW; COX, WOODBURN AND RAE; WADDELL AND FINDLAY; THORNTON; DUNCANSON AND RUTHERFORD.

CELTIC:- MILLER; MALLAN AND BAILLIE; EVANS, BODEN AND MCAULEY; COLLINS AND MCPHAIL; JOHNSTON; TULLY AND HAUGHNEY.

From the Glasgow Herald of Monday, 29th August, 1949:

S.F.A. Inquiry on Ibrox Essential

By Our Football Correspondent

The referee and the Refereeing Committee of the Scottish Football Association will, I imagine, have almost as big a headache in the near future as some of the victims of the deplorable scene at the Rangers-Celtic League Cup match at Ibrox Stadium on Saturday, when but for the prompt action of the police, a riot would have taken place at the west end of the ground.

The Referee Committee will hear the report of the referee Mr A. B. Gebbie (Hamilton) - he was the official in charge, not Mr P. Fitzpatrick (Glasgow) as Rangers' official programme stated - but whether the referee's report will help the committee to apportion the blame for the fighting and bottle throwing at the Celtic supporters' end of the ground is another matter.

CAUSE OF TROUBLE

There is no doubt as to what caused the trouble - the foul committed by Cox, Rangers' right half-back on Tully, Celtic's inside left, after only 30 minutes of play and the astonishing attitude of the referee in ignoring the offence

similar unpleasant scene at the same ground, punished the Celtic club severely because of the behaviour of a section of their supporters. On September 17, 1941, the S.F.A. announced that the Celtic ground would be closed for one month and during that period they would not be allowed to play on opponents' grounds in Glasgow. The Parkhead officials were also ordered to post bills to intimate to their supporters on their reopening that it had been closed by order of the Association because of "the serious misbehaviour at Ibrox stadium on September 6" and to warn supporters that more serious punishment would befall Celtic if there was a recurrence of such behaviour on any ground.

The S.F.A. decision was not at all acceptable to many people besides Celtic, who officially stated at the time that none of their players had given the crowd any reason for creating trouble before the disturbance on the terracing started.

Will Celtic again be held responsible for the actions of a small section of alleged supporters of the club whom and actually waving play on. The referee did appear to take the names of both players some minutes later when they were involved in an incident which compared with the first was trivial, but as he took no action when Cox committed the original offence it is obvious that he cannot report that the original occurrence caused the scenes on the terracing.

Several S.F.A. Council members and Scottish League officials attended the match, however, and I am certain they will press for a much fuller inquiry than is usual after the referee's report is considered.

There is, of course, no excuse for the hooliganism of the section of the Celtic supporters, however much they felt they and their team had been badly treated.

EIGHT YEARS AGO

Almost eight years ago the S.F.A., after inquiring into a neither they nor anyone else wants in football? How, indeed, can this unruly element be kept out of the various grounds? No solution has so far been found. But if clubs ensure that their players do not, by their actions on the field, encourage hooliganism, there will not be so much of it.

In the case of the match on September 6th 1941, there was no inference by the S.F.A. that Celtic players were responsible for the disturbance among the supporters; in fact, the S.F.A. announced along with their findings against Celtic that more than one Rangers player that day had shown dissent from the decision of the referee and that they and all other players in Scotland must cease the practice herewith.

So far as Saturday is concerned neutral members among Scottish Football legislators should have no trouble apportioning the responsibility for the trouble.

Celtic 1, Rangers 2 – Thursday, 13th September, 1949

Celtic v. Rangers Matches Should be Stopped

Hardly six hours after a delegation from the Scottish Football Association had met the Glasgow magistrates to discuss the disturbances at Ibrox Stadium on August 27, Celtic and Rangers were taking part in another scene which should relieve the authorities, both football and civic, of further consideration of the problems of the "Old Firm".

After watching the last five minutes at Parkhead last night I unhesitatingly state that no further matches between the clubs should be allowed this season.

With this view the Celtic officials are in agreement – if, as they say, referees who can completely control play and players are not available to handle such games.

It is perhaps unfortunate that this Glasgow Cup Semi-final was played at all. I can now say that Celtic, immediately after the Ibrox game of unhappy memory, seriously considered scratching from the competition since only a fortnight would elapse between the Ibrox match and the clubs' next encounter (last night) and because they thought that conditions would still be unsettled.

ASTONISHING DECISIONS

Three minutes from time, last night, with the score 1-1, Rangers were awarded a free kick. Milne was adjudged to have handled the ball 25 yards from his goal. I agree with Celtic's players that the left back had breasted the ball down, and was astonished at the decision. But while Celtic were protesting and while in addition the ball was still moving from Milne's return to the spot where the alleged infringement had taken place, Waddell took the kick, passed to Findlay and the ball was in the net before most of the Celtic players had lined up and before, so far as one could see, any signal to take the kick had been given.

Celtic's chagrin knew no bounds then, and to the horror of those who have the interests of the game at heart, Tully was quite clearly seen to be urging his team-mates to leave the field. Almost reluctantly several of them took the wiser council of others and the game was restarted. Within a minute Waddell, chasing Boden for a loose ball, had his legs swept from him in a manner similar to what most of the spectators at Ibrox in the last Saturday in August saw Tully experiencing from Cox.

That neither Tully nor Boden was ordered off was another astonishing decision. Tully did appear to have his name taken for his gestures after Rangers' goal, but Boden received no caution. In fact, a free kick was given against Waddell for his part (which might have been pushing) in the incident with the Celtic centre half. The track round the field seemed to contain all Glasgow's policemen now and there had been more than a liberal sprinkling there and within the terracing all through.

So ended a match that had started on an almost funereal note. Celtic contributed 75% of the football skill there was, led at half-time by a penalty goal scored by McPhail when Shaw acted as goalkeeper to save Taylor's shot, then lost the equaliser to Williamson almost immediately. Rangers had the benefit of the wind in the second half, and then Celtic met an undeserved fate in being beaten as they were.

But whatever their grievances, some of their players – McGuire (for his repeated crude tackles), as well as Tully and Boden – seemed to have no sense of their responsibility. I shall be surprised if the Celtic directors do not seriously consider the position of players who, however much they feel aggrieved, let their club down as these three did last night.

Glasgow Cup Semi-Final

Celtic (1) 1	Rangers (0) 2
McPhail (pen.)	Williamson

CELTIC:- MILLER; MCGUIRE AND MILNE; EVANS, BODEN AND MCAULEY; COLLINS AND MCPHAIL; HAUGHEY, TAYLOR AND TULLY.

RANGERS:- BROWN; YOUNG AND SHAW; MCCOLL, WOODBURN AND COX; WADDELL AND FINDLAY; WILLIAMSON, DUNCANSON AND RUTHERFORD.

Rangers 4, Celtic 0 – Saturday, 24th September, 1949

Rangers-Celtic Match of Unreality

A Rangers v. Celtic match used to be the greatest club game in the world; now it is an anaemic, lustreless fixture – just another fixture.

At Ibrox Stadium on Saturday, Celtic were even more sorely pressed by Rangers to field a side representative of their power; four of the forwards are in their first season of senior football, and one, Rennet (Lochee Harp), was having his senior baptism. The absence from the Rangers team of Thornton and Duncanson and of McAuley and Tully from Celtic's undoubtedly reduced the element of skill. In addition most of the 22 players on view are in my opinion ordinary exponents who would otherwise have found it difficult to retain their place in the respective reserve eleven some ten years ago.

SCARED OF TROUBLE

Nevertheless these are not the reasons for the unreality of the latest "Old Firm" duel. In the first place the respective managements are so afraid of further trouble on the field and terracing that they have scared their players out of the natural expression of their football ability. The magnificent Waddell was one of few on Saturday who seemed capable of combined restraint with venturesomeness and McGuire gave notice that he has no time for namby-pamby ways.

For the rest, the majority displayed an obvious desire to be as unobtrusive as possible and to aid the cause of pacifism. Football, for all the niceties of ball control, is an unsatisfying spectacle without the exhilarating race for the ball and the breathtaking last-second tackle.

And what an atmosphere in which to try to play football! Once the spectator had passed the turnstiles around which were the notices warning him of the penalties of bad behaviour, he entered a ground like a cemetery in which policemen were deployed throughout the terracing as well as on the track. So silent were the throng that a vendor of something akin to the old "Pink Un" was clearly heard in the pressbox as he tried to sell his wares. The Celtic Supporters Association had been successful – the attendance of only 60,000 and the sparse population of the west section of the terracing proved that.

When Celtic appeared, no more than a few dozen pairs of hands clapped a welcome; not a scarf was waved, not a flag unfurled. As the game began, spectators entered from the west turnstile yet making for the east terracing making their way through forlorn groups of neutrals: Rangers followers of the milder variety, and a smattering of green and white rosetted men who had risked being called blacklegs, and made violent gestures to try to dissuade photographers from proving that the Celtic team were not entirely on their own.

When Findlay scored in 42 minutes and Rangers led 2-0 – Rutherford had shot the first goal in five minutes – Rangers' inside right looked almost apologetic. Whether his shyness in receiving the mild congratulations of his team-mates was caused by the realisation that Waddell by his delightful dribble by which he had rounded both Milne and Baillie and by his exquisite pass had done everything but put the ball in the net, or whether Findlay reasoned that the contest was now over, I do not know.

INTERVAL ENTERTAINMENT

During the half-time interval gloom unrelieved reigned on the west terracing, but a show of confidence emanated from the closely-packed eastern slopes. A large blue balloon which the police may have construed as being in the barred banner category was captured, but after a futile attempt at deflation it was allowed to bob away over the heads of men who sang "God Save the King," chanted of following on even to Dublin, and as a piece de resistance bellowed a concoction in which the words "no surrender" were distinguishable.

Waddell reminded us on the restart that we were watching a football match. Several of his swerves and titbits of ball control have rarely been equalled on a Scottish ground; one almost visualised the white-shirted figure of Matthews suddenly blessed with the power of finish. Milne, almost in despair, took his drubbing in as sportsmanlike a manner as was possible. Miller kept his goal in the best Celtic style, and McGuire dispensed his favours impartially. Evans, though far from being his enthusiastic self, Baillie and McPhail strove to remind their colleagues that they were wearing Celtic colours and the referee, Mr M.A. Mann (Perth), efficiently controlled players who would have paid homage to a schoolma'am refereeing a girls' hockey match.

Baillie squandered Celtic's best chance when he headed Collins' cross over the bar with the whole goal gaping, and Waddell scored a beauty which was disallowed on the statuesque signal of a linesman for offside which was as incorrect as it was absurd. Shaw, injured and at outside left, was fouled by you know whom, and Waddell offhandedly smote the penalty kick past Miller. The outside right ended for him a perfect day by laying a cross on Williamson's head and in went the fourth goal.

Three minutes remained and all that was left to see was the handshaking which was so general as almost to be suspect. Rangers' victory could not have been more complete but it was as hollow in the circumstances as it was decisive.

Rangers (2) 4	Celtic (0) 0
Rutherford	
Findlay	
Waddell (pen.)	
Williamson	

RANGERS:- BROWN; YOUNG AND SHAW; MCCOLL AND WOODBURN, RAE; WADDELL AND FINDLAY; WILLIAMSON; COX AND RUTHERFORD.

CELTIC:- MILLER; MCGUIRE AND MILNE; EVANS, BODEN AND BAILLIE; COLLINS AND MCPHAIL; HAUGHNEY; TAYLOR AND RENNETT.

The Fifties

By this time other clubs, notably Hibernian and Dundee, had got their acts together and were able to mount a genuine challenge to Rangers, with Hibernian winning two championships and Dundee two League Cups in the early part of the decade. And, despite the fact that Celtic won the Scottish Cup, beating Motherwell in 1951, Rangers were still the more powerful part of the Old Firm.

Celtic, however, pulled off a master stroke in 1951, when, in an attempt to strengthen their defence, they turned in the unlikely direction of Llanelli in Wales. There, seemingly playing out the twilight of his career, was Jock Stein, a former centre half with Albion Rovers.

Stein was bought for a nominal sum and quickly established himself as a great leader on the field. He captained the side to a Coronation Cup triumph in the summer of 1953 and the following season he led them to a League and Scottish Cup double. It was in a League Cup tie against Rangers in 1956 that he sustained a bad ankle injury which forced his retirement from the playing side of the game, but he had played a huge part in turning Celtic from also rans into winners.

Easily the greatest ever Old Firm triumph for Celtic came in October 1957 when they beat Rangers 7-1 in the League Cup Final. They wrote songs about that victory and to this day, Celtic fans rhyme off the winning team like some kind of litany - Beattie, Donnelly, Fallon, Fernie, Evans, Peacock, Tully, Collins, McPhail, Wilson and Mochan. On that day, Willie Fernie gave one of the finest ever performances by an individual in an Old Firm clash.

That same season, Rangers got a little revenge when they beat their Old rivals in the New Year's Day match at Parkhead. They also beat Celtic 2-0 in the Glasgow Cup, and when the pair drew 1-1 in the Charity Cup, Rangers won on the toss of a coin.

Rangers, however, with Scot Symon in charge, and players such as the brilliant Ian McMillan, Jimmy Millar, Ralph Brand, and Davie Wilson in the side, regained supremacy and won the Championship the following season, having again won the New Year's Day match at Ibrox. That match will be remembered for the dreadful conditions in which it was played. Celtic at one point appealed to the referee to abandon the proceedings, but, after consulting with his linesman., the ref ordered the sides to play on with Rangers winning 2-1. Eric Caldow scored with a penalty for the Ibrox side while Bertie Auld missed from the spot.

Celtic 1, Rangers 1 – Monday, 2nd January, 1950

Gift Equaliser for Rangers

One had to see the distress of Mallan, the Celtic left back, after he had completely missed his kick eight minutes before the end of the match at Parkhead, to appreciate the fortuitousness of Rangers' equalising goal.

Mallan, who had on his return to the first eleven after a long absence played a notable part in Celtic's defensive scheme, had all the time he required to clear a loose ball within his 18-yard line, but astonishingly he lost his balance, completely missed the ball, and McCulloch, far and away Rangers' best forward accepted the Ne'erday gift and equalised the goal scored by Weir after 36 minutes of play.

That goal too was the result of a defensive mistake, for Woodburn should never have intercepted Taylor's though pass to the centre forward.

The lasting impression of the fifty-fourth New Year match between the "Old Firm" rivals must be of deterioration in forward play compared with many memorable displays of the past. And, as is generally the cause of lack of constructive football, weakness at inside forward was principally responsible. Indeed the forward honours can easily be apportioned – to McCulloch for his quick acceleration and accurate crossing, to Weir for his enthusiastic leadership of the Celtic attack, and to Tully for many titbits of ball manipulation.

MCGRORY OUTSTANDING

For the rest the respective defences were much too capable for the edification of the well-behaved crowd. McGrory in particular spiked Thornton's guns in such a manner as to suggest that here is a young player who may go far in the game simply because he concentrates on the ball and refuses to be deceived by intricacies of swerve and dummy. With Evans and Baillie, who on the day were superior to McColl and Cox, McGrory completed a splendid half-back line.

Despite the fact that Celtic made seven positional changes – and three in personnel – compared with Saturday's side, they were the better combination and, accordingly, apart from Mallan's dreadful blunder, worthy of victory.

But from a hard and closely contested match one will remember firstly all the general failure of the forwards – Haughey and Findlay will not soon forget their misses near goal – and the admirable sporting spirit which both teams displayed. While it is true that both are mere shadows of the green-and-white and light blue teams of the past, they have nothing to learn on yesterday's showing of the rudiments of clean, honest, combat.

Celtic (1) 1	Rangers (0) 1
Weir	McCulloch

CELTIC:- BONNAR; BODEN AND MALLAN; EVANS, MCGRORY AND BAILLIE; COLLINS AND HAUGHEY; WEIR, TAYLOR AND TULLY.

RANGERS:- BROWN; YOUNG AND SHAW; COLL, WOODBURN AND COX; MCCULLOCH AND FINDLAY; THORNTON, JOHNSON AND MARSHALL.

The Celtic star of the fifties Bobby Collins scores against the auld enemy.

Celtic 3, Rangers 2 – Saturday, 6th May, 1950

Charity Cup Triumph for Celtic Youth

Celtic ended the 49-50 season as they began it – with a 3-2 victory over Rangers. Their Glasgow Charity Cup success was their first triumph in a major tournament since they won the Glasgow Cup in September 1943, and was all the more welcome on that account.

With less than seven minutes of the second half played, and Celtic three goals up, it looked as if Rangers were destined to suffer a beating such as they have not experienced for many a day; their veteran side appeared jaded and unusually apprehensive in defence. Yet the oldest player on the field almost snatched the Cup from the perhaps too confident Celtic youngsters.

Gillick, fielded at outside right, had made but a token appearance in the first half, in which only a momentary display of petulance when an offside decision was given against his side reminded us that this indeed was Gillick. Just before Celtic scored their third goal he and Paton changed positions and Rangers were soon to recapture some of the forward form that has eluded them for so long.

INSPIRED BY GILLICK

In 67 minutes after he had just failed to score with a left foot shot Gillick, with one of the short sharp bursts for which he was famous, shot a splendid goal from Cox's through pass. Instantly Celtic lost the initiative as another volley from the inside right almost took Thornton's head off; revelling in the confusion his accurate passing and astute sense of position was causing, the veteran of all veterans came within inches of slipping the ball past the outstretched Bonnar to a spot from which Thornton could not have missed scoring. Before Evans was able to restore calmness to the Celtic rear, Thornton headed a glorious goal from Cox's free kick in 78 minutes and there were visions of extra time in a match that Celtic looked to have had in their pockets. The Gillick-inspired spell did not – could not – last, however, as age finally gave way to youth.

HALF-BACK EXCELLENCE

This Celtic youth may be capable of restoring the club's reputation. The half-backs, whose average age is less than 22, were a magnificent unit in all but the short period in which the Gillick craft presented them with a new problem. There is no more improved player in Scotland than the towering McGrory, who refused to be deceived by Thornton's wiles. It was most satisfying to see Woodburn congratulate his opposite number at the close.

Another guardsman-like Celt, Haughney, showed considerable promise in his new position of right back and that despite the fact that Rangers for once had an outside left who looked the part. Hubbard is small and light but knows his limitations, crosses well with either foot and with a Cairns or a McPhail at his elbow might solve an Ibrox problem of long standing.

TIRED WOODBURN

Celtic may have similar hopes of their young Irishman, Peacock, becoming a most profitable inside left. They now know that the centre-forward position can safely be left to McPhail, who worried an obviously tired Woodburn throughout. Tully, particularly in the first half, was a delightful entertainer and so observant of etiquette as to make his critics of a few months ago wonder who is due the credit for the welcome change in his demeanour.

Such a foul as Paton perpetrated on the Celtic outside left shortly before half-time would on a less happy day have caused serious repercussions – especially as the referee did not think the offence called for more than a word of warning.

Celtic's first goal in 41 minutes resulted from an intricate piece of footwork in midfield by Tully and a lobbed pass to McPhail that the centre forward touched with his head before the ball glanced off Woodburn into the net. Their second, in 48, minutes was fortuitous, McPhail's harmless-looking shot being diverted past Brown by Cox, whose display was otherwise almost perfect. Three and a half minutes later one of McGrory's fine clearances from Thornton was gobbled up by Tully, whose cross was foozled by Shaw before being driven through by McPhail.

Glasgow Charity Cup Final

Celtic (1) 3	Rangers (0) 2
McPhail 2	Gillick
Cox o.g.	Thornton

CELTIC:- BONNAR; HAUGHNEY AND MILNE; EVANS, MCGRORY AND BAILLIE; COLLINS AND FERNIE; MCPHAIL, PEACOCK AND TULLY

RANGERS:- BROWN; LINDSAY AND SHAW; LITTLE, WOODBURN AND COX; GILLICK AND PATON; THORNTON, DUNCANSON AND HUBBARD.

Celtic 3, Rangers 2 – Saturday, 23rd September, 1950

Celtic Make Amends

Having castigated Celtic for their exhibition of recklessness against Motherwell in the League Cup quarter-final at Parkhead, I cannot but compliment the club on their greatly improved display against Rangers on the same ground on Saturday. The enthusiasm which against Motherwell degenerated into a riot of careless, unprofitable football has become subservient to skilful play and has immediately earned reward.

Celtic's first goal against Rangers was typical of their desire to show that their blunders of the previous Saturday were not going to be repeated. In midfield Baillie passed along the ground to Peacock, who deceived so able a defender as McColl with his quick change of direction and an unexpected slip to McPhail, while Tully gestured for the ball to be sent in his direction. The move threw the defence off their balance and before they had recovered, McPhail had once again changed the route of attack by flicking out to the left wing. Tully gobbled up the excellent pass and, drawing Young, crossed meticulously for the newcomer Weir to head a perfect goal.

The cheers had hardly died away when Thornton outmanoeuvred Mallan and let Rae in for a shot which gave Bonnar no chance as Fallon deflected it in its flight. Thirteen minutes were left for play when the extraordinary heading ability of Thornton gave Rangers the lead. Findlay glanced with his head a corner kick taken by Rutherford and Celtic's defenders appeared to stand aside as the ball flashed wide of goal. Thornton, who had expected to be the recipient of the kick had began his run from the 18-yard line but without diminishing his speed he swerved and with delicious timing headed a goal in a thousand. Rangers for the first time in the game looked like winning.

PENALTY KICK

There was no panic in the Celtic team, however, and by continued careful approach play Tully was once again placed in position for another of his dangerous crosses. Over the ball went but Woodburn, standing some six yards away intercepted. The referee, with a clear view, signalled for a penalty kick, to the consternation of Rangers. I thought the ball struck Woodburn on the shoulder and saw no sign of him arming or handling, but the referee waved away all protests and McPhail scored from the penalty kick.

The jubilant Celts struck again, five minutes from time, and again Tully's cross led to the goal. So judicious was his job that Brown could only palm out, and after Collins had headed against the underside of the bar Peacock almost burst the net on the rebound.

Rangers will with reason maintain that the penalty incident cost them the match but in view of the referee's leniency on previous occasions they can have no legitimate grievance. Early in the second half Cox prevented a pass from reaching Weir by using his arm. If there had been any doubt about the infringement it was dissipated by Cox's instantaneously crushing the limb into his body and hanging his head as he waited the whistle. Rangers escaped then, when the score was still 0-0 and again before the opening goal when Young foiled Tully with a tackle that reminded one of that far from graceful dance "Boomps-a-Daisy."

Mallan made a timeous return to his best form in Celtic's defence, and that was extremely important from their point of view, for Thornton was once again almost the entire Rangers' attack. The Celtic backs are by no means satisfactory, however, and I am sure a more resolute winger than Rutherford and a more capable one than Rae would have made Milne and Fallon pay dearly for their first-time sliding tackling. Mallan showed remarkable power of recovery when his backs had been left sprawling on the ground. Evans, though less artistic than McColl in the first half, was easily the outstanding wing half-back. Weir took twenty minutes to get the feel of his first important game and then showed splendid promise.

VALUE OF TULLY

The man who made most of the difference to Celtic was, however, Tully. Sometimes his trickery ends on in the deception of himself and his team-mates but when he uses the ball, he really uses it. As he prepares to cross or pass he seems to say, "Put your head and foot to scoring position and I'll not be an inch out with the ball."

I thought Lindsay was Rangers' best player. That Collins was so quiet is a tribute to the intelligence of the reserve left back. There was no sign of improvement in the forward line. Some day Thornton will be off his game, and the men will be saying that the team selection should have stopped at Cox.

Celtic (1) 3	Rangers (1) 2
Weir	Rae
McPhail	Thornton
Peacock	

CELTIC:- BONNAR; FALLON AND MILNE; EVANS MALLAN AND BAILLIE; COLLINS AND WEIR (D); MCPHAIL, PEACOCK AND TULLY.

RANGERS:- BROWN; YOUNG AND LINDSAY; MCCOLL, WOODBURN AND COX; RUTHERFORD AND FINDLAY; THORNTON, JOHNSON AND RAE.

Rangers 1, Celtic 0 – Monday, 1st January, 1951

Celtic Gamble Fails

The roar of approval that greeted the return of McPhail to the Celtic forward line at Ibrox Stadium yesterday indicated that the Parkhead club's followers, despite the success of his deputy McAlinden against Hearts two days earlier, had great hopes of the Internationalist leading his side to victory.

When after only nine minutes he had hit the crossbar with a tremendous free kick from 20 yards it did seem as if McPhail was making a triumphal return. When, however, with Rangers leading through Waddell's goal in 24 minutes, the Celtic team lined up for the second half and McPhail was at outside left, even the most perfervid supporter realised that something was wrong. Something was, for McPhail was hardly able to walk all through the second half. Celtic's gamble in fielding the player while a strain was still troubling him had failed.

As it was, they were perhaps a little unfortunate not to draw. Even after the enforced reconstruction of their attack, with Collins and Tully forming the right wing and Weir at centre forward, they played more combined football on the deplorable ground than did Rangers. They had no such powerful raider as Waddell, however, and no such steady back as Young. These two Rangers, along with Woodburn, were outstanding. Mallan was as capable as Woodburn for all that he had a much harder task than his opposite number. The Celtic centre half was second only to Baillie as his team's best player.

It was not a game to remember. The conditions were appalling, with the centre of the field dotted with puddles of water and with the wing portions hard and greasy. In addition, there was far too much fouling and far too much latitude allowed by the referee. I saw Simpson kicking out at Mallan in the first half when the ball was yards away, and Evans committing a similar offence after he had been awarded a free kick. Young was permitted almost a minute's argument with the referee after he had back-heeled the ball away over the track towards the area where one section of the fanatics had their stance, and one recalled a similar instance of dissent in the same area of the ground as a result of which a Rangers forward was sent from the field.

Lack of common sense and sportsmanship seem to be forever associated with a Rangers-Celtic fixture. No wonder the crowd misbehave. Fortunately, there was no serious incident. Only one bottle so far as I could see was introduced to the arena, though its flight was so close to Weir as he ran to take a corner kick at the north end of the stand that the player must have thought that one was quite enough.

Rangers (1) 1	Celtic (0) 0
Waddell	

RANGERS:- BROWN; YOUNG AND SHAW; McCOLL, WOODBURN AND COX; WADDELL AND FINDLAY; SIMPSON (W.); THORNTON AND PATON.

CELTIC:- BONNAR; FALLON AND MILNE; EVANS, MALLAN AND BAILLIE; WEIR (J.) AND COLLINS; McPHAIL; PEACOCK AND TULLY.

Rangers 2, Celtic 1 – Wednesday, 2nd May, 1951

Rangers' Charity Cup Win at Hampden

Rangers qualified to meet Third Lanark in a quarter-final of the Glasgow Charity Cup on Saturday by beating Celtic at Hampden Park last night. There was no doubt that Rangers deserved their success though mid-way through the first half, when a pall of darkness and hail and sleet made the scene as wintry as any experienced this season, it was touch and go for the game's being abandoned when the Ibrox team were two goals ahead. Celtic's fine rally in the second half just failed to give them a draw.

Before 70,000 spectators, Rangers scored in four minutes, Thornton heading a spectacular goal from Young's free kick taken near mid-field.

Celtic's defence did not impress with their marking on that occasion, and four minutes later they lost another goal through a defensive error. Rollo lost possession to Waddell on the touchline and from the winger's through pass Findlay slipped the ball past Hunter.

Celtic were not dispirited and for the next 15 minutes they forced the pace. Brown had the only close call, however, when he had to dive at Welsh's feet from McPhail's intelligent pass. For 15 minutes before the interval a skilful game appeared likely to be ruined by the conditions.

The light had returned when the second half started, but the pitch bore traces of the first-half storm. Celtic switched Tully and Peacock momentarily but Collins went for good it seemed to outside right. Celtic were much more dangerous with the assistance of the wind which was not, however, of its first-half strength. Rangers had a lucky escape when Tully, easily Celtic's best forward, had his shot directed past the post by Young.

The outstanding forward on the field, however, was Waddell, whose strong running and clever dribbling were too much for the erratic Rollo. Waddell created more havoc in one individual raid than the entire Celtic forward line did in two.

Eight minutes from the end, Tully headed a fine goal from Collins's cross – a goal Celtic fully deserved on their second-half display.

Glasgow Charity Cup

Rangers (2) 2	Celtic (0) 1
Thornton	Tully
Findlay	
Attendance	70,000

CELTIC:- HUNTER; FALLON AND ROLLO; EVANS, McGRORY AND BAILLIE; WALSH AND COLLINS; McPHAIL; PEACOCK AND TULLY.

RANGERS:- BROWN; YOUNG AND SHAW; McCOLL, WOODBURN AND COX; WADDELL AND FINDLAY; THORNTON; SIMPSON (W.) AND RUTHERFORD.

Rangers 1, Celtic 1 – Saturday, 22nd September, 1951
Rangers and Celtic Again in Good Graces

Rangers and Celtic provided a most adequate and welcome answer to the charge that their fixtures are irrevocably linked with disturbances on and off the field. I am breaking no confidences by saying that for probably the first time in the history of this match the result was less important to both managements than ever it has been. The teams were instructed to play football and forget everything else, and the players' response was admirable.

It was not a case of the game being allowed to deteriorate into a namby-pamby affair through fear of the consequences of over-zealous rivalry; indeed, while there was as little quarter asked or given as in the past, both teams contrived to arouse new enthusiasm for Scottish football as it used to be played – the clever dribble, the accurate pass along the ground, the breathtaking shot.

Only the insincere would deny that in the recent past Celtic have been a better disciplined eleven than Rangers, but on Saturday the balance was restored and no one did more to achieve that than McColl, Woodburn or Cox, who took the first available opportunity of making amends for their midweek misdemeanors.

BATTLE OF BEHAVIOUR

The result being of less moment than the manner in which it was achieved, Rangers would have been wholly satisfied with their draw had not they been let down by some of their supporters. It would not, of course, have been an "Old Firm" match, had everything in the garden been lovely. Rangers had commendably made it clear in the press and in their programme that such things as banners, party-tune singing and foul language would not be tolerated.

The outcome was almost incredible, for even when Collins scored his magnificent goal in 21 minutes there was not a sign of a banner associated with Celtic and yet before and throughout the match there was considerable vaunting of flags at the Rangers followers' end of the ground. We do not know all the party tunes, but we have heard some in the past from Celtic supporters. On Saturday we strained our ears in vain to catch a note in praise of Erin's green valleys, but no extra effort was necessary to pick out from the clamour at the Copland Road end the old Ibrox lyrics. From beneath the orange and blue and the Union Jack the faithful promised over and over again to guard old Derry's walls and to follow, follow, even unto Dublin.

Only the waving of a myriad of green and white scarves, a bout of slow hand-clapping that mingled derision almost with dignity, and at half-time the necessarily slight variation in the promises to follow, follow, denoted the opposition's disfavour. Thus was the battle of behaviour clearly won by the Celtic crowd, some of whose components in the past have been decisively out-pointed.

Collins' goal was the most memorable feature of a most satisfying match. It was the more remarkable in that it was scored when Celtic had only ten players on the field, McPhail having retired in the eighteenth minute suffering from a nasty head cut. The remarkable power of the smallest player of the 22 was evident in Collins' sudden shot from 25 yards which Brown may have done very well indeed to have touched. McPhail was absent for 10 minutes, and strangely Rangers had one of their worst spells during that absence. It was then that the splendid stamina of the younger Celts stood their side in great stead. Once McPhail returned, an unhappy wan figure of a man making a token appearance at outside right, Rangers strangely again improved and in view of their early brilliance and the chances they had missed, they were unfortunate to be a goal behind.

They were probably quite thankful for their draw in the end however, and certainly lucky that McPhail was unable to take over his own position. In the first place a fit McPhail would not have permitted Woodburn the command he had in the air, and in the second – and more important – place, his being at outside right against the inexperienced Little gave Rangers respite they certainly would not have enjoyed had Collins, easily the best forward of all, been there.

FALLON'S MISTAKE

The eighteenth minute of the second half proved as unfortunate for Celtic as the eighteenth in the first half had been. Fallon could have allowed Young's high pass to go by for a goal-kick; instead, he duffed a left-foot clearance into the tracks of Findlay, who with one fine raking shot did something to retrieve his reputation. Rangers' claim for a penalty kick for Baillie's alleged handling was refused, as had been Celtic's in the fourth minute of the match when Walsh went down after a tackle by Cox. A flashing header from Peacock struck the crossbar after a delightful Celtic movement in which the ball passed from the feet of six of their players. Findlay had earlier missed from a short range following a similar exquisite attack by Rangers, and in the end justice was served in there being no more goals.

Young, a great player and a great sportsman (who won even the Celtic supporters' praise when he assisted an injured Peacock), Brown, McColl, Woodburn and Gardiner were outstanding Rangers. Rollo (master of Waddell in everything but speed), all three half-backs, Collins and Peacock were the finest Celts. The most entertaining player of all was not Tully, though he performed intelligently and well against Young, but Baillie, who has never had a better match. Nor, I dare say, has the referee.

Rangers (0) 1	Celtic (1) 1
Findlay	Collins

RANGERS :– BROWN: YOUNG AND LITTLE, MCCOLL, WOODBURN AND COX: WADDELL AND FINDLAY: GARDINER: THORNTON AND HUBBARD.

CELTIC :– DEVANNEY: FALLON AND ROLLO: EVANS, BODEN AND BAILLIE: COLLINS AND WALSH: MCPHAIL, PEACOCK AND TULLY.

Rangers 3, Celtic 0 – Saturday, 13th October, 1951

Vital Minute at Hampden

Rangers entered the League Cup final in the 44th minute at Hampden Park – that is, with just over half the game remaining to be played. In that minute Boden, the Celtic centre half-back, was injured, and as he lay unconscious, Johnson, with one of his cannon-ball shots, scored Rangers' second goal. It was evident even to the most perfervid Celtic supporter that this team's chance had gone, for even with 11 fit players they had rather the worse of a match that in the first half-hour promised to be one of the best contests between the famous rivals.

Had not Boden been injured when he was, the superior stamina of the younger Celtic team might have enabled them to stage one of their traditional second-half rallies, particularly as after the interval they had the slight advantage of the wind. Some would have it, too, that the referee should have stopped play when Boden fell, apparently seriously hurt, and that in that event Rangers would not have scored the important second goal.

It is always a difficult task for a referee to decide when to call a halt because of injury, and as Boden, who was much too late in trying to tackle Waddell, contributed to his injury, I do not think Celtic have a legitimate grievance, though there is no doubt that on this occasion they were unfortunate.

FIRST-HALF STANDARD

Boden did not reappear until 12 minutes of the second half had gone, and by that time Rangers were three goals up, Findlay having headed a splendid goal in 54 minutes after Waddell had bamboozled Rollo and crossed with precision. Rangers did not thereafter need to go all out, and that probably accounts for their not maintaining the standard of their play in the first half, which must have been a revelation to the thousands of people who have been lamenting the Ibrox club's recent displays.

The decision to field Thornton at centre forward and Johnson at inside-left contributed greatly to Rangers' victory. Thornton cannot, of course, be expected to provide the complete answer to Rangers' forward problems, for he is approaching the end of his career, but on Saturday this first-class ball-player introduced his most valuable leadership to an attack that has been sadly lacking that asset. Johnson, who throughout was the most dangerous shot on the field, turned out to be another trump card.

Celtic had no forward to compare with these two players or with Waddell, who latterly had Rollo running round in circles. The left-back was extremely lucky not to suffer more drastic punishment than a free-kick when he swung his boot wildly at the winger late in the game. That indeed was not the first offence of this type, for he had made a similar gesture after Waddell had crudely fouled Baillie in the first half.

What with one thing and another, the left side of the Celtic defence had a dreadful day. It was the infringement by Baillie on Waddell that led to Rangers' first goal, Thornton heading it from Young's free kick. When Waddell gained possession before he made the cross from which Johnson scored, it was the result of a pass from Baillie which went straight to McColl's feet, and a replica of the mistake started Waddell on the run that gave Findlay his goal.

MCCOLL OUTSTANDING

There was no comparable weakness in Rangers' defence in which the understanding of Young, McColl and Woodburn was noteworthy. McColl was the best player of the 22, his passing on the ground being consistently accurate and frequently inside the opposing back, which is the most profitable of all.

Brown, who was beaten twice and did not lose a goal – Tully hit the bar in the first half and Boden did likewise from outside left in the second – was masterly in his cutting out of high crosses. He would not have lost the goal that Thornton headed.

Celtic had few distinguished players. McPhail had scant assistance from inside forwards who were seldom up with him and he was well held by Woodburn – and only once unfairly. That incident in the first half should have resulted in a penalty kick, but, judging from the grotesque attempt by Peacock to equalise in the first half and the equally remiss effort by Weir in the second, Celtic might even have missed a penalty kick.

League Cup Final

Rangers (2) 3	Celtic (0) 0
Thornton	
Johnson	
Findlay	

RANGERS:- BROWN, YOUNG AND LITTLE, MCCOLL, WOODBURN AND COX, WADDELL AND FINDLAY, THORNTON, JOHNSON AND RUTHERFORD.

CELTIC:- FALLON AND ROLLO, EVANS, BODEN AND BAILLIE, WEIR (J) AND COLLINS, MCPHAIL, PEACOCK AND TULLY.

Celtic 1, Rangers 4 – Tuesday, 1st January, 1952
Handicapped Rangers' Skill

The disgraceful behaviour of a small section of the 40,000 crowd at Celtic Park almost succeeded in spoiling the pleasure of the vast majority, who could not possibly have expected to see so exhilarating and so skilful a display of football as both teams – and Rangers in particular – provided on a ground that was a sea of melting snow and mud.

When hundreds of spectators were scrambling on the track and even for a moment encroaching on the playing pitch, the players continued to act as if nothing were happening to distract their attention. It is to the great credit of all of them that nothing happened on the field which could have been construed as provocative of the hooliganism at the Celtic supporters' end of the ground.

Rangers gained a richly deserved victory – an almost unbelievably decisive victory in view of the fact that they played with 10 men for almost the last half-hour of the match.

After Shaw had been carried off on a stretcher suffering from a leg injury – he went down in a tackle with Tully, who was penalised – Rangers withdrew Cox to left back and scored almost direct from the deputy defender's free-kick, Cox's punt being glided by Thornton to Paton, who scored his second and his side's third goal with a splendid low shot. In 71 minutes another free kick – conceded this time by Evans, who I thought had reason to be disgruntled for being penalised – was driven to the net with terrific force from 22 yards by Waddell, who thus completed a day of personal triumph.

Celtic's inexperienced youngster, Jack, had little answer to the outside right's speed and ball control. Some of the combined moves of Thornton and Waddell were astonishingly skilful in the circumstances and conditions. Thornton made the passes which led to Rangers' first three goals. Celtic had no chance-maker to compare with him and no goal-taker to compare with Paton.

The introduction of Shaw was an astute move, for the veteran frequently baulked Celtic's best forward, Collins. Woodburn completely mastered Weir, and McColl and Prentice seemed to revel in the heavy going. Late in the match Brown made three exceptionally fine saves. He was fortunate only once, just before half-time, Collins' cross-shot beating the far post with the goalkeeper sprawling.

GIFT GOAL

Bell, another Celtic youngster, cost his side the important opening goal in 15 minutes when he tried to advance and field Thornton's through pass far ahead of Liddell, who accepted the gift with alacrity. Fallon, Evans (Celtic's best player), Baillie, Collins and Tully came nearest to the standard set by Waddell and Thornton, two masterly players indeed.

The conditions obviously were more to the liking of the taller and heavier Rangers, but it was their skill rather than their strength and stamina which brought success.

Tully scored Celtic's goal in 20 minutes with a shrewd lob from 30 yards which mystified Brown. Paton a minute later scored his first goal.

Celtic (1) 1	Rangers (2) 4
Tully	Liddell
	Paton 2
	Waddell
Attendance	40,000

CELTIC :– BELL, FALLON AND JACK, STEIN AND BAILLIE, COLLINS AND WALSH, WEIR (J), PEACOCK AND TULLY

RANGERS :– BROWN, YOUNG AND SHAW, MCCOLL, WOODBURN AND PRENTICE, WADDELL AND PATON, THORNTON, COX AND LIDDELL.

Celtic 2, Rangers 1 – Saturday, 20th September, 1952
Walsh's Great Goal

There have been better Celtic-Rangers games in the past than on Saturday at Parkhead but many more have been worse. So long as such immaculate ball-players as Thornton and Tully are permitted to display their skill a game cannot be dull, and it is to the credit of both teams and to the referee, whose control of play was never in question, that the match was not won and lost, as it had been in the past, by unfair tactics.

If only for the fact that they scored one of the finest goals that has ever been seen in Scottish football, Celtic deserved their victory. In four minutes, after Fallon had fallen over the ball some 30 yards from Rangers' goal, Walsh's speed enabled him to beat McColl to the ball, his intelligent control baffled Woodburn, and his accuracy and power of shot from 18 yards gave Niven no chance to save.

GOALKEEPER'S ERROR

It was a goal that the Celtic followers could only have dreamed about. When five minutes later Niven allowed a speculative cross from the touchline by Rollo to drop over his head to put Celtic two goals up, the position was almost incredible – Celtic, with two full backs in the forward line, and even before that the decision of selection had taken the less fancied team on the road to victory.

Though Rangers twice in the match had goals disallowed for offside – the first, scored by McCulloch, could have been invalid by only the narrowest of margins – they did not look like saving the day until, 18 minutes from the end, a misunderstanding between Meechan and Baillie led to Liddell's scoring. Had Rangers then had another Thornton they might then have profited from the first sign of a Celtic panic, but Thorntons are as scarce in Scottish football as strawberries in December.

Rangers for long periods played attractively in the centre of the field, and McColl and Cox gave their forwards splendid service, but Evans and Baillie had the answer to the Thorne-Grierson plan and Thornton, for all his shrewdness, was rarely permitted to attempt to win the game on his own by a steady centre-half whose success in the air was a potent factor in Celtic's success. Rangers' left-wing problem is still with them and Liddell must still be wondering why he failed to score midway through the first half after a delightful Thornton move had spreadeagled the defence.

Bonnar, who made a magnificent first-half save from Cox's header, and the Celtic backs gave most capable performances. A special word of praise is due to Meechan, whose sense of position countered the superior speed of McCulloch. Evans' anticipation of danger on the right side of Rangers' attack saved his side on several occasions.

Both Walsh and Tully were far from ahead of their opposite numbers. Tully, whose first-half foul on Young was the only annoying infringement, was the man who rallied his side late in the secondhalf through his ability to hold the ball. "We want Tully," the Rangers' end had shouted after the Young incident. They may have been sorry, for they probably got more of him than they wished.

FALLON'S SUCCESS

The playing of Fallon at centre-forward was a successful Celtic experiment, though he was frequently pulled up for his method of charging. Fallon showed however, that he was no mere bludgeon, and if his header in the fourteenth minute had entered the net instead of striking the crossbar, one doubts whether this moderate Rangers side would have prevented a debacle.

There was a general expression of good feeling at the end although Young refused to join Tully in the ceremony.

Celtic (2) 2	Rangers (0) 1
Walsh	Liddell
Rollo	

CELTIC :– BONNAR: BODEN AND MEECHAN: EVANS, STEIN AND BAILLIE: ROLLO AND WALSH: FALLON, TULLY AND PEACOCK.

RANGERS :– NIVEN: YOUNG AND LITTLE: MCCOLL, WOODBURN AND COX: MCCULLOCH AND GRIERSON: THORNTON, PRENTICE AND LIDDELL.

Rangers 1, Celtic 0 – Saturday, 1st January, 1953
Drab Display at Ibrox

Perhaps Rangers and Celtic, like the 65,000 crowd who attended their match at Ibrox Stadium, were taken aback by the spring-like weather that favoured them; perhaps they too were surprised that even the ruder elements of the multitude should behave, generally speaking, in a manner akin to human beings. Whatever the reason, their display was almost completely lacking in distinction.

I cannot recall a less entertaining "Old Firm" game unless it be that of a few seasons ago when, on the same ground, Celtic's supporters boycotted a match and their team played as if they were unwilling participants.

There was little sustained attacking play on either side. Most of the attempts to break down the defence were so orthodox that they were doomed to failure almost before they began. Each one of the ten forwards contributed occasional flashes of skill but rarely did two of one side appear to be in the same mood at the same time.

INSIDE FORWARDS HELD

There was so little between the teams that a goalless draw would have been the most suitable result. Rangers always looked the likelier side in attack, but they rarely impressed when they came within shooting range. Evans, Stein and Rollo mopped up almost every inside forward move; only the sprightly little Hubbard's darts and the crosses of Waddell were dangerous to Celtic.

It was a Waddell cross which led to Rangers' goal – a goal for which Hunter must accept full responsibility. He saw the ball all the way, moved out to intercept it in the air, and then suddenly stopped as if he were mindful of the possibility of being tackled by an inrushing forward.

In any event he was much too late when he renewed his run out, and Simpson headed simply into the net. The goal came in the eighth minute of the second half, and towards the end Prentice hit Hunter's knees with a shot of such speed that the goalkeeper could do nothing more than involuntarily close his legs. Hunter had few other anxious minutes and Niven was similarly free from worry. He made a splendid save soon after Simpson's goal, when Peacock's header from Collins' cross seemed to be sneaking inside his right hand post.

IMMATURE

Rangers' half-backs had even greater mastery over the opposing inside forwards than had Celtic's. Woodburn has seldom had so easy a match, McIlroy's immaturity being evident from the start.

Rangers were lucky on two occasions. In the first half Cox held Collins's leg as the winger was about to shoot from inside the penalty area; the referee did not detect an offence, however, and there was no penalty kick. In the second half Waddell twice within a few minutes fouled Tully and should certainly have been cautioned to say the least. These were the only infringements of an unsportsmanlike nature.

Rangers (0) 1	Celtic (0) 0
Simpson	

RANGERS :– NIVEN; YOUNG AND LITTLE; MCCOLL, WOODBURN AND COX; WADDELL AND GRIERSON; SIMPSON; PRENTICE AND HUBBARD.

CELTIC :– HUNTER; HAUGHNEY AND MEECHAN; EVANS, STEIN AND ROLLO; COLLINS AND FERNIE; MCILROY; PEACOCK AND TULLY.

Rangers 2, Celtic 0 – Saturday, 14th March, 1953

Deserved Victory for Rangers

"It was a great game," said the Rangers supporter as he left Ibrox Stadium on Saturday. "It was a terrible game," said the Celtic supporter as he made his way home from the opposite end of the ground. It was neither, says this reporter who, like the vast majority of the 95,000 crowd, was thankful for the small mercies of football provided and glad that disorderly behaviour was for once absent from the playing field.

It will be a miracle if Rangers and Celtic ever again attain in an "Old Firm" contest the standard of play of some of their predecessors. The present circumstances practically preclude natural, healthy rivalry.

TENSE ATMOSPHERE

It can be taken for granted that both sides on Saturday had strict instructions to refrain from provocative conduct. The demeanour of several of the players indicated that they were so busy trying to be gentlemen that they had little time to carry on their profession, and though there were many skilful touches and odd bouts of admirable combined play, something was missing. It can be said with justification that Rangers and Celtic today carry players who would have been lucky to get the chance of carrying the hamper 20 years ago, but even the best footballer is liable to be upset by such an atmosphere as pervaded Saturday's match.

Policemen on the track and on the terracing were even more prominent than usual and for the first time in my recollection an appeal was made before the start of the match by the police authorities that banners and provocative emblems should not be flaunted. That appeal was unsuccessful for Union Jacks and Orange flags were observed at one end of the ground and Eire tricolours – for a section of the Celtic supporters have resumed their ill-advised ways – at the other. The sash was worn a thousand times and the green valleys of Erin traversed just as often, but there was even less happy harmony than there ever has been in the segregated crowd: one felt that the volcano would erupt at any moment. Such are the depths to which we have sunk.

DOMINATING DEFENDERS

Rangers fully deserved their victory. Though they might have been expected to start under a psychological disadvantage, they played for the most part coolly and, apart from their scoring attempts, intelligently. In the first half hour their defence frequently conceded free kicks – in the match 21 were awarded against Rangers, and 11 against Celtic – and McColl, apparently for disagreeing with the referee's having penalised him for impeding Walsh, had his name taken. There was no sign, however, of the rashness of the previous Saturday.

Woodburn, after two infringements – on two of only three occasions in which Celtic found a way through the centre – played a magnificent game. Young, who was a superb constructive player as well as a defender, and Little, consistently successful against Collins, formed with their centre half a barrier which Celtic found more and more difficult to penetrate.

ESCAPES

The industrious Prentice and the agile Grierson made inroads into the opposing defence that their opposite numbers were not capable of emulating and had Simpson, a clever distributor of the ball, been half as good as when he shot or headed, the Celtic support would have left their pitches long before they did. As it was, Rangers led at half-time only by a goal scored by Prentice in the twelfth minute after the ball had broken favourably to him from a Grierson-McPhail duel.

In addition Rangers survived a remarkable minute just before the interval in which Collins shot against a post. Tully shot against Niven from only six yards, and another Collins shot that had the goalkeeper beaten, was headed from under the crossbar by Little.

Grierson was always the most likely goal-scorer and a splendid left foot shot from the inside right early in the second half beat Hunter completely and rebounded from the base of a post. Hunter was often in trouble through fast orthodox Rangers raids, whereas Niven for almost the entire second half had merely to stand and watch Celtic's forwards cross-passing to their own doom. The final pass would be a foot out and in would step Young, Little or Woodburn and clear almost contemptuously.

Twenty minutes from time Walsh headed incongruously past from Tully's cross and two minutes from the end Grierson showed his rivals how to score when he cut through with Simpson's headed pass, enticed Hunter from his goal and slid the ball into the net.

CHANGE OF POSITION

Had Celtic switched Collins inside earlier than the 75th minute, they might have profited. The change when it was made was much more likely to succeed than all the wanderings of Tully, Walsh and Fernie, who did not play well in their selected positions and "improved worse" as the saying goes, in others.

The best Celts, like the best Rangers, were defenders. Yet Haughney and Stein were rarely so dominating in their positions as were Young and Woodburn. Evans and McPhail – the left-half's shrewd distribution in the second half was to inept forwards – played courageously throughout.

The refereeing was splendid.

Rangers (1) 2	Celtic (0) 0
Prentice	
Grierson	
Attendance	**95,000**

RANGERS :– NIVEN: YOUNG AND LITTLE: MCCOLL, WOODBURN AND COX: PATON AND GRIERSON: SIMPSON, PRENTICE AND HUBBARD.

CELTIC :– HUNTER: HAUGHNEY AND MEECHAN: EVANS, STEIN AND MCPHAIL: COLLINS AND FERNIE: MCGRORY, WALSH AND TULLY.

Rangers 1, Celtic 1 – Tuesday, 1st September, 1953

Rangers and Celtic Draw Enjoyable Match

To the great surprise of the majority of the 60,000 crowd at Ibrox Stadium last night, Celtic not only held the "hot" favourites, Rangers, in a Glasgow Cup semi-final but came within an ace of beating them – and that despite the fact that barely two minutes after Peacock, in the 28th minute, had scored a glorious leading goal with his right foot from nearly 30 yards, Celtic suffered the misfortune of having Bonnar injured. The goal-keeper returned to the outside left position five minutes after half-time.

When, 25 minutes from the end, Walsh flashed through the centre with one of his many superb passes that McPhail distributed to all around him and shot strongly from 25 yards strongly and well away from Niven, one could almost sense Rangers' thoughts that they had lost a game which they had been expected to win. Walsh's magnificent effort struck the post, however, and Bonnar, with his right arm tight to his side, was just not quick enough to steer the rebound into the empty net.

Fourteen minutes from time Hubbard, roaming inside, took on the drop a ball that had been misheaded by Prentice and shot a fine equalising goal – a goal that eventually meant a replay at Celtic Park tomorrow evening.

Celtic's reorganised defence with Evans acting as goalkeeper in a manner that suggested he had been born for the job, Stein a centre half of tremendous power and stamina and the youthful Conroy surprising possibly even his sponsors, have never been more impressive.

McPhail was a masterly centre forward, measuring his passes with grand judgement and disturbing Rangers' defence with his flair for moving out of the supposed normal beat. A splendid save by Niven early in the game prevented McPhail from scoring with one of his swerving free kicks, and sure handling by the goalkeeper denied Walsh more than once when late in the match McPhail was still spreadeagling his opponents by skill and skill alone.

Evans too, made at least one first class save, which stopped a terrific low shot from McColl, far and away Rangers' most prominent player. I thought Young set a very high standard of sportsmanship by refraining from making physical contact with the handicapped Bonnar – on more than one occasion the "lame duck" almost made Young and Rangers pay for their sporting behaviour.

Glasgow Cup Semi-Final

Rangers (0) 1	Celtic (1) 1
Hubbard	Peacock
Attendance	60,000

RANGERS :– NIVEN: YOUNG AND LITTLE: MCCOLL, WOODBURN AND COX: WADDELL AND GRIERSON: PATON: PRENTICE AND HUBBARD.

CELTIC :– BONNAR: HAUGHNEY AND MEECHAN: EVANS, STEIN AND CONROY: COLLINS AND WALSH: MCPHAIL: PEACOCK AND FERNIE.

Celtic 0, Rangers 4 – Thursday, 3rd September, 1953

Rangers Punish Celtic of Many Blunders

Having had approximately a dozen goal-scoring attempts, in 90 minutes play at Celtic Park last night and having succeeded with four, Rangers routed Celtic in their Glasgow Cup semi-final replay and qualified to meet Third Lanark in the Final on September 28 at Hampden Park.

The result was fantastic, but that is not to say that Rangers did not deserve to win. They did, if only for the all-round superiority of their defence, for the fast penetrative raiding of Waddell, and for their ability to snatch the scoring opportunity that a negligent and often panic-stricken opposing defence permitted.

Hunter was beaten four times but had not a single save that was worth noting. Niven, on the other hand, had the save of the match after only five minutes play, and it was from the fourth shot driven by Evans – a right half, mark you – in that brief period.

Mochan, whose dilatoriness had allowed McColl to start Waddell on the first successful run which led to Grierson's shooting a splendid goal in the sixth minute, almost atoned on three or four occasions when his terrific shots with either foot beat Niven but flashed just over or wide. Mochan and the other Celtic forwards had many other efforts not nearly so praiseworthy, and when Rangers, having faced a strong wind, turned two goals up, there was only one outcome probable.

Stein had objected strongly to Rangers' second goal headed by Paton in 12 minutes from a Waddell cross. The centre half may have had reason to complain about the manner in which he was beaten in the air, and one lasting memory of this match is the astonishing superiority Paton enjoyed over him in the heading duels. In any event Stein went from one error to another, paid the penalty of losing control of himself, and must bear the brunt of the defeat.

STEIN'S ERRORS

Fourteen minutes after half-time he allowed a duffed shot by Grierson to roll in on Hunter, and Paton nipped into the muddle of misunderstanding and accepted the gift with alacrity. Six minutes later a huge kick by Young dropped apparently favourably for Stein, and apparently awkwardly for Paton, but the ball spun back on to the Celtic goal and Prentice had more time and room than he may find during the rest of the season to complete Celtic's discomfiture.

Glasgow Cup Semi-Final Replay

Celtic (0) 0	Rangers (2) 4
	Grierson
	Paton 2
	Prentice

CELTIC :– HUNTER: HAUGHEY AND MEECHAN: EVANS, STEIN AND PEACOCK: COLLINS AND WELSH: MCPHAIL: MEECHAN AND FERNIE.

RANGERS :– NIVEN: YOUNG AND LITTLE: MCCOLL, WOODBURN AND COX: WADDELL AND GRIERSON: PATON, PRENTICE AND HUBBARD.

Rangers 1, Celtic 1 – Saturday, 19th September, 1953

Waddell's Great Day at Ibrox

Though the second half of the Ibrox match was tame in comparison with the first, I am not disposed to believe that the players, who had seen nothing of the disturbance at half-time but no doubt knew of it, were affected to the point of not indulging in their natural game.

POOR SHOOTING

Tully made an auspicious return to the Celtic team, and frequently baffled his immediate opponent, McColl, with dexterous footwork and sprayed inviting passes all around. McPhail in particular co-operated and the result was some delightful football on the ground.

Rangers, for their part, were far from idle in attack, though their methods of threatening the Celtic goal were entirely different. Rangers indeed had only one forward of note for all of the 90 minutes – but what a forward he was. Waddell has rarely played a better part for his side. Almost invariably he had the beating of an injudicious Fallon, who seemed short of match-practice, and his crossing with either foot was superb.

Bell was the much busier goalkeeper, although Celtic had more command of the ball in midfield. He was beaten in the twenty-first minute when Paton, taking advantage of a slip by Stein, which resulted either from the treacherous foothold or indecision on the centre half's part, shot intelligently into the corner of the net. Paton had few other intelligent moments, however, and on this occasion his tendency to play the centre half instead of the ball in a duel in the air was not allowed to be profitable. Duncan, who early in the second half changed positions with a Tully whose energy had gone, equalised in the twenty-third minute with a cracking right-foot hook after clever play by Walsh, McPhail and Collins.

The outstanding defenders were Haughney, Evans and Peacock, as well as Bell, on the Celtic side, and Woodburn, Cox and Little on Rangers'. Little is too fond, however, of the sliding tackle, and in the second half it was touch and go for his conceding a penalty kick with his habit. At any rate Cox appeared to be most relieved when the referee dismissed Walsh's claim.

Rangers (1) 1	Celtic (1) 1
Paton	Duncan

RANGERS :– NIVEN: CALDOW AND LITTLE: COLL, WOODBURN AND COX: WADDELL AND GRIERSON: PATON: PRENTICE AND HUBBARD.

CELTIC :– BELL: HAUGHNEY AND FALLON: EVANS, STEIN AND PEACOCK: COLLINS AND WALSH: MCPHAIL: TULLY AND DUNCAN.

Celtic 1, Rangers 0 – Friday, 1st January, 1954

Fine Defence Almost Baulks Celtic

A magnificent display by Rangers' defence almost baulked Celtic of a thoroughly deserved victory at Parkhead. Never has Woodburn, in particular, served his club more capably.

Time and again the centre-half with, superb judgment, foiled a clever attack even though he could not have been fully fit in the second half as the result of stopping with his head a Fernie shot which was driven with astonishing power.

It was cruel luck for Woodburn that his only mistake enabled Mochan to score in 16 minutes after half-time and even that error was partly caused by Young's failure to clear.

So admirably had Rangers defended and so conscientiously had McColl and Cox tried to make their colleagues in front into some semblance of a forward line, that until Mochan's goal the obviously better team seemed unlikely to get material reward. Having tasted blood, however, Celtic took a firm grip of the match and long before the end more than one Rangers player was near exhaustion.

FORWARD SUPERIORITY

Immeasurably superior at inside forward – Collins, with his ability to spread play and Fernie, of the immaculate ball control were a splendid combination – and enjoying at least parity at wing half – the unflagging energy of Evans and Peacock denoted superb physical fitness – Celtic were an attractive team.

I am sure no-one expected to see the mastery of Meechan over Waddell – an ill-supported Waddell, it is true, but as man to man the loser of almost every duel with a most improved young back.

Haughney was just as much the master of Hubbard and Stein dominated his beat, which to Gardiner must have appeared a wilderness, so scant was the support he received. Later in the match the centre forward made a valiant effort to head an equalising goal from a Hubbard free kick, and one felt that had some of his more experienced colleagues in attack been of real Rangers class, Gardiner might have won the match.

The referee, quick to curb the slightest sign of unfair tackling of which both sides were commendably rarely guilty, punishing as the match was, gave a most competent exhibition.

Celtic (0) 1	Rangers (0) 0
Mochan	

CELTIC – BONNAR: HAUGHNEY AND MEECHAN: EVANS, STEIN AND PEACOCK: HIGGINS AND FERNIE: MCPHAIL: COLLINS AND MOCHAN.

RANGERS – BROWN: YOUNG AND LITTLE: MCCOLL, WOODBURN AND COX: WADDELL AND GRIERSON: GARDINER: PRENTICE AND HUBBARD.

Willie Fernie

A player ahead of his time, Fernie would be worth millions in today's transfer market. He was born in Fife in 1928, and although Rangers tried to sign him, he opted to join Celtic in 1949. Although he could play anywhere – he filled various roles for club and country – his best position was in the midfield where he had perfect passing ability and amazing ball control, although some misguided critics thought he was "too greedy" on the ball.

Fernie was a powerful influence in Celtic's Coronation Cup triumph in 1953, but perhaps his finest hour was his complete dominance of the 1957 League Cup Final against Rangers, capped by scoring from the penalty spot in the 7-1 victory. In 1957 he was transferred to Middlesbrough - where he played alongside Brian Clough - but returned to Celtic a couple of years later.

Played his last match for Celtic against Rangers in 1961, then moved to St. Mirren where he gained a Scottish Cup runners-up medal after having helped the Paisley side beat Celtic in the Semi finals. In all, he won 12 caps for Scotland and later tried his hand at management with Kilmarnock.

Sean Fallon

Another of the legendary Celtic side who beat Rangers 7-1 in 1957. Fallon is one of the toughest characters ever to have played in the Scottish game, but was and remains one of the game's real gentlemen. He joined Celtic from Irish League side Glenavon on St. Patrick's Day, 1950. A native of Sligo, he once turned down the chance to play for Northern Ireland, opting to represent Eire.

Fallon, who was later to form a marvellous partnership with Jock Stein, first on the playing field and then in management, was nicknamed "The Iron Man", because he constantly shrugged off injuries to play for the club. On one occasion he played on with a broken collar bone, and dismissed expressions of sympathy by pointing out that it wasn't as if he had played with a broken leg.

He was better known as a full-back, but was, on occasion, switched to centre forward with great effect. He played in the 1954 Cup Final against Aberdeen and scored the opening goal in a 2-1 win. Injury eventually forced him into retirement in 1958 and he became a club coach and later assistant manager to Stein. After Celtic's European Cup win in 1967, Fallon was given the freedom of Sligo.

Bertie Peacock

Born in Coleraine, Northern Ireland, Peacock joined Celtic from Glentoran in 1949, and although he spent most of his first season in the reserves, it finished on a high note when he was included for the Glasgow Charity Cup Final in which Celtic beat Rangers 3-2. The following season, in the first Old Firm League match, Peacock scored his first goal against Rangers in another 3-2 win, and from there on he established himself.

Peacock, originally an inside forward who later switched to left half, was one of the fittest players of his era and played a huge part in taking Celtic out of their post–war slump. He played in the Cup–winning sides of 1951 and 1954, and that famous League Cup victory in 1957.

He won 32 caps for Northern Ireland – he played in the 1958 World Cup finals – and after leaving Celtic in 1961 he had a spell as player-manager with Coleraine. He was also manager of the Northern Ireland international side, and in 1986 was awarded the MBE for services to football.

John McPhail

Another man who came through the barren years with Celtic, signing from the now defunct Strathclyde Juniors in 1941.

Affectionately known as "Hooky", John was a versatile player, but his best position was up front and he gained hero worship when he scored the winning goal against Motherwell in the 1951 Scottish Cup Final, thus ending Celtic's post–war depression.

McPhail, although almost 6ft in height, had a delicate, educated touch on the ball. He was also a courageous player. He won five full caps for Scotland between 1950-54, and scored almost 100 goals for the club before injuries forced his retirement from the game in 1956.

McPhail's younger brother Billy also played for Celtic, joining them from Clyde, and he will always have a place in the hearts of the Celtic fans for his hat–trick against Rangers in the 1957 League Cup Final. John, however, was the more famous McPhail. After his retirement, he took up a career in sports journalism.

Rangers 1, Celtic 0 – Saturday, 1st May, 1954
Non-Favourites' Success

The players of both Celtic and Rangers continue to remain aloof from the atmosphere of the terracing and on Saturday succeeded in producing a reasonably good spectacle. Indeed, one of them, Fernie, made a gesture to his opponents which should have, but did not, put shame to the riff-raff. Early in the match and just after Stanners had been felled by a hard shot from the inside right, Fernie, regaining possession in a position of great danger to Rangers, kicked the ball out of play in order that the centre half might get attention.

COX OUTSTANDING

Rangers showed considerable improvement. The partnership of Young and Cox at back restored confidence to the defence. Cox was far and away the best player afield, and for once Higgins gained no advantage from his intelligent sense of position.

Celtic, it is true, had much the greater share of play in the attack after the opening 20 minutes, in which Rangers played more like Champions and Cup winners than their opponents. Celtic's shooting – and refusal to shoot – was, however, appalling. I cannot recall any footballer spurn such a chance as Fernie did near the end of the first half, by which time Prentice had scored Rangers' goal. The inside right was left in possession confronted only by Niven and not more than five yards from the goal. He seemed to think that side-footing the ball into the net was not a feat of which to be proud, and he invited a despairing late tackle and lost the ball.

A goal at that stage, when Rangers were about to lose the advantage of the wind, would, I think, have given Celtic victory. That they did not deserve, however, because of their deplorable finishing.

Well as young Conroy played as an individual, Celtic undoubtedly missed Evans who has the flair for altering the trend of events. The outfield defenders were at sixes and sevens when Prentice scored with a ground shot in 37 minutes, and Bonnar, who recently has been guilty of advancing from his goal when there is no need for him to do so, was even more blameworthy, for he was fully six yards out when Prentice shot from 25 yards. Bonnar had, however, made several fine saves – notably, one from Simpson which was exceeded in grandeur only by those accomplished by Niven late in the half.

So, as has often been the case then, non-favourites in a Celtic-Rangers' match have upset the odds. Whether the latest turn-up was the result of Rangers' better form or Celtic's lapse into mediocrity I do not know; probably an accumulation of both factors was responsible.

Rangers (1) 1   Celtic (0) 0
Prentice

RANGERS:- NIVEN; YOUNG AND COX; NEILLANDS, STANNERS AND RAE; WADDELL AND GRIERSON; SIMPSON; PRENTICE AND MCCULLOCH.

CELTIC:- BONNAR; HAUGHNEY AND MEECHAN; CONROY, STEIN AND PEACOCK; HIGGINS AND FERNIE; FALLON; COLLINS AND MOCHAN.

Saturday, 1st May, 1954
Reasons for Small Crowd at Hampden

LACK OF ACTION AGAINST HOOLIGANS

The attendance at the Glasgow Charity Cup First-Round tie between Celtic and Rangers at Hampden Park was only 44,000 and it is interesting to hear that Scottish football officials are attributing the smallness of the crowd to the fact that the English Cup Final could be seen on television in Scotland.

If the administrators of the game in Scotland were to pay such assiduous attention to the evils that attach themselves to football as they do to the problem of television, they would have much less need to worry about the latter.

I suppose that of the 130,000 crowd at Hampden the previous Saturday, at least two-thirds would be supporters of Celtic. Where were they on Saturday? The average Celtic supporter does not miss his club's game in fine conditions of weather such as applied on Saturday; no more does he treat a game with Rangers as of less importance than others.

Rangers, too, have tens of thousands of supporters who did not attend the Charity Cup-tie – and there are many of no allegiance to either club who would not have stayed away had they had any form of guarantee that there would be no trouble.

Celtic and Rangers cannot afford to do without the patronage of all three classes. They can afford, however to do without the banner-wavers and the sectarian song-singers who enjoyed another afternoon unmolested by the authorities.

So far as could be seen from the press seats, there was no fighting before or during the game. As the crowds left the ground, however, there was an outbreak of fighting which obviously could have taken place within the ground itself had not the hooligan element segregated themselves as is their usual cowardly habit.

Some will say that fortunately the football season is over and that passions will have cooled during the recess. That may be so, but they will become heated again. Not a day should be lost in exploring every means of eradicating the hooligan element. If that is not done we had better announce that admission to games in which Celtic and Rangers play will be by banner and through ability to voice hatred only, and admit that a few hundred hooligans can hold the city to ransom.

Jock Stein

Arguably the most dominant figure in the history of Celtic. Although he will be best remembered for his achievements as manager of the club – he led them to 25 major trophies, comprising the European Cup, ten Championships, eight Scottish Cups and six League Cups – as a player and captain he was vastly influential in turning Celtic from also-rans into winners.

He was brought from the obscurity of non-League football with Llanelli in Wales in 1951 and quickly established himself as a leader on the field. He led Celtic to the Coronation Cup triumph in 1953 and to the League and Cup Double the following season. He was a member of one of the best–ever Celtic half-back lines of Evans, Stein and Peacock.

Stein sustained a bad ankle injury in a League Cup tie against Rangers in 1956 and that eventually led to his retirement as a player. He became youth coach at the club before moving as manager to Dunfermline, whom he led to a Scottish Cup win. After a spell with Hibs, he returned to Celtic as manager, succeeding Jimmy McGrory, and sparked the most successful period in the club's history. He also managed Leeds United for a short period, 44 days (exactly same as Brian Clough) and Scotland.

Willie Waddell

The fans made up songs about the man – what greater tribute can a footballer hope to receive from the supporters? The Deedle will go down in history as the greatest player-manager-director to serve the Rangers. There may have been better players, there have been better managers and directors, but nobody has given service in all three departments that comes even near his efforts.

Born in Forth in 1921, he joined Rangers as a professional from Strathclyde in 1938. Waddell was a winger of great strength, running and ability. He was an idol with the fans during those years after the war. He became a legend and was to play such an important part in shaping the Rangers as they are today.

As a player he won four Championships, and two Scottish Cups. He played for Scotland in 17 full internationals and three war–time matches, and he had five League caps. On retiring from the playing side in 1956 he joined Kilmarnock as manager, leading them to their only Championship success in 1965. Following that he went into journalism and became manager of Rangers in 1969 where he led them to victory in the European Cup–Winners' Cup against Moscow Dynamo in Barcelona in 1972. He handed over to Jock Wallace and became general manager, and then director. Waddell was also a driving force in building the new Ibrox Stadium.

Celtic 2, Rangers 0 – Saturday, 18th September, 1954

Fernie's Toll of Rangers

So compact had been both defences on Saturday and so ineffective both sets of forwards when the rare chances of scoring did arise, that Walsh's goal, 15 minutes after half time, was more than a little surprising. On this occasion the completion of an attacking movement was, however, superb; few better scoring shots have been seen on the ground.

Evans, after an exhilarating run, passed low through the centre to Walsh who, back to Rangers' goal, wheeled round the close-marking Stanners and as Niven advanced from his goal to narrow the centre forward's angle, shot powerfully and unerringly for the far corner of the net from just inside the 18 yard line.

Many of the spectators must have wondered why Rangers – and Stanners in particular, gesticulated that they were not satisfied, but Rangers had good reason for protesting within the bounds which Mr Mowat permits. I had a perfect view of the situation when Walsh and Stanners made for the ball and I have not the slightest doubt that Walsh nudged his opponent sufficiently to unbalance him. I am equally sure that a most competent referee who was on the Rangers players' flank detected no infringement.

A goal it was and, despite the flaw in its execution, it was thoroughly deserved. It succeeded too in arousing Rangers to their most enthusiastic attacking spell of a mediocre match, and a hitherto almost bone idle Bonnar twice saved the day for Celtic when he baulked McCulloch in the middle of the penalty area, while three minutes from time he saved magnificently at the corner of the post a shot from Simpson which he probably did not see until a few yards from him.

GREAT ASSET

In the final minute Higgins scored a second Celtic goal, and for all Rangers' late rally the result was not unfair to them. They had no footballer comparable with the player who knocked the final nail in their coffin. Fernie, who sometimes causes even his admirers to tear their hair as he refuses to cut the lace which appears to attach the ball to his twinkling feet, produced an astonishing burst of speed in beating McColl, before he chipped the ball into the goalmouth for his colleague to score. Time and again the Celtic inside left had baffled his immediate opponent and if frequently his passing was too long delayed, there is no question that this extremely fit, clever, individualist is an asset that any club would be glad to possess.

Let us temper our criticism of his tendency to selfishness in realisation that he of all forwards is able to run a defence into the ground because of his unorthodoxy.

Mochan, who at least twice in the second half emulated Fernie by outpacing and outmanoeuvring both Young and McColl, and did not score only because he did not shoot quickly enough, was the other Celtic forward who scorned the ordinary and gave his side a great advantage. No Rangers forward and only Higgins of the other Celtic forwards ever deviated from the commonplace methods for which defenders are grateful.

Rangers indeed had only two consistently dependable players, Niven and Stanners, who only on the occasion of Walsh's scoring was the loser of his duels with the centre forward. Young and both wing-halves were deficient in speed and where they did have the requisite pace, Rangers did not have the football brain. McCulloch frequently passed Fallon on the outside, but the back, much more confident now that he has had his day at centre forward, almost always retrieved the position.

Simpson, who late in the first half shot over an empty goal after Grierson's cross-shot had rebounded from the crossbar, and Rangers' inside forwards, were completely mastered. Prentice in particular can never have played worse. Evans beat him on the ground and in the air, and when he did get the opportunity to shoot, he passed the responsibility to someone else. A dreadful day for the inside left ended when he was cautioned for showing dissent – and that in itself indicates Prentice's state of mind for he is not normally a player who finds himself on the wrong side of a referee.

The measure of Rangers' inside forwards' weakness was that Boden, far from comfortable at inside right, was far superior to both.

Haughney was another outstanding Celtic player even although he was opposed to Rangers' most intelligent forward, Hubbard. The home side obviously had more accomplished players than Rangers whose chief attribute was their ability to pack their goal in moments of danger. The great defenders of the past are now, however, "over the hill", and if their forwards cannot ensure them sufficient relief, disintegration must inevitably set in.

Celtic (0) 2	Rangers (0) 0
Walsh	
Higgins	

CELTIC:- BONNAR; HAUGHNEY AND FALLON; EVANS, STEIN AND PEACOCK; HIGGINS AND BODEN; WALSH; FERNIE AND MOCHAN.

RANGERS:- NIVEN; YOUNG AND LITTLE; MCCOLL, STANNERS AND RAE; MCCULLOCH AND GRIERSON; SIMPSON (W.); PRENTICE AND HUBBARD.

Saturday, 18th September, 1954

Reasons for Small Crowd at "Old Firm" Game

Only 44,000 spectators attended the Scottish League match between Celtic and Rangers on Saturday at Celtic Park – a clear indication of the loss of popularity of a meeting of the "Old Firm". The match was all-ticket on the instructions of the police and the limit fixed at 70,000, so that approximately 26,000 tickets were not sold. The public dissatisfaction with the all-ticket system is one of the reasons for Saturday's attendance being so small on a day ideal for watching as well as playing, but it is not the chief reason.

Many of the followers of Rangers and Celtic stayed away because of dissatisfaction with their teams' form, but many more were absent because of the risks attached to attending a match between the clubs. Though there was the usual display by ignoramuses at either end of the ground of colours which are not those of the competing teams, and though the repertoire of the age-old sectarian songs

was employed to the full, that was the extent, as far as could be seen, of bad behaviour inside the ground, except for one case of a spectator at Rangers' supporters' end, compelling the police to make an arrest.

Outside the ground at the end of the match, there was an outbreak of bottle-throwing – the more serious in that it seemed to be indiscriminate and caused casualties amongst those who were not members of the rival factions. Such disorder is the reason for the absence of so many football followers.

Celtic's victory was their first since the opening day of the season; Rangers' defeat, on the other hand, was only their second since the season began. Celtic are one of the seven clubs unbeaten in the League, the lead in which is shared by Aberdeen, St. Mirren and Hearts.

Rangers 4, Celtic 1 – Saturday, 1st January, 1955

Contrast in Defences at Ibrox Stadium

Though Rangers had in Hubbard and Simpson the best forwards on the field at Ibrox Stadium on Saturday – Hubbard achieved the distinction of scoring three goals, and Simpson, who scored his side's first, was only a little less successful – I am certain that Rangers' deserved victory was not so much the outcome of superiority in attack, as of far greater competence in defence.

Though McColl was missing, there was a compactness and a coolness in the performance of Young and his defensive colleagues that provided striking contrast with the nervous display in the Celtic rear lines.

The first to pay the full price for a blunder was Stein, who in the ninth minute grotesquely sliced a clearance to the feet of Grierson, who promptly and accurately gave Simpson a scoring chance which he took gratefully.

For the rest of the match Stein was as unsure of himself and those around him as to make one wonder if this was the Celtic centre half, ripe in experience, and not a youngster playing in his first big game. Twice at least, he and Bell became so confused that although not a Ranger was within speaking distance of them, they almost scrambled the ball into their own net.

There was no such alarm at Rangers' end, even though for the first half Celtic had a monopoly of the ball and were, chiefly because of the tremendous urge of Evans, the likelier-looking team; therefore, though Hubbard and Simpson undoubtedly were the matchwinners, Young and company, by calm, watchful defence broke the Celtic spirit and paved the way for victory.

Easily as Rangers won in the end, it should be noted that only three minutes of the first half were left when Simpson had made his side's second shot. Ten minutes earlier, on practically the only occasion on which Walsh beat Young, the centre half brought him down and Fernie lobbed the free kick over the defensive wall and away from the searching fingers of Niven. That was the only suggestion

of a mistake that Niven made.

The first half had been far from distinguished: the second, by comparison, was almost rich in entertainment. Hubbard and Simpson made it so with the permission of Haughney and Stein, who rarely have failed so often in the tackle.

DELIGHTFUL GOAL

Prentice in 68 minutes added a grey hair or two to his opponents' heads with a tremendous shot which rebounded from a post with all Celtic in despair. Five minutes later, Hubbard took his own particular way of creating even greater despondency, for he jinked round Haughney, Stein and Bell before he walked the ball into the net. Immediately before that delightful effort, Tully had headed a Fernie cross so hard that only the fact that Niven was in direct line prevented a goal.

Boden almost equalised with a shot which Niven fisted over the crossbar after an acrobatic backward leap, and Little kicked a shot from Collins away from the line before Simpson chipped his pass so precisely that Hubbard, intelligently placed in the centre, had merely to direct the ball into a gaping goal. Ten minutes were left, and hardly any more Celtic supporters. In the final minute Grierson was fouled in the Celtic penalty area and Hubbard converted the penalty kick as capably as we expected him to do.

Rangers (1) 4	Celtic (1) 1
Simpson	Fernie
Hubbard 3 (1 pen.)	
Attendance	65,000

RANGERS:- NIVEN; LITTLE AND COX; PRYDE, YOUNG AND RAE; McCULLOCH AND PRENTICE; SIMPSON; GRIERSON AND HUBBARD.

CELTIC:- BELL; HAUGHNEY AND MEECHAN; EVANS, STEIN AND PEACOCK; BODEN AND TULLY; WALSH; FERNIE AND COLLINS.

Celtic 0, Rangers 1 – Saturday, 7th May, 1955

First Rangers-Queen's Final Since 1933

Rangers and Queen's Park will contest the Final of the Glasgow Charity Cup tonight at Hampden Park. The last occasion on which they met in the Final was in 1933 when Rangers won 1-0.

In the Semi-finals on Saturday Rangers beat Celtic 1-0 at Celtic Park – Simpson scored – and Queen's beat Clyde on the toss of a coin after a 1-1 draw at Hampden Park, J. Ward having scored in 15 minutes for the amateurs, and Hill for Clyde 10 minutes from the end.

RANGERS' LUCK

Rangers will probably never have a more fortunate win than they had at Celtic Park. The home team, who more or less monopolised play from start to finish, would with any luck have won by at least half a dozen goals.

Niven was in brilliant form in Rangers' goal but on four occasions when the ball rebounded from the framework of the goal, he was in no position to save, and twice he had his full-backs to thank for clearances on the goal-line. On other occasions he could do no more than parry the ball which, however, invariably spun to the feet of a colleague.

Nevertheless, in spite of the almost constant strain on them Rangers were impressive in defence, with Caldow and Young outstanding. They had their moments of indecision under attack but on the whole looked less vulnerable than the Celtic rearguard did during Rangers'

infrequent menacing raids, which were usually led by Scott or Hubbard.

The goal resulted from a blunder by Stein near the end. He seemed undecided how to dispose of the harmless-looking ball in the penalty area and lost possession to Simpson, who shot into the side-net as Bonnar advanced from his goal. That was Stein's only lapse. With Evans and Peacock, he formed a half-back line much superior to Rangers'.

DESPAIR

Despite its one-sidedness the game, in which the pace was rarely slackened, was always interesting to the non-partisan onlooker, however tantalising it may have been to Celtic supporters; their despair could have been no greater than that of the Celtic forwards as their skilful and persistent efforts failed to produce the result they deserved.

Glasgow Charity Cup Semi-Final

Celtic (0) 0	Rangers (0) 1
	Simpson

CELTIC:- BONNAR; HAUGHNEY AND CONROY; EVANS, STEIN AND PEACOCK; COLLINS AND FERNIE; WALSH; TULLY AND MOCHAN.

RANGERS:- NIVEN; CALDOW AND LITTLE; MCCOLL, YOUNG AND PRENTICE; SCOTT AND MCMILLAN; SIMPSON, RAE AND HUBBARD

Rangers' Simpson celebrates a Murray goal against Celtic in the 4-4 thriller of 1957.

Rangers 1, Celtic 4 – Saturday, 27th August, 1955
Penalty Paid

Some folks got their fingers burned on Saturday at Ibrox Stadium – the fanatics, who, a few minutes before the kick-off, set alight a green flag amid the circling Union Jacks, and the Rangers' officials responsible for the inclusion of Baird in their team.

Twenty minutes before the end of the match, having suffered a humiliation as never before, the hard core of spectators who disgrace the club they follow had gone, the colours they misappropriate and the musical instruments they favour having vanished more quickly even than the flag that had been burned at the stake as a heretic, as was of Hibernian lore, the famous flute.

The course of the play itself proved the folly of the selection of Baird. Almost from the kick-off Baird was as a tortoise among the defenders who cannot be described as hares, and his tackling was so late and crude that it was hardly surprising that someone fell a victim. The unlucky individual was Fernie who, in the twelfth minute, retired to the outside-right position and was unable thereafter to contribute anything like a full share to his side's effort.

Far, however, from Rangers gaining an undeserved advantage from that foul of Baird's, they suffered dreadfully. Into the inside right position came Collins who gave such a display as those on the Continent which astonished Yugoslavs, Austrians and Hungarians and which encouraged the few Scots who saw them in their belief that all is not lost to the Scottish game.

Collins is as pertinacious a player as there is in the land, and he is also so strong a little man that he almost welcomes intimidation. He gave yards of running and a beating to all those he tormented. He passed the ball beautifully and did not wait to see the effect but raced for more open space. He more than once won a tackle with the huge Young and once in the winning toppled him over, and probably caused Young to be even more indignant than he was with the deficiencies all around him. Collins once too dodged another of Baird's sweeps and as he danced his way on, looked over his shoulder and grinned.

Evans, Stein, and Peacock were a magnificent half-back line. Evans gave McMillan hardly a kick at the ball, Stein was beaten only once – and that not in a dangerous position – by Murray, and Peacock had a resounding success in the duel with a fellow-Irishman, Simpson. Celtic's backs were not tested as one imagined they would be, for Rangers' wingers were starved out of the match. Hubbard was particularly unfortunate that his colleagues on the left were so stodgy and unimaginative, for he showed early in the game that he had skill comparable with the Celtic forwards.

Fallon must have played his best game for Celtic for many a day, and Scott, almost as poorly supported as Hubbard, was placed in his proper perspective – a promising youngster who cannot yet on his own take on a defence or even one determined opponent.

INUNDATED

Only McColl, for his efforts to plug the gap on the other side of the field, Young, Murray and Hubbard of Rangers' outfield players, were in any way distinguished. Young latterly became inundated with the waves of Celtic attack, and there were periods in the second half in which had the Celtic forwards shot as accurately as they made the chances, the score would have reached double figures.

Rangers' best scoring opportunity was devised by Simpson after a persevering dribble up the left wing but Hubbard, the player who was in position to score when the inside right crossed, twisted his shot ingloriously askew. It was little wonder – he could hardly have recognised the object which had come to his feet, so little had he been in touch with it.

FINE GOALS

McPhail scored the first goal in 17 minutes, whipping round Caldow as nippily as Collins would have done and smashing a right-foot shot over Niven's head. Twelve minutes later Collins and McPhail made a draught-board of the left side of the field with a bout of almost impertinently short passes. Mochan diverted the last past Young and Smith scored easily. Ten minutes from half-time Fallon and Scott collided as they went for a Baird free kick, and Scott received the congratulations for a fortuitous goal that may well have been unwittingly scored by the back.

Rangers' gleam of hope lasted only two minutes, for another of McPhail's astute inside passes was glided by Smith round the struggling Baird and from 22 yards shot so powerfully that Niven, though he had anticipated the direction, could not prevent the goal.

The goal that emptied the Rangers end of the terracing was scored by Mochan with a bullet-like right-foot shot seven minutes after the interval. For a full minute before it was decided that Mochan would finish the movement, the ball was passed from Celtic foot to Celtic foot across the edge of the penalty area in a remarkable spell of skilful manoeuvring that probably would not have been attempted by a side not thoroughly the masters.

Rangers (1) 1	Celtic (3) 4
Scott	McPhail
	Smith 2
	Mochan

RANGERS:- NIVEN; CALDOW AND LITTLE; MCCOLL, YOUNG AND BAIRD; SCOTT AND SIMPSON; MURRAY; MCMILLAN AND HUBBARD.

CELTIC:- BONNAR; HAUGHNEY AND FALLON; EVANS, STEIN AND PEACOCK; COLLINS AND FERNIE; MOCHAN; SMITH AND MCPHAIL.

Celtic 0, Rangers 4 – Wednesday, 31st August, 1955

Revenge with a Vengeance for Rangers

The results in Celtic-Rangers matches continue to baffle the public. Last night at Parkhead, Rangers, who had been beaten by Celtic at Ibrox Stadium on Saturday more convincingly than the score, 4-1, indicated, gained revenge with a 4-0 victory in one of the second-last matches in the League Cup sectional tournament.

An injury suffered by Stein, Celtic's centre half, handicapped the home side. He had to go outside left before half-time.

Rangers, set to face a slight breeze at Celtic Park, made an excellent start. After Young had repelled two Celtic attacks, Hubbard cleverly beat Haughney and Evans, and passed to Baird. The inside left pushed the ball on to Simpson and, taking the return pass first time round, Baird shot a splendid goal from 20 yards in the fifth minute.

An injury to Stein 10 minutes from the interval caused him to go to the left touchline, Evans to centre half, and Smith to right half.

Just on the interval a Murray cross eluded the entire Celtic defence and Haughney had to concede a corner. It had been an excellent first half.

Stein resumed at outside left, with Evans at centre and McPhail at right half. The Celtic forward line was McVittie, Collins, Mochan, Smith and Stein. Celtic began strongly, but the limping Stein was unable to profit from a Collins cross.

In the 51st minute Baird carried the ball down the left wing and crossed. Simpson and Murray failed to take the chance to shoot, but before Celtic had properly cleared, Baird rushed in and shot with his left foot from eight yards and Bonnar was helpless.

Mochan did pass Young but Niven made a splendid save from the centre forward's shot. Celtic made further readjustments, Smith going to right half, Mochan to inside left, and McPhail to centre forward. From a Mochan corner kick the limping Stein nearly scored with a glancing header.

Rangers were well on top in the closing 15 minutes and in the 76th minute they emphasised their superiority when Simpson collected a long upfield punt, eluded Peacock and Bonnar, and sent the ball into the empty net. Three minutes later Murray added a fourth goal after some lovely passing by the inside forwards. Near the end, Scott struck both the post and the crossbar in quick succession.

Celtic (0) 0	Rangers (1) 4
	Baird 2
	Simpson
	Murray

CELTIC :- BONNAR; HAUGHNEY AND FALLON; EVANS, STEIN AND PEACOCK; COLLINS AND MCVITTIE; MOCHAN; SMITH AND MCPHAIL.

RANGERS :- NIVEN; CALDOW AND LITTLE; MCCOLL, YOUNG AND RAE; SCOTT AND SIMPSON; MURRAY; BAIRD AND HUBBARD.

Celtic 1, Rangers 1 – Saturday, 24th September, 1955

Improved Form of Celtic and Rangers

Celtic and Rangers retrieved their reputations to a great extent yesterday at Hampden Park in the Glasgow Cup Final despite the fact that rain and wind again made the players' task difficult. The 53,600 crowd thoroughly appreciated the change for the better.

Rangers, somewhat fortunate to be only one goal down at half-time, decidedly altered that impression in the second half when, as the wind was now in their favour, they increased in strength, and penned Celtic in defence for long spells. During those periods of anxiety for Celtic, Beattie and Evans were outstanding.

The most improved player of those who contested Saturday's match was undoubtedly McColl, who was easily the most prominent wing half. I do not think Celtic's changes at half-time were profitable, for Tully, the complete footballer in the first half, was much more subdued at inside left in the face of McColl's close marking.

BRILLIANT TULLY

The Tully-Collins wing began the match brilliantly. In 19 minutes, Tully's magnificent ball control and pass to the unmarked Collins brought Celtic's goal, Collins' shot being diverted to the roof of the net by Caldow. Six minutes later Hubbard, Rangers' best forward, crossed low into the Celtic goal, but not a colleague was there to take the chance. Baird, his apparently normal mixture of ball-player and barger, was warned by the referee for a bad foul on Fernie.

In the 51st minute both Haughney and Collins failed to profit from another Tully move but from that point on Rangers were clearly superior. Beattie saved splendidly at the post when Simpson shot from Miller's pass and twice in the next few minutes emulated that when Baird and Caldow shot for a point just under the crossbar.

Eleven minutes after half-time, Rangers deservedly equalised, McColl's low shot from the edge of the penalty area being "dummied" by Simpson and passing through Fallon's legs and under an unsighted goalkeeper's body.

Seven minutes from the end Haughney recklessly stretched out a boot in a hopeless effort to connect with Tully's through pass and Niven was laid low. To the relief of everyone the goalkeeper resumed, after Haughney had been admonished by the referee.

Glasgow Cup Final

Celtic (1) 1	Rangers (0) 1
Caldow (o.g.)	McColl
Attendance	53,600

CELTIC:- BEATTIE; BODEN AND FALLON; FERNIE, EVANS AND PEACOCK; TULLY AND COLLINS; HAUGHNEY; SMITH AND MOCHAN.

RANGERS:- NIVEN; CALDOW AND LITTLE; MCCOLL, YOUNG AND RAE; SCOTT AND SIMPSON; MILLER, BAIRD AND HUBBARD.

Rangers 0, Celtic 0 – Monday, 24th September, 1955

Forwards' Deplorable Day at Ibrox

Most unpleasant weather undoubtedly contributed to the competitively peaceful attitude of the crowd of some 47,000 on Saturday at Ibrox Stadium. There seems nothing so successful as rain in dousing passions. The police, too, had made elaborate plans to ensure reasonable behaviour. Any potential troublemakers in the crowd, however, were rendered harmless by the deplorably bad display of most of the players – for once both Rangers and Celtic followers were fellow-sufferers.

The wind, the rain, the slippery turf, and the skidding ball all combined to make the players' task difficult but the truth is that there were few competent footballers on the field. That was the real reason for the mediocrity. Rangers were more blameworthy than Celtic, who were much below full strength, and had a full back at centre forward, an inside right at right half and a youngster at outside right who appeared to be overawed by the occasion.

SCOTT'S FAILURE.

I can recall two shots by Rangers – a speculative bang by Baird which went yards wide, and a duffed grounder by Prentice – and one instance of a forward movement calculated to provide a scoring chance. That was in the first half when Simpson for once managed to entice Evans out of position and crossed to the unmarked Scott, who seemed to be as flustered as a hen in gathering her chicks around her and permitted to converge on him and ruin the chance no fewer than three Celtic players who should not have got near him before the ball was in the net.

Celtic were slightly superior in ability to fashion scoring chances, but Mochan, the marksman of the forward line, cut and sliced his shots and only once seriously troubled Niven. Rangers' goalkeeper had the save of the match from almost the only worthwhile shot when he tipped over a left-foot shot from Docherty in the first half.

Apart from the opportunity squandered by Scott, the best chance of a goal fell to Haughney, and it was not his fault that he did not take it. Young has never rendered Rangers more valuable service than when he impeded the centre forward two yards outside the penalty area with disaster, even in such a day of forward failings, imminent for Rangers.

I have rarely seen a match in which there was so much reticence to accept the responsibility of shooting. An inside forward would be in unchallenged possession 30 yards from his opponents' goal and invariably he would look around for a chance to get rid of the ball – generally in a backward direction. Baird and Prentice, two of the biggest and strongest men afield, offended in that respect irritatingly frequently.

WINGERS MASTERED

For once Rangers' wingers were mastered, and the attacking plans therefore disintegrated. Fallon once again showed that Scott, ill-supported, can cause him little concern and Boden was even more successful against Hubbard, whom he intelligently played out to the touchline and out of harm's way.

Evans had a magnificent game at centre half and on the day was superior to Young, who found the strong, hard-tackling Haughney an unorthodox opponent. In the ordinary duties of a wing half Rae was a splendid player for Rangers, opposed as he was by one of the few players with constructive ideas, Collins.

BALL-MASTERY

There was no doubt however who contributed the most football in the match. Fernie, the individual whose ways apparently no one can change, played right half as if he were inside right and proved that even in difficult conditions, the ball can be mastered. Rangers were no doubt relieved that Fernie's forays deep into their defence had started farther back than they would have done had he been in customary position.

The most disturbing aspect of an unsatisfactory match was the referee's lenient attitude to blatant fouling. One player, I think, was spoken to – Prentice, for perpetually kicking the ball away after a linesman had signalled it had been out of play, yet two of Prentice's colleagues, McColl and Baird, indulged in an orgy of back-charging and crude tackling which was seldom even penalised; McColl in the second half was almost running amok, and it took a retaliatory breenge by Fallon to bring him to his senses. Such retribution should not have been necessary – it is the referee's duty to bring the unruly player to book.

RANGERS:- NIVEN; CALDOW AND LITTLE; MCCOLL, YOUNG AND RAE; SCOTT AND BAIRD; SIMPSON; PRENTICE AND HUBBARD.

CELTIC:- BEATTIE; BODEN AND FALLON; FERNIE, EVANS AND PEACOCK; DOCHERTY AND COLLINS; HAUGHNEY; SMITH AND MOCHAN.

Celtic 5, Rangers 3 – Monday, 26th December, 1955

Method Prevails in the Grand Hampden Game

CELTIC WIN GLASGOW CUP

Celtic won the Glasgow Cup yesterday at Hampden Park for the first time since the 1948-49 season by beating Rangers in a replay of this season's Final. The 39,000 crowd saw an exhilarating match in conditions of wind and rain which would have provided at least some excuse had the quality of play been mediocre.

That Celtic were by far the more skilful side in attacking football there was no doubt, but in a series of blunders by their defence, apparently on tenterhooks when Kichenbrand was in the vicinity of their goal, enabled Rangers to retain a chance of winning until the last 10 minutes. Then, however, the greater fitness of Celtic, coupled with their advantage in skill, gained full reward.

BEATTIE'S BLUNDERS

One of the most illuminating moments in the match which did not have a dull minute occurred after Fernie had headed the last goal four minutes from time. Beattie left his stance and raced to midfield to join the other Celtic players congratulating the scorer, whereupon he was summarily banished from the scene by his captain.

Beattie was no doubt much relieved that his errors had not lost his side the victory. Rangers' first two goals were directly attributable to the goalkeeper's mistakes, though so nervous did Stein himself seem for a long period in the first half that the much less experienced player was almost inevitably bound to become affected.

Rangers must be concerned with the fact that every Celtic goal was scored through the heart of their defences. It was not a case on this occasion of the sharp-shooting Mochan succeeding with his powerful shots from awkward angles. Yet before a goal had been scored, one of Mochan's few truly-driven shots probably softened the resistance of Young, whose face took the full brunt of the blow.

The first half pace was terrific and the wonder was that both teams were able to maintain it well into the second half. In the twenty-fourth minute came the first of Beattie's lapses. Baird chased the ball to a point midway between Celtic's right-hand post and the corner flag and did uncommonly well to cross – just before the ball went out of play. The flight was no more than three yards from the line and Beattie should have stepped forward and clutched or fisted. Incredibly, however, he stood still and Rangers' centre forward, who must have been momentarily astonished, headed into the net.

The cheers and the groans had not ceased when Collins equalised. Sharkey, who throughout was prepared to tackle the formidable obstacle of Young unaided, sent the centre half the wrong way as he manoeuvred, and though the long leg of Young almost intercepted the through pass, Collins darted in the goal that has escaped him in club matches for so long.

Nine minutes later Young ventured too daringly upfield, lost the ball and was tottering backwards when Collins was repaying Sharkey with a pass which the centre forward converted with a splendid left-foot shot from the 16-yard line, but not before he had indulged in his characteristic caress of the ball.

Two minutes from half time Beattie's judgement was again faulty at a cross ball, and although his team-mate partially cleared, he made a reckless dive at Kichenbrand's ankles and suffered the full deserved punishment – a penalty kick, which Hubbard guided unswervingly away from him.

COOL SHARKEY

In the twelfth minute of the second half, Mochan joined Sharkey in discomfiting Young and McColl and again the centre forward, while the more impatient of the supporters howled for an immediate shot, coolly dribbled until he was satisfied with his position and hit another left-foot shot into the roof of the net.

Rangers equalised within the minute. Baird's ground shot was travelling several feet wide when Fallon, rushing across the goal, diverted it to the net.

With only with minutes left Baird betrayed his state of mind by trying with both hands to stop a cross from Smith in his own penalty area. A minute later another bout of Sharkey ball-play was followed by a replica of his scoring shot and Collins rushed the ball through after it had rebounded from the crossbar. Four minutes from time Fernie headed Smith's cross far out of Niven's reach.

It is to the credit of Kichenbrand, far and away Rangers' best forward, that he was still trying to retrieve the situation in the dying seconds during which he warmed Beattie's fingers with a terrific shot. So long, however as Rangers are relying so much on their centre forward so long will their attacks break down.

The methods of Celtic yesterday are much more likely to succeed over a long period – ball control, intelligent passing, and ability to switch the point of attack.

Glasgow Cup Final

Celtic (2) 5	Rangers (2) 3
Collins 2	Kichenbrand
Sharkey	Hubbard (pen.)
Mochan	Fallon (o.g.)
Fernie	

CELTIC:- BEATTIE, HAUGHNEY AND FALLON; EVANS, STEIN AND PEACOCK; SMITH AND FERNIE; SHARKEY; COLLINS AND MOCHAN.

RANGERS:- NIVEN; CALDOW AND LITTLE; McCOLL, YOUNG AND RAE; SCOTT AND SIMPSON; KICHENBRAND; BAIRD AND HUBBARD.

Celtic 0, Rangers 1 – Monday, 2nd January, 1956

Unpredictable Celtic and Rangers

Celtic and Rangers continue to provide the unpredictable in football. Yesterday at Celtic Park Rangers gained revenge for the 5-3 defeat they suffered in the Glasgow Cup Final eight days ago, and it will be recalled that it was at Celtic Park that they beat their rivals 4-0 after having lost the previous League Cup sectional match 4-1 to them at Ibrox Stadium.

Celtic's choice of outside right was just as surprising as the manner in which the "Old Firm" confound the forecasters of results. If only because young McVittie was brought into the side on the occasion of that 4-0 defeat, it would probably have been wiser to have fielded another player yesterday. This clever, slightly-built boy – he is only 17 – is not ready for the top grade of football.

Both McVittie and his club may argue that there were several others in this latest Celtic-Rangers game who did not appear qualified for the top grade. I have rarely seen a poorer "Old Firm" match and I do not concede that the white ball, which seemed to play captious tricks in flight, was primarily responsible.

That Celtic did not win was entirely their own fault. Their opponents were handicapped for all but the opening half hour through Rae's suffering a leg injury and having to go to the left wing, and yet despite long spells of complete mastery in the second half they could not score.

Rangers were lucky on several occasions – notably when a Fernie shot struck Brown rather than was saved by him, and three minutes from time when Caldow pulled Mochan down from behind in the penalty area and escaped punishment – but Celtic were not unlucky to lose. Their forwards were shockingly ineffective at shots, and only

Collins seemed to appreciate that a little liveliness might save the day.

Brown returned to Rangers' goal and despite an occasional error of judgement in fisting, thoroughly justified his selection. His opposite number, Beattie, did not have half a dozen shots to save, but was involved in the foolish loss of a goal in the twenty-seventh minute.

Kichenbrand was faster than Stein in chasing a high punt by Simpson, Beattie rushed out some 18 yards from his line and Kichenbrand accurately lobbed the ball past him into the unguarded goal. The goalkeeper could well have afforded to stay in his goal as Stein was close enough to hamper the centre forward.

That skilfully-taken goal was Kichenbrand's contribution to the match, apart from a number of crude lunges which Stein in particular suffered with admirable tolerance. The centre half had an almost perfect match. Eliot, the reserve in Young's place for Rangers, was also a convincing player, if not as polished as Stein.

The half-backs on both sides were indeed outstanding players. Evans was second only to Stein in ability, and Baird when he went to left half, played with a poise which he rarely displays as a forward.

Celtic (0) 0	Rangers (1) 1
	Kichenbrand

CELTIC:- BEATTIE; HAUGHNEY AND FALLON; EVANS, STEIN AND PEACOCK; MCVITTIE AND FERNIE; SHARKEY; COLLINS AND MOCHAN.

RANGERS:- BROWN: CALDOW AND LITTLE: MCCOLL. ELLIOT AND RAE; SCOTT AND SIMPSON: KICHENBRAND; BAIRD AND HUBBARD.

Celtic 2, Rangers 1 – Wednesday, 15th August, 1956

Haughney Misses Disputed Penalty Kick

A most aggressive series of raids rocked the Celtic defence early in the match at Celtic Park. Murray beat the defence in the jump and headed just wide. After an excellent Simpson-Scott movement Murray again threatened Beattie's goal with a grounded shot.

Celtic were indebted to Jack for three further Rangers attacks being repelled.

Celtic gradually asserted themselves, and Niven might have been beaten on three occasions had Evans, Peacock and Fernie been accurate in finishing. Young was effectively blocking the direct road to Niven, but when McPhail hoodwinked the entire Rangers defence, Fernie's dilatoriness alone saved Rangers.

Baird and Murray took Rangers deep into Celtic's half where a brilliant Fallon tackle thwarted Hubbard. Then in the thirty-fourth minute McPhail guided a Haughney pass into Collins' path, and Niven was decisively beaten.

Jack was again an effective barrier in Rangers' counter-thrust, but a fine angular shot by Scott hit the crossbar. Murray equalised just on half-time after a goal mouth scramble.

Rangers again were first to attack; after Beattie had saved a softish shot by Rae, Scott ballooned his shot many yards too high.

Jack was constantly on the alert to cover the astute moves of Murray. Simpson shot rashly past after Murray had measured his pass with great accuracy.

Then Niven timed his advance correctly and beat Collins as the inside right ran in on goal.

In the 65th minute Young upset Higgins and Haughney shot the penalty over the crossbar. Young was displeased, disputing the award with the referee even after the kick.

Five minutes later Tully hooked a lobbed shot past Niven for a second Celtic goal.

Celtic (1) 2	Rangers (1) 1
Collins	Murray
Tully	

CELTIC:- BEATTIE: HAUGHNEY AND FALLON; EVANS, JACK AND PEACOCK; HIGGINS AND COLLINS; MCPHAIL; FERNIE AND TULLY.

RANGERS:- NIVEN, SHEARER AND LITTLE; MCCOLL, YOUNG AND RAE, SCOTT AND SIMPSON; MURRAY; BAIRD AND HUBBARD.

Rangers 0, Celtic 0 – Wednesday, 29th August, 1956
Fernie's Late Miss in Goalless Ibrox Game

Large queues were outside Ibrox Stadium when Evans won the toss and set Rangers to play against a strong sun.

Celtic made a promising start and Mochan twice had Niven in difficulty within five minutes with accurate crosses. From the first the goalkeeper failed to grasp the ball, Young and Shearer between them anxiously conceding a corner kick, and from the second Niven was again content to concede a corner kick.

A cunning through pass from Murray left Paton clear but the inside right, after rounding the advancing Beattie, miskicked.

Celtic were much more dangerous and the energetic and clever play of their forwards gave the home defence many moments of anxiety. In attempting to clear a Collins cross, Caldow made a rash back pass, and a less alert goalkeeper than Niven would have been beaten.

Although Rangers' play improved, their forwards rarely gained shooting position. The quick tackling of the Celtic defence was in great measure responsible for that.

INDUSTRIOUS EVANS
Evans, a most industrious wing half, started another Celtic attack and an unexpected shot by Fernie had Niven scampering across goal, but the ball went past.

Towards the interval Rangers had a series of strong attacks, and one splendid shot from Scott brought out an equally good save by Beattie. Murray was clever with conspicuous distribution, but his forward colleagues were too anxious with their finishing efforts. A tremendous shot from McColl from 35 yards was only a foot wide.

Rangers immediately forced a corner kick on either wing, and from the second (Scott's) Simpson headed narrowly past. Rangers claimed a penalty kick when Murray fell in a tackle with Peacock, but the referee correctly ignored the appeal.

Celtic eventually recovered and a dangerously swerving corner kick by Tully was cleverly cleared by Niven. Play was swinging pleasingly from end to end, and only a last minute intervention by Fallon thwarted Paton of a possible score. The defences, although they often cleared hurriedly, were generally in command.

Fallon again baulked Rangers of a goal when he headed an overhead kick from Scott off the goal line after Murray had cleverly given the outside right possession.

BAD MISS
In the seventieth minute Young hesitated in clearing and was dispossessed by Collins, but Mochan's shot from the inside right's pass struck the post. Peacock started a splendid Celtic move with a pass to Tully, the outside right transferred the ball to McPhail, who in turn sent it to Fernie two yards from goal, but the inside left lofted high over when scoring looked easier.

In the closing minutes both sides strove desperately for a winning goal.

SUMMING-UP
Although play did not reach a high standard there were excitement and incident befitting the importance of the game.

The defences, in turn subjected to heavy pressure, were the better divisions of both teams, and the respective right backs, Evans and McColl, the most industrious and accomplished players afield. The forward play generally lacked coolness, and both sets of inside men, Paton and Simpson in particular, should have been more effective.

McColl, Niven, Young and Murray, a most intelligent centre forward, were the outstanding Rangers. Celtic had splendid service from Fallon and the tireless Collins, as well as Evans.

A draw was an equitable result.

Rangers (0) 0   **Celtic (0) 0**

RANGERS:- NIVEN; CALDOW AND LITTLE; MCCOLL, YOUNG AND SHEARER; SCOTT AND PATON; MURRAY; SIMPSON AND HUBBARD.

CELTIC:- BEATTIE; HAUGHNEY AND FALLON; EVANS, JACK AND PEACOCK; TULLY AND COLLINS; MCPHAIL; FERNIE AND MOCHAN.

Celtic 0, Rangers 2 – Saturday, 22nd September, 1956
Young Inspires Rangers at Parkhead

When midway through the second half at Celtic Park on Saturday, Scott went racing through the centre of Celtic's defence and shot low and hard past Beattie, the home team and their followers were dumbfounded. Rangers had been forced to concentrate on defence after half-time when Celtic had the advantage of the wind and monopoly of possession of the ball, but that Rangers should score when they did and consolidate their precarious first-half lead was not surprising, for each time they managed to switch from defence, the speed of Scott and the skill of Hubbard worried the Celtic defenders who, though reasonably sound as individuals, did not seem to have a plan of campaign.

LURED INTO THE WEB
They had, of course, no such leader as Young, a majestic figure who not only gave a magnificent individual display but employed his side's resources in defence to the best possible advantage. Celtic frequently outwitted the players of the outer wings of Rangers' defence - and they were generally strengthened by both inside forwards - but just as frequently they were lured into the web spun by Young.

Celtic's cross-passing game became more ragged as time passed, yet still they seemed unaware of the necessity to spread play and make their opponents turn and run. One long accurate transfer of McColl, Young or Baird in the direction of the corner flag carried more danger than half a dozen of Celtic's intricate movements.

Both in defence and in attack, therefore, Rangers were the more methodical and intelligent. Yet they did not deserve to win. Before Murray headed the first goal in 32 minutes, Celtic were deprived of scores only by superb saves by Niven. He was, I think, lucky when he dived to the left as Fernie shot and the ball struck him, but his leap and deflection of a McPhail shot constituted goalkeeping of the highest class. Rangers' defence would almost certainly not have lost that first-half goal of Murray's. When Little lobbed into goal both Jack and Beattie were in a position to clear, but probably they both expected the other to do the job.

Celtic, too, had their share of luck, however, in the first half, for Logie struck the top of the crossbar with a shot which dipped and deceived Beattie, and Hubbard drove the ball against the angle of the crossbar and the post.

INFRINGEMENTS

Celtic did have one outstanding grievance. I have not for some time seen any footballer allowed the latitude that Baird was, especially in the first half. Twenty-five free kicks for infringements other than offside were awarded during the match - nineteen of them against Rangers, and a high proportion of them against Baird. Yet, though the referee spoke to him in the first quarter of an hour, no disciplinary action was taken.

What should be the reaction of a player who is repeatedly prevented from practising the arts of the game, who beats an opponent as, for instance, Fernie does without causing irritation, and is tripped or bodychecked - Rangers were penalised on no fewer than 10 occasions for infringements against Fernie - and then sees the defence which he has at least partly broken, lining up in full strength for the free kick which is almost always an advantage to the offending side?

Rangers should pause and consider that just such incidents as Saturday's, followed by the retaliatory tactics, have caused most of the crowd disturbance in the murky past of the two clubs.

I was sorry to see the young promising Logie guilty of fouling Rangers' other wing half McColl, who had the brunt to bear of the menace of Fernie and yet never once resorted to unfair tackling. McColl was therefore one of the few distinguished players. One can, it should be remembered, be a great player though an opponent is momentarily one's superior.

McColl was on this occasion a much better player than Evans, who in turn was not half the player Peacock was. Evans may have had some reason for allowing Baird, who is still handicapped with a shoulder injury, so much freedom of movement, but so far as I could see, Baird not only was not tackled unfairly - he was not tackled at all. And Baird concentrating on the ball is too proficient a player not to take full advantage of theoretical and not practical opposition.

Celtic (0) 0	Rangers (1) 2
	Murray
	Scott

CELTIC:- BEATTIE; HAUGHNEY AND FALLON, EVANS, JACK AND PEACOCK; HIGGINS AND COLLINS, MCPHAIL, FERNIE AND MOCHAN.

RANGERS:- NIVEN, SHEARER AND LITTLE; MCCOLL, YOUNG AND LOGIE, SCOTT AND GRIERSON, MURRAY, BAIRD AND HUBBARD.

Rangers 2, Celtic 0 – Tuesday, 1st January, 1957
Celtic Lucky to Escape Heavier Defeat

Celtic at Ibrox Stadium yesterday were almost unrecognisable as the eleven who played exhilarating football at Easter Road Park on Saturday, and they were lucky indeed that Rangers did not take heavier toll of them than the goals scored by Murray in the twelfth minute and Simpson in the seventy-first.

This football is a strange game, for Celtic's outstanding player was Jack, who had a dreadful day against Hibernian. Time and again he prevented goals with strong, well-timed tackling. Had it not been for him and Beattie, who made many grand saves, especially in the second half, Celtic would have suffered a humiliating defeat.

SUSPENSE

Rangers were at once more methodical and more enthusiastic; it is a rare occasion in which a Celtic side are inferior in fighting spirit, but yesterday they were a poor second in that respect.

Niven had in comparison with Beattie an idle 90 minutes. Rangers' backs and half-backs gave most of the Celtic players a lesson in going determinedly for the ball and the long passing of Simpson and Baird was much more suited to the soft turf than Celtic's attempted intricacies.

Baird spoiled a fine display, however, with some coarse tackling which early in the match earned him a reprimand from the referee.

Both Rangers' goals were scored from positions close in on goal, Murray's from Baird's pass and Simpson's from Murray's deflection of a free kick taken by Shearer. Celtic's best chance was squandered by Fernie when, three minutes from half-time, he intercepted a pass back and missed an unguarded goal.

Rangers (1) 2	Celtic (0) 0
Murray	
Simpson	

RANGERS:- NIVEN; SHEARER AND CALDOW; MCCOLL, YOUNG AND LOGIE; SCOTT AND SIMPSON; MURRAY; BAIRD AND HUBBARD

CELTIC:- BEATTIE; HAUGHNEY AND MEECHAN; EVANS, JACK AND PEACOCK; SMITH AND RYAN; MEECHAN, FERNIE AND TULLY

Celtic 4, Rangers 4 – Saturday, 16th February, 1957
Astonishing Changes of Fortune

There is not such a thing as a cheap or a soft penalty kick in the book of Mr M.J. Mowat - nor is there in mine. Long may we have a referee who awards a penalty kick in such circumstances as those in which Mr Mowat gave Rangers theirs at Celtic Park on Saturday and does not shelter under the indirect free-kick rule.

The fact that the infringement committed by Jack might not have been so punished by many a referee is beside the point; the further fact that Rangers were inordinately fortunate to receive a penalty kick is in the same category.

PENALTY KICK

When, seven minutes from time Celtic were leading 4-2, I was firmly convinced that Rangers knew they were beaten, and when Baird from midfield thumped the ball high into the Celtic penalty area he probably did not have the slightest hope that a goal would accrue. Rangers' forwards certainly did not have much hope, for only Hubbard was in a position to challenge Jack for the ball. As I saw the incident, Hubbard made only a half-hearted attempt to jump; indeed, he may not have jumped at all. In any event, Jack seemed to concentrate more on an opponent who had no chance of beating him in the air than on the ball, and clumsily barged into him. Celtic are much less disposed than most teams to dispute a referee's decision; even so, only Jack - and he with no vehemence - seemed to disapprove of the penalty kick award.

Hubbard yet again confounded a goalkeeper with his shot from the spot, and the deathly stillness at the Rangers' followers' end of the ground was shattered. Two minutes later Rangers were, astonishingly, on equal terms - and again through no serious effort of their own. Jack nervously sent an attempted pass back yards too wide and strong and Murray side-footed the equalising goal when Hubbard's corner kick reached the goal area.

The remaining five minutes were obviously spent by Rangers congratulating themselves on their reprieve and by Celtic wondering if it were indeed true. They were the only dull moments of a most exhilarating match - undoubtedly the best I have seen between the clubs in the post-war years. We had four goals inside nine minutes in the first half, and four more in the period of 11 minutes in the second, and in the intervals as much excitement and good football as would suffice for half a dozen games.

In the sixth minute Morrison began his senior career with Rangers by directing Simpson's pass away from Beattie. That pass was one of the best of the match, but it would hardly have split the Celtic defence as it did had not Peacock been alarmingly out of position as a result of his having disputed Rangers' right to a throw-in. Furthermore, Beattie seemed somewhat easily beaten; he would have had more excuse for losing a goal a minute later when Simpson fired the ball much more powerfully for the same corner of the net.

In the ninth minute one of the well-controlled series of passing movements by the Celtic forwards was gloriously completed with a rasping shot by McPhail, but less than four minutes later Fallon was penalised for impeding Scott, and the winger's free kick was headed into the net from 14 yards by Simpson. I did not see a Celtic defender seriously try to deny the inside right his chance; indeed, throughout the match this failing in the air was a grave Celtic weakness.

CHANCES MISSED

In exactly a quarter of an hour Celtic equalised for the second time, Collins moving to the right touchline and enabling Higgins to dart through and score. Just on half time Fernie gave him an even easier opportunity, but the outside right held his head in his hands as he failed to evade Niven's desperate leap.

Higgins was twice in the second half to fail with similar chances - once when Niven was on the ground - and when the score was 4-2 in his side's favour, he was baulked of a goal by a brilliant save by Niven, who managed to get fingers to a header and touch the ball round a post.

Early in the second half, however, during which Rangers had their turn of the wind, Fallon made the save of the day by heading over the crossbar a Scott corner kick propelled beyond Beattie's reach by the Simpson brow. Jack's lack of composure was now apparent and another fine header, this time by Morrison, was magnificently saved by Beattie.

Two brilliant goals in the twenty-ninth and thirty-fifth minutes, however, ended Rangers' one phase of superiority. A venturesome run by Haughney led to the first. Davis hesitated and conceded a corner kick. Fernie sent the ball to the ball to the edge of the penalty area. McPhail, with a tremendous leap, directed it for goal and Collins hooked the ball when it was chest-high past a bewildered defence. Then McPhail, the best footballer afield, twice beat Davis on the right and passed low and true to Fernie, who emulated Collins by swivelling and shooting in the one movement. Then came the Jack blunders.

Fallon, Evans, McPhail, and Collins of Celtic and Caldow, McColl, Scott and Simpson of Rangers were the best players of an unexpectedly fine match. There was none of the namby-pamby play that has been the consequence of instructions given players to avoid trouble in many of the "Old Firm" games of the past.

Scottish Cup - 6th Round

Celtic (2) 4	Rangers (2) 4
McPhail	Morrison
Higgins	Simpson
Collins	Hubbard (pen.)
Fernie	Murray

CELTIC:- BEATTIE; HAUGHNEY AND FALLON; EVANS, JACK AND PEACOCK; HIGGINS AND FERNIE; MCPHAIL; MOCHAN AND COLLINS.

RANGERS:- NIVEN; SHEARER AND CALDOW; MCCOLL, DAVIS AND BLAIR; SCOTT AND SIMPSON; MURRAY; MORRISON AND HUBBARD.

Rangers 0, Celtic 2 – Wednesday, 20th February, 1957

Celtic Worthy Winners of Ibrox Replay

Celtic qualified for the seventh round of the Scottish Cup, in which they will play St Mirren at Celtic Park in March, by beating Rangers in the replay of their sixth-round tie yesterday at Ibrox Stadium. That is the brief factual outcome of the events at the Rangers ground.

Over 80,000 people, their appetites whetted by the excellence of last Saturday's game, obviously expected a repeat performance, but only the Celtic following were not gravely disappointed. On a heavily sanded frost-affected pitch Celtic played almost all of the football in the match; had the verdict been decided on the lines of boxing, the contest would have been stopped long before 90 minutes with Celtic so far ahead on points that it was impossible for their rivals to overhaul them.

COARSE TACKLING

The success of Celtic therefore was thoroughly deserved. It was not only in the matter of the skill of the game, however, that Celtic were superior. There must be unstinted praise for a side who suffered so long as they did from tactics that can at best be described as deplorable. Indeed, I would go so far as to say that Celtic's greatest triumph yesterday was their immeasurable superiority in behaviour. Almost from the start several Rangers players indulged in coarse tackling; even after Simpson had his name taken in the twenty-eighth minute, there was no improvement.

The referee had a most difficult job. His early attitude seemed to be that he was making allowance for the state of the pitch and that if there was any sign of players having committed an infringement because of the treacherous conditions, which frequently caused men to fall long before the ball was in their vicinity, the offence would be adjudged unintentional.

Latterly, however, Mr Mowat became a victim of his own planning; Rangers players committed far worse fouls than that for which Simpson had been cautioned and escaped with a spoken reprimand. The Celtic player who suffered the worst treatment was Fernie, the outstanding ball player on the field. He was bodychecked, back-charged and tripped a round dozen times – it was little wonder that in the second half he was barely able to stand.

The shocking climax came when Higgins, five minutes from time, was flattened by a bull-like rush from Shearer just as he was about to shoot, well inside the penalty area. If the penalty kick awarded against Jack on Saturday was a penalty kick – and I for one had no doubt that it was – this tackle was worth a dozen. Yet none was given. It was not Mr Mowat's day.

The restraint shown by the Celtic players was commendable – indeed, almost astonishing – but as I have indicated already, their triumph was even the greater for that.

Niven, Caldow, McColl, Davis, Scott and Hubbard are the only Rangers players who are entitled to escape censure on the score of conduct, and only Niven, despite his lapse which gave the opposition their first goal, and Caldow, were into the bargain comparable with any of their opponents in the praiseworthy arts and crafts of football.

Celtic, the smaller and lighter side, took full advantage of their greater mobility, and in the first half particularly mastered the conditions with quick accurate passing and individual touches of skill and ball control which Rangers could not match - indeed, rarely attempted to match. Rangers appeared to think that they could cause panic in the Celtic defence with the long, hard, high kick up the centre, but Jack - and I mention him in particular in view of his errors late in the first game - was not to be tempted into rashness or nervousness. The centre half was a model of efficiency; he, Fernie, Evans and Collins were magnificent players in a fine team.

MISJUDGMENT

Higgins scored the opening goal in the fifteenth minute. Both he and Baird stumbled as the winger cut in, but Higgins kept his feet and with his left foot, shot low but not hard. Niven misjudged his downward movement for the ball and succeeded in touching it against a post from which the ball crawled, agonisingly for Rangers, over the line. Ten minutes from half-time Collins chipped the ball shrewdly to Mochan, who, from the edge of the penalty area, swung his famous left foot and sent the ball screeching under the crossbar.

Niven atoned on several occasions for his mistake by making brilliant saves. McPhail hit a post and there were remarkable escapes at Rangers' goal on several later occasions. Beattie had not a semblance of a shot to save until midway in the second half; that in itself is a measure of Rangers' inferiority.

Scottish Cup - 6th Round Replay	
Rangers (0) 0	Celtic (2) 2
	Higgins
	Mochan
Attendance	80,000

RANGERS:- NIVEN; SHEARER AND CALDOW; MCCOLL, DAVIS AND BAIRD; SCOTT AND SIMPSON; MURRAY; MORRISON AND HUBBARD.

CELTIC:- BEATTIE; HAUGHNEY AND FALLON; EVANS, JACK AND PEACOCK; HIGGINS AND FERNIE; MCPHAIL; MOCHAN AND COLLINS.

Rangers 2, Celtic 0 – Monday, 19th August, 1957

Rangers in Glasgow Cup Semi-Finals

CELTIC LACK THRUST AT IBROX

Rangers, the holders of the Glasgow Cup, entered the Semi-finals of this year's competition by defeating Celtic last night before some 55,000 spectators at Ibrox Stadium in the first of the two first-round ties (Partick Thistle and Clyde will contest the second tonight at Firhill Park).

In the final minute of a splendid match Baird, who had scored the opening goal in the thirty-fourth minute, shot a second after his first shot had struck a Celtic player and rebounded fortuitously to him. Baird was probably the second-best forward Rangers had – Scott was eminently the best – but he was not comparable with Tully or Collins as a footballer. He has, however, no hesitation in having a crack at goal, and it was late in the match before Celtic realised that all the skilful approach play in the world could not result in goals if a leavening of straightforward thrustful finishing is introduced.

CHANCE LOST

This was a somewhat lucky Rangers victory, but Celtic cannot attribute to fortune the fact that they did not pierce the last line of Rangers' defence. In the very first minute of the match for instance, Sharkey had a chance in a million to give Celtic the great psychological advantage of the opening goal. Almost from the kick-off Fernie robbed Baird, strode purposefully forward, and laid the ball on the tracks of McPhail; the centre forward took Valentine to the left and then chipped the ball into a yawning space in front of Niven; Sharkey had anticipated the pass, collected the ball and then from 10 yards struck the goalkeeper, who must have had slender hopes indeed of retrieving the position.

Before the end of the firsthalf Beattie had performed splendid feats of goalkeeping – notably saves from McColl and Scott – but they resulted from the superior thrust of Rangers' forwards and the speed of Scott, rather than any success in combined attacking football. Celtic were immeasurably superior in that respect but no-one, not even Collins who played a tremendous game in every other respect, would emulate his opponents' willingness to shoot.

FORTUNATE

Just before half-time Rangers were, however, exceedingly fortunate when Shearer, standing on the goal line saved – I thought with his arm – a Collins shot. Then 19 minutes from time, Tully, venturing deep infield and gesticulating in the old inimitable manner, utterly deceived Rangers' defence by thrusting the ball through to Sharkey when a square pass to Mochan was expected: Sharkey shot under Niven's despairing dive but the ball was slightly deflected by the goalkeeper and Shearer, scurrying back, was able to clear.

Celtic had several consolations in defeat. Donnelly, playing in his first senior "Old Firm" match was intelligent and successful throughout against Hubbard, who has rarely been so subdued by fair methods. Secondly, it was manifest that Tully can still be the architect of victory if he has colleagues who can capitalise on the scoring opportunities he can contrive. McPhail was sadly remiss, however; he seemed to have no zest for the physical side of the game. Valentine, rarely resembling the great Queen's Park centre half, was a vulnerable point in Rangers' defence, but still McPhail was inordinately reluctant to try to pass him.

VALUE OF SCOTT

Rangers were dependent most of all in attack on Scott, whose speed was a deal too much for Fallon – and for Peacock, too. Davis, despite the ordeal of opposing Collins in his most tantalising mood, took the chance to prove that the left half and not the centre half is his position at Ibrox, and McColl, opposed by a Celtic left wing who did not compare with the right, finished one of the strongest players of all.

Rangers (1) 2	Celtic (0 0
Baird 2	
Attendance	55,000

RANGERS:- NIVEN; SHEARER AND CALDOW; MCCOLL, VALENTINE AND DAVIS; SCOTT AND SIMPSON; MURRAY; BAIRD AND HUBBARD.

CELTIC:- BEATTIE; DONNELLY AND FALLON; FERNIE, EVANS AND PEACOCK; TULLY AND COLLINS; MCPHAIL; SHARKEY AND MOCHAN.

Rangers 2, Celtic 3 – Saturday, 21st September 1957

Celtic's Superiority in Ibrox Match

By Our Football Correspondent, Cyril Horne

Though in the closing minutes of a nerve-racking, stamina-testing match Celtic were once somewhat fortunate, and once exceedingly so to withstand Rangers' furious efforts to equalise – Fernie kicked a Simpson header off the goal-line, and Murray headed against the base of a post – the result did not unduly favour Celtic. Theirs was a victory of superior football.

Rangers almost certainly lost the match in the first half, in which with the wind at their backs they were frequently remiss in attack. Perhaps the back and half-backs conceived the idea that strong thrusting inside forwards could provoke errors in the Celtic defence as the long high ball sailed into goal but on almost every occasion this unattractive, potentially dangerous form of thrust was attempted Evans, of the superb heading ability and sound judgement in anticipation, baulked them of the ball, driven ahead with insufficient thought for the power of the wind, and passed over the bye-line far ahead of the pursuing forwards.

GOAL BY COLLINS

A player of Fernie's type would have been invaluable for Rangers in this period and so would one of the McPhail mould; their holding of the ball and refusing to pass until there was a point in doing so provided a pleasant contrast to Rangers' less studied methods.

It was, however, a defender's hard-hit punt downfield which led to Celtic's first goal. Fallon's powerful drive was nevertheless aimed for the head of McPhail who flicked the ball past Valentine in the jump. Then we saw another kind of player Rangers lacked. Collins was sprinting to McPhail's left before even the centre forward made contact and in a few electrifying seconds he had taken the ball in his stride, darted inward and past Shearer, and baffled the out-coming Ritchie with a perfectly placed low shot.

That glorious goal was scored in the nineteenth minute, and not until six minutes from half-time did Rangers pierce the opposing defence. Scott for once escaped the close-marking Fallon and crossed a ball that Beattie surprisingly did not try to cut out and he was beaten where he stood when Simpson, who revels in the heading goal-scoring chance, made contact.

Minutes before, Rangers might have been faced with an ominous two goal deficit and the prospect of playing against the wind in the second half, for Tully with a series of swerves left a trail of dumbfounded opponents behind him, chipped the ball back to two unguarded colleagues a mere 10 yards from goal, and looked appealingly to the sky as both Wilson and McPhail duffed their shots.

DECEIVED

Nine minutes after half-time, one of several free kicks conceded by young Austin, now not surprisingly finding Fernie and Collins too swift for him, cost Rangers a goal. Collins went through the motions of at least felling one of the defenders in the barrier and deceiving all of them by delicately lofting the ball to McPhail, who, standing on the extreme left of the line-up, and astonishingly because of his brilliant heading ability unmarked, directed his header over the hands of Ritchie, who seemed so puzzled by the change of Collins' intention that he made only a half-hearted backward jump.

Collins and Tully 10 minutes later spreadeagled Rangers, and when McPhail near the left touch-line was given a long, low pass he was, as before, isolated. The centre forward had time to change the ball to his right foot, study the goal-mouth position and cross before Valentine was within six yards of him; Wilson headed the pass decisively past Ritchie, who must have wondered where his fellow-defenders had gone.

Simpson gave Rangers late hope by beating Beattie to a back-header by Murray and driving the ball under the diving goalkeeper – I thought Beattie made his advance a fraction too late – but Celtic's defence held out. Baird was the most successful forward. Scott met his master in Fallon, who surely who can never have been a better full back, concentrating on the ball and ignoring the somewhat tentative attempts of Scott to distract him from his purpose. Simpson's scoring was not an inconsiderable contribution, but neither he nor Murray had the ability to control the ball on the ground. Hubbard had lost the nippiness which made full backs tackle nothing but air; too often nowadays, he cannot avoid the challenge.

ADVANTAGES

Celtic had the best full back afield in Fallon, a clearly superior half-back line, and as obvious an advantage in skill and shrewdness in the forward line. Perhaps their disadvantage in physique was to their advantage; in any event they gained the reward of devoting more attention to the arts and crafts of the game.

Rangers (1) 2	Celtic (1) 3
Simpson 2	Collins
	McPhail
	Wilson

RANGERS:- RITCHIE; SHEARER AND CALDOW; MCCOLL, VALENTINE AND AUSTIN; SCOTT AND SIMPSON; MURRAY; BAIRD AND HUBBARD.

CELTIC:- BEATTIE; DONNELLY AND FALLON; FERNIE, EVANS AND PEACOCK; SHARKEY AND COLLINS; MCPHAIL; SMITH AND TULLY.

Celtic 7, Rangers 1 – Saturday, 19th October, 1957

Celtic's Seven-Goal Triumph in League Cup Final

From Our Football Correspondent: Cyril Horne

SKILL AND DISCIPLINE PREVAIL

Eleven football players of Celtic Football Club did more in 90 minutes at Hampden Park on Saturday for the good of football than officialdom, in whose hands the destiny of the game lies, has done in years and years. For with a display of such grandeur as has rarely graced the great vast ground they proved conclusively the value of concentration on discipline and on the arts and crafts of the game to the exclusion of the so-called power-play which has indeed been a disfiguring weakness in the sport, but which has frequently been accredited through the awarding of international honours to the "strong-men".

BRILLIANT FERNIE

So devastating an effect had Fernie, the forward turned wing-half, on Rangers, who before the rout of Saturday were still considered as difficult opposition as could be found in the length and breadth of the football land, that the Scottish International selectors must surely now be considering whether they should destroy forthwith the impression that certain players are indispensable for future internationals and build their sides round this wonderful footballer who achieves his purpose without the merest suggestion of relying on physique and who suffers the rude, unfair attempts of opponents to stop him without a thought of retaliation.

Though Rangers Football Club may not immediately be in the mood to agree, they cannot surely in the near future but decide to change their policy on the field. I am not one who is going to charge their players of Saturday with the ultimate responsibility for the club's humiliation, badly as most of them performed. The culprits are those who have, encouraged by results at the expense of method, not discouraged the he-man type of game that has become typical of the side in recent years. I have seen Celtic teams in years gone by no better disciplined and no better equipped for their task from the point of view of skill than the present Rangers, but the Celtic management have long since realised that constructive football will in the end receive the greater reward.

OTHER MCPHAIL

Not since their brilliant Coronation Cup days at Hampden have Celtic played football of such quality. One recalls that in the 1953 triumph a slightly corpulent John McPhail played havoc with Arsenal, Manchester United and Hibernian through masterly control and passing of the ball; now the younger, slimmer Billy McPhail has joined Fernie, Tully and company in the bewildering of Rangers by the same admirable methods.

Valentine, not long ago a commanding figure on this same ground, was a forlorn bewitched centre half on Saturday, repeatedly beaten in the air and on the ground in a variety of ways, and the disintegration of Rangers' defence undoubtedly stemmed from McPhail's mastery.

But it did not begin with Valentine's plight.

Celtic introduced Mochan to outside left and that player seized his opportunity as if it were his last. His pace and penetrative dribbling and apparently new-found zest for the game had Shearer in a dreadful dither almost from the first kick of the ball. So Shearer decided to test Mochan's physical strength and straightaway was decisively beaten in that respect too. Thereafter McColl was so busily engaged as an extra right back that great gaps appeared on that side of the field.

In the first 20 minutes Celtic might have scored at least four goals and indeed were inordinately unlucky not to score at least two when Collins and the Tully hit the wood around Niven. Rangers' first scoring effort was Murray's in the 20th minute, but it was blocked by the shrewd intervention of Evans, throughout a centre half of absolute competence.

Three minutes later McPhail headed down to Wilson and the inside left, without waiting for the ball to touch the ground, bulged the net from 12 yards. Before Mochan scored Celtic's second goal the frantic leap from Niven and again the crossbar stopped another 30-yard free kick driven with such power by Collins as a stranger would not associate with one of his stature.

FIERCE SHOT

Mochan's goal in the final minute of the half ended fittingly superb play by McPhail, who after engaging in a heading movement with Wilson, lofted the ball over Shearer to the galloping outside left. Shearer went full length in a desperate attempt to tackle and McColl was also stretched on the ground. Mochan cut in and from near the touchline hurtled his shot into the far corner of the net.

Rangers began the second half with the wind in their favour and with the sun now in the eyes of the Celtic defenders but, alarmingly for their followers, with Murray, a knee bandaged, at outside left, Simpson at centre forward and Scott and Hubbard forming the right wing. Murray, be it noted, had injured himself in trying to tackle Evans, from behind and been penalised for his pains.

Soon Fernie was travelling half the length of the field again and running his opponents into the ground, and it was a demoralised defence who lost the third goal, headed by McPhail when Collins crossed. Five minutes later Simpson, with an exhilarating dive and header, scored from McColl's cross; it was noticeable that this was the first chance permitted by Evans who minutes earlier had been injured. Of that injury more will follow.

NAME TAKEN

Baird soon afterwards had his name taken by the referee who apparently detected an infringement committed against Wilson not obvious from the press box, and in the final 23 minutes McPhail (now toying with Valentine), Mochan, McPhail again and Fernie from a penalty kick

George Young

In the present day when Rangers are enjoying such outstanding success on the domestic scene, it must be difficult for the younger generation of fans to envisage that in the late forties and early fifties the club also had giants of men, who were held in the highest esteem throughout Europe. George "Corky" Young was one of them. A right back, who was converted to centre half after the *sine die* suspension of Willie Woodburn, he was the dominant figure in the Rangers defence which was known as the Iron Curtain. Young was born in Grangemouth in 1922 and joined Rangers from Kirkintilloch Rob Roy in 1941, remaining at Ibrox until he retired as a player in 1957–another of those men you could never envisage playing for any other club. Tall, commanding and strong, he also had skill on the ball and was one of the all-time outstanding performers in Old Firm matches.

Young won 53 caps and captained Scotland for six successive seasons, playing against England on nine occasions. He also had 21 League caps and, with Rangers, won six Championships, four Scottish Cups and two League Cups. He had a spell as manager of the now defunct Third Lanark, and on leaving football became a hotelier.

Ian McMillan

Known as the Wee Prime Minister, McMillan was already an established player when he joined Rangers. He began his career with Airdrie in 1948 and signed for Rangers ten years later for a fee of £10,000. After just a couple of days with the club, he made a dream debut, scoring twice in a 4-4 draw with Raith Rovers at Ibrox.

Was one of the best Rangers midfield men ever, with a smooth, silky touch and the ability to open up even the tightest of defences. He was also a gentleman, and highly respected by everyone in the game. After six years, Ian returned to Airdrie for £5,000 and had to retire because of injury in 1967.

He managed the Broomfield club from 1970-76 and two years later became a director. It is something of a mystery why McMillan gained only six full caps and two League honours. But his medal haul at Ibrox was impressive–three Championships, three Scottish Cups and two League Cups.

Bobby Shearer

Another of the great Rangers captains, and an un–compromising right back. Packed inside his 5ft. 7in. frame was dynamism and raw courage. His solidness and his passion for the club typified the spirit at Ibrox during that era in the sixties.

He led Rangers to their historic treble in season 1963-64.

Shearer signed for Rangers from Hamilton in 1955 for a couple of thousand pounds and stayed with the club for ten years, after which he was player-coach with Queen of the South. His career, however, was not all a story of success and triumph. Bobby was unlucky enough to play in the 9-3 defeat by England at Wembley in 1961, and he was also the manager of Third Lanark when they went defunct in 1968. He also managed Hamilton, his first senior, club before being involved in several business ventures. Shearer played only four times for Scotland, and made two appearances for the Scottish League. He played in Europe on 30 occasions for Rangers, and in all made 431 appearances for the club, winning six Championships, three Scottish Cups and three League Cups.

Jimmy Millar

A centre forward of the old–fashioned style, Millar was one of the bravest and most honest strikers ever to play in Scotland. Born in Edinburgh, he joined Rangers from Dunfermline Athletic for a relatively small fee in 1955. After completing three years' active service in Egypt and Greece, he quickly established himself in the first team where his strength and dedication caused all sorts of problems for opponents.

Millar formed a potent front partnership with Ralph Brand and his best season was in 1962-63, when he scored 44 goals in 52 matches. That same season, many regarded his performance against Celtic at Ibrox on New Year's Day to be his best for the club. Millar, who had flu, refused to stay at home and scored in a match Rangers won 4-0.

Jimmy was capped only twice by Scotland and gained four League caps. With Rangers he scored 166 goals in 320 matches and won three Championships, five Scottish Cups and three League Cups. Moved to Dundee United in 1967, and later had a short spell as manager of Raith Rovers.

completed the humiliation. During that period Niven, Shearer and Valentine were so panic-stricken that any one of them might have joined the list of Celtic goal-scorers.

The advantage of the tall goalkeeper over the short was never more clear than in this match. Beattie, whose chief worry was the harassing tactics of opponents – I cannot recall a Celtic player making contact with Niven – gave his fellow defenders confidence with perfect handling and timing of his interceptions. Donnelly continues to make a reputation as the most promising back in Scotland and Fallon again reduced the ill-supported Scott to a hapless young man, prominent after the first 10 minutes only for successful attempts to provoke his stronger wiser opponent.

Never have I seen Rangers so outclassed in half-back play; Fernie, Evans and Peacock were, each in his own distinguished way, tremendous players in everything but brawn and bulk.

TULLY'S FEAT

No one Celt, however, but did not contribute handsomely to the team's glorious day. The effect of the now restrained, but clever as ever Tully, should not be minimised. Perhaps only Fernie of all footballers in Scotland could have emulated Tully's first-half feat of ball manipulation which enabled him to outwit Baird, Davis, Valentine and Caldow. Then as his team-mates poised themselves for the chip back from the goal-line, Tully struck like lightning and the ball cannoned off the very edge of the near post, passed between Niven and the goal-line, and out of play beyond

the post. The goal of a century had been within half an inch of achievement.

I have mentioned the injury to Evans. It occurred when the score was 1-0 and Baird was leading up to his caution. Baird had been admonished earlier for his treatment of Fernie, but when he brought down Evans after the centre half had dribbled round him, the whole Celtic team ceased playing. Astonishingly Mr Mowat waved the game on – one wonders if he had become obsessed with the advantage rule and in a moment of aberration had given the advantage to the offender – and Beattie had to make his save of the day as Murray promptly accepted the gift of a scoring chance.

That was Mr Mowat's one mistake and he can be pardoned that, in view of his excellent refereeing. Without a referee with his power of control we would almost certainly not have seen Celtic's superb football.

League Cup Final

Celtic (2) 7	Rangers (0) 1
Wilson	Simpson
Mochan 2	
McPhail 3	
Fernie (pen.)	

CELTIC:- BEATTIE; DONNELLY AND FALLON; FERNIE, EVANS AND PEACOCK; TULLY AND COLLINS; MCPHAIL; WILSON AND MOCHAN.

RANGERS:- NIVEN; SHEARER AND CALDOW; MCCOLL, VALENTINE AND DAVIS; SCOTT AND SIMPSON; MURRAY; BAIRD AND HUBBARD.

Wille Fernie's penalty for Celtic in the historic 1957 7-1 League Cup final victory.

Celtic 0, Rangers 1 – Wednesday, 1st January, 1958

Brilliant Save by Ritchie Denies Celtic Draw

By Cyril Horne

A most remarkable save by Ritchie midway in the second half at Celtic Park was the principal factor in Rangers' success. McVittie's shot was placed carefully and cleverly far to the right of Rangers' goalkeeper but with nimbleness and courage exceptional on the day of freezing, iron-hard ground he dived headlong and collared the ball on the ground when all the Celtic legions were crying "Goal."

RANGERS THRUST

Had Celtic scored then, after intensive pressure, it would have been no more than they deserved. Yet for all that great effort they were outpointed in attack, and though they probably raided Rangers' goal three times as frequently as the Ibrox forwards menaced Beattie, the Murray-led line was always the more dangerous.

Rangers, too, seemed the more able to master the difficult conditions; no light-blue clad player seemed to be so uncomfortable, for instance, as Mochan or Fallon who late in the match went to centre forward with the obvious intention of introducing thrust to the forward line.

It was significant that the greatest danger to Rangers throughout the match emanated from the huge throw-ins by Ryan who, especially in the second half, caused near panic as he hurled the ball into the heart of the defensive zone.

The outstanding feature of a splendid match – sportingly contested apart from one foolish foul by Baird on Colrain in the dying minutes – was the play of Evans who showed how the defensive duties of a centre half can be combined with constructive ideas.

SUCCESSFUL PLAYERS

Evans, Smith, Kennedy, Ryan and Wilson were fine players for Celtic. Scott, who scored the goal in the 19th minute, Millar, whose play was modelled most intelligently on the conditions, and Wilson were forwards of distinction. Telfer, sure throughout, and Baird, taming the capricious ball admirably for one of his height and weight, were tremendous players in defence.

Celtic (0) 0   Rangers (1) 1
                      Scott

CELTIC:- BEATTIE; FALLON AND KENNEDY; SMITH, EVANS AND PEACOCK; MCVITTIE AND COLRAIN; RYAN; WILSON AND MOCHAN

RANGERS:-RITCHIE; SHEARER AND CALDOW; MCCOLL, TELFER AND BAIRD; SCOTT AND MILLAR; MURRAY; BRAND AND WILSON

Rangers 1, Celtic 1 – Thursday, 8th May, 1958

Toss of a Coin Decides at Ibrox

After a game of many hard knocks, the toss of a coin finally decided that Rangers go forward to the Final of the Glasgow Charity Cup. It was a game in which the arts of football skill were shown at only too rare intervals.

Rangers were superior in the first half and deservedly led by a Murray goal in the fifteenth minute. The Rangers' centre's volleying of the ball into the net was expertly done, but he owed much to the Celtic defence by making the chance, possibly by their hesitance in tackling.

In the second half Celtic switched Collins and McVittie, and a decided improvement was soon apparent. Ritchie's goal survived a barrage until the fifty-ninth minute when Fernie passed back to Peacock who scored from more than 20 yards.

Rangers' defence, which had never been ruffled early on, temporarily lost touch. Shearer was then reprimanded for a bad foul on Wilson.

Apart from an early lapse, Beattie was a clever and confident keeper. Ritchie, with less opportunity to shine, made no errors. Of the four full backs, Shearer was easily the best.

Much of the blame for the game's failing to produce the classic touches must fall on the wing halves. Both centre halves were safe, although Evans failed to produce his Hampden form. Among the forwards, the centres, Murray and McPhail, were outstanding.

Glasgow Charity Cup Semi-Final
Rangers (1) 1   Celtic (0) 1
Murray   Peacock
(Rangers won on the toss of a coin)

RANGERS:- RITCHIE; SHEARER AND LITTLE; DAVIS, TELFER AND SMITH; DUNCAN AND MILLAR; MURRAY; BAIRD AND WILSON.

CELTIC:- BEATTIE; MEECHAN AND MOCHAN; SMITH, EVANS AND PEACOCK; COLLINS AND FERNIE; MCPHAIL; WILSON AND MCVITTIE.

Celtic 2, Rangers 2 – Saturday, 6th September, 1958
Disapproval of Penalty for Rangers
By Cyril Horne

While there was not the slightest excuse for the behaviour of the people at the Celtic end of the ground at Parkhead on Saturday, one cannot ignore how and why the outburst of bottle-throwing occurred. It was clearly the horrid means of expressing disapproval of the penalty kick awarded to Rangers in the forty-first minute.

I was mystified when the penalty was awarded. Was it for McNeil's tackle of Wilson or was it for the later incident in which Brand, like Wilson, went full length? I saw no infringement and the vehement protests of the Celtic team, who for some years have been much less guilty of showing dissent than many others, was a factor worthy of consideration. Undoubtedly, however, their demeanour must have encouraged the bottle boys to make free with their favours.

A penalty kick it was in the end, and Hubbard equalised the goal scored by Collins in 28 minutes. Thereafter one had to have one eye on the field of play and the other on the unruliness of the terracing.

Twenty-seven minutes from time there was another scene of vociferous dissent – this time by Rangers players, and they should be grateful that their badgering of the referee did not result in another fracas on the terracing. Scott had been penalised for one of several fouls on Mochan, and the free kick was taken as Mr. Harvie, in passing, had a word with Rangers' outside right. The ball reached Conway who transferred it to Smith, and the latter, warding off Telfer's tackle, ran in and beat the advancing Niven. As the ball crossed the line the referee was pointing for an infringement presumably committed by Smith but what it had been I had no idea.

Celtic managed to inveigle the referee into a discussion with a linesman as a result of which the goal stood, though Rangers in their turn kept arguing about it.

Brand made the score 2-2 three minutes later, and shortly before the finish, there occurred another inexplicable interpretation by the referee when Collins was sandwiched and held by two Rangers defenders in the penalty area and no penalty kick was given.

The finest player in this match that satisfied no-one was Peacock. There were occasional attractive offerings by Fernie and Tully in Celtic's attack, but it was significant that Fernie was the team's best shot. Shearer and Telfer were splendid defensive players for Rangers, but the forwards, Hubbard apart, were unimpressive.

Celtic (1) 2	Rangers (1) 2
Collins	Hubbard (pen.)
Smith	Brand

CELTIC:- BEATTIE; MCKAY AND MOCHAN; FERNIE, MCNEIL AND PEACOCK; SMITH AND TULLY; CONWAY; COLLINS AND AULD.

RANGERS:- NIVEN; SHEARER AND CALDOW; MCCOLL, TELFER AND DAVIS; SCOTT AND BRAND: MURRAY; WILSON AND HUBBARD.

Rangers 2, Celtic 1 – Thursday, 1st January, 1959
Rangers Lucky to Win
By Cyril Horne

After 35 minutes' play in the second half at Ibrox Stadium, the referee halted the proceedings for a consultation with his linesmen. No one had the slightest doubt about the subject matter, indeed abandonment seemed certain to be the outcome, for a dreadful gale of wind and rain was sweeping over a pitch long since become a quagmire. Not a vestige of goal-line marking could be seen and more than one player seemed sure to collapse from exhaustion.

After the officials' huddle, however, play resumed as it had ceased with Celtic making tremendous efforts to neutralise Rangers' 2-1 lead.

Then, five minutes from time, a penalty kick for Celtic, awarded as unhesitatingly by Mr Mowat as had been one for Rangers in the last minute of the first half. One felt sorry for Auld as he and his colleagues searched for the penalty spot in the morass; Caldow, who had converted his side's penalty at the same end of the ground had much the easier conditions. Auld in the end made a nearly perfect strong shot – no one could have risked trying to side-foot the kick – but the ball struck the crossbar.

Though Matthews missed the last scoring chance of the match, this was indeed Rangers' lucky day; one cannot escape the conclusion that the young Celtic forwards would have run them ragged on a firmer pitch.

Mochan suffered an ordeal, became petulant, conceded a penalty kick through arming the ball, shot by Scott with no apparent danger to Beattie, and latterly had his name taken, presumably for repeatedly infringing the rules.

Peacock began the scoring in 15 minutes with a low shot which was deflected by Telfer past Niven. Midway in the first half Matthew equalised after Beattie had saved from him. This was a splendid match, despite the deplorable conditions. Niven, both Rangers' full backs and McColl can rarely have played better. I thought Smith was the outstanding Celtic player and all their inside forwards were superior to Rangers' three. But lacking even one winger of ordinary straightforward methods Celtic were committed to centre field thrusts and skilfully and enthusiastically as Colrain and Divers conducted them, the mud was a deadly enemy.

Rangers (2) 2	Celtic (1) 1
Mathews	Peacock
Caldow (pen.)	

RANGERS:- NIVEN; SHEARER AND CALDOW; MCCOLL, TELFER AND STEVENSON; SCOTT AND MCMILLAN; MURRAY; BRAND AND MATTHEWS.

CELTIC:- BEATTIE; MCKAY AND MOCHAN; SMITH, EVANS AND PEACOCK; MCVITTIE AND JACKSON; COLRAIN; DIVERS AND AULD.

Celtic 2, Rangers 1 – Saturday, 28th February, 1959

Young Celtic Attack Harass Rangers

By Cyril Horne

ECHO OF 1939 ENCOUNTER

Just over 20 years ago – before at least four of Celtic's Scottish Cup team of Saturday were born – a vast crowd of almost 119,000 assembled for the New Year league fixture of the Old Firm. I can still hear the groaning of the Celtic legions when their team was announced; injury and illness had laid waste a famous forward line. For of Delany, McDonald, Crum, Divers and Murphy, only the first and last were there and Murphy was at inside left, possibly for the only time in his career.

Defeat was Celtic's portion that day in 1939, but as Mr. J.S. Symon, Rangers' manager, will recall, there was glory in the defeat.

At 2.45 on Saturday there was a funereal hush at the Celtic end of Parkhead when the forward line for the Scottish Cup third-round tie echoed out of the loudspeaker; the name of Colrain as well as that of Auld was missing; only Wilson, himself not a regular first-team player this season, was not a mere apprentice of the trade.

CHANGE OF MOOD

But at half-time the Celtic following were deliriously happy, their team a goal up against a full-strength Rangers eleven who began the match with every advantage except in the fact that they were raging hot favourites. When Divers, son of the Divers mentioned heretofore, headed his goal one minute from the interval, the match was probably three-quarters won and lost, for Rangers' limitations had been starkly revealed and Celtic, were clearly climbing per ardua ad astra.

The regular, if hardly rhythmic, chant of "Seven, seven, seven" which developed at the covered enclosure end of the ground – the League Cup final of last season has for some an irresistible and indestructible appeal – was, however, wildly vainglorious; much toil and sweat there had yet to be for Celtic before the victory was sure – 11 minutes from time for instance, when McMillan emerged for once from indolence and crossed invitingly to Murray, and Haffey with a one-handed save in a million diverted the fast-flying header.

That fleeting moment of danger apart, however, Celtic after McVittie's goal in 56 minutes were in quite astonishing command – the utter failure of Rangers' inside forwards to challenge an admittedly magnificent half-back line must have astonished Celtic themselves.

Soon, however, McKay, that delightfully constructive full back, and Mochan, who unlike his partner does not hold with caressing and fondling the ball, gained control of Rangers' wingers. For all that Smith, Evans and Peacock were so devastatingly successful, I am not at all certain that Mochan did not play the greatest part in the Celtic victory. His judgment in the tackle and in the air was excellent; when he had an even chance of thwarting Scott he did not once fail, and when Scott is contained these days Rangers do not appear capable of doing anything about it.

WILSON'S GUIDANCE

Wilson played admirably the role of guide and mentor to the youthful Celtic centre forwards, all of whom thoroughly justified their selection, especially Divers, who might have scored three more goals but for ill-luck and the sprightliness of Niven, one of whose early saves was almost the equal of Haffey's solitary second-half masterpiece.

Shearer and Caldow bore with Niven the brunt of their opponents' intelligent, quick passing on the ground and their constant physical effort. I am sure Shearer especially appreciated how lucky Rangers were to suffer only a one-goal defeat. Rangers' captain's example of making a particular display of congratulating his opponents seemed to indicate that Murray's goal, headed after a minute of overtime – correctly awarded for Peacock's having indulged in time-wasting at throw-ins – was as meaningless a score as is possible to imagine.

The last words must be for orderliness of the crowd and the success of the police planning and administration (though we must compare a 42,000 all-ticket crowd with a 119,000 first-come-first-served attendance) and for Mr Symon, who justifiably could have expected an 11-man effort from his team comparable with Celtic's on that memorable 1939 day.

Celtic (1) 2	Rangers (0) 1
Divers	Murray
McVittie	
Attendance	42,000

CELTIC:- HAFFEY; MACKAY AND MOCHAN; SMITH, EVANS AND PEACOCK; MCVITTIE AND JACKSON; LOCHHEAD; WILSON AND DIVERS.

RANGERS:- NIVEN; SHEARER AND CALDOW; DAVIS, TELFER AND STEVENSON; SCOTT AND MACMILLAN; MURRAY; WILSON AND MATTHEW.

Rangers 1, Celtic 1 – Saturday, 2nd May, 1959
Celtic Win on Toss of Coin

The luck Celtic enjoyed against Rangers at Ibrox Stadium continued even after the game was over: on the toss of a coin, they passed into the final of the Glasgow Charity Cup in which they will play Clyde on Saturday at Hampden Park.

Rangers undoubtedly were most unfortunate to lose, for in the second half when they harnessed the strong west wind more effectively than Celtic had before the interval, they were seldom out of their opponents' half of the field and were denied goals by the brilliant if fortuitous goalkeeping of Haffey and the tough defence of Evans, Peacock and Mochan.

After 64 minutes of play Rangers had the ball in the net for the second time through Scott, but the goal was disallowed after a linesman indicated that Matthew was offside. That decision resulted in a scene in Celtic's penalty are a which reflected no credit on Evans or Telfer.

Mr Mowat smoothed over that incident which was by no means the only instance of unseemly behaviour, but was less lenient 14 minutes later when he took Auld's name for a crude tackle on Telfer near the touchline.

The feuds apart, the game was enjoyable. Rangers had the better forwards, who at times combined delightfully. Celtic, however, never really settled in attack; their second-half partnership of Colrain and McVittie on the right wing, with Smith, their liveliest forward, at inside left, was unsuccessful.

Brand opened the scoring for Rangers in 14 minutes when he headed past Haffey an accurately flighted cross by Scott. Celtic equalised 15 minutes later when Byrne prodded the ball over the line while Rangers' defence were disentangling themselves after a long throw-in by McKay.

Glasgow Charity Cup Semi-Final

Rangers (1) 1	Celtic (1) 1
Brand	Byrne

(Celtic won on the toss of a coin)

RANGERS:- NIVEN; SHEARER AND CALDOW; DAVIS, TELFER AND STEVENSON; SCOTT AND MCMILLAN; MURRAY; BRAND AND MATTHEW.

CELTIC:- HAFFEY; DONNELLY AND MOCHAN; MACKAY, EVANS AND PEACOCK; SMITH AND MCVITTIE; BYRNE; COLRAIN AND AULD

Celtic 1, Rangers 2 – Monday, 17th August, 1959
Rangers Beat Celtic in Glasgow Cup
By Cyril Horne

DECISIVE GOAL BY MILLER

Fourteen minutes from time in the Glasgow Cup first-round tie at Celtic Park last night Millar, Rangers' centre forward, challenged Evans, Celtic's centre half for a long, high pass out of defence by Baird. Evans, first to the bouncing ball, could have cleared at his leisure into touch, but he adopted a cavalier-like attitude to the situation and Millar, much more determined, won the ball. He proceeded to entice Haffey out and score a goal which was in the end to be decisive.

That goal, coolly and intelligently scored by Millar, gave Rangers a somewhat fortunate victory. Their first goal scored six minutes from half-time by Baird, throughout Rangers' most profitable forward, was fortuitous indeed. Duncan struck his cross incorrectly low against Evans, and Haffey was easily beaten by the low shot from 18 yards after Baird had collected the rebound.

In 63 minutes Conway equalised that goal, having cleverly flicked the ball over Telfer's head and delivered a right-foot shot which the nimble Niven all but saved.

The much-changed Celtic played remarkably well last night – especially Jackson and Conway. The centre forward frequently beat Telfer, but in the first half especially, he shot too quickly. But Celtic were dreadfully weak at outside left, and Shearer had an unexpectedly easy task.

Rangers were little better served on the wings – Duncan was easily brushed aside by Mochan – a consistently fine defender – and the attacks of both sides had of necessity to be concentrated in the centre of the field.

Peacock for over an hour was a magnificent wing half – he tired towards the end – and McNeil showed the value of forthright tackling against the tricky Wilson. But the lasting memory of this "Old Firm" game, watched in comparative silence by 38,000 spectators, was the failure of both sets of forwards – the wingers particularly responsible – to outwit close-marking defences.

Glasgow Cup 1st Round

Celtic (0) 1	Rangers (1) 2
Conway	Baird
	Millar
Attendance	38,000

CELTIC:- HAFFEY; MCNEIL AND MOCHAN; MCKAY, EVANS AND PEACOCK; CARROLL AND JACKSON; CONWAY, DIVERS AND MACKIE.

RANGERS:- NIVEN; SHEARER AND CALDOW; DAVIS, TELFER AND STEVENSON; DUNCAN AND MCMILLAN; MILLAR; BAIRD AND WILSON.

Ragers 3, Celtic 1 – Saturday, 5th September, 1959

Rangers Turn the Clock Back

By Cyril Horne

RASH PLAY AT IBROX STADIUM

In bygone but not forgotten Rangers-Celtic matches players of both clubs were, through inflaming spectators with their behaviour on the field, responsible for much of the misconduct on the terracing. In recent years, however, little such provocation has emanated from the field, and now both clubs and the police, through their warnings and through the overwhelming presence of the police on the terracing, have called the hooligans' bluff.

Yet most depressingly on Saturday, the clock was turned back. I cannot reconcile the rashness and recklessness of Rangers players with their club's professed attitude to spectators, some 65,000 of whom had the opportunity to read in Rangers' official programme:- "Each of you today can be the guardian of the game's reputation. The trust is in you. We believe you will not fail." One wonders if a similar pronouncement has reached the eyes or ears of the players.

TRAINER BUSY

Celtic may be a weak, frail collection of players and Rangers strong, hardy specimens of manhood, the one team wilting and the other blooming in the physical jousts that are inevitable in a game such as football. The fact remains that on Saturday, the Celtic trainer was summoned to attend Jackson (twice), Haffey, Auld and Kennedy, whereas the warm sunny afternoon was all serene for Rangers' trainer, who not once had to appear on the field.

Rangers would not have won without the cleverness of their centre forward, Millar, who assisted in the scoring of two of his side's goals and himself scored the other, an exhilarating decisive goal. Millar has the enviable ability of being able to vary the deep centre forward type of play, in which he contrives to make chances, with the sudden, bold individual thrust: one way or the other, he controls the ball most admirably. On Saturday he was the most successful player afield, with the possible exception of a colleague, Niven.

PERSISTENT OFFENDER

But Millar was also a constant offender against the proprieties of football. Having almost at the outset having made no determined attempt to avoid using Haffey as a doormat, he was three times later, in the first 15 minutes, penalised for fouling Evans, and when shortly before half-time he was officially cautioned for a display of dissent – not his first – he was objecting to the seventh instance of his back-charging or impeding Evans having been detected.

Mr Mowat indicated then the direction of the pavilion, but in the second-half Millar did not change his ways, and when shortly before the end he had another lesson on the geography of the place from the referee, he had been the offender in nearly half of the 25 infringements that Rangers committed.

By this time MacKay, Divers, who so far forgot himself as to arm the ball in the penalty area – that and a second-half flagrant push of Conway by Davis in Rangers' 18 yard box went unpunished – and Auld was seeking retribution and playing the type of game their opponents had decreed; one sensed in the increased activity of the police how close we were to a free-for-all.

Mr Mowat must be blamed for some of the distasteful moments of the first half. An early reprimand for Millar would almost certainly have altered the trend of the events – and possibly also the result of the match. Yet, when Evans six minutes from time was adjudged to have played Millar and not the ball – the first and only occasion on which the centre half was penalised – the referee saw fit to reprimand him.

NIVEN IN FORM

Niven, who made three magnificent saves from Conway shots, and one of equal value when Auld directed a header far to his left, Telfer (for all that he was early perplexed by Conway), Stevenson (who admirably combined strong play with scrupulousness), Millar, Baird, Kennedy, Evans, Peacock, Jackson, Conway and Auld contributed the bulk of what skilful football there was.

Haffey, who limped for an hour as a result of Baird's having barged into him, and Evans not for the first time showed little understanding of each other's intentions. Wilson scored in the ninth minute. Millar having beaten Evans in the jump for a long corner kick by Matthew which passed right across Haffey's front. In 65 minutes Millar, challenged to the far left by Evans, whose delayed tackles were rarely successful, sent another cross over to the far post and Haffey, by this time not fully fit, unwisely tried to use only his left hand to try to stop Scott's header.

Evans, Peacock and MacKay in turn directed the ball to Jackson, who scored Celtic's goal in 73 minutes with a fine left-foot shot, but five minutes later Millar, having beaten Evans both in the air and on the ground, turned and twisted his way all of 40 yards, Evans chasing hard behind him and other defenders reluctant to tackle, before he shot Rangers' third goal. One could not have visualised a Celtic player scoring such a glorious individualist goal: long ere the shot, Rangers' defence would have been lining up for a free kick.

Rangers (1) 3	Celtic (0) 1
Wilson	Jackson
Scott	
Millar	

RANGERS:- NIVEN; SHEARER AND LITTLE; DAVIS, TELFER AND STEVENSON; SCOTT AND WILSON; MILLAR; BAIRD AND MATTHEW

CELTIC:- HAFFEY; MCNEIL AND KENNEDY; MACKAY, EVANS AND PEACOCK; MCVITTIE AND JACKSON; CONWAY, DIVERS AND AULD

The Sixties

IN the first half of the decade, Rangers were again the team to beat, and the Championship was won for the 32nd time in the opening year. They lost the title to Dundee the following season, but with players such as the multi talented Ian McMillan, Willie Henderson, Jim Baxter and the emergence of John Greig, who was to become the club's greatest ever captain things looked bright for the Ibrox club.

In season 1962-63, the Old Firm met in the final of the Scottish Cup, with Rangers the overwhelming favourites, but it took them to a replay before they won by a handsome 3-0, thus maintaining a record of never having lost a Scottish Cup final replay since 1905. With Baxter and McMillan in devastating form, the replay result was never in doubt and Rangers were not flattered by the margin of victory, the goals coming from Brand (2) and Wilson.

1963-64 saw five clashes between Rangers and Celtic, with the Ibrox side winning the lot, and the Parkhead side were back in the doldrums.

Then Celtic made what was later proved to be the most significant decision made in the history of the club. In 1965, they persuaded Jock Stein to return to Parkhead as manager to succeed Jimmy McGrory. Stein had set in motion a youth plan at Celtic before moving to Dunfermline as boss, where he led the Fife club to a Scottish Cup triumph - against Celtic - in 1961. He later moved to Hibernian, but when the call came from Parkhead, he could not resist and that sparked the most successful period in the club's history with many of the young players he had worked with blossoming.

Within weeks of returning, he had led Celtic to a Scottish Cup final win, but it was season 1966-67 which was to stun the footballing world. Celtic, at their first attempt, became the first British club to win the European Cup - and everything else they entered for that term.

The decade also saw the emergence of the exciting and brilliant Jimmy Johnstone and there were others who were to become legends - Simpson, Craig, Gemmell, Murdoch, McNeill, Clark, Wallace, Chalmers, Auld, Lennox, McBride, Hughes.

Celtic won the championship in 1965-66, sparking off their record-breaking nine-in-a-row, and in the last year of year decade, Kenny Dalglish was to make his first team debut

Celtic 0, Rangers 1 – Friday, 1st January, 1960
Late Goal Beats Celtic
By Cyril Horne

Less than half a minute from time at Celtic Park, Millar gave Rangers their fifth successive win with a splendidly taken goal, a goal which Celtic – their captain Peacock in particular – did not think should have been granted.

Evans had dived low to head out from his penalty area and Baird immediately prodded the ball forward to Millar, who shot hard and high with his left-foot as Haffey somewhat hesitantly left his goal to narrow the centre forward's angle. Celtic prevailed upon the referee to consult the linesman on the stand side, presumably appealing that Millar had been offside, but the score stood.

Magnificent goalkeeping by Haffey time and time again baulked Rangers earlier in the match. His first-half saves from Brand and Millar were equalled only by his diverting for a corner kick a penalty kick shot hard to his right by Little in the fifteenth minute of the second half.

Yet just before Millar's goal and in the only anxious moments Niven had, Celtic almost snatched victory. Davis cleared on the goalline a header from Carroll which had beaten his goalkeeper, and Mochan astonishingly did not shoot when he was provided with Celtic's best scoring chance of the game.

I cannot recall a Celtic-Rangers match of such mediocrity of forward play. Only Brand and Millar of Rangers, and Carroll for Celtic – and the new centre forward was badly supported – gave sound defences trouble. Brand played very well as deputy for Scott, whose usual partner, McMillan, was also missing.

| Celtic (0) 0 | Rangers (0) 1 |
| | Millar |

CELTIC:- HAFFEY; MACKAY AND KENNEDY; MCNEIL, EVANS AND PEACOCK; AULD AND SMITH; CARROLL; MOCHAN AND BYRNE

RANGERS:- NIVEN, SHEARER AND LITTLE; DAVIS, PATERSON AND STEVENSON; BRAND AND BAIRD; MILLAR, WILSON AND HUME

Celtic 1, Rangers 1 – Saturday, 2nd April, 1960
More Excitement than Skill at Hampden Park
By Cyril Horne

Those who watch matches between Celtic and Rangers these days are, one supposes, grateful for the small mercies – reasonable behaviour on the field, the absence of violence on the terracing and a semblance of football of the standard of Old Firm games of long ago. The Cup Semi-final on Saturday, having passed these tests, was therefore not an unsatisfying match; indeed, I believe that the Celtic and Rangers of today would rarely provide better.

But for all the excitement of Saturday, there was little sustained play of distinction. The strong swirling wind was partly responsible, but the inability of many of the players to defeat the wind by keeping the ball on the ground was equally evident. Davis, McMillan and Millar of Rangers and Peacock, Mochan and Divers of Celtic of the players in a team primarily responsible for setting up attacks did on occasion introduce intelligent ground passing, but there was a great deal more lofted kicking which caused an irritating succession of shies.

Celtic had first lease of the wind, and in only the third minute, when Mochan shot wide a free-kick from fully 25 yards, the advantage of shooting from longer range than usual when extra force was to be gained without effort was apparent for the ball flew shoulder-high over the vast half-moon of turf behind the goal, and hit the terracing wall first bounce. But rarely did Celtic put a strong shooting foot to the ball. Chalmers headed their goal in 23 minutes from Colrain's corner kick when Rangers, not for the first time, left a player unmarked for a cross and just before half-time, Niven diving low to his right, made a super save of a Divers header.

Celtic deserved their half-time lead but in the secondhalf Rangers were able to attack even more, and they at least more often cracked the ball for goal. Haffey was three times as busy as Niven had been in the first half, and the taller goalkeeper made not a single mistake; indeed, he made saves from McMillan, Scott and Millar which saved the day for his side.

Rangers' goal came from a header, as did the best Celtic scoring attempts. Twenty-one minutes from time, during a period of clear Rangers superiority, Wilson crossed hard and chest-high from the left corner of the field and Millar scored a magnificent goal from no fewer than 15 yards.

Peacock was a splendid player during Celtic's second-half strain and the entire defence was much less erratic than Rangers' throughout the match. One could hardly have believed that Rangers' right back in the first half was Caldow, so many errors did he make, and Paterson, although he was not nearly so culpable, carried safety-first tactics to extremity.

Scottish Cup Semi-Final

Celtic (1) 1	Rangers (0) 1
Chalmers	Millar
(at Hampden Park)	

CELTIC:- HAFFEY, MCKAY AND KENNEDY; MCNEIL, EVANS AND PEACOCK; CHALMERS AND COLRAIN; MOCHAN; DIVERS AND BYRNE.

RANGERS:- NIVEN; CALDOW AND LITTLE; DAVIS, PATERSON AND STEVENSON; SCOTT AND MCMILLAN; MILLAR; BAIRD AND WILSON.

Rangers 4, Celtic 1 – Wednesday, 7th April 1960
Rangers Qualify for Cup Final
By Cyril Horne

CELTIC'S DEFENSIVE ERRORS

Few of the crowd of 71,000 who attended the Scottish Cup Semi-final replay yesterday could have visualised the astonishing events of the second half during which Celtic's defence played like novices and tossed away the advantage they and their forwards had gained in the first half.

Rangers qualified to play Kilmarnock in the Final, but as much because of their opponents' blundering as through their own ability. As in the first match, the wind mastered most of the players, some of whom would hardly have been allowed to carry the hampers 20 years ago, so deplorable were their efforts to accomplish the elementary tasks of trapping and controlling the ball.

EXCHANGE OF GOALS

Celtic, who kicked against both wind and sun at the start, were the better side in the first half. They lost the first goal to Wilson in 28 minutes – and lost is the operative word, for the outside left ran past a dilatory MacKay who may have expected Haffey to advance for Baird's free kick. Eight minutes later Mochan, one of the few skilful ones, shot an equalising goal and at half-time Rangers, who had had not more than three shots which demanded Haffey's attention, must have been in the doldrums. With wind and sun behind them Celtic, as they began the second half, were clearly favourites.

But four minutes after half-time Peacock struck McMillan on the face as he attempted to drive the ball upfield towards Mochan, and as the inside right staggered near the centre circle, the ball rebounded fortuitously to Millar who, having exchanged a quick ground pass with

Scott, side-footed a leading goal. Celtic's defence again looked unaccountably mystified.

In 71 minutes they were positively bewildered when Wilson headed almost out of Haffey's hands an orthodox cross by Scott while Kennedy and Evans in close proximity acted as spectators. Colrain almost immediately struck the crossbar and when Davis had to be taken off on a stretcher, this Celtic team still seemed to have a chance though the wind had dwindled and the sun gone down.

But Baird, now at right half, was up to support one of Rangers' now rare attacks, and when his cross dropped in the Celtic goal area, Millar in 78 minutes headed another goal, no doubt wondering again why he was not even challenged.

Only Ritchie, Rangers' wing halves McMillan, Millar, McNeil (only in the first half), Mochan and Colrain, gave some distinction to the match. Most of the others ought to have had to suffer the torrent of rain that descended on supporters not long after the final whistle.

Scottish Cup Semi-Final Replay

Rangers (1) 4	Celtic (1) 1
Wilson 2	Mochan
Millar 2	
(at Hampden Park)	
Attendance	71,000

RANGERS:- RITCHIE; CALDOW AND LITTLE; DAVIS, PATERSON AND STEVENSON; SCOTT AND MCMILLAN; MILLAR; BAIRD AND WILSON.

CELTIC:- HAFFEY; MCKAY AND KENNEDY; MCNEIL, EVANS AND PEACOCK; CHALMERS AND COLRAIN: MOCHAN; JACKSON AND DIVERS.

Rangers 1, Celtic 1 – Monday, 9th May, 1960
Coin Gives Victory to Poor Rangers Team
By Cyril Horne

Rangers qualified last night at Ibrox Stadium for the final of the Glasgow Charity Cup, having beaten Celtic on the toss of a coin. No more than 12,000 people saw last night's match. This was yet another dreadful display by Rangers who would surely have been severely punished for their lack of ability had Celtic not been grossly inefficient in their shooting, and unlucky as well.

In only one respect were Rangers clearly superior – in the challenge for the ball – and it is in that respect that they will never make any impression on the world of football, for foreign sides are becoming less and less intimidated by the purely physical challenge.

When they scored through Brand in 47 minutes, Fallon, handicapped like Scott with a leg injury, could not get down quickly enough to stop the low 20 yard shot; in the previous ten minutes they had survived most fortuitously, especially when Auld, having outwitted two opponents, lobbed the ball beyond Niven but against the far post.

Crerand, who had struck a post in the first half, was one of several young Celtic players of great promise and

he at least was not overawed. Six minutes from time he scored one of the finest goals ever seen at Ibrox, breasting down a Paterson clearance in midfield and thrusting through and leaving three Rangers players in his wake before shooting with his left foot from inside the penalty area with such accuracy and power such as no Celtic forward showed throughout the match. When Rangers and Celtic with all their resources are so far behind world club standard, it is no wonder that Scotland international teams are so far behind the top class.

Glasgow Charity Cup Semi-Final

Rangers (0) 1	Celtic (0) 1
Brand	Crerand
Attendance	12,000

RANGERS:- NIVEN; CALDOW AND LITTLE; MCCOLL, PATERSON AND STEVENSON; SCOTT AND MCMILLAN; MILLAR; BRAND AND WATSON.

CELTIC:- FALLON; MCKAY AND KENNEDY; CRERAND, MCNEILL AND PEACOCK; CARROLL AND CHALMERS; MOCHAN; DIVERS AND AULD.

Celtic 4, Rangers 2 – Monday, 15th August, 1960
Rangers Beaten at Celtic Park
By Cyril Horne

Celtic qualified for the Semi-finals of the Glasgow Cup when they beat Rangers last night at Celtic Park in a first-round tie. The Celtic contingent in the 50,000 crowd were almost delirious with delight at the end; I hope they can appreciate that their young, promising team defeated one of the worst elevens ever to have worn Rangers jerseys.

On this dull, rainy evening only Celtic – and Crerand in particular – reminded us of the great Celtic and Rangers players of the past. Crerand was far and away the best player of the 22; he mastered Rangers' expensive purchase, Baxter, in the air – though he is shorter – and on the ground, and he passed the ball as Rangers' wing halves never contrived to pass – into the space left by retreating defenders and inviting a colleague to race clear through the defence.

In the end, Rangers were thoroughly outclassed; the wonder was that they did not suffer an even heavier defeat.

Celtic scored first through Auld in 13 minutes, Divers distracting Niven as Auld's right-foot lob passed into the far corner of the net. Millar equalised in 18 minutes, his right-foot shot deceiving Haffey, who moved much too late. Auld, the best forward of the 10, made Celtic's second goal when he tricked Davis and crossed for Chalmers to head precisely past Niven.

Five minutes after half-time Kennedy armed a shot from McMillan that Haffey could not have saved, and Caldow hit the penalty kick too straight. Haffey saved, and Rangers thereafter were committed to defence, and none too graceful defence at that. The fouls perpetrated by Baxter on Chalmers and by Davis on Auld – the latter not detected by the referee – probably caused some of the booing which greeted the Rangers team at the end.

After an astonishing series of escapes at Rangers' goal, Divers scored the goal of the match three minutes from time when he finished a splendid Crerand-Carroll passing bout with a rollicking shot from 15 yards.

Millar headed a goal for Rangers almost immediately when Haffey failed to cut out a cross by Scott but Davis headed past his own goalkeeper in the closing seconds.

Glasgow Cup 1st round

Celtic (2) 4	Rangers (1) 2
Auld	Millar 2
Chalmers	
Divers	
Davis (o.g.)	
Attendance	50,000

CELTIC:- HAFFEY; MACKAY AND KENNEDY; CRERAND, MCNEILL AND PEACOCK; CARROLL AND CHALMERS; MOCHAN; DIVERS AND AULD.

RANGERS:- NIVEN; CALDOW AND LITTLE, DAVIS, PATERSON AND STEVENSON; SCOTT AND MACMILLAN; MILLAR; BAXTER AND WILSON.

Rangers 2, Celtic 3 – Saturday, 20th August, 1960
Hughes Hero of Celtic Win
By Cyril Horne

It is some considerable time since Celtic have had a player of the physique of Hughes in their team let alone in their forward line; it is reasonable to believe that the bigger-than-average-man is rarely a better-than-average footballer.

Hughes, who is only 17, caused havoc in Rangers' defence on Saturday. The even bigger, heavier Baillie was time and again confused as his much more nimble opponent beat him for speed and for control of the ball.

It appears that Hughes has not only much football ability but splendid temperament, for he was not tempted into physical jousting though he must have wondered, as many of us did, how often Baillie would have to pull him down before the referee called a serious, warning halt.

Five minutes of the cool, calculating Hughes would have won the match for Rangers during their second-half command, in which the wing halves added their not inconsiderable force to the barrage of attack. Rangers' unmethodical play was frequently interrupted by Crerand, who with one carefully judged ground pass to Hughes initiated a much more promising attack.

Shortly before Brand in 61 minutes scored Rangers' second goal, a typical Crerand-Hughes raid necessitated the save of the game – and not by the goalkeeper. Hughes beat first Baillie, then Caldow and then Ritchie and was baulked of a goal by Shearer who, racing back, got his left foot to the ball and swept it away from the goal-line.

Before Carroll scored the first goal in 14 minutes, Rangers might have had a penalty kick for McKay impeding Wilson, and Millar shot grotesquely high after a fine cross by Wilson. Carroll's goal resulted directly from the ability of Hughes to beat Baillie, and in 25 minutes Divers shot a second Celtic goal when Baillie again was baffled by the centre forward.

Eight minutes from half-time, McNeil successfully tackled Millar but lost the ball when he tried to dribble round his opponent, and Millar scored with a ground shot which went through the advancing Haffey's legs. But just on half-time Mochan for once beat Shearer, Carroll carried on the attack on the left, and when Rangers expected Hughes to direct the movement further to the right, he suddenly wheeled and shot the goal of the match. Such a goal Rangers never seemed likely to score, for all – and probably, because of – their fierce determination.

Rangers (1) 2	Celtic (3) 3
Millar	Carroll
Brand	Divers
	Hughes

RANGERS:- RITCHIE; SHEARER AND CALDOW; DAVIS; BAILLIE AND BAXTER; SCOTT AND BAIRD; MILLER, BRAND AND WILSON.

CELTIC:- HAFFEY; MACKAY AND KENNEDY; CRERAND, MCNEIL AND PEACOCK; CARROLL AND CHALMERS; HUGHES; DIVERS AND MOCHAN.

Ronnie Simpson

There will, no doubt, be arguments as to who has been Celtic's greatest–ever goalkeeper, with good claims for men such as Johnny Thomson, Joe Kennoway, Willie Miller and Pat Bonner. Simpson also has the proper credentials – and the medals to back up his claim. His story is also a sort of fairy tale, which appeals to the romantics among football fans.

Simpson, born in Glasgow in October 1930, is the son of former Ranger Jimmy Simpson and made his senior debut for the amateurs Queen's Park at the age of 14. He also played for Great Britain in the 1948 Olympic Games. He joined the professional ranks at Third Lanark, then moved to Newcastle United where he won two FA Cup–winners medals in 1952 and 1955. Out of football for almost two years because of serious injury, he joined Hibs and it was Jock Stein who sold him to Celtic for £2,000.

That was to prove one of the all-time bargains. Apart from the European Cup triumph in 1967, Simpson won four Championships, one Scottish Cup and three League Cups. He also became the oldest player to make his debut for Scotland when, at the age of 36, he played against England at Wembley in 1967. Retired in 1970 and had a brief spell as manager at Hamilton.

Bobby Collins

Apart from Jimmy Johnstone, Collins will go down as the greatest "wee man" to wear the hoops over the last 50 years. He was just 5ft. 4in. tall and he took a size 4 in boots, but had the heart of a lion, and a brilliant football brain to go with it.

Born just a short distance from Hampden in 1931, Collins was wanted by Everton – he was to sign for them later in his career – but instead joined Celtic in 1948.

He made his debut before 71,000 fans in a 3-2 win over Rangers at Parkhead in a League Cup tie the following year. In September 1953, when Celtic beat Aberdeen 3-0 at Parkhead, Collins became one of the few players to score a hat-trick of penalty kicks.

Collins was transferred to Everton in 1958 and then to Leeds United four years later. He became the first Scot to win England's Footballer of the Year in 1965. That was the year he also broke a thigh, but in typical fashion, he battled his way back to fitness and went on to give service to several English clubs, including Hull, Bury and Blackpool. In all, Collins won 31 full caps and 16 League caps.

Pat Crerand

A Gorbals boy, Patrick Timothy Crerand joined Celtic from Duntocher Hibs in 1958 and went on to prove himself one of the finest passers of a ball ever to grace the Scottish game. His was a marvellous football talent which overshadowed his lack of pace. Also struck up a great friendship with Old Firm rival Jim Baxter and was part of one of the best half-back lines seen in Scottish jerseys – Crerand, McNeill and Baxter.

Crerand's temperament was a bit suspect. He was once sent off in a World Cup qualifying tie in Czechoslovakia, and also in a five-a-side tournament at Brockville, Falkirk. His last match for Celtic was in a 4-0 New Year's Day defeat by Rangers at Ibrox in 1963.

Talk of unrest behind the scenes at Parkhead led to his transfer to Manchester United for £56,000 in February, 1963. Ironically, he won a European Cup medal with Manchester United in 1968, the year after his beloved Celtic triumphed in Lisbon. Other honours included 16 full caps, seven League caps, two English First Division Championships and an FA Cup medal.

Steve Chalmers

Like Tommy Gemmell, there will always be a special place in the history of Celtic for this pacey, brave striker. While Gemmell scored the equaliser in Lisbon, Chalmers came up with the winner when he diverted a shot from Bobby Murdoch away out of the reach of the Milan goalkeeper.

He was a junior international when he joined Celtic from Ashfield in 1959, and played regular first team football for the club for a decade. His honest and dedicated work on the field made him a big favourite with the fans, and he went on to win five full caps for Scotland, scoring in the 1-1 draw with Brazil at Hampden in 1966.

While Celtic fans will always remember him for his strike in Lisbon, there are those who will also recall him being one of the elite to have scored a hat-trick against Rangers, that coming in a 5-1 win at Parkhead on January 3, 1966. After a leg break in 1969, Chalmers was never quite the same player and he moved to Morton two years later. He also had a spell with Partick Thistle.

Celtic 1, Rangers 2 – Saturday, 3rd September, 1960
Rangers' Second-Half Rally
By Cyril Horne

At half-time at Celtic Park on Saturday, Rangers' prospects were as dismal as the weather. Their left half, Baxter, had driven more shots – two of those of no great merit – toward the Celtic goal than all five forwards together, and only the wretched shooting of Celtic's forwards had denied the more raucous of their supporters their realisation of their hope of "Seven, seven, seven." One must say in passing that this habitual reference to a League Cup final of three years ago is exceedingly tiresome, as well as rash tempting of providence.

Rangers were indeed fortunate to be only a goal down at the interval – a goal which they with some justification claimed should have been disallowed on the ground of offside before Chalmers shot. But Hughes soon afterwards hit more turf than ball when Ritchie must have been as much in fear of his person as of his chance of saving; the big centre forward almost immediately stood fascinated at the sight of Mochan for once beating Shearer on the outside and failed to appreciate that the object of the intrusion along the bye-line was to tee him up to goal, and Mochan himself shot wildly after one of three sublime passes from Divers that split the defence.

BIGGEST BLUNDER

All that was as nothing, however, compared with the blunder of Chalmers in the nineteenth minute. Carroll cleverly headed the ball down to his partner, who, only three yards from the goal-line and onside but isolated from challenge, swung his right foot and missed.

Celtic, so clearly the more skilful side in the first half, were to pay dearly for their forwards' finishing failure – and also, incongruously, for the success of their young centre half, Kurila, who tackled Millar so quickly, strongly and accurately that Rangers' centre forward contributed practically nothing to his side's attack which emanated almost entirely from the ill-supported Scott. Millar so disliked the cramping of his style that he had to be lectured by the referee for his treatment of the centre half.

Shortly before half-time Chalmers headed a cross from Hughes into the net, but the referee, well up with play, had no doubt that the ball had been beyond the bye-line before Hughes released it. And shortly after Rangers had equalised in the third minute of the second half, Chalmers headed against the crossbar.

But that was almost the last Celtic scoring chance, so transformed were Rangers. The power and pace of their second half attack seemed to surprise Celtic who certainly became more and more perplexed by the change in Rangers' methods.

Davis having headed the equalising goal – Brand dummied the ball and deceived Fallon – Millar decided, or had the decision made for him, to retreat from Kurila and as both McMillan and Brand moved into the centre of the field, Millar from either wing half position foraged for the ball with great determination and then redistributed it to his colleagues in a variety of pleasing ways.

Millar's success in his new role should have compelled Celtic to alter their defensive strategy; if Kurila was to stay in the stopper position, which almost always he did, someone else should have had the job of following Millar. In any event Rangers revelled in their new scheme and their play improved remarkably.

WINNING GOAL

Twenty minutes from time Millar was momentarily back in the middle when he beat Kurila in the air and enabled Brand to race in and shoot from 16 yards so fast and so accurately for the far post that Fallon was beaten where he stood. Celtic switched Hughes and Mochan then, but the value of the change would barely be tested, so much were Celtic committed to defence.

Davis who would have been an even better player had he not persisted in giving Scott the short ball, and Millar were principally responsible for their side's second half display; for more than an hour, however, Shearer, who time and again interrupted Celtic attacks with successful tackling of the much too deliberate Mochan, and Paterson taking the minimum of risks and blocking the middle successfully if unattractively, kept Rangers in the game with a chance. Crerand and Peacock were the inspiration of Celtic's first-half superiority, but only Divers of the forwards seemed to have the stamina as well as skill in the second half. Hughes probably handicapped himself through holding on to the ball too long. Ten minutes of a fit Auld with his speed and shot would almost certainly have precluded the possibility of a successful Rangers rally.

Celtic (1) 1	Rangers (0) 2
Chalmers	Davis
	Brand

CELTIC:- FALLON; MACKAY AND KENNEDY; CRERAND, KURILA AND PEACOCK; CARROLL AND CHALMERS; HUGHES; DIVERS AND MOCHAN.

RANGERS:- RITCHIE; SHEARER AND CALDOW; DAVIS, PATERSON AND BAXTER; SCOTT AND MCMILLAN; MILLAR; BRAND AND WILSON.

Celtic 1, Rangers 5 – Saturday, 10th September, 1960

Rangers' Rampant Finish

For more than an hour it was anybody's game at Parkhead, but after Rangers scored their second goal in 65 minutes, they romped into an unassailable position. It was not that Celtic collapsed, rather that Rangers struck irresistible form.

The score flattered the winners, but all credit to their forwards for seizing their chances. Two of their goals followed blunders by the Celtic goalkeeper, Fallon, and another came when Celtic's deputy centre half, Kurila, lost the ball and let Rangers through.

Within two minutes of the start of the game, Rangers scored. Wilson swung in a corner kick and Fallon punched the ball straight to the feet of Scott, who shot into the net. In brisk retaliation by Celtic Hughes just missed the goal and Chalmers hit the crossbar, then the post, and at the interval it could fairly be said that Rangers were lucky to be leading.

After 65 minutes' play Kurila, who had trailed Millar very successfully, took on both the centre forward and Wilson. In the end he battered the ball against Wilson from whom it rebounded to Millar, who rounded McKay before beating Fallon at the second attempt: in a vain attempt to stop the ball as it rolled over the line, Kennedy merely speeded its progress.

Rangers, now playing with the confidence of a two-goal lead, really settled to a game, and bamboozled Celtic with their crisp and accurate football. In 78 minutes Millar, out on the right with Scott, crossed a ball which Fallon mishandled, and Brand scored. In 84 minutes Wilson took a pass from Brand and scored Rangers' fourth goal, and a minute later Davis, the most accomplished player of all, headed a fifth after a corner kick by Scott.

Almost at the last minute Chalmers' perseverance was rewarded, when taking a pass from Divers, who had hitherto flitted in and out of the game, he beat Ritchie from close range.

Celtic (0) 1	Rangers (1) 5
Chalmers	Scott
	Millar
	Brand
	Wilson
	Davis

CELTIC:- FALLON; MCKAY AND KENNEDY; CRERAND, KURILA AND PEACOCK; CONWAY AND CHALMERS; CARROLL; DIVERS AND HUGHES.

RANGERS:- RITCHIE; SHEARER AND CALDOW; DAVIS, PATERSON AND BAXTER; SCOTT AND MCMILLAN; MILLAR; BRAND AND WILSON.

Rangers 2, Celtic 1 – Monday, 2nd January, 1961

Celtic's Misfortune at Ibrox

By Cyril Horne

For more than an hour yesterday at Ibrox, Celtic were the team who played as if they were confident leaders of the League. They led 1-0 at half-time, Divers having scored in 28 minutes after Baxter chose to indulge in frills of ball control almost on his own penalty spot, and just after Brand had equalised in the sixty-second minute, a misdirected pass by Scott having been deflected by a Celtic player who inadvertently played both Brand and Wilson onside, Rangers were remarkably lucky not to lose more goals.

Paterson, who had been worried into a series of fouls of obstruction as Conway's speed time and again threatened Rangers' goal, was beaten by the centre forward in the jump, and sprawled on his back as Conway raced through, sidestepped Niven and ran the ball into the net. But the referee had blown for a free-kick against Conway who, if he made unfair contact with the centre half, did so to elude the octopus-like grasping of his opponent.

Yet again a linesman's flag waved Fernie offside as he ran in to head a clever lobbed pass from Divers, Celtic were not surprisingly disappointed because Fernie had run past Caldow for the scoring chance.

But before Wilson headed the decisive goal 10 minutes from time the game had clearly swung in Rangers' favour almost entirely because since the thirtieth minute of the first half, Byrne, holding his left arm close to his chest,

was unable to make any contribution to his side's effort. Byrne, who before he was twice fouled in as many minutes – on each occasion Rangers were penalised – had been the best winger of the four but the handicap inflicted on Celtic through the second foul enabled their opponents to have such freedom on the right side of the field as they had not enjoyed when the teams were on level physical terms.

So as Celtic tired, a winning goal for Rangers could almost be seen coming. Yet in the end it was an error of judgement by Haffey, who hitherto had made not the suggestion of a mistake, which lost Celtic the match. Davis advanced up the exposed side of the field and let Scott run for the corner; over came the orthodox high cross, and Haffey, though the ball descended less than two yards from his own goal and he was not hampered, missed it completely and Wilson headed into the net.

Rangers (0) 2	Celtic (1) 1
Brand	Divers
Wilson	

RANGERS:- NIVEN; SHEARER AND CALDOW; DAVIS, PATERSON AND BAXTER; SCOTT AND MCMILLAN; MILLAR; BRAND AND WILSON.

CELTIC:- HAFFEY; MACKAY AND KENNEDY; CRERAND, MCNEILL AND PEACOCK; CHALMERS AND DIVERS; CONWAY: FERNIE AND BYRNE.

Rangers 2, Celtic 2 – Saturday, 16th September, 1961
Sporting Contest at Ibrox

Despite a strong, whirling wind in which the ball hovered or drifted unpredictably, Rangers and Celtic gave a remarkably good performance at Ibrox Stadium, and a draw was an equitable result.

Rangers were the superior team in the first half, during which Christie spearheaded attacks which had the Celtic defence bemused, but after the interval the initiative lay mostly with Celtic, McNeill having taken command in midfield and his forwards showing much more liveliness and enterprise.

On pressure Rangers should have been well ahead in the first half-hour. Christie, chasing every ball, was a constant menace to the Celtic defenders as he sought to add to the goal he headed from a cross by Wilson after five minutes' play which he might have done but for the lack of support from the men on either side of him, McMillan and Brand, both of whom had an off day and latterly faded out of the game.

Celtic, too, were unimpressive in attack until the persistent Divers, taking the home defence by surprise after 28 minutes' play, scored from a pass by Chalmers; from then until half-time they frequently had their opponents worried.

Three minutes after the interval Celtic took the lead when Fernie, who had seldom been in the picture, was in position to jab the ball past Ritchie from close range after Shearer blocked a shot from Chalmers.

Thereafter the contest developed on stern but sporting lines, with both sides having opportunities to score, but it was not until two minutes from the end that Rangers equalised through Baxter with a shot from 25 yards.

Rangers (1) 2	Celtic (1) 2
Christie	Divers
Baxter	Fernie

RANGERS:- RITCHIE; SHEARER AND CALDOW; DAVIS, PATERSON AND BAXTER; SCOTT AND MCMILLAN; CHRISTIE, BRAND AND WILSON.

CELTIC:- HAFFEY; MACKAY AND KENNEDY; CRERAND, MCNEILL AND PRICE; CHALMERS AND JACKSON; HUGHES, DIVERS AND FERNIE.

Celtic 1, Rangers 1 – Monday, April 9th, 1962
Wilson Saves Day for Rangers
Now Ahead of Dundee Only on Goal Average

A late goal by Wilson gave Rangers a rather fortuitous but valuable point last night at Celtic Park. They were outplayed for most of the game, but were able to salvage the point which keeps them at the top of the First Division Championship table on goal average from Dundee (2.86 against 1.63).

Both have two fixtures to fulfil – Rangers away to Aberdeen and at home to Kilmarnock, Dundee at home to St Mirren and away to St Johnstone.

On a surface made treacherous with heavy rain, Celtic adopted the proper tactics of moving the ball swiftly from man to man and employing their wingers to full advantage. Rangers elected to play much too closely, which served merely to ease the situation of a Celtic defence which even without Crerand was always tightly-knit and well-marshalled by the commanding McNeill.

The only Rangers forward who caused any discomfort to them was the diminutive Henderson who, although missing the experience and promptings of McMillan, did enough to justify his being preferred to Scott.

HUGHES DANGER

It was appropriate that Hughes should score Celtic's only goal of the game in 23 minutes, for he, more than any of his forward colleagues, frequently perplexed Rangers' defence. McKinnon at centre half had an unhappy match against Hughes, and his name was taken for an infringement against the centre, as was that of McKay for a particularly vicious tackle on Henderson in the first half.

Although Celtic could claim territorial advantage, Rangers' fighting qualities were revealed in the last half-hour, and it was this rather than their skill which brought them the equaliser in 78 minutes, when the persistent Wilson warded off the challenge of Haffey, who had rushed out to intercept, and trundled the ball into the net.

Although Rangers deserved this goal, if only for their pluck, Celtic could have made victory secure had they accepted the chances offered, particularly in the first half, when Hughes, Carroll and Divers all missed scoring opportunities.

Celtic (1) 1	Rangers (0) 1
Hughes	Wilson

CELTIC:- HAFFEY; DONNELLY AND KENNEDY; MCKAY, MCNEILL AND CLARK; CHALMERS AND CARROLL; HUGHES; DIVERS AND BROGAN.

RANGERS:- RITCHIE; SHEARER AND CALDOW; DAVIS, MCKINNON AND BAXTER; HENDERSON AND GREIG; MILLAR; BRAND AND WILSON.

Celtic 0, Rangers 1 – Saturday, 8th September, 1962

Old Firm Disappoint

The game at Parkhead on Saturday, surely one of the least distinguished in the long series of matches between Celtic and Rangers, seemed to be ending in a goalless draw, such had been the futility of both sides in attack.

But with seven minutes remaining for play, Rangers' outside right, Henderson, operating on the left, had the better of a tackle by McKay, shook himself free of the back's despairing clutch at his jersey, and shot from 10 yards.

It was not a powerful shot and Haffey had it covered, but in the goalmouth flurry the ball was deflected the other way. Kennedy, with a desperate lunge, attempted to stop the ball squirming over the line but could do no more than batter it into the back of the net.

Apart from settling the issue, if somewhat luckily, in Rangers' favour, the move illustrated the difference in approach between the two sets of forwards on a day when the defences were dominant.

Whereas Rangers' forwards, by switching the point of attack, at least tried to find a weak spot, Celtic moved on orthodox lines, their hopes apparently pinned on their bustling centre forward, Hughes. The idea was sound enough for Rangers' centre half, McKinnon, was less comfortable against Hughes, who, however, seldom got the ball in open position.

After about half an hour of inconclusive play, Crerand thought he would show his forwards the way. First he seriously tested Ritchie from long range, and then strode powerfully into Rangers' penalty area where Brand, in hot pursuit, tripped him.

There was some delay while several Rangers players argued that the ball was not placed exactly on the spot for the penalty kick and Crerand threw the ball into a group of opponents, clearly inviting one of them to place it. But the referee, who had a good game, was having none of it, retrieved the ball and handed it to Crerand.

Whether or not he was in the right frame of mind to take the kick after his bickering, and considering he was badly jarred by his fall, Crerand nevertheless took the responsibility. Ritchie saw the ball coming all the way and pushed it round his left-hand post.

In the second half Celtic continued to have most of the ball, but oddly enough Haffey had more direct shots than Ritchie. There was, however, little in the play to arouse enthusiasm and the final whistle came as a relief.

| Celtic (0) 0 | Rangers (0) 1 |
| | Henderson |

CELTIC:- HAFFEY; MACKAY AND KENNEDY; CRERAND, MCNEILL AND PRICE; LENNOX AND GALLACHER; HUGHES; MURDOCH AND BYRNE.

RANGERS:- RITCHIE; SHEARER AND CALDOW; DAVIS, MCKINNON AND BAXTER; HENDERSON AND GREIG; MILLAR; BRAND AND WILSON.

Rangers 2, Celtic 2 – Monday, 15th October, 1962

Drawn Match at Ibrox Stadium

By Cyril Horne

A Celtic team seriously handicapped through injury – McNeill limped at outside left for the last 15 minutes and Kennedy, twice the victim of fierce tackles, played only by instinct in that period – deserved their draw in the Glasgow Cup first-round tie last night at Ibrox Stadium.

Celtic twice equalised after having been a goal down, and they atoned for deficiency in forward skill with great enthusiasm.

For fully half an hour before the start, the 50,000 spectators almost burst their lungs as they shouted and chanted their slogans and songs of intolerance from the ends of the ground; one could not help but notice that the area of reasonable neutrality between the furthermost parts of the terracing was half-empty and almost shamefacedly quiet. One is glad to report, however, that there appeared to be no physical violence within the ground.

Celtic's unexpected choice at centre forward, McNamee, displayed only strength and enthusiasm and even before he had to take over at centre half, he had exchanged places with Carroll. Divers was the best Celtic forward, but that is a tribute easily earned these days.

BEST GOAL

Divers scored the most deserved goal of the four 18 minutes from time when he jockeyed for position with a pass from Chalmers and shot from 20 yards through a crowd of players. Wilson had scored the first goal in 34 minutes with a shot that went under the body of the advancing Haffey and McNamee had equalised two minutes after half-time with another shot of power but little direction, the ball beating Ritchie almost as Wilson's shot had eluded Haffey.

In 60 minutes McNeill astonishingly missed a clearance from hand by Ritchie which bounced much closer to him than to Millar, and the centre forward strode through unchallenged for a leading goal. The unceasing urge of Crerand drove Celtic on to their second equalising goal by Divers.

Glasgow Cup 1st Round

Rangers (1) 2	Celtic (0) 2
Wilson	McNamee
Millar	Divers
Attendance	50,000

RANGERS:- RITCHIE; SHEARER AND CALDOW; GREIG, MCKINNON AND BAXTER; HENDERSON AND MCMILLAN; MILLAR; BRAND AND WILSON.

CELTIC:- HAFFEY; MACKAY AND KENNEDY; CRERAND, MCNEILL AND O'NEILL; CHALMERS AND CARROLL; MCNAMEE; DIVERS AND BYRNE.

Celtic 3, Rangers 2 - Wednesday, 21st November, 1962
Celtic in Glasgow Cup Semi-Final
By Cyril Horne

LATE GOAL IN EXTRA TIME AGAINST RANGERS

Celtic beat Rangers in the third-last minute of extra time in the Glasgow Cup first-round replay at Celtic Park and will meet Partick Thistle in the Semi-finals at Firhill Park on Tuesday, December 4.

Some 24,000 – a splendid attendance on a foggy, frosty day – saw Celtic triumph – a triumph especially of their younger players. "Saw" is perhaps the wrong word to use, as darkness aided fog in the battle against the floodlight. It was the teenage inside forward, Murdoch, deputising for Craig, who scored the winning goal, having moved characteristically quickly and intelligently through the defence for the measured pass of Divers, who had baffled Baillie with neat ball control.

NEAR MISS

That was not the final exhilarating incident in a match that was remarkably good on treacherous ground, for Jeffrey, Celtic's latest addition to a young forward line, raced purposefully past Shearer and cracked a shot against a post.

Divers, playing the deep-lying centreforward game, was a constant worry to the bulky Baillie who perhaps more than most found keeping his feet on the hard slippery surface a hard task indeed.

The greatest menace to Celtic was the extremely clever Henderson, especially in the second half, but the Rangers were innocuous at inside forward and a great deal of the winger's skill was not rewarded.

Ritchie, like Haffey, made several exceptionally fine saves. He had no chance whatever of preventing the first goal, scored in 26 minutes by Crerand from a free kick from just outside the penalty area which struck the defensive wall and spun away from the goalkeeper.

Haffey was equally blameless when Henderson, three minutes from half-time, scored. After eight minutes of the second half Divers made Murdoch's first goal with a shrewd low cross from the right wing, and midway through the second half Brand was allowed to score from a palpably offside position. All of us were reconciled to a draw after extra time – and although Celtic deserved to win a draw would have pleased all but those who cannot appreciate good football when it is played by the club they do not support – when the combination of Divers, who in the first period of extra time had hit the crossbar, and Murdoch, decided the issue.

Glasgow Cup 1st Round Replay

Celtic (1) 3	Rangers (1) 2
Crerand	Henderson
Murdoch 2	Brand
(after extra time; 90 minutes 2-2)	
attendance	24,000

CELTIC:- HAFFEY; YOUNG AND KENNEDY; CRERAND, MCNEILL AND O'NEILL; CHALMERS AND MURDOCH; DIVERS; GALLAGHER AND JEFFREY.

RANGERS:- RITCHIE; SHEARER AND CALDOW; MCKINNON, BAILLIE AND BAXTER; HENDERSON AND GREIG; MILLAR; BRAND AND WILSON.

Rangers 4, Celtic 0 – Tuesday, 2nd January, 1963
Vulnerable Celtic Defence

FINE DISPLAY BY RANGERS

For more than an hour at Ibrox Stadium, it seemed that the freakish goal scored by Davis in the eleventh minute would be Rangers' only reward for greater superiority to Celtic than they have displayed in an Old Firm match for several years. But in 14 minutes – from the 66th to the 80th – Millar, Greig and Wilson severely punished a defence that had been vulnerable throughout and in which more than one player, like more than one of his forwards, did not appear to have much liking for his task.

Rangers – and Davis, Baxter, Millar, and Wilson in particular – played much splendid football on a ground which was iron-hard and slippery and which I thought was unplayable, if only because it was dangerous for even the most skilful. The least successful Rangers player was Shearer, and that was because Brogan was far and away the best Celtic player. The outside left, however, received nothing like the service on which Wilson prospered.

I have no wish to detract from the merit of Rangers' performance when I say that this was one of the worst Celtic elevens for many a day. Certainly, they had none of the luck of the game – they were undoubtedly most unfortunate just before Rangers' second goal when McKinnon prevented Hughes from running straight in on Ritchie by handling the ball as it bounced on or around the 18 yard line – but lack of ability, far more than lack of fortune, caused a deservedly heavy defeat.

Davis's scoring shot struck Crerand and was diverted out of Haffey's reach, and he could not hold Brand's shot before Millar scored. The goalkeeper had not the slightest chance of saving the third or fourth goals.

Rangers (1) 4	Celtic (0) 0
Davis	
Millar	
Greig	
Wilson	

RANGERS:- RITCHIE; SHEARER AND CALDOW; DAVIS, MCKINNON AND BAXTER; SCOTT AND GREIG; MILLAR; BRAND AND WILSON.

CELTIC:- HAFFEY; MCKAY AND KENNEDY; CRERAND, MCNEILL AND PRICE; CHALMERS AND MURDOCH; HUGHES, GALLAGHER AND BROGAN.

Celtic 1, Rangers 1 – Saturday, 4th May, 1963

Haffey's Fine Goalkeeping

It is to be hoped that before Celtic and Rangers replay the 1963 Scottish Cup Final, which on Saturday at Hampden Park neither deserved to win, stringent measures are adopted to encourage the art of goalscoring.

Haffey was the man of the match, although in the rain and wind of Hampden this was hardly a goalkeeper's day. Haffey's sense of anticipation, his agility and his sureness of hands saved his side. His diverting, of a second-half shot of Brand, one of the few which were shot strongly and confidently, was the *piece de rèsistance*.

MISSED CHANCES

Haffey was beaten twice – when Brand flicked past him Henderson's cross in 43 minutes for Rangers' goal, and when midway in the second half the little outside right flighted a cross over his outstretched arms and on to the top of the crossbar. Wilson, who is rightly considered the best taker of scoring chances of all the wingers in Britain, shot incredibly badly from no more than eight yards, and with only Haffey between him and success.

Celtic did not shoot badly – they hardly ever shot at all. Divers did not beat Ritchie from half-a-dozen yards though the goalkeeper was on the ground; Brogan, having romped past Shearer, was even more dilatory in shooting; and Johnstone, much less blameworthy because of his lack of experience than all of the others who failed as marksmen, lobbing wide of the goal when Ritchie was spreadeagled, having saved Celtic's one exhilarating shot – that of Price from a 25-yard free kick.

It was not then an occasion for celebration by the forwards. Murdoch, who scored the Celtic goal just on half-time after Hughes, for once, had taken the direct road and Johnstone, as tricky a player as Henderson and just as inadequately assisted, vied with Rangers' wingers as the attacking players of greatest potential. What the game lacked most of all was a Cunningham, Bob McPhail, McGrory or Napier: a forward who could take the responsibility of shooting and revel in the opportunity to shoot, especially with the wind behind him.

Rangers depend a great deal these days on the inspiration in attack provided by Baxter, but though the left half mastered the wet ball and swirling wind better than most, he was not allowed to exert his usual influence. For that Celtic must be indebted to the industrious McNamee, who, along with McNeill, a commanding centre half, and the cool Price, formed the superior half-back line.

Scottish Cup Final

Celtic (1) 1	Rangers (1) 1
Murdoch	Brand
(at Hampden Park)	
Attendance	130,000

CELTIC:- HAFFEY; MACKAY AND KENNEDY; MCNAMEE, MCNEILL AND PRICE; JOHNSTONE AND MURDOCH; HUGHES; DIVERS AND BROGAN.

RANGERS:- RITCHIE; SHEARER AND PROVAN; GREIG, MCKINNON AND BAXTER; HENDERSON AND MCLEAN; MILLAR; BRAND AND WILSON.

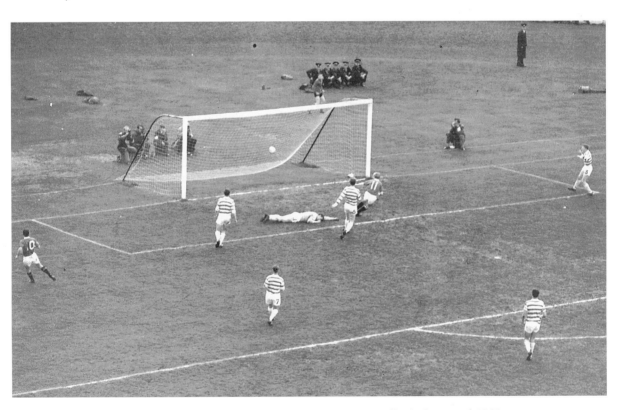

Davie Wilson scores the second in the 3-0 cup final victory of 1963.

Rangers 3, Celtic 0 – Wednesday, 15th May, 1963
Rangers Again Win Scottish Cup
By Cyril Horne

CLIMAX OF GLORIOUS SEASON OF IBROX CLUB

Rangers won the Scottish Cup for the seventeenth time when, in a replay of the 1963 Final at Hampden Park last night, they not only defeated but outclassed Celtic, who themselves have been Cup winners on seventeen occasions.

This had been a glorious season for Rangers, who easily won the Scottish League Championship. Their Scottish Cup record in modern times is remarkable. Since 1930 they have been in 12 finals and won them all.

As early as 25 minutes before the end of last night's match, many thousands of the Celtic proportion of the 120,000 crowd streamed out of the ground. They appreciated that after the third goal, scored at that point by Brand, Celtic could not possibly retrieve the position.

Henderson has never played so successfully against Kennedy. He revelled in the pass thrust inside the back by McMillan. The outside right's cross after Millar had passed down the touchline was swept past Haffey in the seventh minute by Brand, and only tremendous defence by McNeill, throughout the best Celtic player, denied Rangers a second goal until the last minute of the first half.

The loss of the second goal was the result of McNamee's trying to help his forwards and forgetting that a wing-half's primary duty is to defend. He was far from his best when Millar passed to Brand who, as McKay retreated, closed in and shot. Haffey could not hold the fast, low shot, and Wallace took the easy scoring chance in his stride.

Once Brand with his left foot from 25 yards had surprised Haffey with a shot which dropped as it came to the goalkeeper and bounced over the line, Rangers toyed with their opponents.

I cannot recall a Celtic team of so many players timid and lacking in skill. The forward line, Chalmers apart, were easily brushed off the ball by players who had no physical advantage. The right wing, as first Murdoch and then Divers formed a most undistinguished partnership with Craig, not only did not contribute much to attack, but failed to prevent the skilful thrusts of Baxter. He, Shearer, McMillan, Millar and Wilson, were magnificent players in a Rangers team that did not need to be world beaters.

Rangers (2) 3	Celtic (0) 0
Brand 2	
Wilson	
Attendance	**120,000**

RANGERS:- RITCHIE; SHEARER AND PROVAN; GREIG, MCKINNON AND BAXTER; HENDERSON AND MCMILLAN; MILLAR; BRAND AND WILSON.

CELTIC:- HAFFEY; MCKAY AND KENNEDY; MCNAMEE, MCNEILL AND PRICE; CRAIG AND MURDOCH; DIVERS; CHALMERS AND HUGHES.

Celtic 0, Rangers 3 – Saturday, 10th August, 1963
Failure of Celtic Forwards

A game in which Celtic had the opportunities to win in the first 25 minutes ended with Rangers completely on top, even toying with their opponents.

Now presumably, as last season when results were not forthcoming, we can await permutations of the forwards Celtic have at their command, for the combination on Saturday was a failure.

With Hughes and Murdoch rarely eluding the vigilant McKinnon and hard-tackling Shearer, the spearhead of the Celtic attack became Chalmers, but unfortunately his eye was not in and he dissipated at least a dozen chances to score, half of them during the team's early dominance.

Probably his least excusable lapse was that after 80 minutes of play, when left in the clear a few yards out after Greig had misjudged the weight of his pass back to Ritchie, he shot straight at the goalkeeper.

Fifty minutes earlier with just such an opportunity, McNeill being the culprit on that occasion, Forrest swooped on the ball, drew Haffey from his goal and gave Rangers a lead as unexpected as it was undeserved.

RANGERS TAKE COMMAND

From that moment Rangers, hitherto uncertain in defence and far from incisive in attack, struck the game which led ultimately to the disintegration of Celtic and the end of the proceedings as a contest – a fact acknowledged by the crowds at the Celtic end of the ground who began to drift away long before time-up.

Overall it was not one of the great Celtic-Rangers occasions. The home crowd probably expected too much from the newcomer at inside right, Turner, who showed ability, especially in passing, but could not be said to stand head and shoulders above the other forwards.

Baxter? Well, he was just Baxter. Supremely confident throughout, he made the opening for McLean to score Rangers' second goal in 62 minutes. Six minutes later it was all over when Forrest, anticipating the dummy sold by Brand as Henderson crossed, slammed the ball past Haffey.

Celtic (0) 0	Rangers (1) 3
	Forrest 2
	Mclean

CELTIC:- HAFFEY; MCKAY AND GEMMELL; MCNAMEE, MCNEILL AND PRICE; JOHNSTONE AND TURNER; HUGHES; CHALMERS AND MURDOCH.

RANGERS:- RITCHIE; SHEARER AND PROVAN; GREIG, MCKINNON AND BAXTER; HENDERSON AND MCLEAN; FORREST; BRAND AND WILSON.

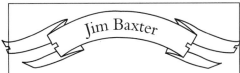

Davie Wilson

One of the great Rangers wingers of all time. Wilson joined the Ibrox club from Baillieston Juniors in 1956 and played more than 350 matches, scoring 150 goals. He was a small, strong man with pace and outstanding skills. Had an amazing strike rate for a winger, but could also play at centre forward. He was moved there for a League match against Falkirk at Brockville in 1962. Rangers won 7-1 and Wilson scored six.

Wilson was capped by Scotland 22 times, and his finest hour in a dark blue jersey came against England at Wembley in 1963. Left back Eric Caldow suffered a leg break and Wilson had to move back to defence. He was outstanding as the ten-man Scottish side won 2-1.

Wilson won five Championship medals, four in the Scottish Cup and two in the League Cup. A broken leg ended his international career and he moved to Dundee United in 1967. In 1972 he was transferred to Dumbarton, where he also had two spells as manager of the club. Was also assistant manager at Kilmarnock.

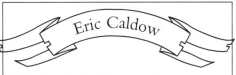

Eric Caldow

This Ayrshireman was, without doubt, an exceptional full-back with electric pace and great timing in the tackle. He joined Rangers from Muirkirk Juniors in 1952, making his first team debut the following season. In all, he played 436 matches for the club and was also a member of the side which won the domestic treble in 1963.

Caldow was also a great servant for Scotland, winning 40 caps before a terrible leg break against England at Wembley in 1963 ended his international career. Rangers have had many brilliant full-backs down through history, and Caldow was certainly one of them. A very popular man with the fans, he is still seen around Ibrox, helping to entertain patrons in the corporate hospitality suites.

Caldow left Rangers for Stirling Albion in 1967 and a year later he had a spell as player–manager with Corby Town. He was also manager of Stranraer. As well as full caps, he also had 14 appearances for the Scottish League and two for the under-23 side. With Rangers he won five Championships, two Scottish Cups and three League Cups.

Jim Baxter

Slim Jim was quite simply an outrageous, wonderful talent; one of the few Scots of his time who could be termed as genuine world class. He played left half or inside left, and what he lacked in discipline, he more than made up with his amazing skills on the ball. Born in Hill of Beath, Fife, in 1939, he will always have a special place in the history of Rangers.

He joined the club in 1960 from Raith Rovers for a fee of £18,000 and although he spent only five seasons at Ibrox in his first spell with Rangers, his feats, both on and off the field, were legendary. He recovered from a bad leg break playing for Rangers in a European Cup match in Vienna in 1964, and was then transferred to Sunderland a year later for around £75,000. A £100,000 move to Nottingham Forest followed two years later, and in 1969 he returned to Rangers. The old magic was missing and Baxter retired to enter the licensed trade in 1970.

Baxter had many wonderful matches against Celtic–the 1963 Scottish Cup Final replay springs to mind immediately–and he also produced great memories in a Scotland jersey. He won 34 full caps and his medal collection at Ibrox was three Championships, three Scottish Cups and four League Cups.

Ron McKinnon

A centre half in the classic mould, McKinnon was, despite being under 6ft, commanding in the air and a quick, intelligent player on the ground. He was also a good reader of the game. He played in two Scottish Cup Final victories over Celtic and was particularly effective in the replay of 1966 when the Parkhead side were strong favourites, but were beaten by a goal from Kai Johansen.

McKinnon joined the club from Dunipace Juniors in 1959 and was with them until 1973 when he emigrated to South Africa, where he also played for a while. His great rival was Celtic's Billy McNeill and for years they shared the job of playing at the centre of the Scotland defence. McKinnon gained 28 full caps and McNeill just one more.

McKinnon also played in the Rangers side which was beaten in the final of the European Cup–Winners' Cup in 1967, but his major triumphs were two Championships, four Scottish Cups and three League Cups.

Gentleman Jim Baxter, a player of immense talent, who graced the Scottish game in the early sixties.

Ralph Brand slips the ball past Haffey for the opener in the 1963 Scottish Cup Final Replay.

Rangers 3, Celtic 0 – Saturday, 24th August, 1963
Celtic Finish Poorly

Celtic's lack of punch in attack was again apparent at Ibrox against Rangers, who, although under pressure for most of the first half, yet turned with a goal lead, and finished up toying with dispirited opposition.

Rangers had the strong wind behind them to begin with, but made poor use of it, their upfield punts from the rear being intercepted by a diligent defence who, when in trouble, did not hesitate to put the ball into touch.

UNLUCKY CHALMERS

Meanwhile Celtic's forwards, off to an indifferent start, began to move the ball about intelligently. Chalmers was outstanding in their raids and he was unfortunate to be baulked of a goal first by Greig, then by Shearer on the goal-line.

Similarly Jeffrey had cause to be disappointed when Provan bobbed up to clear his header after Chalmers had again weaved his way through Rangers' defence, but in general the Celtic attack had neither the guile nor the strength to turn their territorial superiority into goals.

So, against the run of play, Rangers scored seven minutes before the interval when Wilson got his head to a corner kick by Henderson, and then took command of the game in 54 minutes when Brand scored with a penalty kick.

The award was conceded when Forrest, boring though on the left flank, had his feet pulled from him by McNeill, who had an unstable afternoon. He was again outwitted in 62 minutes by Forrest, who with a quick wheel 10 yards out, shot past Haffey.

This third reverse took much of the heart out of Celtic, who, although they continued to fight stubbornly, never recaptured the rhythm which characterised much of their play in the first half.

There was no repetition of the dilly-dallying tactics which Rangers adopted after they had clinched the issue at Celtic Park a fortnight previously, but it was painfully obvious before the close that there was only one team in what was, by and large, a disappointing game.

Rangers (1) 3   Celtic (0) 0
Wilson
Brand (pen.)
Forrest

RANGERS:- RITCHIE; SHEARER AND PROVAN; GREIG, MCKINNON AND BAXTER; HENDERSON AND MCLEAN; FORREST; BRAND AND WILSON.

CELTIC;- HAFFEY; MACKAY AND GEMMELL; CLARK, MCNEILL AND PRICE; GALLAGHER AND TURNER; DIVERS; CHALMERS AND JEFFREY.

Rangers 2, Celtic 1 – Saturday, 7th September, 1963
More Spirited Celtic

Of the three games between Rangers and Celtic since the season opened, that on Saturday at Ibrox Stadium in the League competition was the liveliest and most entertaining, mainly because the Celtic team contested the issue until the final whistle.

Rangers, proving again how difficult they are to beat, came from behind in the second half, equalised in 52 minutes, took their lead in 65, and thereafter never looked like losing.

NARROW ESCAPE

Yet, their task could have been harder, for with two minutes to go in the first half Chalmers got his head to a cross by Lennox, directed the ball well to Ritchie's left, and was chagrined to see it rebound to safety from the post.

Thus Rangers turned, luckily, only one goal down, for after Celtic scored in 11 minutes, when MacKay and Turner made the opening from which Chalmers scooped the ball past Ritchie, they were the dominant team. With Chalmers as spearhead and Divers playing a deep-lying role, the Celtic attack fully extended the Rangers' defence.

But Rangers, even facing into the strong wind, were not wholly committed to defence and indeed, were denied the equaliser midway in the first half only by MacKay's fortuitous intervention on the goal-line when Brand worked himself into the clear 12 yards out and shot powerfully for the angle of post and crossbar.

There was no mistaking Rangers' purpose in the second half – attack. Haffey effected a brilliant point-blank save from Baxter, but had no chance when McLean levelled the scores.

The tall inside right, whose play after the interval showed marked improvement on recent performances, galloped into an open space in pursuit of a ball released perfectly by Forrest and guided it out of Haffey's reach.

The leading goal came from a similar move by Forrest who, as Celtic defenders retreated instead of tackling, held onto the ball until Brand had raced into ideal position for the pass, and again Haffey was powerless to prevent a score.

Excitement did not end there. The goalkeepers were seldom idle; Ritchie distinguished himself with saves from Divers and Brogan, and Haffey denied Brand a second goal with a splendid interception. To add to the interest Rangers' right half, Greig, joined in a late barrage, three shots from him hurtling just wide of the target.

Rangers (0) 2   Celtic (1) 1
McLean   Chalmers
Brand

RANGERS:- RITCHIE; SHEARER AND PROVAN; GREIG, MCKINNON AND BAXTER; HENDERSON AND MCLEAN; FORREST; BRAND AND WILSON.

CELTIC:- HAFFEY; MCKAY AND GEMMELL; CLARK, MCNEILL AND O'NEILL; LENNOX AND TURNER; DIVERS; CHALMERS AND BROGAN.

Celtic 0, Rangers 1 – Wednesday, 1st January, 1964
Rangers Win Against Run of Play

Rangers succeeded in snatching a victory at Celtic Park yesterday which on football skill and run of play they certainly did not merit. For Celtic it was a sad tale of success that might have been theirs and, if justice had been done, would have been.

With Rangers' inside forwards Greig and McLean once again failing to strike form, the Ibrox club were constantly struggling to find cohesion, and much of their passing lacked accuracy. McKinnon, supported as he was by Davis, had a very unsound game and the defence, which started shakily, never fully recovered its poise. Only in the first half was Baxter able to add a few grace notes; he was too often in defence afterwards.

Celtic had several chances to score, but a mixture of bad luck, hesitancy at the vital moment, and fine saves by Ritchie thwarted all their efforts. Clark's absence for a few minutes in the second half – he was carried off on a stretcher, apparently suffering from concussion – did not noticeably restrict their attacks, but in the end they had to leave the field not having scored a goal for the first time since September.

CLEVER WINGERS

The players who most often sparked life into the match were the two outside rights, Johnstone and Henderson, the Celtic player making the larger contribution simply because he saw more of the ball. In nine minutes Johnstone beat Ritchie with a left-foot shot which hit a post, and Celtic might well have had a penalty kick awarded to them in 21 minutes when Chalmers was brought down from behind by McKinnon as he pursued the outside right's pass. Henderson, too, struck a post with a hard shot.

The decisive goal was struck by Millar in 63 minutes. From Henderson's free kick, taken just outside the penalty area, Brand drove the ball against a defender; when it came out to Millar, the centre forward turned quickly and hooked it past Fallon.

As so often happens after tension has been released by a score, the game became freer and goalmouth incidents, which had been rare events, came in rapid succession. There was more interest for the 60,000 spectators in the last half-hour than there had been in most of what had gone before, but it all amounted to frustration for Celtic.

Celtic (0) 0	Rangers (0) 1
	Millar
Attendance	60,000

CELTIC:- FALLON; YOUNG AND GEMMELL; CLARK, MCNEILL AND KENNEDY; JOHNSTONE AND MURDOCH; CHALMERS; DIVERS AND HUGHES.

RANGERS:- RITCHIE; PROVAN AND CALDOW; DAVIS, MCKINNON AND BAXTER; HENDERSON AND GREIG; MILLAR; MCLEAN AND BRAND.

Rangers 2: Celtic 0 – Saturday, 7th March, 1964
Off-Form Rangers Still Win

As the second half progressed and Celtic saw their ambition of preventing a fifth successive defeat by Rangers this season frustrated, unwelcome pique crept into their play and Murdoch and Chalmers had their names taken by the referee, who took exception to bad-tempered tackles on Wilson and Henderson.

Rangers' progress did suffer from an unexpectedly lifeless display by Baxter, and Wilson and Forrest were marked out of the game by Young, who is rapidly becoming one of the best right backs in Scotland, and McNeill, who apart from a few needless fouls on Forrest in the first half, eventually emerged as the outstanding player of the two sides. The centre half could not be blamed for the first goal, which Forrest headed when Fallon allowed Wilson's corner kick to bounce out of his arms.

It was on the right side of the field that Rangers were strongest. McMillan made up for lack of pace by accurate passes which gave Henderson the ball when and where he liked it. Taking the game as a whole, the winger's performance was only second to McNeill's, and it was appropriate that Henderson should score. His goal was brilliantly taken. Receiving the ball 40 yards out, Henderson ran through a retreating Celtic defence and from the penalty spot drove the ball past Fallon with his left foot.

The reorganisation of Celtic's team, whereby Murdoch took the place of the injured Clark at right half and Johnstone went to inside right, was not a success.

CLEVER RUN

In a first half of great promise Johnstone made a delightful weaving run, and for a time had Baxter turning in pursuit as he swept past the left half. But this unexpected weakness in Rangers' left flank was never fully exploited since Greig and McKinnon bottled up the centre of the field, where Chalmers waged a lonely war, cut off from supplies from Divers, who was dreadfully slow, and Hughes, who came off second best when the crunch came with Shearer.

Eventually Johnstone's physique proved to be too slight for continuous inside-forward play and reformation was forced on an increasingly ragged Celtic attack. But it came on paper only, for the new line of Johnstone, Chalmers, Hughes, Divers and Brogan proved no more of a threat to Rangers' dominant defence than the old.

Rangers (1) 2	Celtic (0) 0
Forrest	
Henderson	

RANGERS:- RITCHIE; SHEARER AND PROVAN; GREIG, MCKINNON AND BAXTER; HENDERSON AND MCMILLAN; FORREST; BRAND AND WILSON.

CELTIC:- FALLON; YOUNG AND GEMMELL; MURDOCH, MCNEILL AND KENNEDY; BROGAN (F) AND JOHNSTONE; CHALMERS; DIVERS AND HUGHES.

Celtic 3, Rangers 1 - Saturday, 5th September, 1964

Splendid Win for Celtic

Celtic provided further proof that they will be a power to be reckoned with this season, when on Saturday at Parkhead they recorded an emphatic victory over Rangers after 90 minutes of excitement on a pitch soaked by incessant heavy rain.

Rangers, played far below their best form. Beaten to the ball regularly, they seldom had the opportunity to move as a team in attack, and their defence was too often outwitted by the massive Hughes and the diminutive Johnstone.

The latter, indeed, was the personality of the day, although he was closely challenged for that distinction by Henderson on Rangers' right wing, but the men who had most to do with Celtic's success in attack were the inside forward trio, with Divers the master schemer, who completely outshone their Rangers counterparts.

Celtic lost the opportunity to open the scoring after eight minutes' play when Gallagher failed with a penalty kick after Provan impeded Johnstone, but the overdue goal came in 34 minutes when Chalmers put his head to a ball crossed by Johnstone after Divers made the opening.

Rangers were out of luck shortly before the interval when Fallon failed to cut out a corner kick by Henderson, and Wilson's shot was blocked on the goal-line by Young, and early in the second half McLean struck the crossbar.

But Celtic quickly regained the initiative and scored again in 52 minutes. Ritchie, probably with one eye on Hughes, was unable to clutch a ball crossed by Johnstone, and as it spun loose, Chalmers slammed it into the net.

Five minutes later Hughes took on the entire Rangers' defence in a dribble from left to right into the penalty area, and when he shot from 12 yards, Ritchie allowed the greasy ball to squirm through his fingers and roll over the line.

Rangers made a spurt towards the end of the game, and after 82 minutes' play Wilson scored from an acute angle after combination by Henderson and Baxter. The outside left was soon afterwards presented with what appeared to be a less difficult chance, but on this occasion he headed the ball which soared wide of the mark; with it went any slight hope that Rangers might save a point.

Celtic (1) 3	Rangers (0) 1
Chalmers 2	Wilson
Hughes	

CELTIC:- FALLON; YOUNG AND GEMMELL; BROGAN, CUSHLEY AND KENNEDY; JOHNSTONE AND DIVERS; CHALMERS; CALLAGHAN AND HUGHES;

RANGERS:- RITCHIE; HYND AND PROVAN; GREIG, McKINNON AND BAXTER; HENDERSON AND McLEAN; FORREST; BRAND AND WILSON.

Celtic 1, Rangers 2 – Saturday, 24th October, 1964

Rangers' Gallant Display

Rangers retained the League Cup with as gallant a performance as they have ever produced on the big occasion when they held off Celtic's challenge in the first half, if at times fortuitously, created goal-scoring opportunities later which their opponents never so simply contrived, and in the end emerged as masters.

Behind the success was the influence of Baxter, who laid on the second goal for Forrest after 62 minutes, the centre forward having 11 minutes earlier swooped after an indecisive clearance by Gemmell.

CELTIC GOAL

When Johnstone scored for Celtic after 72 minutes after leading-out work by Clark and Chalmers, the stage was set for the grandstand finish which had the crowd of 91,000 in almost continuous uproar.

But Rangers, as they have demonstrated so often in the past, once they get their noses in front, are extremely hard to pass and this Celtic forward line, weak in the inside positions, just could not beat down Rangers' defence.

Hughes and Johnstone exchanged their outside forward positions, but Baxter, Rangers' captain, cunningly countered this move by switching Provan and Caldow, so that Chalmers, ill-supported by Murdoch and Divers, never got the ball in such favourable positions as Forrest.

In the second half, with not a goal on the scoreboard,

Celtic's defence, not now so sure of itself, was early in trouble as Rangers' outside forwards began to swing the ball into the middle, and Fallon, who just before the interval held a terrific drive by Baxter, had some anxious moments as his outfield colleagues showed signs of panic.

The scene was further transformed when Forrest scored the opening goal and, despite spirited retaliation by Celtic, in the course of which Ritchie had lucky saves from Murdoch and Chalmers, the issue was sealed when Forrest scored again.

By and large, it was an engrossing game in which fortunes alternated with astonishing rapidity. It had its rough and tough moments, in two of which Millar fell foul of the referee and had his name taken, but will be remembered as one of the great encounters between these two Glasgow clubs.

Scottish League Cup Final

Celtic (0) 1	Rangers (0) 2
Johnstone	Forrest 2
Attendance	91,000

CELTIC:- FALLON; YOUNG AND GEMMELL; CLARK, CUSHLEY AND KENNEDY; JOHNSTONE AND MURDOCH; CHALMERS; DIVERS AND HUGHES.

RANGERS:- RITCHIE; PROVAN AND CALDOW; GREIG, McKINNON AND WOOD; BRAND AND MILLAR; FORREST; BAXTER AND JOHNSTON.

John Hughes puts Celtic one-up in the 1965 League Cup final.

The young John Greig is tackled by Celtic's Gemmell and Kennedy.

Rangers 1, Celtic 0 – Friday, 1st January, 1965

War of Attrition at Ibrox

By Raymond Jacobs

On the evidence of yesterday's game at Ibrox Stadium, the reputation of Old Firm encounters is continuing to rest on former glories and the controversial incidents which seem to occur either on or off the field.

This time it was the players' self-discipline which broke down in a match which, to say the least, was red-blooded throughout.

Johnstone was ordered off for charging down Beck in injury time just before the interval, Hughes had his name taken for a foul on Ritchie, and Provan after one on Kennedy.

FEW SHOTS

Neither side gave the impression of being able wholly to dominate play in what emerged as a war of attrition rather than a display of the arts and crafts of the game. Exciting and well-executed movements were scarce and neither Ritchie nor Simpson had to deal with more than a handful of shots each.

Rangers, who through no fault of their own had not had a game for almost a fortnight, were sluggish and their forwards lacked ideas, even to penetrate depleted opposition. Johnston was the most purposeful of the five, but the absence of Baxter's influence could almost be felt.

It was only appropriate that the winning goal should have been initiated by the young winger. In 12 minutes his corner-kick was headed forward to Forrest by Millar and the centre forward, turning quickly, shot home from about six yards.

BEST PERIOD

Celtic, as so often happens, were spurred to intense exertions by the loss of Johnstone, and they played their best football when they were a man short. Two excellent scoring attempts by Murdoch at the peak of Celtic's revival just failed, and a fine opportunity missed by Divers after a fine run by Hughes, were almost forgotten in the moments which followed the inside right's unexpectedly bad penalty miss.

Ranger's best players were Ritchie, Caldow, Greig and Johnston. Simpson, who used the ball particularly intelligently in the second half, Gemmell, McNeill and Gallagher took the eye for Celtic.

Rangers (1) 1	Celtic (0) 0
Forrest	

RANGERS:- RITCHIE; PROVAN AND CALDOW; GREIG, MCKINNON AND WOOD; WILSON AND MILLAR; FORREST; BECK AND JOHNSTON.

CELTIC:- SIMPSON; YOUNG AND GEMMELL; CLARK, MCNEILL AND KENNEDY; JOHNSTONE AND MURDOCH; HUGHES; DIVERS AND GALLAGHER.

Jim Forrest: goal scorer in the Ne'er Day game.

Celtic 2, Rangers 1 – Friday, 30th April, 1965

Celtic Beat Handicapped Rangers in Glasgow Cup

In theory 11 fit men should be capable of trouncing nine on the football field, but Celtic had the greatest difficulty in even establishing a lead against a crippled Rangers side in the Glasgow Cup tie last night at Parkhead before a crowd of 41,000.

In the closing minutes of the first half Hynd was carried off with an ankle injury, Martin was given attention for a damaged left hand and McLean was seen to be nursing a hand.

Thus Rangers turned out after the interval with nine men. Provan was in goal, Hynd and McLean were missing, and Martin, his hand bandaged, wore Provan's No. 2 jersey but played as a forward.

WILSON EXCELS

Although McLean resumed after 61 minutes the scene seemed set for slaughter, but with Wilson repeating at left back the great performance he gave against England two years ago when Caldow's leg was broken at Wembley, and McKinnon blocking the route through the centre, Celtic were unable to pierce Ranger's defensive barrier until 15 minutes from time when Provan allowed to slip through his fingers a shot from Auld which a regular goalkeeper would have clutched.

At that stage of the game, however, Celtic were worried, for 10 minutes earlier Wilson sent Henderson speeding up the left wing. The outside right suddenly veering to the right, tricked two opponents whose eyes were on Martin, and with his left foot hit the ball past Fallon from within the penalty area.

GOAL FROM REBOUND

Thereafter Celtic applied heavy pressure, and it was no more than their due when Chalmers in 79 minutes put them in the lead when he collected the rebound of a ball which Gemmell had driven against a post.

But this was not a convincing Celtic side in attack. All the forwards were guilty of rash thinking in open positions; perhaps they thought it was only a matter of time until Rangers' defence crumbled, but that, as everyone knows, will be the day.

Celtic will now meet Clyde in the Semi-final at Parkhead on Monday night. Queen's Park are already in the Final.

Glasgow Cup	
Celtic (0) 2	Rangers (0) 1
Auld	Henderson
Chalmers	
Attendance	41,000

CELTIC:- FALLON; YOUNG AND GEMMELL; MURDOCH, MCNEILL AND CLARK; CHALMERS AND GALLAGHER; HUGHES; LENNOX AND AULD.

RANGERS:- MARTIN; PROVAN AND CALDOW; HYND, MCKINNON AND GREIG; HENDERSON AND WOOD; MCLEAN; BRAND AND WILSON.

Rangers 2, Celtic 1 – Saturday, 18th September, 1965

Rangers Uncertain Victory

The cheer which erupted from the terracing at Rangers' end of Ibrox Stadium was as much one of relief as of joy, for in the last ten minutes of the game it was touch and go whether Rangers would be able to hold on to their narrow lead over Celtic.

As the boxing fraternity would say, it was a win on points, built up by Rangers in the first half in which, with the aid of a strong but capricious wind, they dominated the proceedings and with a little luck, might have been more than one goal ahead at the interval.

CLOSE MARKING

The game indeed was moving towards the last half hour before Celtic gave the home defence any cause for anxiety, and it was then that Rangers were greatly indebted to Ritchie and McKinnon for holding together a defensive structure in which cracks began to appear.

Although the general standard of play was not high, the exchanges in a game which was notable for close marking and, at times, ruthless tackling, were always interesting with just that spice of uncertainty towards the end which kept the crowd rooted to their places.

All the goals were scored in the first 20 minutes. McLean was fortunate to retain possession in a joust with Young near the by-line after just six minutes of play, but when he crossed into the goalmouth, Forrest beat Gemmell and Fallon to the ball and prodded it into the net.

Celtic equalised in 18 minutes. Greig pulled down Lennox and Hughes scored with the penalty kick. Two minutes later Forrest was boring though when he was impeded by McNeill. McLean made as satisfactory a job of the penalty kick as Hughes had done earlier.

Celtic were handicapped in their second-half rally by a leg injury to McNeill, who alternated between centre forward and outside right positions before hirpling back to his beat, but Rangers too had to rearrange their forces when Sorensen, also with a leg injury, switched to outside left.

On a day in which the forwards were not given much time or space in which to plan, the outstanding contributors to the entertainment were Henderson and Johnston of Rangers, and Johnstone of Celtic.

Rangers (2) 2	Celtic (1) 1
Forrest	Hughes (pen.)
McLean (pen.)	

RANGERS:- RITCHIE; HANSEN AND PROVAN; WATSON, MCKINNON AND GREIG; HENDERSON AND SORENSEN; FORREST; MCLEAN AND JOHNSTON.

CELTIC:- FALLON; YOUNG AND GEMMELL; MURDOCH, MCNEILL AND CLARK;. JOHNSTONE AND DIVERS; HUGHES; LENNOX AND AULD.

Celtic 2, Rangers 1 - Saturday, 23rd October, 1965

League Cup Final an Orgy of Crudeness

By Raymond Jacobs

FIVE PLAYERS' NAMES TAKEN

Except for the manner in which victory was achieved, the League Cup Final exceeded the worst traditions of Old Firm matches. Two penalty goals were scored and five players had their names taken. When Celtic meet Rangers the meek do not inherit the earth; and war correspondents rather than sports writers, should be despatched to these violent fronts.

The physical aspect of the match must take precedence over any other because that is what the match is all about. There was only a passing nod to the most elementary skills of the game, and that came largely from Rangers. Power, stamina and scarcely containable vigour rode roughshod over any consideration of disciplined and thoughtful football.

Some of the tackles were intimidating. Man went for man. Tripping, kicking, hacking, and jersey-pulling were rife. How can Scottish football raise its hands piously in horror against the same gambits of continental players when the two leading teams in the country indulge in the orgy of crudeness which made this so unpalatable a spectacle?

TENSE OCCASIONS

Within four minutes, the names of Young and Johnston were in the referee's book, and those of McKinnon, Murdoch and Johnstone followed at intervals. Mr Phillips' first penalty award was inevitable, the second justifiable. His whistle was seldom silent and so any hope of the game developing a rhythm was destroyed.

Only when it was all over could one look back and say that the match was won and lost in the first half-hour. Before Celtic scored, Forrest had missed two gilt-edged chances, created in a way which suggested that McNeill, in the centre of Celtic's defence, was highly vulnerable on the ground.

The match indeed confirmed an impression of Scottish football as a whole – that the art of creative inside-forward play is now a largely neglected one. It is the wingers, and to a lesser extent the half backs, who are the mainsprings of attacks nowadays.

Rangers were still very much in command when in 17 minutes McKinnon, surely not realising where he was standing, handled a harmless free kick, an appalling mistake which stopped Rangers in their tracks. Hughes scored with an assured kick, and McKinnon was left to go distraughtly from one colleague to another, apologising

for this costly error of judgment.

Twelve minutes later Provan sold his side into more lasting bondage. Beaten by Johnstone, he gave chase and brought the winger down from behind. Ritchie got a hand to Hughes' shot, but could not stop it going into the net. But even this double blow did not entirely weaken Rangers' grip.

As the half drew to a close Greig emerged as their most valuable player. In defence he covered vast tracts of the field, in attack he helped to flog his forwards to more intense effort, and gave them an example by bringing out a brilliant save from Simpson from 25 yards.

POSITIONAL CHANGES

After the interval Johnston and Wilson changed positions, but although they contrived an occasional movement of incisiveness, Henderson's influence on the game was severely curbed by Gemmell. And with McNeill steadying himself on Murdoch's broad shoulders, the teeth of Rangers' attack were drawn.

Celtic, to be sure, made penetration exceptionally difficult by packing their defence. They preferred the dangerous tactics of a holding operation, relying on Hughes' mastery of Johansen for an occasional relieving breakout. Even Johnstone and McBride were called back to help strengthen the bulwarks.

The plan finally worked out, although its application produced a long period of frustratingly scrappy football. Simpson had a good save from Johnston and confirmed that Wilson's reflexes have slowed immeasurably by beating the Rangers forward to a pass he would have turned into a goal not so long ago.

Rangers' persistence was at last rewarded with a goal when Henderson took a free kick just outside the area, and with Greig rushing at the ball, it spun past Simpson off Young's face. That was seven minutes from the end, and it was too late to salvage the match.

Scottish League Cup Final

Celtic (2) 2	Rangers (0) 1
Hughes 2 (2 pens.)	Young (o.g.)

CELTIC:- SIMPSON; YOUNG AND GEMMELL; MURDOCH, MCNEILL AND CLARK; JOHNSTONE AND GALLAGHER; MCBRIDE; LENNOX AND HUGHES.

RANGERS:- RITCHIE; JOHANSEN AND PROVAN; WOOD, MCKINNON AND GREIG; HENDERSON AND WILLOUGHBY; FORREST; WILSON AND JOHNSTON.

Old Firm Victory Laps Should be Banned

By Raymond Jacobs

To the victor go the spoils, and in football a recent addition to the booty is the lap of honour. In normal circumstances it is a harmless conceit, but when Celtic meet Rangers it should be banned, preferably through mutual agreement between the clubs, or, if necessary, by magistrates and the police.

This can be the only reaction to the scenes at Hampden Park after Celtic had beaten Rangers in the Final of the League Cup. They were frightening and dangerous, and could have led to a very difficult situation.

The Celtic players having received tribute from their supporters' end of the terracing, were on their way back to the middle of the field when a horde of spectators from the Rangers end burst on to the pitch. More than one Celtic player came close to being assaulted, and if any one attack had succeeded, the subsequent events do not bear thinking about.

LOATHING

It was probably never the intention of Celtic to complete a circuit of the field, thus running the gauntlet of the Mount Florida end of the ground. Presumably the players, like the rest of us, have ambitions to live to a ripe old age. But there is no doubt that the loathing of one camp for the other breeds on these occasions an atmosphere so explosive as to be combustible when victory of one is flaunted in the face of the other.

Two further disagreeable aspects of a disagreeable afternoon also must be mentioned, for one of which there is probably no known remedy. The other can, and should be, put a stop to by the clubs.

The tone of the game was set when Celtic supporters attempted to drown the playing of the National Anthem with prolonged cheering, and the opposition responded by singing the words with a fervour which one suspects had little connection with sentiments of loyalty to the crown.

IMPLICATION

And when Celtic were given their second penalty award, the congratulations bestowed upon one another by McBride and Johnstone were not only provocative, but implied that the referee had been cleverly deceived.

No official, it has to be hoped, will have a more difficult task this season than had Mr Phillips on Saturday; he is to be recommended for his skill in performing it.

Chalmers puts the ball past Ritchie for his third and Celtic's fifth in the second half of the 1966 New Year derby.

Celtic 5, Rangers 1 – Monday, 3rd January, 1966

Celtic's Five Goals in Second Half

By Raymond Jacobs

HUMBLING DEFEAT FOR POOR RANGERS TEAM

Celtic, a goal down after little more than a minute, scored five times in the second half at Celtic Park, three of the goals from Chalmers, but well before the fifth goal Rangers were an outclassed, outplayed side. Indeed, few Rangers teams of the past can have been as thoroughly dissected as this one.

There were two crucial differences between the teams. Celtic, wearing training boots, strode the sanded surface of the frostbound pitch with comparative assurance. Rangers' players, conventionally shod, were much less sure-footed and thus could never really come to terms with the difficulties presented by the conditions.

Chiefly, however, Celtic emerged quite simply as the better side, fluent and inventive where Rangers were hesitant and orthodox. Both at wing half and at inside forward, where constructiveness begins, Celtic were infinitely superior, and on the wing Hughes made life as uncomfortable for Provan as he did for Johansen in the League Cup Final.

NEWCOMER

Celtic's advantage also held in defence. Under almost continual pressure, McKinnon and Greig managed generally to keep their heads and their feet, while all around were losing theirs, but eventually they were over-run. Rangers' clearances too were astonishingly aimless and hurried. In front an attack lacking in physical strength bobbed as corks on water, and Setterington, tossed in at the deep end for his first League appearance, was manifestly out of his depth; not that the young inside right was set any inspiring example by his more experienced colleagues.

To add to a day that Rangers will surely want to forget, and as surely will be reminded of frequently, Johansen, Setterington and Provan had their names taken. It was not surprising that, even more rapidly than at Hampden Park in October, the faithful were departing in droves from the Rangers end of the ground.

A little less than ninety minutes earlier, however, their spirits were understandably high. Rangers set off with unexpected confidence and took the lead, according to a colleague with a stop-watch, in 1 min. 40 sec. precisely. Greig shot and the ball broke off a defender to Wilson who, with his left foot, shot past Simpson's reach from an angle.

For the remainder of the half – indeed, for the remainder of the game – Simpson was largely untroubled, whereas activity bubbled and frothed around Ritchie. With a little more care from Johnstone and Hughes, Celtic might not have had to wait until five minutes after the interval for the equalising goal. Among a welter of incidents, the best chance was squandered by Hughes when Hynd miskicked the ball to his feet a few yards out, and the winger shot over the crossbar.

After the interval the goals came, and it is unlikely that five better will be seen anywhere for a long time. The deluge was begun in 50 minutes when McBride dummied Gemmell's cross, and Chalmers shot home from six yards. After 67 minutes McBride missed an opportunity when Ritchie and McKinnon collided, leaving the goal vacant, but a score came only a minute later as Chalmers put Celtic in the lead, heading in Gallagher's corner kick.

FREE KICK

Still Celtic pounded on, and five minutes later Hughes slipped past Provan on the touchline and cut the ball back to the edge of the area, where Gallagher drove the ball past Ritchie off the underside of the crossbar. The fourth notch was cut after 80 minutes as Johnstone touched a free kick to McBride, and the centre forward's square pass, through the referee's legs, was hammered into the net by Murdoch from 30 yards.

Ritchie, only temporarily it turned out, forestalled a fifth goal with a brilliant save from McBride, but there was nothing he or anyone else could do to prevent Johnstone from hitting a post and Chalmers from scoring from the rebound a goal that completed a total and humbling rout.

Celtic (0) 5	Rangers (1) 1
Chalmers 3	Wilson
Gallacher	
Murdoch	

CELTIC:- SIMPSON; CRAIG AND GEMMELL; MURDOCH, CUSHLEY AND CLARK; JOHNSTONE AND GALLAGHER; MCBRIDE; CHALMERS AND HUGHES.

RANGERS:- RITCHIE; PROVAN AND JOHANSEN; HYND, MCKINNON AND GREIG; WILSON AND SETTERINGTON; FORREST, MCLEAN AND JOHNSTON.

Celtic 0, Rangers 0 – Saturday, 23rd April, 1966

Defences on Top at Hampden

By Raymond Jacobs

There was a rough as well as an unfinished quality about the Scottish Cup Final on Saturday at Hampden Park. The mind was given few images to capture, and the memory little to store away, to be gratefully recalled on some day of less vivid light, mildness and colour.

Tension kept the game absorbing, with the knowledge that just one bold slash might be enough to cut the stiff knot of deadlock and bring with it the mingling of irrevocable triumph which sets competition by elimination apart.

The widening trend in modern football was all too evident – that defence must be organised and in control, for then the likelihood of defeat is diminished. Celtic and Rangers both made the point; one or other, of course, will eventually concede, which is always the consolation to be taken away from drawn Cup matches.

The caution of Celtic's approach was conditioned, one suspects, by the kind of games in which they have recently been engaged. They have been obliged, as it were, to be unnatural and to walk softly, but the big stick with the notches of that century of goals and more carved on it seems to have been mislaid. One goal in four games and one brief intense application of pressure on Saturday suggest that for the time being at least, the springs of enterprise have dried up.

BRILLIANT SAVE

McBride had a header brilliantly touched away by Ritchie but Celtic's leading scorer was, for the most part, an anonymous figure. Murdoch's siege gun was silent. Chalmers challenged energetically but without being able to get in a shot, and Gallagher, who did, was badly off target, save once when his drive lifted itself over the crossbar like an aircraft at take-off.

Thus the forwards were, for the most part, kept at arm's length from goal, and were allowed little scope if ever they did penetrate behind the opposing screens and into the penalty area.

In the event, two defenders – McNeill, who sent a header thudding against the crossbar, and Greig, forestalled at the end of a typical forceful run by a courageous dive of Simpson's – came as close as anyone to scoring. To that further extent the forwards were overshadowed.

The result was a hard midfield battle in the expected, apparently inevitable, tradition of Old Firm games when to avoid defeat is held almost as desirable as actually winning. The tackling was seldom openly ruthless, but always uncompromising, for this was no occasion for taking prisoners.

The referee whose control was unexceptionable and undisturbed by the need for controversial decisions, had to warn Young and Provan against perpetrating the grosser excesses of Henderson and Johnstone, and McNeill never used to have to fling his weight about as he occasionally did on Forrest. Otherwise the onlooker might flinch at the fierceness of it, but still keep his eyebrows in place.

It was therefore disappointing that only Johnstone of the four internationalists playing as wingers was able to impose more than a fleeting influence on the play. Had they done so, the point of attack could perhaps decisively have been taken more often away from the centre, where McNeill and McKinnon and their attendant sweepers, Clark and Greig, were impregnable.

POSITIONAL CHANGES

Henderson and Wilson switched wings at once and permanently, except for a short period in the second half when Henderson changed places with Johnston. But Henderson revealed scant enthusiasm for the fray and Wilson, aside from curbing Gemmell's inclination to move upfield, was short of the pace needed to prise open such a tight defence as Celtic's.

Hughes this time met his match in Johansen. At the very start Celtic, obviously remembering the indignities inflicted on Johansen by Hughes in the League Cup Final, set out to test the right back's mettle. Johansen weathered the storm and showed his increased maturity in not only subduing Hughes, but also in parting intelligently with the ball.

And so it all has to be gone through again. Celtic will still be expected to retain the trophy on the grounds, no doubt, that the reserves of match-winning potential at their disposal are stronger than Rangers'. But Rangers may have proved, at least to themselves, that Celtic are by no means invincible.

Scottish Cup Final

Celtic (0) 0	Rangers (0) 0
(at Hampden Park)	

CELTIC:- SIMPSON; YOUNG AND GEMMELL; MURDOCH, MCNEILL AND CLARK; JOHNSTONE AND MCBRIDE; CHALMERS; GALLAGHER AND HUGHES.

RANGERS:- RITCHIE; JOHANSEN AND PROVAN; GREIG, MCKINNON AND MILLAR; HENDERSON AND WATSON; FORREST; JOHNSTON AND WILSON.

Rangers 1, Celtic 0 - Saturday, 27th April, 1966

Scottish Cup Won by Rangers

By Raymond Jacobs

JOHANSEN SCORES ONLY GOAL OF 180 MINUTES' PLAY

Rangers won the Scottish Cup for the nineteenth time last night at Hampden Park when, watched by a crowd of 96,862, they beat Celtic in the replay of the final. The vital goal was scored by their Danish right back, Johansen, 20 minutes before a relentless, at times ruthless, battle would have had to go into extra time.

It was a goal worthy of winning any trophy, and its quality was matched only by its unexpectedness. Johansen wriggled his way to the byeline and when McLean missed the ball a few yards out, it ran to Henderson. The winger's shot was cleared off the line by Murdoch out to Johansen, who let fly from 25 yards, and the ball flew low and hard into the net.

Thus are cups sometimes won and in this instance the deed was done by a defensive member of a side whose forwards, compared with the opposition, had given little indication that they were capable of doing such damage themselves.

Rangers' triumph, against all the predicted odds, was built on a magnificent defence and some fortune since Celtic came close to scoring on many occasions. The outstanding figure was Millar, always there when he was needed most, supporting Greig, McKinnon and Johansen, and also finding time and energy to urge his forwards on. Behind them Ritchie was safe and sure in goal.

Celtic, always the more fluently moving side, had their opportunities, but the fact is that this was their fourth successive game in which they failed to score a goal, and so all the effort and the leading-up work, much of which was skilfully directed by Auld, came to nothing.

Johnstone was again the most enterprising of their forwards. He made life a misery for Provan after the Rangers left back had had his name taken for a third foul on the winger in the first half. But Hughes was once more subdued, and the channelling of attacks though the middle ran into a stone wall.

TOUGH TACKLING

The strongest impression of the first half was the hardness and recklessness of many of the tackles. Bodies and boots flew with scant regard for life and limb, and there were ceaseless stoppages for free kicks. In this war no one kept their powder dry.

The battle raged to and fro, and once Johansen and Hughes held hands as they raced down the touchline, but neither was trying to be familiar.

Rangers struggled hard and unsuccessfully to find a rhythm whereas Celtic, moving with cohesion and purpose, almost found the target more than once. Auld laid on three chances, of which Chalmers missed two and Hughes the other, and McBride had a shot diverted from the mark.

Rangers' response was limited almost wholly to a shot from Greig which dipped over, and another from Watson which was deflected from its course for a corner by Clark.

The start of the second half was almost identical to that of the first game as Celtic, now with the strong wind at their backs, swept down looking for the goal which would break this agonising stalemate. McNeill headed just wide. Ritchie saved a shot from Johnstone, and when McBride flicked the ball to Chalmers, the centre forward hit it over the crossbar.

RITCHIE'S SAVES

Then came what proved to be the decisive goal, but immediately after it Ritchie, who had previously saved from Chalmers when he stuck out a leg to the ball, again saved from the centre forward, and for good measure stopped another attempt by McNeill.

McBride, who was by this time limping, changed places with Hughes, but it was Rangers, in a breakaway from the heavy Celtic pressure, who almost scored again, Simpson thwarting Johnston with a splendid save.

Celtic kept up the pressure as they desperately sought the equalising goal and Hughes, Auld and McNeill were not far off turning the trick.

But as the crowds melted away from the Celtic end, Rangers continued to hold out, sometimes kicking the ball anywhere to keep it away from the goal, sometimes indulging in time-wasting tactics. But Celtic, who were so confidently expected to retain the trophy, instead saw it pass once more into the hands of their greatest rivals.

Scottish Cup Final Replay

Rangers (0) 1	Celtic (0) 0
Johansen	
(at Hampden Park)	
Attendance	96,862

RANGERS:- RITCHIE; JOHANSEN AND PROVAN; GREIG, MCKINNON AND MILLAR; HENDERSON AND WATSON; MCLEAN; JOHNSTON AND WILSON.

CELTIC:- SIMPSON; CRAIG AND GEMMELL; MURDOCH, MCNEILL AND CLARK; JOHNSTONE AND MCBRIDE; CHALMERS; AULD AND HUGHES.

Ronnie Simpson claims the ball in the 1966 League Cup final.

The victorious 1966 Celtic team display the League Cup.

A clean sweep for Celtic as Rangers are stuck in the mud. The 2-2 draw at Ibrox secures a clean sweep of all competitions in the 1966/7 season.

Provan takes the ball from Steve Chalmers.

Celtic 2, Rangers 0 – Saturday, 17th September, 1966

Rangers Flounder at Parkhead

CELTIC TAKE CONTROL IN OPENING MINUTES

It may be presumed that at Ibrox as well as Parkhead, the training includes tactical exercises, but there was very little evidence of planning in Rangers' display against Celtic at Parkhead.

The hopeful upfield punt associated with Rangers' attack in what were known as their "iron curtain" days, was the main weapon in their armoury, and whereas they used the bludgeon, Celtic preferred the rapier.

Rangers' defence was run though twice before they even took guard. Murdoch in the first minute whipped a long ball through the middle to Lennox, who beat McKinnon to it and crossed. McBride clean missed with his swipe at the ball but Auld, following up, hit it past Ritchie and in off the post.

SECOND ATTEMPT

Barely three minutes had elapsed when Murdoch put Celtic further ahead with a clever goal. After a shot from him had been blocked on the 18-yard line, he regained possession and chipped the ball into the net well out of Ritchie's reach.

Thus Celtic had thrown down the gage. It was certainly picked up by Rangers, but it was always an unequal duel. The main difference between the teams was an ability to exploit the open space, at which Celtic were adept; they also moved with a smooth efficiency in attack and defence which Rangers never achieved.

In view of Celtic's all-round superiority, their supporters probably expected them to run up a big score; that they did not do so was attributable less to the tightening up in Rangers' defence than to Celtic's tactics of inviting the challenge in the full confidence that they would repel it.

Put another way, there was no reason why Celtic should exert themselves. They knew they had the game won and need do no more than contain the opposition, as they did without undue trouble.

But a side effect was that in the second half particularly, the standard of entertainment was low. Things might have been different if in the sixty-third minute Rangers had scored, as they should have. McLean from the edge of the penalty area on the right slung the ball to the far post, where Johnston appeared to have no more to do than to nod it into the net, but unaccountably headed wide of the target.

On the other hand, Celtic's latent power was exemplified later when a ball driven powerfully by Auld hit the bar over Ritchie's head, and again when McBride just failed to get his head to a ball from Lennox with only the goalkeeper to beat.

Celtic (2) 2	Rangers (0) 0
Auld	
Murdoch	

CELTIC:- SIMPSON; GEMMELL AND O'NEILL; MURDOCH, MCNEILL AND CLARK; JOHNSTONE AND LENNOX; MCBRIDE; AULD AND HUGHES. SUBSTITUTE – CHALMERS.

RANGERS:- RITCHIE; PROVAN AND GREIG; MILLAR, MCKINNON AND SMITH (D.); WILSON AND SMITH (A.); FORREST,; MCLEAN AND JOHNSTON. SUBSTITUTE – SETTERINGTON.

McNeill stops Forrest in his tracks.

Celtic 1, Rangers 0 - Saturday, 29th October, 1966

Celtic Outplayed by Rangers but Retain League Cup

By Raymond Jacobs

Celtic retained the League Cup on Saturday, but not in the manner expected. One opportunity was brilliantly taken, but for almost all of the remainder of the game, Rangers outplayed them and pushed them relentlessly back into defence.

The lamentations of Rangers' supporters as they trudged disconsolately away from the ground would be worth printing if they were repeatable. A polite paraphrase would be:- "We wuz robbed". And so they were.

But for all the injustice of the result, many of them must have given thought to the principal reason for defeat. And it was certainly not because two claims for a penalty were turned down, or because Watson had an apparently genuine score obscurely disallowed.

BEST FORM

No side, even if they do reveal their best attacking form of the season, can expect to find an ally in Fate if they so consistently scorn the chances which through their own ability and persistence they make for themselves. The opening words of the next Rangers' song cribbed from that famous line from that doucer literature of cricket might be:- "Oh, my Thornton and my Millar long ago." With the goal light which used to gleam so brightly in these players' eyes, Rangers would surely have found an end to the road for the openings they made.

The inefficiency near goal of this generation of inside forwards would have appalled their predecessors. It was underscored most heavily in the dying minutes: McLean shot over from five yards and A. Smith, with the ball at his feet and Simpson beaten, stumbled as he shot so that O'Neill was able to clear.

Throughout, indeed, McLean was his most irritatingly cumbersome self. Neither in the air nor on the ground could he master McNeill. A. Smith was never intended to be a striker, and though Watson toiled with courage and industry, it was symptomatic of a fatal flaw that Simpson's finest save should be induced by a long drive from Greig.

REMARKABLE RUN.

So much for Rangers' failure. Celtic after all were the winners and all credit should go to them for that, particularly since they extended their remarkable run of consecutive victories in competitive matches to 21 in quite alien circumstances to those of their previous successes.

Only the first 20 minutes or so did they carry the fight in a lively, sometimes tempestuous match with as much authority as Rangers. It was during that period that Auld flighted a cross beyond the far post and McBride headed in down and back for Lennox, who hammered it past Martin into the net.

That simple sequence of action caught Rangers' defenders exposed and badly out of position in a way that was never to occur again. Certainly McKinnon did not look fully in command even in the very occasional moments when Celtic contrived a breakaway, but a long Auld shot over the bar some long time after the interval constituted Celtic's only other scoring attempt of consequence.

Instead they became involuntarily and increasingly committed to defence. McBride, Auld, Murdoch, Johnstone and Chalmers, who substituted for Hughes shortly after half-time, were more and more concerned with reinforcing their rearguard, which, from clearing their lines with alert composure, they were obliged to be less discriminating the longer the game lasted.

That Celtic had to adopt, in the military jargon, so defensive a posture, may have come as much of a surprise to them as it did to onlookers accustomed to flat-out aggression which has subdued and overwhelmed a lengthy succession of opponents. This time, however, it was Rangers who seized the initiative and held it virtually without challenge to the end.

In this unfamiliar pattern Gemmell looked far less happy than when he is playing behind a dominant attack. Johnston, finally serviced by D.Smith, gave Gemmell an uncomfortable afternoon, and if Henderson had been fitter than he evidently was, O'Neill might have been more severely put to the test.

As it was, O'Neill, McNeill, Clark and Simpson emerged from their ordeal battered but unbowed by the constant pressure exerted on them by the tremendous form of Rangers' attack, whose inspiration derived from a magnificent display at wing-half.

FINEST DISPLAY

Greig's urgency is a factor to be taken for granted but always admired. But D. Smith's use of the ball proclaimed his best display for Rangers since he was transferred from Aberdeen. Provan and Johansen took up the challenge forcefully, and thus anxiety to avoid a third successive defeat in a season from their greatest rivals was powerfully upheld.

Where it broke down was in the middle, close to goal. With one swift uncomplicated move Celtic achieved in less than a quarter sweep of a second hand, more than Rangers could in over an hour of striving. And it is goals, not sweat and lost opportunities, that show in the record books.

Scottish League Cup Final

Celtic (1) 1   Rangers (0) 0
Lennox

CELTIC:- SIMPSON; GEMMELL AND O'NEILL; MURDOCH, MCNEILL AND CLARK; JOHNSTONE AND LENNOX; MCBRIDE; AULD AND HUGHES. SUBSTITUTE - CHALMERS.

RANGERS:- MARTIN; JOHANSEN AND PROVAN; GREIG, MCKINNON AND D. SMITH; HENDERSON AND WATSON; MCLEAN; A. SMITH AND JOHNSTON. SUBSTITUTE – WILSON

Rangers 2, Celtic 2 – Saturday, 8th May, 1967

Celtic's Clean Sweep in Scottish Competitions

By Glyn Edwards

Seven defeats and two draws in their last nine league visits to Ibrox is a pretty dismal record by any standards. Yet Celtic will have no thoughts on that account this morning, as the one point they attained on Saturday not only won them the League Championship for the twenty-second time, but also made them the first Scottish club to win every home competition in the last 20 years.

Before any irate supporters hasten to point out that the Ibrox side have twice won the League Cup, Scottish Cup and League Championship in a season, in 1948-49 and in 1963-64, let me remind them that on each occasion they failed to win the Glasgow Cup (or, in the days when it was open to the Glasgow clubs, the Charity Cup).

With just one point needed to achieve their record-breaking feat, Celtic might have been expected to adopt defensive tactics against their arch-rivals. But, commendably, they decided otherwise with the result that the crowd of some 78,000, including Mr Helenio Herrera, manager of Internazionale of Milan, Celtic's opponents in the forthcoming European Cup Final, and the Russian touring party, were provided with a level of entertainment and skill which reflected considerable credit on both sides.

On a sodden pitch and in constant heavy rain, which made virtues of sure-footedness and confidence, the players gave their all, and it was not surprising that before the end several of them were leg-weary and the pace slackened slightly. But even in the last few minutes, someone could always summon up the energy to go through on his own in search of a decisive goal.

It would, though, have been a travesty had either side managed to win the game, for each skilfully contrived move by one team, either collectively or individually, was more often than not matched by the other for the entire 90 enthralling minutes.

Indeed, it was glaringly obvious that the teams themselves thought that a draw was the ideal result, for with the last shrill of the referee's whistle came sincere and spontaneous arms-round-each-other congratulations from all of the rival players – a lesson to those among their supporters who caused the game to be held up for a minute or so in the second half, as spectators spilled onto the track to avoid being struck by flying bottles.

VITAL MINUTE

One minute in the first half was undoubtedly the most vital in the game. In those 60 seconds Rangers gained the lead which they so badly wanted – and then proceeded to throw it away.

It began when in 40 minutes D. Smith began a long, meandering run down the left touchline in search of an opening. He held off one challenge and then pitched the ball across to the unmarked Jardine, who, given ample time to control it by a strangely hesitant Celtic defence, drove an unsavable shot from fully 25 yards into the net via the underside of the crossbar.

Had Rangers been able to carry that lead into the second half things might have turned out differently, but more by their own carelessness than anything else, they conceded the equaliser only 45 seconds later. A Wallace shot was stopped by Martin, and although two or three Rangers defenders had the opportunity to clear, none did. The ball bobbed around tantalisingly on the six-yard line until Lennox pushed it onto a post and Johnstone shot home the rebound.

JOHNSTONE'S SECOND

If that goal was something of a scrambled affair, the same could certainly not be said of Celtic's second, again scored by Johnstone, who vied with Auld, McKinnon and Greig for the distinction of being the most accomplished player afield. The little winger, having received the ball from a throw-in by Chalmers in 74 minutes, made for the penalty area, evading McKinnon's tackle in the process, veered left as other defenders closed in, and then smacked a glorious shot into the roof of the net.

Although the goal did not win the game for Celtic – Hynd scored Rangers' second 10 minutes from the end when he scliffed home a Henderson cross – it is a safe bet than no better has ever won a League championship.

Rangers (1) 2	Celtic (1) 2
Jardine	Johnstone 2
Hynd	
Attendance	78,000

RANGERS:- MARTIN; JOHANSEN AND PROVAN; JARDINE, MCKINNON AND GREIG; HENDERSON AND A. SMITH; HYND; D. SMITH AND JOHNSTON. SUBSTITUTE – WILSON.

CELTIC:- SIMPSON; CRAIG AND GEMMELL; MURDOCH, MCNEILL AND CLARK; JOHNSTONE AND WALLACE; CHALMERS, AULD AND LENNOX. SUBSTITUTE – O'NEILL.

Rangers 1, Celtic 1 – Wednesday, 16th August, 1967

Late Penman Goal gives Rangers Draw with Celtic

By Glyn Edwards

The first Old Firm match of the season is over, and, at the risk of being presumptuous, I would say the unanimous opinion of the crowd of some 80,000 who thronged out of Ibrox Stadium last night was – roll on the next.

If the return match is only half as exciting and entertaining as last night's encounter, then the paying customer can have no qualms about delving into his pocket for that extra shilling admission charge imposed for the new season. It will be cheap at the price.

SOLID DEFENCE

Although Rangers had most of the pressure and enough scoring chances to win the game, Celtic performed so magnificently in defence, particularly in the second half, that it seemed for all the world that their goal scored via the penalty spot in 38 minutes would be sufficient to carry them through.

But in the best tradition of Rangers' Cup ties their players, notably Jardine, Penman and Greig, stuck to their guns and with just two minutes remaining for play Penman, who earlier had failed to score with a penalty kick, brought the Ibrox house down when he rammed the ball home direct from a free kick awarded some 25 yards from goal.

That, to my mind, brought a fitting end to this grim tussle, for such it was as the players fought hard for the ball, taking knocks and giving them, with as many as three men at a time prostrate – not that these occasions were in the main attributable to rancour. Only once did the referee see fit to take a player's name, and that was when Johnstone blotted his copybook somewhat by crudely bringing down Ferguson.

SOLO RUN

It was Rangers who looked the more settled team at the outset, and in three minutes Jardine, after having taken the ball right in on Simpson from about the midway line, was dispossessed by Craig at the last moment.

But gradually Celtic came more and more into the game and in 19 minutes Gemmell had two glorious shots at goal, the first being brilliantly saved by Sorensen and the other slipping inches wide of an upright.

Those were narrow escapes from Rangers, but they were nothing compared to an incident which occurred at the other end in 27 minutes. Penman sent the ball low across goal and Ferguson, while stumbling forward, hooked the ball onto the top of the crossbar with Simpson a mere spectator.

Thereafter Rangers continued to enjoy the lion's share of the ball, but they were set back on their heels in 38 minutes when Smith pulled down Lennox from behind and Gemmell sent Sorensen the wrong way with the resultant penalty kick.

PENALTY AWARD

In the second half it was almost all one-way traffic – toward Simpson's goal – but the Celtic defence were equal to everything Rangers could throw at them, including a penalty kick awarded when after an hour, Auld barged Jardine off the ball. Penman took the kick, but Rangers' supporters were in utter dejection when Simpson threw himself across goal and saved the ball shoulder-high at the post.

In 70 minutes Rangers had another great chance to score, but again Penman from a delightful through pass by Smith, miskicked with no one to beat but the goalkeeper. In the outfield none was better than the former Dundee player, but at close quarters it just was not his night – until that is, he smacked home the great equalising goal in the dying minutes.

Rangers (0) 1	Celtic (1) 1
Penman	Gemmell (pen.)
Attendance	80,000

RANGERS:- SORENSEN; JOHANSEN AND PROVAN; JARDINE, MCKINNON AND GREIG; HENDERSON AND PENMAN; FERGUSON; D. SMITH AND PEARSON. SUBSTITUTE – HYND.

CELTIC:- SIMPSON; CRAIG AND GEMMELL; MURDOCH, MCNEILL AND CLARK; JOHNSTONE AND WALLACE; CHALMERS; AULD AND LENNOX. SUBSTITUTE – GALLAGHER.

Celtic 3, Rangers 1 – Wednesday, 30th August 1967

Three Late Goals give Celtic Victory over Rangers

By Glyn Edwards

Rangers' right back, Johansen, will carry on his back for many a long day the responsibility for his team's defeat by Celtic last night at Parkhead, and their consequent failure to qualify for the quarter-final stage of the League Cup competition.

With but 14 minutes left for play and Rangers grimly holding on to a one-goal lead established early in the game, Johansen was presented with the best opportunities to put his side into a strong position.

Henderson, in full flight for goal, was brought down in the penalty area by a late tackle by Clark, but the Dane's kick struck the underside of the bar and came out. Even then the odds looked on a Rangers' goal as the ball bobbed around on the six-yard line, but before the inrushing Penman could put his boot to the ball Johansen unthinkingly headed it forward and the referee had no hesitation in awarding a free kick to Celtic.

A costly mistake that was to be, for just two minutes later Wallace emerged from a group of players with his right hand held high, and the ball in the back of the Rangers' net. How it got there I am unsure. All I know is that from a corner on the left the ball bounced lazily into the net, and Celtic's inside right appeared to be getting the credit for it.

Instead of being 2-0 ahead, Rangers now found themselves on level terms – and for them worse was to follow. Just five minutes later Lennox teed up a ball for Murdoch on the edge of the penalty area and the wing half sent it hurtling into the roof of the net with Sorensen marooned on his goal-line.

As vast empty spaces appeared on the terracing where only minutes before Rangers' supporters had been cheering their team, as they thought, to victory over Celtic for the first time since the replayed Scottish Cup final 18 months ago, Lennox nipped in between two hesitant Rangers defenders and coolly clipped the ball home for Celtic's third goal.

Was there any wonder that Johansen left the field with his head held low? Yet the Dane, who incidentally scored the winning goal against Celtic in that replayed Cup Final, must not be made the whipping-boy. Basically, the blame for Rangers' defeat rests on all their shoulders. It was, to my mind, unwise of them to adopt a defensive policy after

Henderson had shot them into the lead in nine minutes from a pass by Penman.

OFFSIDE

That goal brought vigorous protests from several of the Celtic players, who clearly thought that Henderson was offside – and a similar occurrence was to happen in 31 minutes when Lennox scored what looked like a perfectly good goal, only to have it disallowed for offside.

Three minutes later a delightful Penman flick left Ferguson with only Simpson to beat, but he wildly shot past and the first half, which at times had been unduly abrasive, came to an end with Rangers hanging desperately on to their slender lead.

In the second half Celtic continued to exert great pressure, but somehow Rangers held on and even at times looked dangerous when they made the break from defence, as was illustrated when Johnston, in 52 minutes, struck the junction of the crossbar and the upright with a high floating cross.

Hereabouts the tacking on both sides made one wince, but the referee saw fit to take only the names of Gemmell, for an act of retaliation on Penman, and of Ferguson, for an over-zealous tackle of a Celtic defender.

Seconds after Ferguson's booking a young spectator uprooted a corner flag and, brandishing it in his right hand, dashed on to the field in front of the stand. A rugby tackle by Provan soon put an end to the intruder's capers, and he was escorted from the ground between two policemen.

Then it was back to the game and the continuance of the Celtic siege, interrupted only by the penalty kick miss which proved so fatal to Rangers and so beneficial to Celtic.

Scottish League Cup

Celtic (0) 3	Rangers (1) 1
Wallace	Henderson
Murdoch	
Lennox	

CELTIC:- SIMPSON; CRAIG AND GEMMELL; MURDOCH, MCNEILL AND CLARK; JOHNSTONE AND WALLACE; CHALMERS; AULD AND LENNOX. SUBSTITUTE – O'NEILL.

RANGERS:- SORENSEN; JOHANSEN AND PROVAN; JARDINE, MCKINNON AND GREIG; HENDERSON AND PENMAN; FERGUSON; D. SMITH AND JOHNSTON. SUBSTITUTE – WATSON.

Billy McNeill

The most successful club captain in the history of the British game, and one of the all-time greats as a powerful, dominating centre half, with the happy knack of coming forward to score vital goals, such as the winner in the 1965 Scottish Cup Final against Dunfermline. McNeill was Jock Stein's general on the field, and the man, known by his team mates as Caesar, led by example as Celtic totally dominated the domestic scene for almost a decade, and became the first British club to win the European Cup by beating Inter Milan 2-1 in Lisbon on May 25, 1967.

Born in Bellshill in 1940, he joined Celtic from Blantyre Victoria in 1957. He made his first team debut in a 2-2 League draw against Rangers at Parkhead in September 1958 and went on to take over from Bobby Evans as the regular centre half. McNeill has won more medals than any other British player – one European Cup, nine Championships, seven Scottish Cups, and six League Cups. He retired in 1975 after his last Scottish Cup Final appearance, against Airdrie, having played 831 matches for Celtic. He won 29 Scottish caps, was voted Footballer of the Year in 1965 and awarded the MBE in 1974. After retiring he managed Clyde, Aberdeen, Celtic (twice), Manchester City and Aston Villa.

Jimmy Johnstone

Arguably the greatest winger ever produced by Celtic, and one of the best ever seen on a footballing stage. Johnstone, born in Viewpark, Lanarkshire, in 1944, also had a fiery temperament to go with the red hair. If his talent had not been so exceptional, it is doubtful if any manager would have put up with him for very long, but Jock Stein stuck with him and was rewarded by magnificent consistency from the wee man.

It is a pity that Johnstone did not gain more than 25 caps for Scotland and that he never played in the World Cup Finals, but his achievements at club level included a European Cup medal, nine Championships, five Scottish Cups and five League Cups.

Johnstone scored more than 100 goals for the club, and after leaving in 1975, he had spells with San Jose Earthquake, Sheffield United, Dundee, Shelbourne and Elgin City before being reinstated as a junior with Blantyre Celtic, the club whom Celtic farmed him out to in the early sixties to gain experience. Jock Stein once remarked that one of his biggest achievements in football was in keeping Johnstone at the top level for as long as he did.

Tommy Gemmell

A swashbuckling, exciting left back who was really an extra forward for Celtic. His great strength in getting forward and his tremendous shooting ability brought him many vital goals for the club, including the equaliser in the 1967 European Cup Final against Inter Milan in Lisbon. He signed from Coltness United in 1961 and, apart from the European Cup, he went on to win six Championships, three Scottish Cups and four League Cups in more than 400 games for the club.

Gemmell also scored a spectacular goal in the 1970 European Cup Final which Celtic lost to Feyenoord in Milan, and played for Scotland 18 times.

He left Parkhead in December 1971 to join Nottingham Forest for a fee of £40,000 and two years later moved to Dundee, where he helped them win the League Cup in his first season – beating Celtic in the Final. Gemmell later managed Dundee and Albion Rovers.

Harry Hood

One of those players who took a long time to get where he should have been much earlier. Hood, born in Glasgow in 1944, was, and still is, a total Celtic man, yet he took a roundabout road to Parkhead, starting his senior career with Clyde before moving south to Sunderland in 1964. He didn't settle in the north-east of England, and within two years he was back with Clyde.

It wasn't until March 1969 that he eventually got the move he had been waiting for, a £40,000 transfer to Celtic under Jock Stein. The striker spent seven successful seasons at Parkhead, scoring more than 100 goals for the club. Was a big favourite of the fans, helped by the fact that many of his goals came in Old Firm games. In 1971 he scored the winner from the penalty spot in a replayed Scottish Cup Final against Rangers, but will best be remembered for his hat-trick against the Ibrox club in a 3-0 win in the Semi-finals of the League Cup in 1973.

With Celtic he won five Championship medals, three Scottish Cup and two League Cup winners' medals. Left the club on a free transfer in 1976 and played for Motherwell before trying his hand as manager at Albion Rovers and Queen of the South. Now a successful hotelier.

Rangers 1, Celtic 0 – Saturday, 18th September, 1967

Rangers Pay High Price for Victory Over Celtic

By Glyn Edwards

Rangers had to pay a high price for their victory over Celtic at Ibrox Stadium, their first against their arch-rivals since the replayed Scottish Cup Final of April of last year.

After the match it was confirmed that their Scottish internationalist left back, Provan, carried off after a tackle on Auld in four minutes, would be out of football for some three months with a broken leg. The actual injury is a traverse fracture of the tibia of the left leg, which is now in plaster.

CASUALTY LIST

Provan's injury was the worst of a tough, unrelenting Old Firm struggle, though others this morning will be nursing knocks of some description. Fortunately, with the European Cup tie with Kiev Dynamo coming up at Parkhead on Wednesday, Celtic escaped with only minor injuries, but Henderson required four stitches in a gash on his left shin as well as treatment to a scalp wound suffered in a clash of heads with Gemmell, and Johnston, who came on as substitute for Provan, finished the game with a twisted ankle. Both, however, expect to be fully fit by Wednesday, as indeed does Celtic's Craig who missed Saturday's match with a bruised foot.

With such a casualty list, no one will be surprised that the Old Firm game must take precedence over any other, because that is what the match is all about. Only a passing nod was given to the most elementary skills of the game; for the most part power, stamina and scarcely contained vigour rode roughshod over any consideration of disciplined and thoughtful football.

Some of the tackling was intimidating to say the least, and in this respect several players could feel extremely fortunate not to have had their names taken. As it was, a somewhat lenient Mr Syme saw fit to book only Chalmers, for the relatively minor offence of booting the ball away in anger after a free kick had been awarded against him.

One glaring misdemeanour which went unpunished was perpetrated by a Celtic defender midway in the second half, when with the ball nowhere in the vicinity, Johansen felt the full force of an unfriendly boot. How the referee, standing no more than 10 yards away and facing in the right direction, saw nothing untoward I will never know.

This is not to say that Celtic were the instigators of all the ankle-tapping, tripping, body checking, and verbal baiting which persisted. Far from it. Few of the Rangers players were knights in shining armour, as is proved by the fact that the Ibrox club had the doubtful distinction of being penalised for more fouls than their opponents.

In a game such as this which gave Rangers their narrow but deserved victory enterprise just had to bear the stamp of genius. Unless one did the unexpected at speed, there was little chance to evade the flying feet of the challenger – and Pearson's goal in 47 minutes was certainly the result of enterprise and fleetness of foot. McKinnon began the move with a deft lob to Pearson who, given instructions to make the whole field his beat, had wandered into the inside-right position. In a devastating run of some 30 yards he beat Gemmell on the inside, swerved past Murdoch and Clark, who moved in to challenge almost simultaneously, and then again side-stepped Gemmell, who had chased back to cover the route to goal.

Even then a goal seemed distinctly improbable as the angle was acute and the range about 18 yards, but Pearson, showing admirable control and coolness, wheeled round and cracked an unsavable left-foot shot past Simpson, who had made to come out.

Thereafter, as before, Rangers created – and scorned – more clear-cut chances than Celtic, and a particularly bad blunder at close quarters by Penman – he shot wildly over after a neat Ferguson head-flick had left the goal at his mercy – might have proved costly when in the dying seconds Johnstone burst through and made an equally sorry hash of a splendid opportunity to equalise. It was little wonder that Chalmers and Wallace, who were in better scoring positions, were annoyed with the little red-head after this wasteful act.

But in the end justice was done. The points were taken by the team who, on the day, had the least number of failures and the most accomplished players afield in Pearson, McKinnon and Smith, who, somewhat ironically, in falling back to left half after Provan's injury, had probably his finest game for Rangers.

Rangers (0) 1   **Celtic (0) 0**
Pearson

RANGERS:- SORENSEN; JOHANSEN AND PROVAN; JARDINE, MCKINNON AND GREIG; HENDERSON AND PENMAN; FERGUSON; D. SMITH AND PEARSON. SUBSTITUTE – JOHNSTON.

CELTIC:- SIMPSON; CATTENACH AND GEMMELL; MURDOCH, MCNEILL AND CLARK; JOHNSTONE AND WALLACE; CHALMERS AULD AND LENNOX. SUBSTITUTE – O'NEILL.

Celtic 2, Rangers 2 – Tuesday, 3rd January, 1968

Fallon Blunders Twice and Rangers Snatch Point

By Raymond Jacobs

It would be no surprise to learn that Fallon's complexion was a shade whiter for the last two minutes of the game at Celtic Park yesterday. For with that time remaining Simpson's deputy allowed a long shot from Johansen to pass under his body and Rangers to snatch what seemed like certain victory from Celtic's grasp.

Fallon was also at fault when Rangers scored their first goal, and so Celtic must have felt they were cruelly robbed of the points they needed to catch up with their rivals for the League Championship. Still, their own first goal was not exactly out of the footballer's manual.

Overall then, a drew was not an unfair ending to what had been a characteristically tough Old Firm battle. Rangers did not dominate the second half to quite the same extent as Celtic did the first, but from looking a well-beaten side at the interval, they forced themselves determinedly back into the game.

Up to half-time it looked as if Rangers' team, evidently chosen with gaining a draw in mind, would fail in their task. In the use of space and the fluency of their movements, Celtic had a decided edge and deserved to win even through a goal tinged with an element of luck.

Auld's free kick after 18 minutes was deflected by Jardine into his own net with Sorensen stranded out of range – a quick and savage retribution paid by the wing-half for having conceded the kick with his foul on Johnstone. Jardine's offence was, however, typical of Rangers' play at that stage.

Rangers were harassed by the unsettling influence on McKinnon of Hughes' power, and the running of Lennox, but above all by Johnstone's tortuous dribbling. The winger was brought down by Rangers' defenders almost on a rota system; the referee might have given him more protection than he did.

Yet for all that, Sorensen looked uncertain. He had few direct shots to deal with. Fallon, of course, had fewer, but this deficiency was soon corrected and it was Johnston, the most penetrative of Rangers' forwards in the first half, who began a stirring revival.

UNDER STRESS

Ten minutes after half time Johnston got a second shot at the ball and his shot squeezed between the kneeling knees of Fallon and rolled over the line. Celtic's defence than came under real stress for the first time and did not look so composed as Rangers' confidence grew.

In the next few minutes Penman and Watson came close and a corner from Persson almost went in direct at the far post. From another corner Johnston's header glanced wide, and so the battle raged up and down – hard and uninhibitedly tough.

But with 12 minutes remaining Celtic scored the goal they and most others thought was the winner. Brogan found Murdoch in the area, and the inside man, turning on less space than a handkerchief would cover, drove a magnificent left-foot shot away from Sorensen.

Before that Quinn had substituted for Auld, and A. Smith came on for Watson. But neither newcomer was concerned in the last dramatic minutes which were wrung from the game.

Celtic (1) 2	Rangers (0) 2
Jardine (o.g.)	Johnston
Murdoch	Johansen

CELTIC:- FALLON; CATTENACH AND GEMMELL; BROGAN, MCNEILL AND CLARK; JOHNSTONE AND MURDOCH; HUGHES; LENNOX AND AULD. SUBSTITUTE – QUINN.

RANGERS:- SORENSEN; JOHANSEN AND GREIG; JARDINE, MCKINNON AND D. SMITH; PENMAN AND WATSON; HYND; JOHNSTON AND PERSSON. SUBSTITUTE – A. SMITH

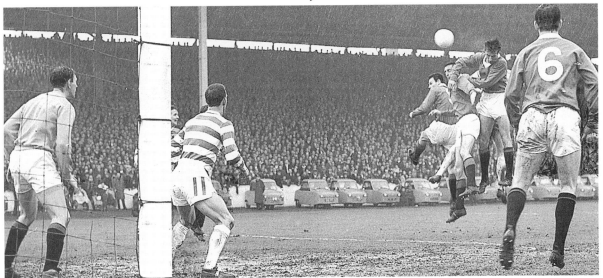

Provan and McKinnon clear a Celtic attack.

Rangers 0, Celtic 2 – Saturday, 10th August, 1968

Greig's Mistakes Lead to Celtic's Two Goals

By Glyn Edwards

"When all the breaks are going to the other side, there is nothing to do but wait for the luck to change." Such was the philosophical comment of one of Rangers' supporters as he left Ibrox on Saturday after his team's League Cup defeat.

In the circumstances, the viewpoint was understandable. He was referring to the fact that both Celtic goals, scored at vital stages of the game, were the direct result of uncharacteristic uncertainty by Greig and that, given a modicum of luck, Rangers might have drawn or even won a game which was sternly contested throughout but, apart from one or two isolated occasions, not unduly violent.

Yet, to me, this supporter failed to grasp the lesson. True, Celtic's goals could and should have been avoided. True, Simpson had three phenomenal saves in the second half and Hughes once headed off his own goal-line. But in fundamental ability, Celtic were the superior side. Whereas Rangers merely guessed, the Cup-holders appeared to know most of the answers, even to the amount of slack they could allow their opponents before they took the bait.

Not for one moment do I believe that Rangers enjoyed such territorial advantage as they did in the second half simply through their own efforts, spirited though they were. I am of the view that Celtic were so profoundly sure of themselves that they deliberately adopted a policy of containment.

Whether this was the right course of action to take is arguable, but the fact remains that Celtic were the winners, even if Simpson had to pull them out of a spot of bother on occasion. That is what he is there for in any case.

GOOD CHANCE

And for all Rangers' second-half pressure they could not create a scoring chance as positive as that which befell Lennox near the end. Put through by Johnstone, for this game Connelly's inside partner, Lennox was left all on his own with only Martin to beat.

This, for once, he could not do, but the move demonstrated the difference between the sides. Celtic, with thoughtful use of the ball, could create open space for themselves. Rangers had, or were allowed, so little room in which to manoeuvre that their shots at goal had almost invariably to travel upwards of 20 yards through a ruck of green-and-white jerseys.

BEST FORWARD

It could not be disputed either that more Rangers than Celtic players fell, for greater or lesser periods, below the standard of which they are known to be capable. Murdoch, McNeill and Brogan, for instance, were head and shoulders above their opposite numbers and Hughes was, in my view, the most productive forward afield.

And they had, too, the more secure goalkeeper in Simpson. Martin had several fine saves but his concentration seemed to lapse on occasion, such as when he allowed Lennox to block his kick-out and only a desperate retrieving act at the feet of the inside forward prevented a first-minute goal.

But if the first blunder went unpunished, not so Greig's eight minutes later. Connelly's pass intended for Johnstone, instead found Greig, who inexplicably allowed the ball to slither between his heels. Johnstone, on to it in a flash, failed in his attempt to round Martin, but the ball broke to Wallace, following up, and into the unguarded net it went.

PASSBACK

Greig's other tragic mistake came in 35 minutes. Under pressure by Lennox, Rangers' captain cut the ball back to his goalkeeper, only to see it swing away from him in flight and land tantalisingly in front of an empty goal. It looked to me that Martin should have saved, swerve or not, but in the event it was Wallace who got to the ball first, and that was Celtic two up.

That said, it only leaves for me to mention the bout of can throwing which led to hundreds of spectators behind the Celtic goal spilling over on to the track midway in the second half, the frequent arrests made by the police, and near the end an unwarranted act of aggression from Johnstone on D. Smith that should have led to his being booked, or, more suitably, sent from the field.

Scottish League Cup

Rangers (0) 0	Celtic (2) 2
	Wallace 2

RANGERS:- MARTIN; JACKSON AND MATHIESON; GREIG, MCKINNON AND D. SMITH; HENDERSON AND A. SMITH; PENMAN; FERGUSON AND PERSSON. SUBSTITUTE – JARDINE.

CELTIC:- SIMPSON; GEMMELL AND O'NEILL; MURDOCH, MCNEILL AND BROGAN; CONNELLY AND JOHNSTONE; WALLACE; LENNOX AND HUGHES.

Willie Johnston shoots past Clark to score in the 1968 Ne'er Day game.

Willie Wallace scores the only goal in Celtics 1-0 win in late August 1968 and his third against Rangers in a fortnight.

George Connelly scores Celtic's third in the 1969 Scottish Cup final.

Willie Henderson and Bobby Lennox.

Celtic 1, Rangers 0 – Saturday, 24th August, 1968

Power and Stamina Take Precedence Over Skill

By Glyn Edwards

The reputations of Rangers and Celtic are, one would have thought, worth at least trying to live up to. On Saturday at Parkhead, both teams gave the impression that they did not think so.

Power, stamina and scarcely contained vigour rode roughshod over any consideration of disciplined and thoughtful football, with the result that only a passing nod was given to the most elementary skills of the game, three players had their names taken, and others were fortunate not to be similarly dealt with.

Regrettably, this orgy of crudeness was not entirely unpredictable. There has been growing evidence recently that the viciousness on the terracings is beginning to communicate itself to the players and when the stick of anxiety not to lose is rubbed against that intense desire to win, sparks may quickly be expected to fly. Fortunately, the referee exerted enough authority to prevent a full scale fire.

The game had gone but 30 seconds or so when crudeness began to raise its ugly head, Jackson bringing down Lennox with a crushing tackle as the inside forward threatened to run clear of the entire Rangers defence. Thereafter, until the interval when, presumably, the players were instructed to calm down and thankfully obeyed, there were regular stoppages for infringements, the most serious of them leading to the booking of Hughes, Murdoch and Ferguson.

Why the two Celtic players had to be so dealt with was painfully obvious, especially to the man on whom they sought vengeance, Ferguson. Why the Rangers' inside forward was also brought to heel by the referee was less so, for after Murdoch had swung an ill-judged boot at him and both were summoned to be disciplined, the game was restarted with a free kick to Rangers.

But if the referee appeared to treat Ferguson somewhat harshly here, who could really blame him. The tense and emotionally-charged atmosphere at these games makes his job difficult enough without the hooliganism on the terracings spreading itself to the players.

Is it not about time anyway that the clubs themselves took steps to ensure that no violence creeps on to the field of play? How can they reasonably expect their supporters to pay heed to their appeals when some of the players show scant regard for the safety of others?

That said, Celtic, holders of the League Cup for the past three years, deserved to win and, to all intents and purposes, qualify for a quarter-final meeting with the winners of Section 7. What technique, ability and attacking ideas there were on view belonged almost entirely to them and, but for some splendid goalkeeping by Martin, they might well have scored sooner than they did.

The Rangers goalkeeper even saved a penalty by Gemmell, awarded in 73 minutes when Mathieson rashly upended Wallace near the bye-line, but he had no chance of saving the goal scored 18 minutes earlier. A snap-shot by Hughes from some 20 yards was touched onto the crossbar by Martin, and when the ball came down there were three Celtic players, Johnstone, Wallace and Lennox, waiting for it. The privilege of putting the ball in the net was given to Wallace who, thus, has now scored eight goals in four games.

DISMAL PERFORMANCE

It is not easy to be charitable to Rangers after such a dismally unimpressive performance. It may be presumed that at Ibrox as well as Parkhead, the training sessions include tactical exercises, but there was very little planning of their play here.

To have the diminutive Johnston at centre forward in direct opposition to the towering McNeill and then more often than not swing high balls into the goalmouth makes no sense at all to me. Nor does the dropping of Alex Smith in favour of Hynd. The one game this season in which Rangers were convincing was against Partick Thistle, and the former Dunfermline Athletic player had no small part to play then.

And when it was seen that Johnston was having so little success, why was Hynd not moved up to give added height and weight to the forwards? It looked like the obvious tactic to employ when so much emphasis was being placed on the lofted cross.

Scottish League Cup

Celtic (0) 1	Rangers (0) 0
Wallace	

CELTIC:- SIMPSON; GEMMELL AND O'NEILL; MURDOCH, MCNEILL AND BROGAN; JOHNSTONE AND CONNELLY; WALLACE; LENNOX AND HUGHES. SUBSTITUTE – JOHN CLARK.

RANGERS:- MARTIN; JACKSON AND MATHIESON; GREIG, MCKINNON AND HYND; PENMAN AND FERGUSON; JOHNSTON; D. SMITH AND PERSSON. SUBSTITUTE – A. SMITH.

Celtic 2, Rangers 4 – Saturday, 14 September, 1968

Rangers Victory gives Scottish Football New Life

By Glyn Edwards

The cheer which erupted from the terracing at Rangers' end of Parkhead when, in 89 minutes, Johnston headed in a lofted cross by Jardine was as much one of relief as of joy. In the preceding 10 minutes or so, it was touch and go whether Rangers would be able to hold on to their slender lead over Celtic.

In those dying moments of a game of which I have nothing but praise, having twice been two goals down, Celtic were summoning up all their reserves in a determined bid to salvage a point.

Then, just as they had done on umpteen occasions beforehand, Rangers broke quickly from deep defence with telling effect. From Henderson out on the left, the ball went across to the edge of the penalty area to Johnston, who in turn whipped it out to Jardine on the right. The Celtic defence was completely caught out and when the ball came back to the middle, there was Johnston to nod it in at Simpson's left hand post.

It was a goal from which Celtic had no time to recover, and one which ensured Rangers' first victory in an Old Firm match for exactly 12 months and their first at Parkhead since New Year's Day 1964. Moreover, it was a goal and a victory which must inject new life into the Scottish game, for had Rangers been defeated yet again by their arch-rivals the League Championship might well have been over before it had time to get off the ground.

They wisely decided to engage Celtic in the fresh air of open conflict, and with the champions' defence more easily harassed than might have been expected, it was a policy which paid off handsomely. With Celtic having to give best to Penman and Greig in midfield, Rangers' strikers, Persson and Johnston, enjoyed a field day.

POWERFUL PERSSON

During the Ibrox depression those two have come in for their share of criticism, but this time they amply justified their selection. Gemmell has rarely had a more uncomfortable afternoon than he had against the powerful Swede, and Johnston, showing the sharpness which made him the scourge of defences a season or two ago, was ever there or thereabouts to carry the fight to Simpson.

It was Persson who first brought hope to Rangers' followers that at last this was to be their day, when in fifteen minutes he completely flummoxed Simpson with a header. Having failed to penetrate Celtic's right flank, Mathieson changed the point of attack to the right, and when Henderson returned the ball into the middle Persson sent it hurtling diagonally past Simpson and in at the far post.

Barely a minute later Wallace, having taken the ball to the bye-line whipped it away from Martin and across an open goal, but Lennox was far too fast off the mark for his own good, and was in the back of the net before the ball arrived.

It was a glorious chance missed and one which was to be punished almost immediately, for a peach of a Penman pass caught McNeill off balance and sent Johnston darting through the middle with only the goalkeeper to beat. This he did by gliding the ball past Simpson as he rushed out to intercept.

Thus Rangers were two goals up, and to say that their supporters were ecstatic would be putting it mildly. Several even had to receive medical attention behind the goal after being caught up in the delirium.

SECOND CHANCE

But they were soon to be brought back to earth. In 29 minutes Connelly dispossessed Persson and sent a glorious pass out to Johnstone, who drew Martin to him and then clipped the ball across to the waiting Wallace. He had merely to tap it home. And four minutes later Lennox had the ball in the net again, but the goal was disallowed, presumably for offside.

Incident crowded upon incident thereafter. Johnstone struck the bar in the course of producing several mesmeric runs, and Martin and Simpson pulled off one magnificent save after another, but there were to be no more goals until, in 63 minutes, Penman hit home, at the second attempt, a Jardine cross.

But still Celtic were not finished. Wallace immediately reduced the arrears, swivelling round on a Lennox pass and deceiving Martin with a shot which slithered underneath his body.

Hereabouts Chalmers substituted for the tiring Connelly, but try as they did Celtic could not again produce the telling blow.

Celtic (1) 2	Rangers (2) 4
Wallace 2	Persson
	Johnston 2
	Penman

CELTIC:- SIMPSON; GEMMELL AND O'NEILL; BROGAN, MCNEILL AND CLARK; JOHNSTONE AND LENNOX; WALLACE; CONNELLY AND HUGHES. SUBSTITUTE – CHALMERS.

RANGERS:- MARTIN; JACKSON AND MATHIESON; GREIG, MCKINNON AND HYND; HENDERSON AND PENMAN; JARDINE; JOHNSTON AND PERSSON. SUBSTITUTE – D. SMITH.

Rangers 1, Celtic 0 – Thursday, 2nd January, 1969

Rangers Victory with Penalty Goal by Greig

By John Downie

Perhaps it is never wholly satisfactory to win by a goal from a penalty, and it is even less so to lose by one, but I do not imagine Rangers' supporters will have much fault to find with the means of beating Celtic in a stirring battle yesterday at Ibrox Stadium, and on the run of the match as a whole the followers of Celtic can have little to complain.

The goal came after exactly an hour's play, Greig scoring from the spot after McNeill had allegedly deflected a Henderson shot with his hand. Whether either side would have scored without such an award is open to speculation. Yet the goalless passages of the contest were in other respects by no means barren.

EAGER STEIN

With Watson at left half for Rangers and Penman in the forward line, both Persson and Greig found better form than they have shown for some time, and with a good supply of the ball from behind, such as Stein, Johnston and Henderson can be relied upon to keep things lively in attack.

Yet Celtic might well have scored first, for Johnstone produced one of those spectacular runs with the ball at his feet from some 20 yards inside his own half and finished it with a short pass to Wallace. But the centre forward was clearly offside as he shot into goal.

Celtic's wingers seemed their only hope. Their half-backs and backs, usually prolific contributors to attacks, were thoroughly pinned down in defence as Watson sent a stream of splendid passes down the left flank to Persson and the winger kept sending shots, crosses and cross-shots into Celtic's goalmouth. From one Watson-Persson move Stein beat Fallon after 15 minutes, but the whistle had sounded even as he shot, and Mr Webster indicated that he was awarding a foul for pushing.

RECOVERY

The next big scare for Celtic, one of the worst of the match, came in 22 minutes when Fallon's hands merely slowed down a hard, high drive from Persson, but the goalkeeper recovered like lightning, turning to pounce on the ball before Stein could get a foot to it just short of the line.

Wallace again looked at fault when he shot wide from in front of goal after a great run to the goal-line and cut-back pass by Hughes in 24 minutes, but a minute later Fallon magnificently saved a ground shot by Henderson at the post. After McNeill had tripped Stein, there was a furious Rangers onslaught in which Johansen struck the underside of the bar with a shot that beat the advancing

Fallon, and further shots by Persson, Johnston and Penman struck defenders, some of whom knew little about them. In 35 minutes Fallon just managed to touch over an angled shot by Stein.

When again Johnstone raised the hopes of Celtic, his cross found Wallace again offside. Perhaps the centre forward was nonplussed at a Rangers side so totally committed to attack that he just could not believe it.

CLEARANCE

Ten minutes after the interval Stein beat Fallon from a Johnstone cross, but his shot was acrobatically kicked out of goal by Brogan. Fallon then did well to kill Stein's short sharp pass into the goalmouth after a run to the bye-line. Hughes got clean away from the clearance, but as he ran in on Martin he shot straight at the goalkeeper.

Then came what proved to be the decisive Rangers attack. It ended when Henderson, some 20 yards out from goal, shot hard and straight. The ball ricocheted off McNeill and went away past Fallon's left post but the referee walked straight to the penalty spot, indicating that a hand had been used, and Greig's penalty kick gave Fallon no chance. Just how bleak the situation then looked for Celtic, even with half an hour to go, could be judged by the fact that their habitually cocky supporters were immediately silenced while the other end of the ground went wild with delight.

PACE DIES

Their apprehension was justified, for although their team was seen more in attack from then on, there was neither fire nor sparkle in their efforts. Chalmers, who replaced Wallace after 27 minutes of the half, seemed almost too literally determined to put up a fight, but did not receive the response one has come to expect from his team-mates.

Rangers, too, damped down their efforts somewhat – the pace they had set could not be maintained forever, especially in their second match in successive days. Yet most of the late shots of any consequence came from them. The game had already run into injury time when Provan was carried off with a knee injury and Jardine briefly took his place.

Rangers (0) 1	Celtic (0) 0
Greig (pen.)	

RANGERS:- MARTIN; JOHANSEN AND PROVAN; GREIG, MCKINNON AND WATSON; HENDERSON AND PENMAN; STEIN; JOHNSTON AND PERSSON. SUBSTITUTE – JARDINE.

CELTIC:- FALLON; CRAIG AND GEMMELL; BROGAN, MCNEILL AND CLARK; JOHNSTONE AND MURDOCH; WALLACE; LENNOX AND HUGHES. SUBSTITUTE – CHALMERS.

Celtic 3, Rangers 4 – Friday, 11th April, 1969

Johnston Scores Three Goals in Rangers' Win

Johnston was the architect of Rangers' victory last night at Parkhead in the Glasgow Cup Semi-final against Celtic, holders of the trophy, who were beaten in the last minute by a characteristic goal scored by the Ibrox club's inside left to make his tally for the night three.

Although decried in advance as a "second eleven" encounter because of the absence of regular players from both sides on World Cup preparations, the game was full of interest and had the 39,000 spectators on tenterhooks until the last kick.

The disadvantage of "absenteeism" seemed to rest more heavily with Celtic for whom Wallace and Chalmers, playing without customary support, lacked their usual fire. Rangers had less cause for complaint, because after a shaky start Jackson and Jardine struck a rich game and emerged triumphant when Celtic appeared set at least to draw.

Celtic took the lead in 13 minutes when Jackson faltered in clearing 30 yards out and Hood ran on to score, but soon afterwards Penman shook the crossbar with a powerful drive, and from the rebound Ferguson beat Fallon to the ball and equalised.

Just on the interval with a flash of inspiration, Rangers took the lead. Jardine swept the ball out to Persson, who, atoning for previous lapses, laid it on for Johnston, who glided it past Fallon.

Rangers were subjected to intense pressure after the interval, but having resisted it, at times luckily, they went further ahead after 30 minutes' play. Penman put through a perfect pass to Johnston, who hammered the ball past Fallon.

MARTIN BLUNDERS

Just after the hour Callaghan pulled back a goal for Celtic, and in 72 minutes they equalised as the result of a blunder by Martin, who fumbled a shot from Brogan and was beaten to the ball by Chalmers.

The issue swayed in the balance till the last minute, when Persson broke away on the left and crossed for Johnston to run the ball into the net and give his club the right to meet Partick Thistle in the final tournament.

Glasgow Cup Semi-Final

Celtic (1) 3	Rangers (2) 4
Hood	Ferguson
Callaghan	Johnston 3
Chalmers	
Attendance	39,000

CELTIC:- FALLON; CRAIG AND O'NEILL; BROGAN, HAY AND CLARK; WALLACE AND CONNELLY; CHALMERS; HOOD AND CALLAGHAN. SUBSTITUTE – McMAHON.

RANGERS:- MARTIN; JOHANSEN AND MATHIESON; JARDINE, JACKSON AND D. SMITH; HENDERSON AND PENMAN; FERGUSON; JOHNSTON AND PERSSON. SUBSTITUTE – A. MILLAR.

The young Fergie.

An Auld Celtic favourite.

Celtic 4, Rangers 0 – Saturday, 26th April, 1969

Celtic Take Heavy Toll of Rangers Blundering

By Glyn Edwards

Rangers got off on the wrong foot and Lennox finished hirpling painfully on one at Hampden Park on Saturday. That, in a nutshell, sums up the 1969 Scottish Cup Final. Celtic, with ruthless professionalism, took a heavy toll of their opponents' blunders and technical naivety, and play was noted more for its violence than artistic content.

Bluntly, the first half was a disgrace to football. Tackles were intimidating, even brutal. Man went for man, tripping, kicking, hacking, and jersey-pulling were rife. How on earth can the management of both sides raise their hands piously in horror against the hooliganism among their supporters when the players themselves indulge in the orgy of crudeness which made this so unpalatable a spectacle.

The pattern of viciousness was set in the first minute, when McNeill rose from a tackle badly shaken and needing treatment to his face. Thereafter foul came upon foul. Players faced up to each other angrily at all points. Murdoch was twice fouled within the space of a few minutes. Brogan was booked after three abrasive tackles in quick succession. Ferguson was given a stern warning, another went to Chalmers, and still another to McKinnon . . . and so it went on. For such violent fronts as these, war correspondents should be employed and not sports writers.

SMALL MERCY

Thankfully much – though by no means all – of the football mayhem disappeared in the second half, though doubtless the state of the game then was responsible for that small mercy.

In the short time that was devoted to football as it should be played, we were able to admire the calm assurance of young Connelly, brought in as the suspended Johnstone's replacement at outside right, but employed almost solely in midfield. His was the one cool head on the field, and, fittingly, his mature appraisal of the situation was greatly responsible for the almost humiliating downfall of Rangers.

Connelly it was who, a minute from the interval, intercepted Persson's intended pass to Mathieson near the halfway line and clipped the ball forward to Lennox, lurking in the clear. Off Lennox went like a scalded cat, pausing only briefly in his stride just inside the penalty box, shooting in at the far post as Martin came out to narrow the angle.

And Connelly it was who applied the coup de grace seconds later – again by kind courtesy of the men in blue. Martin attempted a short kick-out to the unsuspecting Greig. He lost possession to Connelly, who ambled in on Martin, took the ball past him easy as you please and, before it had crossed the line, was waiting, matador fashion, to receive the acclaim he undoubtedly deserved.

Three-nothing for Celtic. It seemed scarcely believable. For until that fateful minute it had seemed only a matter of time before Rangers nullified the goal scored by McNeill

in the second minute, when the centre half rose unchallenged to Lennox's corner kick and sent a curving header in off the far post while the Rangers defenders were marking no one but their own team-mates.

With a quarter of an hour gone Fallon dropped to his left to save superbly from Persson when Mathieson and Smith had combined to destroy Celtic's defensive curtain. In 33 minutes Fallon could only push out a powerful Greig shot, and Ferguson fell over as he rushed to meet the rebound. In 38 minutes Henderson, right through on a pass from Ferguson, slammed the ball high over, and six minutes later Johnston, in an ideal position to score from another Ferguson pass, made a sorry hash of the kick.

BEST GOAL

Predictably, with Rangers resigned to their first defeat in a Scottish Cup Final in 40 years and Celtic assured of their third major trophy of the season, the second half was merely a case of players going through the motions. Yet it did provide the best goal of the game, some astonishing goalkeeping at both ends, a hard-luck story for Lennox and, sadly, more ill-temper and a break-in.

The break-in occurred immediately after Chalmers scored Celtic's fourth goal in 76 minutes. The sight of the inside right boring in on Rangers' goal from the left, after Auld had done the initial damage, and chipping the ball into the net over Martin's right shoulder, was apparently too much for certain individuals on the Mount Florida terracing, and hundreds spilled over on to the track to avoid the trouble behind.

Lennox's ill luck came shortly after Clark had substituted for the injured Brogan in 56 minutes – and yet again it derived from blundering play by Rangers' defence. Martin and McKinnon both tried to clear a cross by Gemmell, both failed lamentably, and Lennox head-lobbed the ball onto the junction of crossbar and post as the goalkeeper strove to regain his ground.

Not did it matter a hoot that Fallon brought off a superlative save from Johnston in the dying minutes – except that it could have convinced the Celtic contingent in a crowd of 132,000 that the goalkeeper can now be trusted implicitly.

Scottish Cup Final

Celtic (3) 4	Rangers (0) 0
McNeill	
Lennox	
Connelly	
Chalmers	
(at Hampden Park)	
Attendance	132,000

CELTIC:- FALLON; CRAIG AND GEMMELL; MURDOCH, MCNEILL AND BROGAN; CONNELLY AND CHALMERS; WALLACE; LENNOX AND AULD. SUBSTITUTE – CLARK.

RANGERS:- MARTIN; JOHANSEN AND MATHIESON; GREIG, MCKINNON AND D. SMITH; HENDERSON AND PENMAN; FERGUSON; JOHNSTON AND PERSSON. SUBSTITUTE – JARDINE.

Rangers 2, Celtic 1 – Wednesday, 13th August, 1969

Baxter Shines in Rangers' Cup Triumph

Rangers, playing with great spirit and determination, shattered the more fancied Celtic in their League Cup sectional tie last night at Ibrox Stadium.

The turning point came when, in the third and fourth minutes of the second half, Rangers levelled and then drew ahead. Thereafter they were the dominant team and did not allow Celtic to develop the rhythmical game of which they are capable.

Another Celtic triumph appeared a possibility when they took the lead after eight minutes' play through Hood, who made the most of a careless back-pass by Provan and scored at his leisure.

Justifiably they led at the interval, for they had been a much more composed and workmanlike side than Rangers, who, apart from brief spells of militancy, seemed to have no settled plan of campaign.

INSPIRED

It was a very different story in the second half. The equaliser scored by Persson, and the leading goal nodded in by Johnston from Greig's service after a Baxter free kick, inspired the home side.

Masterminds in Rangers' triumph were Baxter and Johnston. Once the team had snatched the lead Baxter took command, spreading play coolly and efficiently and dictating the pace of the game.

Given all the time and space he needed by an unsettled Celtic defence, he revelled in this freedom and was the outstanding player in midfield. Unfortunately for him, he fell foul of the referee for an act of gamesmanship late in the game when Celtic were preparing to take a free kick, and had his name taken.

Earlier Gemmell was booked for disputing the referee's decision when Celtic players claimed a penalty kick.

Johnston, whether operating on right or left, had Celtic's defence in the jitters and they never pinned him down.

What came over Celtic? They lost Murdoch early in the game with a leg injury, whereupon Auld came on, but that had no great bearing on the ultimate issue.

The fact is that Rangers' swift and incisive tackling knocked them out of their stride. For Rangers the result was a great boost for their morale, and for Celtic a reminder that they may not get things all their own way in the sterner tasks which lie ahead in the League competition.

Scottish League Cup - Section

Rangers (0) 2	Celtic (1) 1
Persson	Hood
Johnston	

RANGERS:- NEEF; JOHANSEN AND PROVAN; GREIG, MCKINNON AND BAXTER; JOHNSTON AND WATSON; STEIN; JARDINE AND PERSSON. SUBSTITUTE. SMITH

CELTIC:- FALLON; HAY AND GEMMELL; MURDOCH, MCNEILL AND CLARK; CONNELLY AND HOOD; WALLACE; LENNOX AND HUGHES. SUBSTITUTE – AULD.

Celtic 1, Rangers 0 – Wednesday, 20th August, 1969

Gemmell Takes Advantage of Blunder by Neef and Gives Celtic Victory

A blunder by goalkeeper Neef cost Rangers the League Cup sectional tie last night at Celtic Park.

He failed to hold the ball after Murdoch had taken a free kick from the angle of the penalty area, and Gemmell bobbed up to nod it into the net.

The goal, scored midway in the second half, came at a time when Celtic appeared likely to have to settle for a draw, for their forwards were making little or no impression on Rangers' defence, in which the half-back line was rock-like in its solidarity.

Not that Rangers' attack was any more potent. For the first 60 minutes or so the team looked more composed than Celtic but, like their opponents, they were short of ideas when it came to breaching the dykes.

What was lacking originality in attack; progress was made – on orthodox lines – and barred within shooting distance by defenders who read the game perfectly.

After they had scored, Celtic were a much more confident side and Johnstone, who earlier tried to take on too many opponents and ran into trouble, switched play adroitly, so that Celtic finished the stronger and more accomplished team.

It was a hard game, in which the tackling by several players on both sides was less than scrupulous, but it was great entertainment for the 70,000 crowd, even though the proceedings were marred by the bookings of Murdoch, Hughes and McKinnon.

Within the last quarter of an hour Brogan came on for Lennox and Penman replaced Henderson, but the changes had no effect on the result, which leaves the sectional championship in the balance between Rangers and Celtic – with perhaps the latter qualifying on goal average.

Scottish League Cup - Section

Celtic (0) 1	Rangers (0) 0
Gemmell	
Attendance	70,000

CELTIC:- FALLON; CRAIG AND GEMMELL; MURDOCH, MCNEILL AND CLARK; JOHNSTONE AND HOOD; WALLACE; LENNOX AND HUGHES. SUBSTITUTE – BROGAN.

RANGERS:- NEEF; JOHANSEN AND PROVAN; GREIG, MCKINNON AND SMITH; HENDERSON AND JARDINE; STEIN; JOHNSTON AND PERSSON. SUBSTITUTE – PENMAN.

Rangers 0, Celtic 1 – Saturday, 20th September, 1969
Craig Ordered off in Stormy Game
By Glyn Edwards

What is it about Willie Johnston of Rangers that makes him the prime target for the wrath of Celtic? A month ago at Parkhead, it was he who was involved in the incident with Hughes which was to have such regrettable repercussions. It was also Johnston who on Saturday at Ibrox fell victim to the ruthlessness which led to the ordering off of Craig midway through the second half.

Three players had already been booked – Brogan, Hay and Jardine – and others, including the two captains, McNeill and Greig, had been given stern warnings when this tough, uncompromising struggle suddenly and unexpectedly developed into open warfare. Johnston and Craig chased the ball unavailingly to the touchline, and the winger was in the process of retrieving it for the throw-in when he was cruelly struck down from behind.

What prompted Craig to indulge in such wilful barbarism only he – and perhaps Johnston – knows, but certainly it was completely out of character with the player. He normally has the most placid of temperaments, and of all the players on the field, he is the one who would be least expected to involve himself in the troubles which invariably surround Old Firm games.

Still, he did aim a kick at Johnston on this occasion, with such viciousness that there could only have been one outcome. So Celtic were left to defend a one goal lead for 23 minutes a man short.

DROPPED BACK

Ironically the best football of the afternoon came from Celtic when they were thus undermanned. Hay, a surprise choice at inside left, dropped back to his accustomed position of right back, but no call went out from McNeill for his men to man the barricades. There was no need to for, apart from Johnston, none of the Rangers forwards looked disposed even to make a fight of it.

This aspect of Rangers' performance was undoubtedly the most galling for the Ibrox management. A goal down against a team reduced to 10 men, Rangers would have been expected to launch a full-scale offensive, but none materialised. Too many Rangers players seemed all too ready to accept defeat – ignominious defeat too, for their opponents to start with were far below recognised full strength.

It is perhaps an indictment of Rangers' deficiencies that a half-back, Greig, came nearest to nullifying the goal

scored in 49 minutes by Hood, who cleverly controlled McNeill's lofted clearance, hoodwinked McKinnon and then, as Neef wondered about coming out and Greig rushed in to challenge, cracked a great shot from eight yards just inside the goalkeeper's right-hand post. Four minutes later Greig burst past three Celtic defenders on the right flank, but his shot was just an inch or so too high and the ball thudded against the face of the crossbar and came back into play.

Had Greig equalised then, or had Baxter (significantly, another half-back) scored as he should have done when in 24 minutes he was put clean through by Jardine, things might well have turned out differently. But the plain fact was that even without Murdoch, Connelly, Hughes and the others, Celtic were the better team and thoroughly deserved their first League win at Ibrox for 12 years.

FINE SAVES

For Rangers, only Neef (who distinguished himself with several magnificent saves), Johansen, McKinnon, Provan, Greig and Johnston took any lasting credit from the game, played in unceasing rain and on a slippery surface. Their efforts were not nearly enough to bring victory over Celtic, whose outstanding talents were more evenly spread throughout the team.

If Fallon, McNeill, Gemmell and Clark were pillars of strength in the Celtic defence, they were complemented in the fine play in attack by Hood, Johnstone and Lennox – and herein, of course, lay the basic difference between the two sides.

Yet, for all that, the star man afield was, to my mind, the referee. When the stick of anxiety not to lose is rubbed against the intense desire to win (generally speaking in the case of Rangers) sparks may quickly be expected to fly. They duly did – but thankfully Mr Wharton exercised enough authority to prevent a full-scale fire.

Rangers (0) 0	Celtic (0) 1
	Hood

RANGERS:- NEEF; JOHANSEN AND PROVAN; GREIG, MCKINNON AND BAXTER; HENDERSON AND JARDINE; STEIN; SMITH AND JOHANSEN. SUBSTITUTE – WATSON.

CELTIC:- FALLON; CRAIG AND GEMMELL; CLARK, MCNEILL AND BROGAN; JOHNSTONE AND HOOD; WALLACE; HAY AND LENNOX. SUBSTITUTE – CHALMERS.

Murdoch grabs the ball after the referee had given a foul against Rangers.

Colin Stein scores just before the final whistle in the 1971 New Year game.

The Seventies

This decade saw not only great change for Scottish football as a whole, but for the Old Firm in particular. League reconstruction saw the introduction of a ten-club Premier Division, and, subsequently, the emergence of the New Firm of Aberdeen and Dundee United. The national side qualified for two World Cup finals and managers came and went at Ibrox and Parkhead.

Willie Waddell, who guided Rangers to their dramatic European Cup Winners' Cup triumph over Moscow Dynamo in Barcelona in 1972, made way for Jock Wallace, who steered the club to two trebles. Wallace then surprisingly left for Leicester in 1978 and the reins were handed to club captain John Greig. At Parkhead, the great Stein era also came to an end in 1978. Never quite the same after being involved in a horrendous car accident, he stepped aside in 1978 to make way for former club captain McNeill, who was then manager of Aberdeen.

One of the great Old Firm matches of the seventies was the centenary Scottish Cup final of 1973 when Tom Forsyth scored the winning goal for Rangers in a 3-2 triumph. Mind you, the big fellow almost did the impossible which would have been missing from two feet.

With Jock Wallace at the helm, Rangers then halted Celtic's incredible run of nine successive titles by winning the Championship in season 1974-75, the last before league reconstruction. They also won the first ever Premier Division title before Celtic struck back in 1977. That season Celtic won two of the Old Firm league matches and drew the other. The Parkhead men also won the Scottish Cup, beating Rangers 1-0 in the final at Hampden, with Andy Lynch scoring from the penalty spot.

That success for Celtic was sandwiched between Rangers' two Trebles under Wallace, and the decade drew towards a close with two dramatic Old Firm matches in season 78-79. The first was in a League Cup Semi-final at Hampden in December when Rangers' won 3-2 with goals from Sandy Jardine, Colin Jackson and Jim Casey (o.g.). Johnny Doyle and Tom McAdam scored for Celtic. Then in the last league match of the season, on May 21, the teams met in what was a league decider before a crowd of 52,000 at Parkhead. This time Celtic triumphed with Roy Aitken, George McCluskey, Murdo MacLeod and Colin Jackson (o.g.) scoring in a 4-2 victory.

Celtic 0, Rangers 0 – Saturday, 3rd January, 1970

Rangers Recharge Themselves for Even Greater Effort

By Jim Parkinson

Celtic and Rangers were subdued by the frost-bound conditions at Parkhead in their opening duel of the 1970's and, almost out of character, the match will be remembered for its sporting friendliness and being completely free of controversy.

Nothing vitally important in the League Championship situation was decided and, in keeping with the mood, the behaviour of the 72,000 spectators could hardly have been better.

As a spectacle, the greatest club match in the world shrank to ordinary proportions, but it was not the fault of the players, who had to guard against serious injury on the icy bone-hard surface.

In the circumstances neither team will quibble at the no-scoring draw, although Rangers, the underdogs on this occasion, will, perhaps, exact a great deal more satisfaction from the game. They prevented Celtic from taking an overwhelming points lead in the table and psychologically have recharged themselves for even greater effort in their remaining 13 Championship matches.

Mr Willie Waddell, Rangers' manager, could not praise his players highly enough in this game, which was his first Old Firm engagement since he took charge of the team.

Dave Smith was certainly the complete footballer. He refused to be dominated by the opposition or the conditions, and gave a display that surely must rank as his best in a Rangers jersey.

It is only within the last few weeks that Rangers followers have taken the ex-Aberdeen player to their hearts, and now he has really made his niche. The sheer elegance and skill of Smith did not end with his defensive work. Self-assuredly he built up many of Rangers' attacks.

Alex MacDonald and Billy Mathieson, two other players who have not been wholly accepted by Rangers in the past, also can look forward to a more stable future. MacDonald had an excellent first half against young David Hay, and Mathieson was always the master of Jimmy Johnstone.

It was one of the surprising features of the match that Johnstone and Willie Henderson should be so out of touch on conditions that might have been more suitable for them than some of the heavier-built players. Henderson was replaced in the second half by Sandy Jardine. Billy McNeill, for instance, did not show the slightest concern on the slippery pitch, and with Jim Brogan provided Celtic with their top partnership.

The centre half had only one regret and that came a minute from the interval when it appeared his enterprise for going downfield for corner kicks had paid off again. He headed the ball into the net, but referee Mr John Paterson, who handled his first Celtic-Rangers match competently, promptly disallowed it because of a prior infringement. It was the nearest Celtic came to winning the game, apart from a Bertie Auld corner kick which was played onto the post by Neef in the second half.

TWO BOOKINGS

Brogan's scurrying style contrasted with the majestic McNeill, but the wing half effectively repelled many of Rangers' raids; his only flaw was the foul on John Greig which brought him a booking in the second half. It was the second caution of the game. Ronnie McKinnon had earlier been dealt with by the referee for a harsh tackle on Willie Wallace.

The two incidents were completely isolated in an otherwise well-mannered game. Mr Paterson's quick action on both occasions prevented the tension from building up.

Celtic bravely pitched Evan Williams into the arena for this important match and the ex-Wolverhampton Wanderers goalkeeper did not give them any anxious moments. He was probably the busier of the two goalkeepers and showed plenty of agility in cutting out high crosses and, in the first half, in turning a Johansen lob over the bar.

Rangers' unsuccessful transfer on the eve of the match for Bobby Clark, the Aberdeen goalkeeper, must have had an inspiring effect on Gerry Neef. Apart from being beaten by McNeil's header, he was in complete command. He was dazed momentarily near the end when he made a daring save and collided with John Hughes.

Williams also took some hard knocks in the second half and had to have attention from the trainer.

After the match both managers said they had no injuries to cause them concern.

Celtic (0) 0	Rangers (0) 0
Attendance	72,000

CELTIC:- WILLIAMS; HAY AND GEMMELL; MURDOCH, MCNEILL AND BROGAN; JOHNSTONE AND HOOD; WALLACE; AULD AND HUGHES. SUBSTITUTE – CRAIG.

RANGERS:- NEEF; JOHANSEN AND MATHIESON; GREIG, MCKINNON AND SMITH; HENDERSON AND PENMAN; STEIN; JOHNSTON AND MACDONALD. SUBSTITUTE – JARDINE.

Celtic 3, Rangers 1 – Saturday, 21st February, 1970

Celtic Triumph but Old Firm Cup-Tie Best Forgotten

By Jim Parkinson

Perhaps we should feel relieved at being spared the harassing ordeal of an Old Firm Scottish Cup replay on another battleground this week, with its attendant risk of an even greater outbreak of football violence.

In one of the most hateful confrontations between the Glasgow sides for years, few players emerged with any lasting credit in this best forgotten quarter-final tie at Parkhead.

The referee, Mr Tom Wharton, was always in the midst of ugly controversy, and there was even severe criticism of his decision to send off Alex MacDonald without a reprimand for Jim Brogan when he became involved in the incident.

In the circumstances, it would be inevitable that trouble should spread to the terracings. It may be tremendously difficult for players to detach themselves from the high-powered tension of the game and all that is at stake. There was, however, no excuse for the thoughtless act by two Rangers players which, to my mind, set the seal for the fierce enmity which followed.

The flame was put to the powder-keg when Jim Craig headed the ball into his own goal in six minutes. His misery was mirrored in head-down bewilderment when Willie Johnston ran to him and ruffled the Celtic full-back's hair. In mock congratulations, Colin Stein then supplied the second provocative act by running over to give Craig a "well done" slap.

The referee overlooked the incident, but sternly rebuked Billy McNeill, for his overbearing protest about the Rangers pair. McNeill was booked later for dissent, and John Greig and Billy Mathieson were also cautioned.

A tactical switch turned the game in Celtic's favour. David Hay, fielded at inside left in place of Bertie Auld, exchanged roles with Bobby Murdoch. The youngster was allotted the task of checking the forward surges of Greig, and he not only succeeded in this but crowned his day by shooting the magnificent 25-yard match-winning second goal four minutes from the end. Murdoch had a comparatively easy time against Alfie Conn, who was replaced early in the second half by Willie Henderson.

Hay's play was a revelation, although Rangers probably possessed the most skilful player of all in Davie Smith. The wing half's class and accuracy in passing on a heavy ground that cut up badly shone beacon-like through Rangers' best period, in the opening 15 minutes, and did not diminish even when his depleted side were trying to hold out for a replay.

LUCKY ESCAPE

Whereas Neef was constantly in action in Rangers' goal, Williams was seldom troubled. Neef was particularly fortunate in the fourth minute when a Lennox shot beat him and was kicked out by MacDonald. The Celtic players protested that the ball had gone over the line, and certainly this seemed to be the case.

Hughes having earlier hit the post, Celtic deservedly equalised in 39 minutes with a Lennox shot that deflected off Neef into the net.

In the second half Lennox collided with Neef, and though the goalkeeper required treatment, the referee saw nothing remiss in Lennox's challenge.

The incident may, however, have influenced MacDonald to go in with a leg outstretched on Williams, smothering the ball on the ground, in 62 minutes. While the goalkeeper lay on the ground, surrounded by jostling players, Brogan appeared to push MacDonald off his feet. The referee broke up the melee and, once calm was restored, sent MacDonald off. Rangers waited for further action from the referee, but none came and they were then committed to playing for a draw. They looked like achieving their aim too – until Hay settled the issue with his spectacular goal. Celtic's third goal, scored by Johnstone a couple of minutes later, merely emphasised the superiority of the Cup-holders.

The toughness of the encounter can be assessed from the fact that Celtic have four casualties – Williams, Murdoch, Hughes and Wallace – and only the last-named has any reasonable hope of playing against Raith Rovers on Wednesday.

The Rangers players who required treatment were Johnston, Mathieson and Henderson. Greig and Penman also took knocks, but did not find it necessary to report to Ibrox yesterday for treatment.

Scottish Cup Quarter-Final

Celtic (1) 3	Rangers (1) 1
Lennox	Craig (o.g.)
Hay	
Johnstone	

CELTIC:- WILLIAMS; CRAIG AND GEMMELL; MURDOCH, MCNEILL AND BROGAN; JOHNSTONE AND LENNOX; WALLACE; HAY AND HUGHES. SUBSTITUTE – HOOD.

RANGERS:- NEEF; JOHANSEN AND MATHIESON; GREIG, MCKINNON AND SMITH; PENMAN AND CONN; STEIN; MACDONALD AND JOHNSTON. SUBSTITUTE – HENDERSON.

Celtic 2, Rangers 0 – Saturday, 12th September, 1970

Celtic Technique Commands Respect

By Glyn Edwards

If Jock Stein looked on Saturday as something of an anniversary, being as it was the twenty-fifth time Celtic had met Rangers since he took over the managerial reins at the Parkhead club five-and-a-half years ago, he could not have wished the occasion to be more fittingly marked.

Not only did his team register their fourteenth win over Rangers under his direction, they did so in a manner which left little room for doubt that they can yet again sweep the boards in domestic competition.

Frankly, the two teams were poles apart in technique. Whereas Rangers relied almost solely on hopeful endeavour to carry them through, Celtic were both authoritative and composed – indeed, too composed.

EXCEPTIONAL TALENTS

McGrain, McNeill, Connelly and Brogan formed a seemingly impenetrable barrier in front of the goalkeeper, Williams, and if Connelly is singled out for special mention, it is because his exceptional talents are not restricted to defence. No-one on either side has his in-born gift of being able to read a situation so correctly and play so severely on the frailties of the opposition.

It was Connelly who set the pattern for the game when in six minutes he first broke through a Rangers attack and pushed through a low pass to Johnstone which had the Ibrox defenders scurrying back in desperate retreat. All Miller could do was concede a corner, from which Hughes headed into the net through the legs of Jardine.

Considering that Brogan had made a sorry hash of a penalty kick four minutes earlier, after Hughes had been the victim of a singularly late tackle by McKinnon, it was quite remarkable that Celtic were able to maintain their equilibrium and take command of the game so early.

There was little wrong with Rangers' defensive play, but with Greig taken out of the game completely by Hay and with Conn only slightly more in evidence, it was largely down to MacDonald to provide a midfield foundation on which the Ibrox forwards could build.

Celtic's forwards, on the other hand, were rarely without adequate support, and this point was forcibly emphasised when, in 55 minutes, Murdoch came up to put the issue beyond all doubt with a shot from the edge of the box so venomous that the noise of it hitting the stanchion behind McCloy reverbated all around the ground.

Celtic (1) 2	Rangers (0) 0
Hughes	
Murdoch	

CELTIC:- WILLIAMS; MCGRAIN AND HAY; MURDOCH, MCNEILL AND BROGAN; JOHNSTONE AND CONNELLY; HOOD; LENNOX AND HUGHES. SUBSTITUTE – DAVIDSON.

RANGERS:- MCCLOY; JARDINE AND MILLER; GREIG, MCKINNON AND JACKSON; FYFE AND MACDONALD; STEIN; JOHNSTON AND CONN. SUBSTITUTE – PENMAN.

Celtic 0, Rangers 1 – Saturday, 24th October, 1970

Rangers Transform League Humiliation into Cup Jubilation

One of the most remarkable aspects of the Scottish League Cup Final at Hampden Park was that, with only two exceptions, Rangers' winning side was composed of the men who were humiliated on the previous Saturday by Aberdeen at Ibrox Stadium.

The transformation in their play in relieving Celtic of the trophy they had held for five seasons in a row was indeed astonishing. With a great team effort, particularly in the first half, they almost incessantly had Celtic on the defensive.

Indeed, there were two spells – just before the interval and in the last 10 minutes– when Celtic seized the initiative and Rangers' supporters were on tenterhooks as Murdoch and Johnstone urged on their forward colleagues.

Also contributing to the victory were the tactics employed in attack – to harry the opposition by striking them on the flanks. Johnston and Henderson did just that and, with the 16-year-old Johnstone D. leading from the orthodox (or should it be "old-fashioned") centre-forward position, the line had a fluency Celtic lacked.

The goal which settled the issue was nicely conceived and executed. From Henderson's pass MacDonald passed the ball out to Johnston and when the cross came over Johnstone D. crisply headed past Williams.

The goal, scored after 40 minutes play, was just the tonic Rangers needed, and after the interval they showed great determination in holding on to their lead, although they were lucky to retain it when Murdoch, with four cunningly-placed free kicks, had the Ibrox defence in temporary confusion on the six-yard line.

The escapes then were as naught compared to the one around the 70-minute mark. Murdoch dribbled past four opponents inside the penalty area and laid the ball on for Wallace, who shot high over the bar; with it went Celtic's hopes of the equaliser.

Scottish League Cup Final

Celtic (0) 0	Rangers (1) 1
	Johnstone D.
(at Hampden Park)	
Attendance	106,263

CELTIC:- WILLIAMS; CRAIG AND QUINN; MURDOCH, MCNEILL AND HAY; JOHNSTONE J. AND CONNELLY; WALLACE; HOOD AND MACARI. SUBSTITUTE – LENNOX.

RANGERS:- MCCLOY; JARDINE AND MILLAR; CONN, MCKINNON AND JACKSON; HENDERSON AND MACDONALD; JOHNSTONE D.; STEIN AND JOHNSTON.

Bobby Lennox

Another of the Lisbon Lions, "Lemon", as he was nicknamed, signed a provisional form for Celtic in 1961 while with Ardeer Recreation. He made his League debut against Dundee the following year and that was the start of a remarkable career which spanned more than 500 matches, bringing him 272 goals. He was, without doubt, the quickest player of his era and a great favourite with the fans.

His medal haul resembles a treasure trove – one European Cup, nine Championships, eight Scottish Cups and four League Cups. He also won ten caps for Scotland, scoring a goal in the 3-2 defeat of the then World Champions England at Wembley in 1967. Season 1966-67 was, in fact, a memorable one for the little Ayrshire flier. Apart from the European Cup, and that goal against England, he scored the winning goal against Rangers in the League Cup final, and a hat-trick against the Ibrox side in a Glasgow Cup tie.

Lennox, who was also the first man to score a hat trick in the Premier Division, retired from the playing side in 1980 and took up a post as reserve team coach at Parkhead. The following year he was awarded an MBE.

John Hughes

Big Yogi, born in Coatbridge, was a member of the most successful Celtic squad ever, but missed out on the glory of Lisbon, although he played in the side beaten in the European Cup Final three years later. He was a bit of an enigma, either blowing hot or cold, but when he was on form, the striker was virtually unstoppable, because of his strength on the run and an uncanny, delicate touch on the ball.

Joined Celtic from Shotts Bon Accord in 1960, and spent eleven years at Parkhead before being transferred to Crystal Palace along with Willie Wallace in 1971. In his time with Celtic, Hughes won six Championship medals, one Scottish Cup badge and was successful in four League Cup Finals. In the League Cup Final of season 1965-66, he scored with two penalty kicks in the 2-1 win over Rangers.

Probably his finest display, however, was in a league match against Aberdeen in January 1965, when he scored five times in Celtic's 8-0 victory at Parkhead. After being transferred to Crystal Palace, Hughes moved to Sunderland before retiring due to injury in 1973. He gained eight full caps and was the first ever manager of the Scottish Junior international side.

Kenny Dalglish

There are those who will tell you that Dalglish was the best player ever to have worn the hoops and few would argue with that. He was the complete player – and one who got away from Rangers. Sean Fallon signed him as a 16-year-old in 1967, despite the fact that Kenny, at that time, was a Rangers fan.

What he lacked in pace, he more than made up with a razor-sharp footballing brain, tremendous strength, and an outstanding ability on the ball. He scored more than 100 goals for Celtic and won four Championships, four Scottish Cups and a League Cup before signing for Liverpool in 1977 for a fee of £440,000 – then a record transfer between two British clubs. He also scored more than 100 goals for the Anfield side, and his honours with them included three European Cups and six Championships.

Dalglish, on the 102 mark, is the most-capped Scottish player. He was appointed player-manager of Liverpool in 1985 and steered them to a League and Cup double in his first season. Quit at the top with Liverpool, and, after a rest, returned to manage Blackburn Rovers, taking them to the Premiership title in 1995. He has an MBE and was made a Freeman of Glasgow.

Roy Aitken

There may have been some equal, but none more committed to the Celtic cause than Aitken, who was with the club for 15 seasons after signing as a full professional in 1970. He could perform equally well in the midfield or in defence, and he had much more skill than many critics gave him credit for. Many a time his driving force and uncompromising attitude turned a match for Celtic.

He was an inspirational player and that was typified on the night Celtic beat Rangers 4-2 at Parkhead to clinch the Championship in 1979. He was also outstanding in 1988 when, in the club's centenary year, he captained the side to the League and Cup Double. Club honours included five Championship wins, three Scottish Cup triumphs and a League Cup winners' medal. Aitken left Celtic to join Newcastle United for a fee of £500,000 in 1990, but returned to Scottish football within a year by signing for St. Mirren. He then moved to Aberdeen as player-coach and when Willie Miller lost his job as manager in 1995, Aitken was appointed in his place and he steered the club to Premier Division safety. Aitken also played for Scotland 50 times.

Rangers 1, Celtic 1 – Saturday, 2nd January, 1971
Tragedy Overshadows Good Behaviour of Ibrox Crowd

By Jim Parkinson

By an ironical twist of fate, the Old Firm match that, at long last, proved to be a milestone for exemplary crowd behaviour, and, in any case, would always have been remembered for the sheer breathless excitement of the final 60 seconds, paled insignificantly against Britain's worst football ground disaster.

Throughout the history of Rangers-Celtic duels football legislators and civic authorities have sought a solution to stamp out the violence and hooliganism that have become traditionally associated with the fixture. With only two arrests – for drunkenness – in an 80,000 all-ticket crowd, they could have congratulated themselves that the had been achieved at Ibrox Park.

The segregated spectators exchanged their rival chants and taunts between one terracing and the other; in comparison to previous years, these were minimal outbursts. Players of both teams contributed wholeheartedly to the mood of the occasion and Bill Anderson, the referee, controlled the game without incident.

On a bone-hard pitch, which was later to become an eerie clearing station in the freezing fog for the injured and the dead, mistakes were accepted tolerantly not only by the spectators, but by the players of the respective teams.

The strain gradually faded as the final minutes approached, both teams deadlocked without a goal and resigned to draw. The tightness of the contest kept the crowd inside the ground until those 60 seconds from the end which had unprecedented and tragic consequences.

With a single minute remaining, Jimmy Johnstone headed Celtic into the lead after Bobby Lennox's shot rebounded from the crossbar. Whereupon at the traditional Rangers end the disillusioned, disconsolate supporters turned to go down the steep terracing exit.

For them their team had gone past the point of no return; yet with a surging spirit Rangers did rally and Colin Stein, with a mere 15 seconds of the game remaining, equalised. The transformation on the terracings was incredible. Those down the exit steps made an attempt to clamber back into the ground and share in the jubilation. They were met by a flood-tide of their happy fellow supporters sweeping down uncontrollably on top of them.

It was a match Glasgow, Scotland, and, perhaps, the football world will never forget.

Rangers (0) 1	Celtic (0) 1
Stein	Johnstone J.
Attendance	80,000

RANGERS:- NEEF; JARDINE AND MATHIESON; GREIG, MCKINNON AND JACKSON; HENDERSON AND CONN; JOHNSTONE D.; SMITH AND STEIN. SUBSTITUTE – MACDONALD.

CELTIC:- WILLIAMS; CRAIG AND GEMMELL; BROGAN, CONNELLY AND HAY; JOHNSTONE J. AND HOOD; WALLACE; CALLAGHAN AND LENNOX. SUBSTITUTE – MACARI.

Glasgow Herald editorial leader from Monday, 4th January, 1971
Ibrox Park

The Ibrox Park disaster not only killed 66 people and injured many more – that would be tragedy enough – it was a tragedy exacerbated by appalling irony which, with cruel hours of uncertainty, tormented hundreds of thousands of relatives and friends who knew so quickly of the catastrophe, yet had so long to wait before they could be certain whether their own folk were safe. A tragedy on an epic scale, it befell one of the most famous, and notorious fixtures in the world of sport. After a contest which could easily have gone down in history as a triumph for sportsmanship and civilised spectating, with only two arrests from a crowd of 80,000, disaster struck, with a death-toll and innocent suffering which quite overshadow the violence and turbulence which in former years gave the contest its unhappy reputation. The people of Scotland, and perhaps those elsewhere in Britain, will understand that this was just a terrible coincidence of fate, that such imminent danger lurks wherever tens of thousands of people gather in an emotional atmosphere. Those further afield may not.

How recently, it seems, hooliganism was identified as the curse that afflicted professional sport. Until the final whistle yesterday there was hope that all the discussions, the innovations, the committees – among them the Lang working party – were bearing fruit – and so they were. But now the entire concept of ground safety as it stands today has been challenged. And the challenge is impressive not merely in the scale of the consequences, but in the scale of cost and effort required to attain new standards. In British sport, as in British industry, the penalty is now being paid for pioneering in the past. What were once considered the acme of sports arenas are now outdated in the light of modern building technology and standards of spectator amenity and safety. Alterations, such as tunnels to obviate the rush over-the-top to the exits, or seating under cover to stabilise the crowd, are of course desirable but the cost, on a national scale, would be astronomic.

These considerations must loom large in the deliberations of whatever type of inquiry the Secretary of State ultimately decides to set up. And yet Saturday's tragedy, triggered so innocently by the whim of human nature, is the kind which regulations and inspections can never entirely obviate. Nor will the future safeguards obviate the suffering of the survivors and the bereaved. The material wellbeing of the dependants can confidently be left to the generosity of the people of Glasgow, Scotland, and beyond; the emotional wounds can be healed by no gifts, or inquiries, legislation or words.

The scene at Ibrox Stadium after the tragedy when 66 people lost their lives on
2nd January 1971.

Celtic 1, Rangers 1 – Saturday, 8th May, 1971
Derek Johnstone Earns Rangers a Second Chance

By Jim Parkinson

Rangers' claim that this season they are a side more suitably geared to the rigours of Cup football does not sound nearly so extravagant now. With a great sense of occasion, they lifted their game to the heights again before 120,092 spectators in the Scottish Cup Final at Hampden, and although it required a remarkable goal by their 17-year-old substitute, Derek Johnstone, to keep them in contention, a replay on Wednesday night was no more than they deserved.

Johnstone, who last October scored the winning goal in Rangers' League Cup triumph over Celtic at the same ground, was brought back into the team to replace Penman in the final 20 minutes and completed a modern football fairy tale by heading the vital equaliser to give his team another life.

Celtic had been bafflingly thrown out of stride in the first half by a passionately determined Rangers team who wanted to prove themselves anything but underdogs. There is no doubt they succeeded and the Ibrox players revealed astonishing confidence, powerful running and intelligent passing which we do not see often enough from them.

It would have been a measure of their superiority had they gone three goals ahead before half-time. They had three outstanding chances and Willie Johnston could have made this Cup Final his own. Two of these wonderful opportunities fell to him, and there was another after the interval which he must sorely regret missing.

Penman whose skilful passes had seriously troubled Celtic, gave Stein and Johnston the first chance with a low cross. Both of them missed the ball. Then Johnston streaked through on his own only to be dispossessed by Williams throwing himself at the winger's feet.

With Celtic showing surprising hesitance, Rangers kept in control and a Jackson header flew across an empty goal with Stein reaching it just too late. The atmosphere was electrifying and crackled all the more with the impetus and drive of Rangers.

Then, with basic simplicity, Celtic scored in 40 minutes. The ball was played from their own goal, hooked on by Wallace to Hood, and he slanted the ball through to Lennox, who moved past Miller and shot into the far corner of the net. It seemed incredible as Celtic's only other worthwhile contribution in attack had been a fiery shot from Hood which McCloy saved early in the game.

The goal transformed Celtic. They became more sophisticated, whereas Rangers lost their earlier poise and became over-hurried in their attempts to move the ball downfield. Jimmy Johnstone began to show his trickery

and Lennox's speed caused more anxiety for Rangers on the other flank.

Celtic's composure resulted in Lennox cutting loose on two occasions. The first time he had no one to beat but McCloy, but the goalkeeper blocked the shot, and on his next attempt he shot into the side of the net. Had goals accrued then, the trophy would surely have gone to Celtic.

DEFIANT

When Celtic were in the ascendancy, McKinnon and Jackson were steadfastly defiant, and the young Ibrox full backs worked tremendously hard, perhaps not successfully all of the time, to cope with Jimmy Johnstone and Hood.

Faced with going for a life-saving equaliser, Willie Waddell decided to take off Penman and put on Derek Johnstone, and from the moment the youngster headed his first ball, Celtic were a little apprehensive in the air.

Rangers should have scored through Stein, but his shot from a Henderson back-heeled pass flew inches wide. And at the other end Jimmy Johnstone also shot from a good position after one of the best runs of the day.

Then, when all looked over for Rangers, a goal was engineered out of nothing. A throw out by McCloy to Willie Johnston was lobbed speculatively to the edge of the Celtic penalty area. The ball was allowed to bounce and Connelly was caught on the wrong side of young Johnstone, who with extra spring in his jump, nodded over the advancing Williams.

It was significant, too, that the main outbreak of crowd hooliganism occurred at the Mount Florida end when both teams were in their dressing rooms at the interval. When the teams reappeared the police were still dealing with the offenders, but the referee took one glance at the troublesome section and promptly restarted play, whereupon the terracing row immediately subsided. Perhaps on Old Firm occasions the S.F.A. and Scottish League should sanction a serious curtailment of the time allowed for an interval.

Scottish Cup Final

Celtic (1) 1	Rangers (0) 1	
Lennox	Johnstone D.	
Attendance	120,092	

CELTIC:- WILLIAMS; CRAIG AND BROGAN; CONNELLY, MCNEILL AND HAY; JOHNSTONE J. AND LENNOX; WALLACE, CALLAGHAN AND HOOD. SUBSTITUTE – MACARI.

RANGERS:- MCCLOY; MILLER AND MATHIESON; GREIG, MCKINNON AND JACKSON; HENDERSON AND PENMAN; STEIN; MACDONALD AND JOHNSTON. SUBSTITUTE – JOHNSTON D.

Celtic 2, Rangers 1 – Wednesday, 12th May, 1971

Celtic's Double with Two Goals in a Minute Against Rangers

By Jim Parkinson

As Arsenal have done in England, so Celtic completed the Scottish League and Cup double last night. Before 103,332 spectators at Hampden Park they won the Scottish Cup for the twenty-first time when, scoring two goals in a minute midway in the first half, one from a penalty, they beat Rangers in the replay of the Final.

The double blow broke Rangers, who had courageously introduced Jim Denny, a 21-year-old novice from the junior ranks, into the intense heat of an Old Firm duel. Denny, a former Yoker Athletic player, who has had only half a dozen reserve matches, was never overwhelmed, and certainly his inclusion did not contribute to his team's defeat.

Celtic, after their first two golden goals, might have coasted to an effortless victory but for the undaunted spirit of their rivals and the amazing young Derek Johnstone, who has a penchant for scoring goals on Cup Final occasions at Hampden. Johnstone came within a fraction of doing his life-saving act after coming on at the interval; he created a goal which breathed new life into his team mates, and from then on it was touch and go.

David Hay dominated the midfield area and his aggressiveness often put pressure on Rangers. Billy McNeill was supreme, especially in the first half, but again the Celtic defence seemed apprehensive once Rangers brought on the tall, gangling Johnstone.

Celtic's experienced players naturally attempted to exert incessant pressure on young Denny, but the boy did not display the slightest sign of Cup nerves or greenness. Jackson was probably the mainstay of the defence, and Greig was as resolute and iron-hard as ever. Greig was booked two minutes from the end, and Tom Wharton, the referee, had to caution also Jim Brogan – he was booked on Saturday as well – in the tenth minute of the game.

In the late rally Rangers almost forced extra time when a Colin Stein shot hit Evan Williams on the chest and rebounded clear. It was as close as that; perhaps that miss made Rangers' players look forlorn as they watched from the Hampden pitch – Greig sitting at the trackside, head bowed – while Celtic's players collected their winner's medals.

EARLY SHOTS

Rangers desperately tried to follow up their first-half effort of Saturday's match. Stein almost caused a surprise with two efforts in the opening minutes. Brogan, a tireless worker throughout, conceded a corner intentionally the first time and then miskicked over the bar.

Harry Hood had the first real chance after a long angled pass from Jim Craig. It was here that Willie Waddell's faith in the young Denny was proved. With the assurance of a veteran, Denny showed uncanny interception, and that probably settled him. Celtic continued to try to put the boy under pressure, but often their best attempts came from elsewhere.

In 24 minutes a Lennox cross was dummied by McNeill, the ball skidded deeper into the goalmouth, and Macari side-footed it into the net. Before Rangers could recover, they were two goals down. Their defence could not clear from the edge of the penalty area, and when the ball broke loose to Jimmy Johnstone he hurtled through, only to be caught around the waist in a rugby tackle by Ron McKinnon. There was no doubt it was a penalty, and Hood converted less than a minute after Macari's goal.

SUBSTITUTE

It was at half-time that Mr Waddell decided to bring Derek Johnstone out of the reserve, and as though he possessed a magic formula, the Ibrox club cut their deficit in 58 minutes. Greig hooked the ball onto Johnstone, whose first shot was blocked by Williams. The boy tried again, and this time the ball struck Craig, who turned it into his own goal.

The match was in the balance again. McCloy tipped a Macari shot over the bar. Henderson flashed into the game, accurately passing to Johnstone, whose header was fractionally wide, and when McNeill misheaded, Johnstone and Williams had a race for the ball with the goalkeeper winning.

In 74 minutes Willie Wallace had substituted for Hood, but the best chance thereafter fell to Stein, whose shot was blocked by Williams. The Cup was firmly in Celtic's hands and, for the first time, Celtic had beaten their traditional rivals in a Cup Final replay.

Scottish Cup Final replay

Celtic (2) 2	Rangers (0) 1
Macari	Craig (o.g.)
Hood (pen.)	
(at Hampden park)	
Attendance	103,332

CELTIC:- WILLIAMS; CRAIG AND BROGAN; CONNELLY, MCNEILL AND HAY; J. JOHNSTONE AND MACARI; HOOD; CALLAGHAN AND LENNOX. SUBSTITUTE – WALLACE.

RANGERS:- MCCLOY; DENNY AND MATHIESON; GREIG, MCKINNON AND JACKSON; HENDERSON AND PENMAN; STEIN; MACDONALD AND JOHNSTON. SUBSTITUTE – D. JOHNSTONE.

Rangers 0, Celtic 2 – Saturday, 14th August, 1971

Murdoch Returns to Celtic Team with Masterful Display

By Jim Parkinson

Britain's biggest crowd – 72,500 – for the official start to the new season assembled at Ibrox Stadium on Saturday, and appropriately reserved for the occasion was the best Old Firm match in years.

Celtic, shaping like European Cup-winning prospects, confirmed, above all, by beating Rangers with two second-half goals, that they will be the team that other Cup and Championship aspirants will have to chase for honours.

On his performance Murdoch disproved the old axiom that they never come back. He has had his full share of injury and, more seriously, weight trouble, but he is in the team again, fitter than ever and without having lost his immaculate passing skill. When he is directing the flow accurately Celtic are at their peak, and this was how they secured the initiative in their League Cup section.

The return of Murdoch and John Hughes to the first team was a refreshing sight. It reflected the amazing depth of the Parkhead club's resources. A roll-call of the more established men who were not called on or even in the reserves on Saturday would have included the names of Jim Brogan, Harry Hood, Tommy Gemmell, Willie Wallace and Lou Macari.

Despite the undoubted delight at the team's opening success, Jock Stein does not assume that the men who defeated Rangers will become automatic choices for later games. He estimated it will be October at least until he has a settled side.

However he could not wish for better than to have the consistency of this match maintained. There was no obvious weakness in the side against strong opponents who did not have the Celtic cohesion. Particularly in midfield was this evident, as Murdoch, Tom Callaghan and Jimmy Johnstone's individual genius provided a springboard for attacking operations.

At times David Hay and George Connelly, the pure essence of coolness, stepped out of the rear to lend extra fire-power to the offensive.

The assault on Rangers' goal was at its height when little Johnstone flighted a cross to the unmarked Lennox, whose shot hit the post. It was only minutes later – the sixty-eighth – when this quicksilver pair reversed the procedure, Lennox sending a corner kick to Johnstone and the winger shooting through a chink in the packed defence to score.

Rangers' defence surprisingly fell for their own offside trap a minute later, and Hughes was pulled down for what was undoubtedly a penalty. Billy McNeill, Celtic's captain, signalled Ken Dalglish to take the kick. It was the youngster's first Old Firm game, and yet he showed no strain. He even took time to lace a boot tighter before he placed the ball away from Peter McCloy.

The two-goal blow terminated Rangers' hope and left them to wonder about the openings they missed when they were potentially more dangerous. Alex MacDonald might have scored in the first few seconds, as might Willie Mathieson when he twice accelerated from the full-back position to the front.

At times, too, the game could have been turned, although the Ibrox side did not have Celtic's fine balance, especially in midfield. Tommy McLean's play was not so sustained as it has been in the challenge games against Everton and Tottenham Hotspur, although the delicate touches that may mean so much to Rangers are still there.

SUBSTITUTE

Rangers were reluctant to use Derek Johnstone's height and jumping power. The young centre forward who troubled the Celtic defence in the club's meetings last season was replaced early in the second half by Colin Stein.

Colin Jackson and Ronnie McKinnon had difficult tasks, but both played well, even in defeat. They were relieved near the finish not to concede another goal when Hughes hit the bar with an explosive shot after one of the best moves of the match.

Although three people – Greig, MacDonald and Hay – were booked for fouls, there could be few complaints about field misbehaviour. Bill Mullan kept firm control.

Scottish League Cup section

Rangers (0) 0	Celtic (0) 2
	Johnstone J.
	Dalglish (pen.)
Attendance	72,500

RANGERS:- MCCLOY; JARDINE AND MATHIESON; GREIG, MCKINNON AND JACKSON; MCLEAN AND CONN; JOHNSTONE D.; JOHNSTON AND MACDONALD. SUBSTITUTE – STEIN.

CELTIC:- WILLIAMS; CRAIG AND HAY; MURDOCH, MCNEILL AND CONNELLY; JOHNSTONE J. AND LENNOX; DALGLISH; CALLAGHAN AND HUGHES. SUBSTITUTE – DAVIDSON.

Willie Henderson

One of the fans' all–time favourites, Henderson, like his Celtic counterpart Johnstone, was a winger of amazing trickery and tremendous resilience against tough–tackling defenders. He was just 5ft. 4in. and joined Rangers in 1960. Despite the experienced talent at Ibrox in those days, they just couldn't hold back Henderson, and he was in the first team as a 17-year-old, and was capped by Scotland when he was just 18.

Henderson starred in many Old Firm matches and was outstanding in the 3-0 win over Celtic in the Scottish Cup Final replay of 1963. He was also a controversial figure, but any waywardness was tolerated because of his ability on the field. Henderson joined Sheffield Wednesday in 1972, went to Hong Kong Rangers in 1974 and had a brief spell at Airdrie before retiring. He had 29 full caps, six League caps, under-23 honours and, indeed, once captained the Hong Kong national team. With Rangers his medal collection consisted of two Championships, four Scottish Cups and two League Cups.

John Greig

Probably the greatest captain in the history of Rangers, Greig led the club to their first–ever European honour, the Cup–Winners' Cup in Barcelona in 1972. He joined the club from Whitburn Juniors in 1960 and after taking over from Baxter at left half, he was moved to the defence, where he proved versatile. He was an inspirational player and captain, never giving less than 100 per cent, and expecting nothing less from those around him. Greig had magnificent battles with Jinky Johnstone in Old Firm matches. "I used to play keepy–uppy with the wee man", he used to joke, and the two rivals still retain a mutual respect for one another.

Greig amassed an amazing 857 first team appearances. He also captained Scotland and will be remembered for his great goal, three minutes from time, at a packed Hampden when Scotland beat Italy in a World Cup qualifying match in 1965.

Greig gained 44 full caps and apart from the Cup–Winners' Cup triumph, his medals included five Championships, six Scottish Cups and three League Cups. He retired in 1978 and became manager of Rangers until 1983. After a spell in the travel business, he returned to Ibrox where he is now the club's public relations executive.

Alex MacDonald

A little midfield dynamo, who was one of the most enthusiastic players ever seen in this country. A bundle of fun off the pitch, he was a tiger during matches, with amazing energy and the happy knack of popping up in the right position to score vital goals. He joined Rangers from St. Johnstone for a fee of £50,000 in 1968 and spent twelve successful years at Ibrox.

"Doddie" was in the side which won the European Cup Winners' Cup, and was one of those players who relished an Old Firm match. Probably the one which gave him the most satisfaction was the League Cup Final of season 1975-76 in which he scored the only goal of the game.

MacDonald was capped only once, against Switzerland in 1976, and with Rangers he won a Cup-Winners' Cup medal, three Championships, four Scottish Cups and three League Cups. Joined Hearts for £30,000 in 1980 and a year later became player-manager. In 1986 he was voted Manager of the Year when he took Hearts to within minutes of the Championship and to the Scottish Cup final. Is now manager of Airdrie and has taken them to two Scottish Cup Finals.

Derek Johnstone

One of the most prolific scorers in the club's history, and the youngest British player ever to play in a major Cup Final. In only his second match for the club, the 16-year-old Johnstone was pitched into the 1970 League Cup Final against Celtic at Hampden, and scored the only goal of the game. If he had done nothing else for the club, that moment alone would have made him a legend, but there was much, much more to come from Derek.

Equally comfortable at centre half and centre forward, he was superb in the air and another of those inspirational players. Played in the win over Moscow Dynamo in Barcelona, and was also a member of Rangers' two Treble winning squads in the late seventies. Joined Rangers on a schoolboy form in 1968 and became a full professional two years later.

He played 14 times for Scotland and his domestic honours with Rangers were three League Championships, five Scottish Cups and four League Cups. He was transferred from Rangers to Chelsea for £30,000 in 1983 and also had a spell on loan to Dundee United before returning to Ibrox in 1985. Had a short spell as manager of Partick Thistle, and is now a successful broadcaster.

Rangers 0, Celtic 3 – Saturday, 28th August, 1971

French Manager Tips Celtic as Europe's Outstanding Team

By Jim Parkinson

Jean Prouff, manager of Rennes, the French team who play Rangers in the European Cup-winners' Cup in a few weeks time, is one of those characters wholly appreciative of the best in football. His trip to the Old Firm's second League Cup confrontation at Ibrox Stadium was undertaken to assess his Scottish opponents, but he departed singing the praises of Celtic.

Perhaps he had forgotten the exact nature of his mission, having become so enraptured with the Parkhead team's skills, the sort of display that prompted him to predict that they will be Europe's outstanding team this season.

The Frenchman was silent about his impression of Rangers, who, although playing well since they set out to defend their League Cup title, have been unfortunate to run into Celtic at their peak twice within a fortnight.

UNDISPUTED MASTERS

Celtic were undisputed masters. They are virtually assured of their place in the quarter-finals. One point against Ayr United at Parkhead tonight will secure the section.

This match between Glasgow's great rivals and watched by a 74,000 all-ticket crowd further disproved the theory that we cannot have a good Old Firm contest.

We have now had two exciting games in quick succession in which the brand of football, particularly that of Celtic, has overshadowed the rougher aspects of the duel. The referee cautioned only one player, David Hay, at the weekend. He was booked in the first game as well, but in both instances I feel he was somewhat unlucky to be singled out. There had been worse offences previously but, as in the previous tie, Hay committed his infringement at a time when the official was determined to stamp his authority on the match and prevent any escalation of trouble.

The incident did nothing to upset the free-running Hay. He was following the team's example. Jock Stein told his players before the match that the defeat by Morton last week which threw the section wide open should be erased from their minds. Not for a minute did they play like a worried side. They took the field confident that what they did two weeks ago at Ibrox, they could do again.

Yet for all Celtic's sophistication and penetration, they have not scored before the interval in any of their five League Cup ties. Mr Stein is attaching no special significance to this shortcoming, although he would prefer to see the goals coming early and making things easier in the later stages.

Celtic did not have a bad player. They fielded Jim Brogan for the first time in over three weeks with Hay but reversed their full-back positions. They had instructions to change over if it was not working but there was never any need. Billy McNeill had his best game of the season and George Connelly ambled from defence to attack without ever causing a gap.

MIDFIELD CONTROL

It was in the midfield, however, that Celtic exerted their authority. Bobby Murdoch directed passes with rare judgement, but in my opinion there was no one to surpass Tom Callaghan. Celtic are now deriving the benefit of this tall wing half who takes a defence apart by the power of his thrusts. It is a tribute to his perseverance that he has established a place in the top team, and on current form cannot be dispossessed.

Callaghan scored the second goal in 71 minutes, and it will rank as one of the most spectacular for an Old Firm encounter. The goal that completely disillusioned Rangers, however, was scored by Ken Dalglish three minutes after the interval. Dalglish's intelligent positioning was always menacing and he distributed the ball excellently to Lennox, Macari and Jimmy Johnstone.

Rangers' defensive pair, Ronnie McKinnon and Colin Jackson, were under the severest pressure. Neither was in the vicinity when Williams, with a fine throw, gave the ball to Murdoch. The latter flighted up the middle where only Mathieson was left to cover Lennox and Dalglish, and the young centre ran on to make the most of his chance.

Both sides had made substitutions because of injuries: Hood for Murdoch and Conn for MacDonald – before Callaghan's goal, and there were vast spaces in the terracings at the Rangers end before Lennox scored the third near the end.

Peter McCloy, the giant goalkeeper, was undoubtedly Rangers' best player and this is a commentary on how hard-pressed the Ibrox defence were, especially after the interval.

Rangers swung the ball about and played an open game at the start, but did not possess the smoothness or technique of Celtic. Their approach to goal was not so controlled as that of their rivals, and their forwards did not have the lightning reflexes to take what chances cropped up. One in particular could have made a difference shortly after Celtic had scored. Derek Johnstone tried to trundle the ball over but Jim Brogan marked his comeback by sliding along the goal-line and clearing.

Scottish League Cup section

Rangers (0) 0	Celtic (0) 3
	Dalglish
	Callaghan
	Lennox
Attendance	74,000

RANGERS:- MCCLOY; JARDINE AND MATHIESON; GREIG, MCKINNON AND JACKSON; MCLEAN AND MACDONALD; STEIN; JOHNSTONE D. AND JOHNSTON. SUBSTITUTE – CONN.

CELTIC:- WILLIAMS; BROGAN AND HAY; MURDOCH, MCNEILL AND CONNELLY; JOHNSTONE J. AND LENNOX; DALGLISH; CALLAGHAN AND MACARI. SUBSTITUTE – HOOD.

Rangers 2, Celtic 3 – Saturday, 11th September, 1971
Controversy Rages as Celtic Snatch Victory
By Jim Parkinson

Rangers now know what the lesser first-division clubs mean when they say the first two points are always the most difficult to secure. Ruefully, they glance at their League position, and reflect on three defeats from Celtic within five weeks, all at Ibrox.

In the previous League Cup games they were well beaten in the end, and there could be no complaints. But this Old Firm encounter, watched by a crowd of 67,000 was bitterly different. It was a curious mixture of a match, containing less skill than the other ties but more controversy.

Rangers claim that the game was won and lost midway in the second half by the referee's decision to disallow a goal by Colin Stein. My initial reaction was that it was a good goal, Stein managing to take advantage of hesitancy by Williams, raise a leg chest high, and tap the ball over the goalkeeper into the net.

Mr Paterson had other thoughts – dangerous play – and penalised the centre, who was indeed unlucky considering he did everything he could to play the ball. Williams hurt his arm in a late attempt to avert a goal and the injury no doubt contributed to the terracing arguments.

Apart from the fact that a goal would have pushed Rangers into the lead, the timing of it was vitally important. Only a moment or two earlier they had been left with 10 men as Alfie Conn, who was booked in a rash spell of play in the first half, was ordered off for a foul tackle on Tommy Callaghan. If Rangers required their morale to be strengthened, then what better way than a goal quickly after their setback?

As so often happens in these situations, the depleted Rangers gave Celtic a run for it, but in the very last minute little Jimmy Johnstone somehow managed to out-jump the tall Rangers defenders and head the winner.

Rangers will have to ask themselves why this should happen. They conceded the first goal after eight minutes to another header by the diminutive Lou Macari, and the other goal was scored by Kenny Dalglish after the ball had travelled across the disorganised lines of the defence.

John Greig and several of his colleagues protested loudly about Dalglish's equalising effort in the fifty-fifth minute.

The Celtic youngster took the chance in fine style, but Greig and company claimed that Bobby Lennox had been in an offside position on the goal-line. Mr Paterson, however took no notice.

There were other arguable incidents in a match in which Sandy Jardine, Conn and David Hay were booked for infringement. When Willie Johnston equalised for Rangers after Jim Brogan had handled, there were those who believed that the Celtic full back had slipped and involuntarily threw out his arms. And a Jimmy Johnstone "goal" that was disallowed for offside seemed a strange decision. Immediately before the right winger took possession Murdoch handled but was allowed to play on.

After Stein had put Rangers ahead for the first time in their three meetings with Celtic with a goal just before half-time, Celtic revised their tactics. They withdrew Jimmy Johnstone from the middle area and placed him in a deeply-lying position on the right wing. Rangers, for their part, were forced to replace the injured McLean with Willie Henderson, but he was no more successful than his predecessor.

SMOOTHER TEAM

The smoother game was played by Celtic, who had two exceptional players in George Connelly and Callaghan. All the Parkhead team's attacking moves from defence radiate from Connelly, who could easily hit a fly on a wall from 50 to 60 yards, so accurate and precise is his passing. Callaghan, who eats up the ground with that looping stride of his, is tremendously powerful and is not easily knocked off the ball in the hurly-burly of a tough match.

Rangers (2) 2	Celtic (1) 3
Johnston (pen.)	Macari
Stein	Dalglish
	Johnstone J.
Attendance	67,000

RANGERS:- MCCLOY; JARDINE AND MATHIESON; GREIG, JACKSON AND MACDONALD; MCLEAN AND PENMAN; STEIN; CONN AND JOHNSTON. SUBSTITUTE – HENDERSON.

CELTIC:- WILLIAMS; HAY AND BROGAN; MURDOCH, MCNEILL AND CONNELLY; JOHNSTONE AND LENNOX; DALGLISH; CALLAGHAN AND MACARI. SUBSTITUTE – GEMMELL.

Celtic 2, Rangers 1 – Monday, 3th January, 1972
Rangers Stunned by Injury-Time Winner from Jim Brogan

By Raymond Jacobs

The biters were badly bitten at Parkhead yesterday. Rangers, who had beaten Partick Thistle with a goal in the second minute of injury time, were themselves stunned in the same way by Celtic when everyone had become reconciled to a draw.

Of all the instruments that might have inflicted on Rangers their first defeat after seven successive victories and their fourth in as many games against Celtic this season, the least likely to have been chosen was the head of Celtic's left back, Brogan.

With the game heading towards the draw that surely would have soothed the strongest passions, McNeill took a free kick. The ball came to Hood and, as he brought it under control, Brogan began a run into the area which he timed perfectly to infiltrate in front of McCloy, meet Hood's lob, and glance the ball home.

By appearing as he did, apparently from nowhere, Brogan brought an unexpected climax to a game which, on their endeavour in the second half, Rangers hardly deserved to lose.

Before the interval Celtic had established a rhythm and, through Dalglish and Callaghan, a useful measure of control in midfield. Rangers, who had optimistically begun the game with four men up front, were gradually forced to withdraw as Celtic exerted pressure.

Celtic thus made more chances for themselves, and before Jimmy Johnstone opened up the scoring in 35 minutes Deans, Lennox and Hood had all gone close. Apart from that, Rangers put themselves into difficulty by needlessly giving away free kicks in dangerous positions.

It was from one of these that Celtic's first goal came, almost by way of being a punishment. From the left side of the arena Hood flighted the ball to the far side, and there was Jimmy Johnstone, standing completely unmarked so that he only had to stoop to conquer McCloy with his head.

For their part, Rangers showed splendid willingness to carry the fight. McLean passed the ammunition effectively and Stein and Derek Johnstone gave Connaghan more than one uncomfortable moment as they ran on to the high through ball with which Rangers tested the nerve and judgment of the goalkeeper.

FLUENT PLAY

Together, then, the sides put together a first half of football as fluent and entertaining as anyone can hope for in a match where the usual tendency of the occasion is for the tension to subvert normal skills into rushed passing, uncompromising tackles and trigger-happy shooting.

The second half was much more of a patchwork. Rangers swung all their considerable weight into their attempt to beard those formidable lions in their den. The pressure was then on Celtic, and Connelly, just as Smith had done for Rangers, stood out as the cooling influence in defence.

Yet despite Rangers' exertions Hood twice had shots stopped by McCloy, and Mathieson had his name taken for bringing down Lennox as he broke clear – not by any means the worst foul of a match that was controlled with commendable lack of fuss by Mr Mullan.

EQUALISER

But with nine minutes left, Rangers were at last rewarded with what seemed likely to be the equalising goal. Mathieson pushed the ball forward and Stein and Johnston took it almost in tandem with a rush that broke through Celtic's defence. It was Stein's shot that Connaghan put his hands to but could not stop.

And that, we thought, was that – until Brogan's bolt from the blue of a goal brought the game to its stirring end and left the masses at the Celtic end of the ground to exult over their rivals, who stood in mute disbelief at the other end.

Celtic (1) 2	Rangers (0) 1
Johnstone J.	Stein
Brogan	

CELTIC:- CONNAGHAN; HAY AND BROGAN; DALGLISH, MCNEILL AND CONNELLY; JOHNSTONE J. AND LENNOX; DEANS; CALLAGHAN AND HOOD. SUBSTITUTE – MCGRAIN.

RANGERS:- MCCLOY; JARDINE AND MATHIESON; GREIG, JOHNSTONE AND SMITH; MCLEAN AND D. JACKSON; STEIN; A. MACDONALD AND JOHNSTON. SUBSTITUTE – CONN.

The referee separates the players after a foul on Rangers' Neef.

Alec McDonald and Lou Macari kiss and make-up.

Brogan's goal-line clearance denies Derek Johnstone.

Harry Hood closely watched by McKinnon of Rangers in the 1971 Scottish Cup final.

Celtic 3, Rangers 1 – Saturday, 16th September, 1972

Celtic so Much on top that Fans Laugh off Missed Chances

By John Downie

The final score gave very little indication of Celtic's superiority over Rangers in Saturday's match at Hampden. That was far better demonstrated by the displays of "keepy-uppy" with which Connelly in the first half and Macari in the second, entertained the crowd and the good nature with which the Celtic supporters laughed off the many chances missed by their teams in the last quarter and cheered the last-minute goal of Rangers' captain, Greig.

Even the fiercely competitive Greig apparently, had by then accepted the situation, for he acknowledged the opposition salute with a wave of a hand. It was a pity that he had lost his aplomb for just long enough to spoil an otherwise heroic performance.

Immediately after Celtic's third goal had confirmed Rangers' fears that had been growing from the scoring of the first in three minutes, Greig conceded a foul for tripping Dalglish. Within a minute he was in far worse trouble when he initiated a bout of jostling with Callaghan. Both Greig and Callaghan were booked, which on the visual evidence of those out of earshot, seemed hard on the Celt. The name of Stein had preceded theirs into the book in 19 minutes when McCluskey was hurt in a tackle.

Celtic immediately gained the whip hand by announcing Jimmy Johnstone's return as outside right, issuing him with shorts bearing the number 7 and then playing him at outside left. This ruse persuaded Rangers to transpose their backs so that Mathieson, as usual, faced Johnstone, and it seems more than a probability that the switch contributed to the defence confusion that overcame Rangers at various stages of the game.

QUIET GAME

Johnstone himself has often been more consistently active. Yet he was directly involved in the scoring of the first two goals, and it seems likely that wondering what Johnstone was up to behind his back led to the weak pass to his goalkeeper with which Jardine teed up the third for Macari.

After only three minutes, however, a wide arcing cross by Macari drew McCloy out to the right of his goal. Jimmy Johnstone headed the ball back over the goalkeeper and Dalglish touched it into goal.

The next quarter of an hour was exciting, with good shots by Jardine and Greig for Rangers on either side of a splendid save by McCloy at the feet of Dalglish. But in 18 minutes the Johnstone-Dalglish partnership again went into effective action. Jardine fell as Dalglish beat him on the

outside, and before the back could fully recover, Dalglish cut in along the goal-line and pushed the ball towards Johnstone. The winger's first attempt to meet the pass landed him flat on his back in the goalmouth alongside the fallen goalkeeper, but Johnstone got a second stab, which put the ball into the net.

COMPLEX

Celtic, with Connelly, McGrain, Murdoch and Callaghan fetching and carrying for those in front, could have had two more in quick succession as Macari and Deans came close to success. Rangers responded with a complex advance in which Denny, Greig, Smith, MacDonald, Stein, Willie Johnston and Derek Johnstone combined to set up a chance for MacDonald, who scooped over.

But three minutes into the second half Macari knocked the bottom out of the match. His lob over Jardine looked like an invitation to Jimmy Johnstone to cut in, but the wing hung back and when Jardine passed too softly back for McCloy, Macari himself was quickly in to clip the ball into goal.

The most outrageous of a number of incidents in the Rangers goalmouth thereafter was a pile-up in 54 minutes with the ball jammed against the front of McCloy's left-hand post. Jackson eventually persuaded the goalkeeper to release enough pressure to let him scrape the ball round for a corner.

All the action was towards Rangers' end, where three shots were stopped on the line by the backs, Jardine once blocking a shot by Macari by the right post and immediately getting over to the other side in time to meet a drive by Deans that winded him painfully.

So it went on until in the last minute a fine run and a pass by Smith enabled Greig to gain Rangers' goal and that Celtic cheer, which one suspects, was not entirely ironic.

Celtic (2) 3	Rangers (0) 1
Dalglish	Greig
Johnstone J.	
Macari	

CELTIC;- WILLIAMS; MCGRAIN AND MCCLUSKEY; MURDOCH, MCNEILL AND CONNELLY; J. JOHNSTONE AND DALGLISH; DEANS; MACARI AND CALLAGHAN. SUBSTITUTE – HOOD.

RANGERS:- MCCLOY; JARDINE AND MATHIESON; GREIG, JACKSON AND SMITH; STEIN AND DENNY; D. JOHNSTONE; A. MACDONALD AND JOHNSTON. SUBSTITUTE – CONN.

Rangers 2, Celtic 1 – Saturday, 6th January, 1973

Wallace Earns the Plaudits as Rangers Triumph over Celtic

By Ian Archer

Jock Wallace asked us yesterday to forget that he might have made some contribution to Rangers' victory over Celtic. "Don't write about me – and I mean that," he said. "Just tell them I'm a good-looking chap and leave it at that."

It was well in keeping with the style of the Rangers' manager that he should prefer the players to reap the praise, but I have to ignore the man's instructions and write about him.

Wallace works 14 hours a day for Rangers and when he goes to bed, it is a fair guess that he reproduces the patterns of a football match on the ceiling of the room.

He will hear of no criticism of those who work around him and he has never, even privately, taken one to the side and explained how a defeat was no fault of his own.

While the going was rough, he shouldered the blame, and now that Rangers have achieved a result he must come forward and take the plaudits.

The victory was hard earned and well deserved. The best defender on the field was Tom Forsyth of Rangers, the best attacker Alfie Conn of Rangers. Derek Parlane also played a large part in the game and Alex MacDonald seemed to have refound much of the flair that has been missing for some months.

When Rangers took the lead it was no more than they deserved, because Conn and MacDonald had earlier found space inside the penalty area against a suspect Celtic defence.

McCluskey rugby-tackled MacDonald from behind and Parlane needed a lucky rebound from Williams' legs before a penalty landed in the back of the net. His salutes to the crowd were too prolonged, but this was a great moment for a young player.

Celtic were only effective in a period around half-time, traditionally the spell in which they do their damage. Their equalising goal was, in fact, fortunate, because McCloy had Deans' shot covered before a wicked deflection off Smith carried it out of his reach.

But gradually Celtic ran out of steam, and Conn's persistence finally brought him reward in the last minute when he headed home a Young cross. Hay, handicapped after an earlier injury, just could not rise to challenge him. The terraces went berserk and 10 minutes after the end of the match they were still there, still as noisy.

Rangers have started their centenary year at Ibrox with one victory that really matters. There is much work to be done and Wallace knows that his team have still to prove themselves. But the first part of his Ibrox task has been accomplished, and now he can expect to move towards greater triumphs. This is a nice thought for those of us who know the man.

Rangers (1) 2	Celtic (1) 1
Parlane	Smith (o.g.)
Conn	

RANGERS:- MCCLOY; JARDINE AND MATHIESON; GREIG, JOHNSTONE AND SMITH; CONN AND FORSYTH; PARLANE; MACDONALD AND YOUNG. SUBSTITUTE – MCLEAN.

CELTIC:- WILLIAMS; HAY AND BROGAN; MCCLUSKEY, MCNEILL AND CONNELLY; JOHNSTONE AND DEANS; DALGLISH; CALLAGHAN AND MACARI. SUBSTITUTE – HOOD.

Bobby Lennox scores Celtic's goal in the 1971 Scottish Cup final.

Rangers 3, Celtic 2 – Saturday, 5th May, 1973

Seven Years in the Wilderness End for Rangers

By Ian Archer

The text must be taken from the book of Genesis, Chapter 41, verses 1-38, that part of the Bible which describes Joseph and the seven lean years.

On Saturday night, the Scottish Cup lay in the boardroom at Ibrox, taken there by a Rangers team who knew that history demanded heroics, and tradition some tangible evidence of their glories. It was their first triumph since 1966.

In their centenary year, the club brought Scotland's most famous trophy back to their own impressive building and there the champagne flowed. Moses McNeil, that Victorian oarsman from the Gareloch who stopped rowing long enough to found this Glasgow institution, would have loved and understood every minute of it all.

TELEGRAM

On Sunday morning the only sign of celebration was an empty Coca-Cola bottle in the marble foyer. Jock Wallace knocked on a locked door and waited to be let into The Stadium. A telegram awaited from the supporters' club in Canberra who wished to send Antipodean congratulations. A telephone call from Sweden followed.

The Cup, it is true, was won on a Hampden field by a Rangers team every bit as famous as those which had gone before it. It had been gained in front of an audience of 122,000, just as harshly committed as their grandparents had been on other days. The men who made it possible were John Greig, who stood in tears at the end, Derek Johnstone, so cool he might have been refrigerated and Alfie Conn, that oddly arrogant successor to men of previous generations who understood that football can enable anyone to strike poetic attitudes. Tom Forsyth and Derek Parlane played notable parts, and no others should be forgotten.

LANDMARK

But these people yesterday we did not see. Wallace we did and soon the Cup Final of the SFA's one hundredth year was put in perspective. What follows will embarrass the man for he wants credit to go elsewhere, but it needs to be said at a weekend that was a landmark for the Scottish game.

The Rangers team manager talked reluctantly. "I've said too much . . . I've said too much," he kept repeating. "Give praise to the players. No one knows how hard they have worked. They were down, they picked themselves up. They're the men." He agreed, however, to fill in some details.

At the end of a torrent of a match, played in the middle of the kind of pandemonium that would have made a Concorde landing seem almost silent, the players of both sides had collapsed into embraces that showed even the bitterest rivals in sport understood the limits of that antagonism, the basic truth that football elevates all of them.

Wallace went first to Bobby Murdoch of Celtic. "When we won the League Cup Final, I walked past him when he wanted to shake my hand. I didn't mean to. I was just carried away. That night I got a row from my mother who saw it on television. I remembered it.

"Afterwards Jock Stein came up to me. He said, 'Well done. You deserve it.' I think a lot of Jock Stein. And then John Greig arrived with the cup, thrust it towards me and shouted: 'You asked for the Cup – here it is.'"

These things Wallace told us, and then we asked what it all meant to him. For the first time, a man who believes that three words constitute a lengthy speech started stringing together his thoughts.

'When I was eight or nine I would hang about at Wallyford with no money waiting for the Rangers bus, going up to the people and saying: 'Mister, will you give us a lift.' Sometimes they took me, sometimes they didn't.

"I knew all about that side – Brown, Young and Shaw; McColl, Woodburn and Cox; Waddell and Gillick; Thornton; Duncanson and Caskie. One week I went to Tynecastle and couldn't resist buying a rosette for a shilling. That was my bus fare home so I had to walk fourteen miles."

Then, like a professional manager, he remembered: "Waddell wasn't playing that day. Rutherford was on the wing."

Such talk made one recall that story he had told a few months before: "When I was a boy, I had this friend and together we had a ball. He stood on the wing crossing them. He was Waddell. I stood and headed them into the net. I was Waddell."

These anecdotes – and I will be seriously abused for repeating them – rather prove that this game is never played in this country by highly paid and cynical professionals, rather it is inhabited by people who understand about the glory of it all. It is part of the culture of the country, a kind of national consciousness possessed in club boardroom, managers' office, and most importantly, upon the terraces.

So, at last, to the match. Celtic, with eight successive Championships behind them, against a team beaten this season on their own Ibrox turf by St Mirren and Stenhousemuir of the Second Division, but who in recent months had persuaded their fans that they were worthy of huge support. A contest between Scotland's finest teams.

Celtic, attacking first, took the lead in 24 minutes. Dalglish, scampering on to a Deans pass, struck a shot past McCloy and turned in celebration.

After 35 minutes Mathieson pushed a shrewd ball forward and MacDonald beat Connelly, drawn wide. His chipped centre to the near post brought Parlane away from his defender for the header that tied the match and bruised our eardrums with the noise that followed.

Half-time was not long enough for our pulse rates to drop and suddenly, 17 seconds later, Rangers took the lead. Young passed forward, Parlane flicked on, and Conn was left with a clear run at goal.

McNeill looked tired and could not catch him. As in Budapest earlier this season when Celtic were knocked out of the European Cup, a certain lack of pace in defence betrayed them. Conn shot past the advancing Hunter.

But it was still the Parkhead team who made sure that this would be a great Final rather than a very good one by equalising after Greig, in a grand impersonation of a goalkeeper, fisted Deans shot off the line. Connelly, as cool as ever, ignored 65,000 whistlers behind the goal, and struck the penalty home with authority.

So an hour had proved nothing. The tension had apparently abated and the 1973 Final was there to be won by the team with the most skill. That was Rangers.

MacDonald hit a post with a header, an overture to the vital goal that gave Rangers the Cup. McLean slanted over a free kick. Johnstone headed against a post, and as the ball crept across the line and on to the other upright, Forsyth pushed it into the net. "I was so excited, I nearly missed it," he said afterwards.

For the last half hour Rangers cut holes in Celtic's style and morale. Conn and Young should have scored and such was their confidence that extra attacking players seemed to swarm about Hunter, who became a goalkeeper under siege.

And at last it was over. Greig and Parlane wept and seven fat years seemed round the corner. Referee John Gordon left the field, a good day's work done. The Rangers fans were a lot slower in departing, reluctant as they were to desert the battlefield.

Technically the match was won with MacDonald's surveillance of Murdoch, Parlane's selfless running which kept McNeill and Connelly at full stretch, as well as Forsyth and Johnstone's strength and skill against Deans and Dalglish. But this is no time to remember tactics.

Celtic were forced in the end, though an injury to Brogan, to play Callaghan at full back, push Connelly forward, and ask Johnstone to sprint through the middle. They looked confused but this was not their day. They will find their feet again and be a better side for knowing their greatest rivals are reawakened. This was a great side beaten, not an ordinary team destroyed. They share the glow that radiated from the match, even if their medals are only those of losers.

Scottish Cup Final

Rangers (1) 3	Celtic (1) 2
Parlane	Dalglish
Conn	Connelly (pen.)
Forsyth	
(at Hampden Park)	
Attendance	122,000

CELTIC:- HUNTER; MCGRAIN AND BROGAN; MURDOCH, MCNEILL AND CONNELLY; JOHNSTONE J. AND DALGLISH; DEANS; HAY AND CALLAGHAN. SUBSTITUTE – LENNOX.

RANGERS:- MCCLOY; JARDINE AND MATHIESON; GREIG, JOHNSTONE D. AND MACDONALD; MCLEAN AND FORSYTH; PARLANE; CONN AND YOUNG. SUBSTITUTE – SMITH.

Rangers 1, Celtic 2 – Saturday, 18th August, 1973
Missed Chances Prove Costly for Rangers
By Ian Archer

It is not in the nature of the Glasgow football fan to find comfort in defeat. Rangers supporters will look at the scoreline from the latest Old Firm Match and draw vast, worthless conclusions.

Yet, not for the first time, the scoreline conceals the truth. Celtic were rather fortunate to escape from Ibrox having stopped the third successive defeat from Rangers this year. They were, at least on this occasion, a little lucky.

Four times in the match Conn and Young mis-hit shots that would have guaranteed goals. Once Brogan handled in the penalty area, but the claims were ignored by the referee. Fluent and dangerous throughout a match in which the tension could not stop the football showing through, Rangers showed the continuing improvement that marked the later stages of the previous season.

Forsyth in defence was the best player on the field. Greig and MacDonald burned up energy in midfield. Rangers moved with firm authority up to the edge of the penalty area, then squandered the outfield play with indecisive finishing.

Celtic rather improvised. They stuck Johnstone forward alongside Lennox to exploit the offside experiment. Dalglish had a magical period which climaxed with a twisting run and a shot that bounced off a post, but for 80 minutes this match seemed to be producing no more than a high class draw. Then it became the day of the substitutes.

Hood, the late arrival for Celtic, turned Smith, the Rangers replacement, inside out and crossed for Lennox to shoot so unexpected a goal. Then Smith rather foolishly drove a free kick into a defensive wall, with all his defenders lining up at the far post for the cross Celtic used two passes to allow Hood to score at the other end.

The goals were not only unexpected, but unwanted. They provoked the crowd and made the last-minute Rangers reply – an own goal from McNeill, under pressure from Scott – little more than an empty gesture.

There is a danger in too many Old Firm matches devaluing their importance and a goalless draw would have acted as a delaying force until such times as the teams play for real – in the League later this month.

And every player who had placed skill before physical endeavour would have been able to know that his endeavour had been rewarded.

Rangers (0) 1	Celtic (0) 2
McNeill (o.g.)	Lennox
	Hood

RANGERS:- MCCLOY; JARDINE, MATHIESON, GREIG, JOHNSTONE, MACDONALD; MCLEAN, FORSYTH, PARLANE, CONN AND YOUNG. SUBSTITUTES – SCOTT AND SMITH

CELTIC:- HUNTER; MCGRAIN, BROGAN, MURRAY, MCNEILL, CONNELLY; MCLAUGHLIN, JOHNSTONE, DALGLISH, HAY AND LENNOX. SUBSTITUTES – CALLAGHAN AND HOOD.

Celtic 1, Rangers 3 – Saturday, 25th August, 1973
Equation is Balanced
By Ian Archer

In terms of unneeded energy it was similar to using an atomic device to open an infant's money box. Such were the unnecessary explosions at Parkhead on Saturday.

Celtic reintroduced their fans to the style and joy that has sometimes been missing in their play for the last two years. Rangers gave their fans a fine display of fighting spirit and uncompromising attitude.

A week ago I said that Celtic were a shade lucky to win at Ibrox. To balance the equation, it must now be stated that Rangers were wildly lucky to win at Parkhead.

For 53 minutes Celtic lanced and pierced Rangers, but the blows did not sever the arteries of the bears. Murray, made his presence felt, Dalglish was superb, Lennox tireless and McLaughlin precocious.

Lennox scored one goal, and had another disallowed. Greig might have handled inside his own penalty area. Derek Johnstone had to head off his own line.

After half-time Lennox and Hay missed side-footed shots when it seemed a goal might be scored as easily with blow football equipment as a boot. Our notes were cataloguing great football, when Rangers were ready to make all that skill count for nothing.

Suitably it was MacDonald who won the match for them, scoring the first, and making the second and third. For the last week his manager had been saying he was the best midfield man in Scotland. Now MacDonald proved him correct.

A vicious volley from Jardine's cross brought Rangers level. A MacDonald cross, a Conn back-header and a Parlane lunge took them in front. A MacDonald through ball a little later confirmed the almost unbelievable transformation.

Even in that period when Johnstone was sent off and Celtic were reduced to 10 men, the game held further marvels as Dalglish dredged the bottom of his stamina in trying to equalise, and the whole side fought against the impossible odds.

But over a period of seven days, these two results have largely left honour satisfied and the First Division match, as it should, will now decide the late summer rubber. There is little to choose between the country's two best sides.

Scottish League Cup Section

Celtic (1) 1	Rangers (0) 3
Lennox	MacDonald
	Parlane 2

CELTIC:- HUNTER, MCGRAIN, BROGAN, MURRAY, MCNEILL, CONNELLY, JOHNSTONE J., MCLAUGHLIN, DALGLISH, HAY AND LENNOX. SUBSTITUTES – HOOD AND CALLAGHAN.

RANGERS:- MCCLOY, JARDINE, MATHIESON, GREIG, JOHNSTONE D., MACDONALD, YOUNG, FORSYTH, PARLANE, CONN AND YOUNG. SUBSTITUTES – SCOTT AND SMITH.

Rangers 0, Celtic 1 – Saturday, 15th September, 1973
Rangers Frozen by Caution
By Ian Archer

As one observer remarked, "Davie Hay's knee-high centre was met by Jimmy Johnstone, who rose and headed the winner." Thus Celtic won the 153rd first division match between Glasgow's Old Firm.

A solitary goal sent half the Ibrox audience piling out of the stadium in a cloud of dust, their green and white choruses proclaiming another title won.

This was a poor match. The excitement of the earlier league cup ties evaporated as fear replaced freedom. Rangers froze because they understood the strategic implications of defeat; Celtic produced a minimal amount of fluency because half their forward line was missing.

So a crowd of 69,000 saw one goal and a few other penalty-area incidents.

If Celtic sowed little and reaped an enormous harvest, Rangers' seed was scattered largely on stony ground. They could have won the match in the first half, yet rather they surrendered it completely in the later stages. Parlane went largely unsupported in a game where all attacking forces were staffed in small numbers.

There were plenty who said afterwards that modern football was not to their liking, for each side had a token amount of men upfield. For Celtic – with McLaughlin, Deans and Lennox in the grandstand and Dalglish unfit on the pitch – there was some excuse. Rangers were simply far too cautious.

Rangers looked more often at the sunlight in the first half. Young had a long swinging shot saved and a header parried by Hunter, who also dived at the feet of McLean when he hesitated over the game's best opportunity. The goalkeeper earned his money and the eventual victory with a little help from Parlane, who headed over the bar from six yards out, and later shot weakly from the same range.

In the second half Murray stood on the toes of MacDonald, who disappeared for long periods. Hay was released to move forward down the left side where he does most of his best work. After 71 minutes his low cross was headed underneath McCloy's body by Jimmy Johnstone who made his presence felt in the most decisive movement of all.

Rangers (0) 0	Celtic (0) 1
	Johnstone J.
Attendance	69,000

RANGERS:- MCCLOY, JARDINE, MATHIESON, GREIG, JOHNSTONE D., MACDONALD. MCLEAN, FORSYTH, PARLANE, CONN AND YOUNG. SUBSTITUTES - SMITH AND SCOTT.

CELTIC:- HUNTER, MCGRAIN, BROGAN, MURRAY, MCNEILL, CONNELLY, JOHNSTONE J., HOOD, DALGLISH, HAY AND WILSON. SUBSTITUTES – CALLAGHAN AND MCCLUSKEY.

Celtic 3, Rsngers 1 – Wednesday, 5th December, 1973

Hood's Three Goals give Celtic Decade of League Cup Finals

By Ian Archer

Celtic, with absolute assurance and occasional arrogance, last night trampled over Rangers and thus walked into their tenth successive Scottish League Cup Final. It was easy at a rain-swept Hampden Park.

Victory was accomplished with hardly a worry in the world throughout a Semi-final watched by 54,864 sodden spectators.

The Old Firm affair was a small personal triumph for Harry Hood, that accomplished Celtic forward, who scored three goals and joined that select band of players who have done so in these intense confrontations between Glasgow's bitterest rivals.

If Hood was outstanding on a wild night, every one of his colleagues supported him well. Of the 10 others Dalglish was clearly exceptional and Wilson justified the faith of manager Jock Stein, who preferred him to the pair of talented internationals – George Connelly and Jimmy Johnstone.

The Ibrox side played a curious Semi-final. Kicking into the wind in the first half they looked composed, but after the interval, with the elements acting to their advantage, they fell away. Tactically, the switching of Alex MacDonald to the left wing robbed the side of his talent where it was most needed, farther back.

It was, for Rangers, a bad defeat as one doorway to another season of European competition was shut in their face. But to the end they fought, spirit unbroken.

But Celtic, on the Hampden evidence, remain by some distance Scotland's best club team of the present time, much as they have done for over the last decade. Ten in a row is too long a chain of events to be ascribed to coincidence.

This was another hard and unrelenting Old Firm game, full of indiscreet and indecent tackles, which ended with three men – Jackson, MacDonald and Wilson – being booked.

Celtic contrived the start they wanted, using Wilson at centre-forward, held up-field to exploit the off-side experiment and under orders to run the pace out of Rangers' legs. He did so and left others to exploit the gaps.

After 34 minutes his side struck. Dalglish drove a low cross and McCloy, diving awkwardly, full of angular limbs, could not gather the ball. Mathieson kicked off the line as it spun clear, but contrived only to give Dalglish another creative chance. This time the ball was floated into the centre, and Hood pushed the header into the empty net.

But it was not, for a while, to be easy for Celtic. Rangers found an ally in adversity and three minutes later they were deservedly level. Grieg, as always at the heart of every matter, broke up the midfield play and edged towards the penalty area.

Once there he played the pass square to MacDonald on the left and the winger hit a vicious curving cross that shot across the face of Hunter, before spiralling into the corner of the net – the game's best goal.

There it rested until half-time with Rangers, the favourites, downwind. But the expected never happened as Celtic locked up the middle, tackled even harder and eventually sucked their opponents dry.

They scored again after 55 minutes when Jackson was forced into a desperate tackle on Wilson which left the winger almost on the track. Callaghan took the free kick and McNeill, having stolen silently to the far post, headed strongly and accurately back across the goal. Hood again was present to stick the ball over the line. This time there was no reply, for Hay's damaging tackles had taken effect and Rangers were short of inventive ideas.

Manager Wallace threw on Derek Johnstone as an extra striker in place of McLean who had disappeared but the teenager had hardly arrived before Hood scored his third goal to take the Semi-final beyond recall. Again it was a Dalglish pass, and there was a suspicion of offside as he strode across the penalty area to place the ball out of reach of McCloy.

But that luck was balanced by another Hood shot from what looked like an onside position that was disallowed a few seconds later.

So the terraces were cleared with Celtic songs being sung enthusiastically if untunefully. Once more out of a period of some concern inside the club, the right answers had been found and the side had beaten Rangers for the third time out of four meetings this season.

Scottish League Cup Semi-Final

Celtic (1) 3	Rangers (1) 1
Hood 3	MacDonald
Attendance	54,864

RANGERS:- MCCLOY, JARDINE, MATHIESON, GREIG, JACKSON, HOUSTON, MCLEAN, FORSYTH, PARLANE, CONN, MACDONALD. SUBSTITUTES – JOHNSTONE D. AND SMITH.

CELTIC:- HUNTER, MCGRAIN, BROGAN, MCCLUSKEY, MCNEILL, MURRAY, HOOD, HAY, WILSON, CALLAGHAN AND DALGLISH. SUBSTITUTES – JOHNSTONE J., CONNELLY.

Celtic 1, Rangers 0 – Saturday, 5th January, 1974

Rangers' Spirit Bows to Celtic's Sophistication

By Ian Archer

Quietly, as if they always feared the worst, Rangers' fans took the punishment like men. Hardly a word of encouragement, scarcely a hymn of defiance arose from the royal blue end of Parkhead.

Their team came and were vanquished by Celtic. The scoreline looks marginal, but it lies. There was but one side playing football, the composed intelligent and graceful Scottish game. The other was huffing and puffing, but had no chance of blowing down Jock Stein's castle.

A goal by Bobby Lennox in 27 minutes was all that separated Celtic and Rangers and the effort proved what the First Division table already showed before this 154th meeting of the Old Firm. Glasgow has one good team, and one that is not quite so good.

Here were Celtic, close passing under the pressure, finding two and three men available in support of every ball carrier, and waiting patiently for the Ibrox defence to commit itself foolishly in a flurry of anxiety.

DESPERATE

And here were Rangers, a desperate side, running away from the man in possession, heaving long and hopeful balls upfield, a team of remarkable stamina and spirit, but a collection of players without corporate understanding, lacking that sophistication bred by eight successive titles and a ninth to come.

I leave it to the tacticians to analyse Rangers' problems and there will be many ready to do so, for there is no more fashionable sport than kicking a stricken giant when he is down. Many will be the instant remedies, but I cannot bring myself to criticise Jock Wallace, whose only fault is that he works too hard.

There is only one long term point worth making after a bad defeat – and that concerns the quality of the Ibrox playing staff, which old-timers tell me stands no comparison with its predecessors.

There is a reason why Rangers cannot find players like Dalglish, Hay, McGrain and McCluskey. There is good cause to believe that over the next few years Celtic will continue to discover multitudes of young talent annually to defend their perennial title of Champions.

Most boys now want to play for them, as they are Scotland's premier team. Celtic will be only too pleased to acquire them, and when they go in search of them, they look at their ability alone.

They have no need to ask that polite discreet question about which school the lad is attending, the pertinent question that decides whether he would be suitable Rangers material or not.

Given that Celtic's scouting system in so thorough, given too, that English clubs are spending so much time and money on dragging schoolboys south, Rangers' future problems could be severe.

With success breeding success, Celtic will increasingly find it easier to draw volunteers to Parkhead and Rangers more difficult to persuade boys that Ibrox is a suitable place of apprenticeship. And so, with money hard to find for the transfer market, it is not difficult to assess which of Glasgow's clubs stands more chance of acquiring the next 10 Championships.

One hesitates to give advice, but the respectful submission must be that Rangers no longer forgo the chance of some of Scotland's brightest prospects merely because of an accident of birth.

FEW CHANCES

So back to the better players, McCluskey in particular, a warrior at centre back, Murray and Hay, the guiding midfield lights, and Dalglish, the class attacker. Throughout this match they kept tight control and the goal, which started as far back as McNeil and Brogan, continued through Murray and Hood, and was finally trundled over the line, underlined their ability to play accurately all over the field.

Rangers, to their credit, were a better team than the one defeated at Hampden Park in the League Cup for their heart and lungs were made to count for a full 90 minutes. But they made few chances. Greig, that great man, sent Hunter tumbling to stop one shot low at the post, and not even MacDonald's insistence kept them in the game as possible winners.

Celtic, the longer the match lasted, were content to draw them recklessly forward and then hit on the break. Lennox and Deans might have scored the late goals that would better have reflected the difference in class. If another Championship was not quite won by Celtic, then surely another title was lost by Rangers.

Celtic (1) 1	Rangers (0) 0
Lennox	

CELTIC:- HUNTER, MCGRAIN, BROGAN, MCCLUSKEY, MCNEILL, HAY, HOOD, MURRAY, DEANS, DALGLISH AND LENNOX. SUBSTITUTES – CONNELLY AND JOHNSTONE J.

RANGERS:- MCCLOY, JARDINE, MATHIESON, GREIG, JOHNSTONE D., HOUSTON, YOUNG, FORSYTH, PARLANE, MACDONALD AND SCOTT. SUBSTITUTES – SMITH AND HAMILTON.

Celtic 1, Rangers 2 – Saturday, 14th September, 1974

Old Firm Game One to Forget

By Ian Archer

Rangers shrugged off historical precedent which said they had no right to win at Parkhead, carried themselves above Celtic in the First Division's infant table and, in doing so, brought no great honour in the direction of their own Ibrox Stadium.

A tetchy Old Firm match in which players of both sides scuffled and feuded, and in which the referee was vague and tolerant to a fault, ended with the first Rangers victory at Parkhead since 1968. It was a nasty, brutish little triumph in a nasty, brutish little game.

If there is ever justification for Old Firm business which many dislike intensely, it comes in the realisation that the two clubs act as a safety valve for the bigoted. If there is one essential requirement for the competitors, it is to remember that in such a poisonous atmosphere, only the highest standards of sportsmanship will suffice. Rangers first, and Celtic later, forgot that first principle of Glasgow football.

EXEMPTIONS

First of all we will make the exemptions – and there were many – for no two teams ever deserve blanket condemnation. We will say that men like Jardine, Greig and McDougall, McGrain, Murray and Dalglish, as always were a credit to their clubs and their profession. There were others whose conduct was beyond reproach.

But there were some who were not so saintly and honesty demands that Parlane should be singled out in this context. His attitude was essentially unsporting as he kicked at players when the ball was away, refused to retreat 10 yards when ordered, contested balls when they were out of play and made mock gestures of trying to butt Celtic goalkeeper Connaghan when he had the ball in his hands.

There was also Alex MacDonald, who took a kick at McNeill from the back and then dived theatrically to the ground as if he himself had been the victim of an assault – which he had not.

On the Celtic side, Brogan seemed to speak unnecessarily to Derek Johnstone and was booked rightly. The other, smaller Johnstone appeared to aim a blow at Kennedy and was booked, rightly, and perhaps, leniently. There were angry gestures at the end by the Celtic captain and manager to the referee.

Mr Gordon's honesty and integrity are not in doubt. He has refereed the Old Firm well before – notably in the centenary Scottish Cup Final – but here he had a bad day, ignoring the first danger signs, particularly from Parlane, and then chasing the guilty ones when it was too late.

He should have awarded Celtic a penalty in the first minute when Forsyth blatantly pushed Dalglish off the ball in the area. He should not have sent off Brogan in the incident with Parlane, for the Celtic defender was merely trying to take a throw-in while the centre forward obstructed him. His eventual dismissal of Parlane came at least a half hour too late.

As a FIFA referee he seemed to ignore that body's new instructions that handling and failure to retreat 10 yards at free kicks are offences punishable by cautions. He lapsed into Scottish leniency when European authority was needed, on this day above all others.

Of the game itself, Celtic should have had it won in the first half. Dalglish's marvellously quick and instinctive goal after 31 minutes seemed to have put his side elegantly on the way to victory. But how Davie Hay's drive was missed later in the match.

Rangers, on the football that was seen, fully deserved to win on their second half performance, even if they were helped by Celtic's lack of confidence in the referee. They continued to press and those slight signs of fallibility already seen in the Champions this season betrayed them.

Critically, Connaghan made two mistakes, misreading McDougall's cross shot, hit with a lack of weight and precision which scuttled into the far corner of the net, then completely failing to leave his line and cut out the McLean corner which Jackson headed unimpeded into the net. The Rangers fans kept up a barrage of noise throughout this period which helped.

REMINDER

So, thankfully, to the end. There is now a clear need in both clubs to remind their players of the impeccable standards of behaviour needed on the field, as well as the terraces. Under a referee in better form the game might have proceeded more satisfactorily.

But officials, like players, are allowed their bad days and it remains the first moral law of football to accept a referee's decision, however wrong. The alternative in the short term is a match like Saturday's, in the long term, anarchy.

Celtic (1) 1	Rangers (0) 2
Dalglish	McDougall
	Jackson

CELTIC:- CONNAGHAN, MCGRAIN, BROGAN, MCCLUSKEY, MCNEILL, CALLAGHAN, JOHNSTONE J., MURRAY, DALGLISH, DAVIDSON AND WILSON. SUBSTITUTES – LENNOX AND HOOD

RANGERS:- KENNEDY, JARDINE, GREIG, MCDOUGALL, JACKSON, FORSYTH, YOUNG, JOHNSTONE D., PARLANE, MACDONALD AND FYFE. SUBSTITUTES – SCOTT AND MCLEAN.

Kenny Dalglish holds off Colin Jackson.

Jimmy Johnstone scores for Celtic.

Alfie Conn scores Rangers' second in the Centenary Scottish Cup final.

Tom Forsyth prods the ball over the line to win the Centenary Scottish Cup final.

Rangers 3, Celtic 0 – Saturday, 4th January, 1975

The Plot Thickens in Old Firm's League Drama

By Ian Archer

The thousands of Rangers fans who, in the pouring rain, grudgingly refused to leave one end of Ibrox long after Tommy McLean and his colleagues lay seeping in the dressing room bath, were content to forget history and let the future wait. It was time enough to live for the present.

At the same moment tame historians were flicking through the records books to find the last occasion on which Rangers had planted the ball three times in a Celtic net and found no reason to shout at their own goalkeeper. They supplied the answer that it was 12 years since such a happening occurred.

It would be nice, but not honourable, to say that on a Saturday of heavy rain, on a pitch like a ploughed field and in front of a demanding audience, Rangers and Celtic played a game which showed all the old virtues of Scottish football – bravery, skill and character.

It would be pleasant but cowardly, merely to say that the result leaves two major clubs deadlocked as makes no difference at the top of the table with 14 matches left in the title race, and that the real winners will be the massive crowds which follow them up and down the country as the struggle continues.

But everyone wants to know whether the trophy which has resided at Parkhead for the past nine years is to be taken across the city on April 26. The latest evidence leaves the mind confused. Rangers won – but so could have Celtic. One match has not made all that much difference.

It was ironic that Celtic's persistent weakness in recent years should have cost them this latest Old Firm match. So often in the past they have needed to create dozens of chances for every goal scored, and although such wastefulness has not mattered much, it rebounded upon them in this tight contest.

If Hood could have trundled a ball over the line from three yards and Dalglish placed an eight yard shot inside a post during the first half, they would surely have gained a draw. If Dalglish, again, could have got a foot to a Wilson header after Rangers had scored their second goal, there was still time for them to gain a point.

But that was not to be as the match dragged on as both Glavin and Murray became bogged down in the mud while Wilson, after a perceptive, brilliant first half, began to tire. Johnstone's anonymous spell as a substitute made no impression.

So Rangers won well and deservedly, the great merit in their performance being that they contrived to play near to the top of their form on an afternoon when they knew that nothing else would be good enough – and on which defeat would render them rather impotent in the latter stages of this championship.

For long enough, ever since he took the Rangers players up to those sand dunes at Gullane, Jock Wallace has been unfairly branded as a man who is more suited to commanding a bunch of Foreign Legionnaires than a team of footballers. The man, in fact, conceals an astute tactical brain under an uncompromising exterior.

His match-winning stroke was to play without a left back, recognising that Celtic were playing without a right winger. Greig moved into a defensive midfield position, cutting off Dalglish's work at source and leaving Forsyth to mop up if that special player moved into the space behind the captain. Celtic, except for a small period during the first half, could not get players into that untended area for Scott was always keeping McGrain too preoccupied to consider anything other than the occasional overlap.

But tactics are a boring subject. This 72,000 crowd wanted heroics. They will have toasted Tommy McLean late into Saturday night, but I prefer to concentrate the praise on Stewart Kennedy, that remarkable goalkeeper.

Football teams only begin to play with forward assurance if they know that the back door is locked. Kennedy, astonishingly in his first season, controls his area and orders his defenders, and from this rock of a base Rangers go forward with confidence.

TRAINING

One Kennedy save from McGrain was remarkable and a series of dives at Celtic feet was bravery in extremis. He is as good a goalkeeper as any in Britain, better certainly than that over-rated and overpriced Shilton.

McDougall, the other novice, looked better the longer the game lasted – a credit to training schedules. And then there was McLean curling over a cross for Johnstone to head one goal, Parlane another, and in between times, scoring himself from one of MacDonald's many well-weighted passes.

In retrospect, a grand match. I suppose that some 30,000 of the crowd hardly enjoyed a single minute, but no one disturbed the leisure of the police, nor the enjoyment of others. This is to be a Championship of epic proportions.

Rangers 3	Celtic 0
Johnstone D.	
McLean	
Parlane	
Attendance	72,000

RANGERS:- KENNEDY, JARDINE, GREIG, JOHNSTONE, JACKSON, FORSYTH, MCLEAN, MCDOUGALL, PARLANE, MACDONALD AND SCOTT. SUBSTITUTES – YOUNG AND MILLER.

CELTIC:- HUNTER, MCGRAIN, BROGAN, MURRAY, MCNEILL, MCCLUSKEY, HOOD, GLAVIN, DALGLISH, CALLAGHAN AND WILSON. SUBSTITUTES – JOHNSTONE AND MCDONALD.

Celtic 2, Rangers 2 – Saturday, 10th May, 1975
Old Firm Turn on a Final Classic

By Ian Archer

Celtic will meet Rangers next season to settle the ownership of the Glasgow Cup. Their committed ranks of followers will talk of little else as summer takes them to Largs or Lloret de Mar, Troon or Torremolinos.

There is a principle in showbusiness much understood by the late Lex McLean that the customers should always be left a little frustrated, wanting more. The comedian used to scuttle from the Pavilion to catch his train to Helensburgh while the audience chanted for another encore.

On Glasgow's 800th birthday the Old Firm played the same trick. They disappeared down the tunnel deadlocked and so the Scottish club season came to a close with the argument unresolved. We shall never know whether Rangers or Celtic were the better side before the curtain came down with a bump.

PENALTIES

The Rangers players were, in fact, prepared for a period of extra time. Jock Wallace had not told them that 90 minutes was all the rules of the competition allowed and he sent them on to Hampden Park with typical instruction; "Just go out and win." They thought they were due some overtime – and were looking for that additional half hour.

Before the Final I thought that the game deserved a solution, that extra time and penalties should be added to allow the Cup to go to one place or another on Saturday evening. Now I am not so sure – for few will want to miss the next instalment, so good and furious was this latest chapter in world football's most famous quarrel.

Next season, these teams could meet nine times. Some will say that there is a danger in over-exposure, a menace to public order and the very uniqueness of the Old Firm will be undervalued by so many meetings. That, too, I begin to doubt.

For Saturday's match was again exceptional. A hard first half was followed by a good second. Funny goals were followed by nice goals. And all of this was contrived on an afternoon of slate grey skies with water splashing over the feet of forwards and defenders alike.

PERFECT MATCH

There is a guarantee of satisfaction given to spectators these days when the Old Firm collide. Their styles encourage and stimulate each other, Rangers relying on fitness and total aggression, Celtic preferring to await and make the counter attack.

They are the perfect match for each other, the entrepreneur's dream. They sell tickets and some 70,000 risked pneumonia to watch them. This city is occasionally cursed by the excesses of their fans, but recently a football lover has been privileged to have them among us.

The incident and chronology of this Glasgow Final meant more than the tactics, fascinating as they were. Who would have written a script that gave the first humorous line to Sandy Jardine, the Footballer of the Year. He helped the ball towards his own net in the third minute when it could have been put just about anywhere else. Wilson pushed it into the net.

Five minutes later in our rooftop eyrie we were deafened from a different direction. McLean's corner kick was headed by both Johnstone and Jackson before Stein glanced the equaliser into the net. Roddy MacDonald, at fault with others here, went on to play well.

CLASS GOAL

Wilson scored his second – and the final class goal – a little later, rounding Jackson and Kennedy, and dragging the ball wide of Greig before shooting high into the net. Dalglish and the improving Lynch had helped to fashion it.

When one MacDonald's shot ricocheted off the other McDonald to give Rangers a second equaliser, parity was restored for the second time. And in that same first half Kennedy knocked a Wilson shot away with his legs, Jackson cleared a Lennox attempt off the line and Johnstone was booked.

"A titanic struggle," said someone at half time, a correct if slightly dubious analogy on such a watery day. And the match raged on as the surface became worse. There were no more goals, but good individual performances from Stein playing deep and studiously, Murray and Jackson.

Finally this highly strung Final was over and the rain eased off. This correspondent made no prediction beforehand and even now refrains from saying which was the better side on the day.

There was little to choose between them, and the city of Glasgow and the game of football were the victors. The summer will soon be over and we can start again, invigorated.

Glasgow Cup Final

Celtic (2) 2	Rangers (2) 2
Wilson 2	Stein
	McDonald (o.g.)
Attendance	**70,000**

CELTIC:- LATCHFORD, MCGRAIN, LYNCH L., MCCLUSKEY, MCDONALD, BROGAN, HOOD, MURRAY, DALGLISH, LENNOX AND WILSON. SUBSTITUTES – JOHNSTONE J. AND CALLAGHAN.

RANGERS:- KENNEDY, JARDINE, GREIG, MCKEAN, JACKSON, FORSYTH, MCLEAN, STEIN, PARLANE, MACDONALD AND JOHNSTONE D. SUBSTITUTES - YOUNG AND MILNE.

Rangers 2, Celtic 1 – Saturday, 30th August, 1975

Football Takes Another Beating

By Ian Archer

Rangers met Celtic on Saturday in the first match of the new Premier League, beat them by the width of a cigarette paper, and some 69,000 thronged to Ibrox to watch this game of football. The clubs meet three more times before next summer rescues us again.

The Celtic goal was scored by Kenny Dalglish. In the second half Derek Johnstone equalised. Quinton Young gave Rangers the lead, and Alex MacDonald was despatched to the pavilion by competent referee Ian Foote. Peter McCloy played with exceptional skill to protect the slenderest of leads. The match finished at 4.43 p.m.

There were three battles among the supporters as the game was in progress, and as the crowd drifted away the terraces were littered with thousands of beer cans, and hundreds of whisky bottles, while on the pitch itself a large bottle of fortified wine stood in glorious isolation. It was unsafe to leave the ground until 5.30 p.m.

Rival fans battered each other outside the nearby Ibrox House; another rammy in which knives and bottles were used was reported on Paisley Road West. At Central Station someone was stabbed, for there was a pool of blood lying in the concourse.

Police reported that 84 fans were arrested inside or within the immediate environs of Ibrox, between 70 and 100 spectators needed treatment after injuries, and several people lay in the city's hospitals on Saturday night after fights, some in public houses a distance from the ground.

A Rangers fan was thrown 30 feet off a parapet and at least one train was halted outside Glasgow because a supporter had pulled the communications cord. At least one subway train was wrecked. Police in Hope Street stopped fans from trying to rend a bus asunder.

My generation was brought up on stories of the wild Glasgow of the Thirties. I read books about that time, of Saturday nights when the dance halls were alleged to run with blood, when a "claim" could produce such markings that a sewing machine rather than a doctor with a needle and thread could have patched up the victims more effectively.

But now, I would suggest, this is a cruder, more vicious city even further behind the rest of Europe in terms of civilised behaviour, cleanliness, housing, culture and education. It may have been, as the apologists say, a minority who made Saturday so awful, but the blame attaches to all of us.

ALLEGIANCE

I saw a boy at Ibrox, only 15, and he was wearing a scarf proclaiming his allegiance to the Ulster Defence Association. He was talking to two policemen and then he made his way into the ground. Why was that allowed?

And what is the cost to the community? Will I bear the burden of the policing on my rates? Will I pay for all that stitching on my taxes? And what happens to the old and infirm who need attention in the casualty wards and find the place besieged by those in blue and green scarves needing attention to their broken heads? Is there a priority in these matters?

Will the SFA invoke article 130 and punish Rangers and Celtic?

These steps are unlikely for Glasgow has long regarded this problem as insoluble, the football clubs issuing ritual appeals, councillors making pious statements, and magistrates dishing out the fines.

COARSE

The game itself was coarse and enthralling. Those players whom one would expect to overstray the boundaries between legitimate aggression and naked hostility did so, and Mr Foote caught some and missed others. There was too much shirt-pulling, pushing, high and late tackling as well as off-the-ball incidents for the neutral.

Rangers probably won because Dalglish was patrolled so well in the first half by Jardine – despite the goal – and so brilliantly in the second half by the young O'Hara. The other green 10 could not quite overcome the blotting out of their best player, despite McGrain's energy on the overlap.

Lennox, with one missed chance, might have settled the contest the other way, and it was only McCloy who kept Celtic from the equaliser in the last desperate stages when the substitutes Ritchie and Connelly inspired a rally against a Rangers side reduced to 10 men after McDonald's dismissal.

COURAGE

Rangers scored an unchallengeable goal with Johnstone's shot but Young pushed McCluskey before starting the run which gave them the second. Their courage was not in doubt as, hemmed back, they kept Celtic out as they waited with anxiety for the final whistle.

The pity remains that a match which was in no little way rewarding should be marred by the circumstances surrounding it. The violence will further persuade people that football can struggle towards its depressing future without requiring their attendance on the terraces. The Premier League had its worst possible start.

Rangers (0) 2	Celtic (1) 1
Johnstone D.	Dalglish
Young	

RANGERS:- MCCLOY, JARDINE, GREIG, FORSYTH, JACKSON, MACDONALD, MCLEAN, MCKEAN, STEIN, JOHNSTONE D. AND YOUNG. SUBSTITUTES – MILLER AND O'HARA.

CELTIC:- LATCHFORD, MCGRAIN, LYNCH, MCCLUSKEY, MCDONALD, EDVALDSSON, MCNAMARA, WILSON, DALGLISH, CALLAGHAN AND LENNOX. SUBSTITUTES – RITCHIE AND CONNELLY.

Rangers 1, Celtic 0 – Saturday, 25th October, 1975

Rangers' Cheers after Sober Old Firm Final

By Ian Archer

The Scottish League Cup trophy lies at Ibrox. By mid-afternoon on Saturday the large Rangers division in a small crowd of 58,000 were wandering the streets of Glasgow, drinkless but delirious after the first Rangers triumph in this tournament for five years.

The invitation to attend Hampden Park at 12.30 for 1 p.m., it turned out had been for a quiet lunch rather than the usual booze-up. This was a sober Old Firm match, both on the terraces and on the field. There were neither giant hangovers nor joyful memories after the most downbeat Final of recent times.

Rangers won with a mildly spectacular goal from Alex MacDonald, the villain of St Etienne, suddenly the man whose name was chanted the length of Somerville Drive and much further afield as the blue-noses dispersed to various base camps scattered throughout Scotland. They won the hard way.

It was the first time John Greig had handled the League Cup as captain; it gave Rangers their eighth hold on the trophy, and it gave Jock Wallace the only Scottish competition to elude him in his time as manager. It ended the club's recent losing run and gave them automatic entry to Europe again next season.

For Celtic, it was a sad day for Sean Fallon, wanting his own deserved and private victory in the club's twelfth successive final. Kenny Dalglish could not go forward to receive a cup for the first time as captain, and he looked close to despair as he watched the other team climb the stand steps to receive the winners' medals.

Leg weary from Oporto and St Etienne, Celtic and Rangers asked to kick-off two hours early. Both seemed to have risen from their beds on the wrong side and not rubbed the sleep out of their eyes in time for the match. The goalkeepers were largely redundant, the passing was erratic, and tackling snapped down on genius like a mousetrap claiming its unwary victim.

Rangers won a day when their own traditions of persistence, energy and single-mindedness counted for more than the usual Celtic virtues of neat, tidy and attractive football.

There was one decisive – and controversial – contest within the contest. Rangers, who had worried about Dalglish and who had, in previous meetings opposed him with MacDonald or Jardine, this time elected Tom Forsyth for the task of turning out the light of the Final's one and only truly exceptional talent. He not only flicked the switch but, for safety's sake pulled out the whole fusebox as well.

SOME MAN

Forsyth, as they say, is some man. He was not born but forged by blacksmiths. In this Final he collided with Parlane and received a head cut the size of a match box. Tom Craig, the Rangers trainer, went on, came back to the dug-out and reported: "I stuck two fingers in it. Boss. It's bad." "Tell him to get on with it," replied Wallace.

Later, even John Greig was worried: "The blood's pouring out," he shouted to the bench. "He doesn't tackle with his head, does he?" shouted back the manager: "Stop moaning." Wallace told Forsyth in the dressing room as he complained of a sore head, "Away and get it stitched." It needed five loops of needle and thread before it was patched.

DEFENDED

His manager defends him. "If Forsyth ever went over the ball, I would tear the head off him. I would stake my life on the fact that he never goes over the ball." It is impossible from the distance of the Hampden press box to judge that thin dividing line between the indiscriminate and the malicious. As a person, Forsyth in a sportsman. Of that I am sure. With Dalglish burdened by his patrol, Celtic looked loose and uncoordinated. They lost the midfield and Edvaldsson, after an early knock, was not much help. In attack, Lennox and Wilson had no chance to use their legs and run the Rangers defence into a state of distraction.

SCORING HEADER

Rangers were adequate most of the time, and good in bits and pieces, especially in the first part of the second half, when for once they were able to string passes about a Hampden which looks dangerously underknitted. After 67 minutes they scored the only goal.

Parlane beat MacDonald well on the left byeline and his cross was headed away by Edvaldsson in the general direction of Young. It looked as if the winger was going to volley, and that intention was picked up by Celtic. As they closed in to block, Young headed across goal and MacDonald ducked forward to head strongly into the net. It was all – and quite enough.

"The last 20 minutes, they were all running on their guts," Wallace added. Celtic's late charge was resisted and to thunderous applause Greig put the trophy in his hands and carried it into the dressing room, where it was filled with champagne. By three o'clock, the traditional witching hour for football, Hampden was quiet and deserted, and they pulled down the flags.

Scottish League Cup Final

Rangers (0) 1	Celtic (0) 0
MacDonald	
Attendance	58,000

RANGERS:- KENNEDY, JARDINE, GREIG, FORSYTH, JACKSON, MACDONALD A., MCLEAN, STEIN, PARLANE, JOHNSTONE AND YOUNG. SUBSTITUTES – MCKEAN AND MILLER.

CELTIC:- LATCHFORD, MCGRAIN, LYNCH, MCCLUSKEY, MACDONALD R., EDVALDSSON, HOOD, DALGLISH, WILSON, CALLAGHAN AND LENNOX. SUBSTITUTES – MCNAMARA AND GLAVIN

Celtic 1, Rangers 1 – Saturday, 1st November, 1975

Old Firm are back in Business

By Ian Archer

Rangers scored an odd and unfair goal. Celtic scored an awkward goal. Some 55,000 stayed sober and stupefied at the intensity of an Old Firm match that will long be treasured. The Premier League came of age on November 1, 1975.

A lunch-time kick-off at Parkhead meant that by three o'clock the desperate football citizens of Glasgow were walking the streets composing themselves, and waiting for the drink shops to open so that after-match seminars could be conducted with their usual solemn decorum. But that was not all.

The nicest aspect of the Old Firm collision – a sweet course after the Saturday's sour League Cup Final – was that, for once, it was not a match on its own, a piece of ritual blood-letting, a private battle. It had, this time, to be put in context with what was happening in the Lothians and Ayrshire.

At the orthodox kick-off time, Celtic were the league leaders. In the next two hours it was possible for Motherwell to overtake them or Hibernian and Hearts to join them. For once Scottish football – and the leadership of it – were a matter of broad horizons.

By the time the classified results were heard and interpreted, Celtic retained that leadership, but that trio of aspirants, together with Rangers, were clustering just a single point behind. The top of the Premier League table this morning looks as crowded as the last bus to Drumchapel on a Saturday night.

It is a long time since interest in absolute leadership has been scattered so geographically wide. We are now impatient to see what next weekend's results will produce. There is a throbbing excitement about the club game which has not been present for a long time past.

Even the Old Firm match was a grand occasion, for on the field it raged and roared, and off the field it was watched noisily but without too much rancour.

We needed a good Old Firm match and were rewarded with just such a game. The previous Saturday's match had, after all, been a Cup Final and those are always apart. In the context of two points for the winner, both Celtic and Rangers relaxed a little. One felt there had been some dressing-room talks about responsibility and good play.

REWARDED

Thus Celtic had a good first half and their decision to include young George McCluskey, only a year ago a Scottish schoolboy internationalist, showed faith in the club's belief in its own high standards and a willingness to use all of the width of the park to entertain.

McCluskey's wing play was a fresh ingredient and Young's better form also made Rangers a more potent side coming forward. Such ideals tested the two goalkeepers, Latchford and Kennedy, but neither was found wanting and both made saves of the highest class. The ball bobbed around the goalmouths for all but a brief period in the second half when the game became technical and a little coarse.

The battle between Tom Forsyth and Kenny Dalglish was again fascinating and this time played in good spirit. Dalglish was used in a more forward position. Forsyth was taken into deep defence and, therefore, the middle of the park was a place of creativity rather than destruction.

The draw was clearly fair, even if the Rangers goal wasn't. Lynch took a short free kick and Callaghan was dreaming. McLean, standing no more than five yards away, stole and pushed the ball forward to Parlane, who may have been offside. Celtic waited for the first whistle and, when it never came, were naked as the centre forward dribbled round Latchford to score his first Premier League goal. That explained how he came to be lying on his back under the weight of corporate congratulations.

One end was looking forward to the third successive Rangers victory when, three minutes later, McCluskey junior, who had started, understandably, to tire, came up the right wing, hit a fast cross and Wilson, running in at the far post, pushed the ball over the line with his stomach. It was an abdominal equaliser. That left the game shared.

Parlane, who had earlier hit the bar, was booked for a spectacular kick at McCluskey senior and Johnstone for another unfriendly act on the same Celtic defender. But that happened in the one niggling period of a free, full-blooded match.

I can merely say that Old Firm occasions usually make me nervous before they start and offend me when they are under way. This time it was just possible to stand back and admire two fine teams in a fine footballing country play a fine match. No discount warehouses offer better bargains than games like this at 60p a head.

Celtic 1	Rangers 1
Wilson	Parlane
Attendance	55,000

CELTIC:- LATCHFORD, MCGRAIN, LYNCH, P. MCCLUSKEY, MACDONALD, EDVALDSSON, G. MCCLUSKEY, DALGLISH, DEANS, CALLAGHAN AND WILSON. SUBSTITUTES – HOOD AND LENNOX

RANGERS:- KENNEDY, JARDINE, GREIG, FORSYTH, JACKSON, MACDONALD, MCLEAN, STEIN, PARLANE, JOHNSTONE AND YOUNG.

Rangers 1, Celtic 0 – Thursday, 1st January, 1976
Ne'erday Game

The Glasgow Herald did not appear on the first two days of 1976. These traditional Scottish holidays were part of the festive season's non-publication days. Football, if not the presses, however, moved forward and by the time the newspaper was back on the streets, on January 3rd, the Ne'erday games were very much yesterday's news. The following text is extracted from Ian Archer's observations on the Scottish football scene, published that day.

Rangers' victory over Celtic at Ibrox, gained from the same Derek Johnstone head that has done so much damage in Old Firm matches, meant that the Parkhead club failed to break that 31-year losing Ne'erday sequence at the ground and stretched Rangers' unbeaten lead over their bitterest rivals to seven games.

A match that failed to attract a capacity gate, which never really stirred a miserable crowd, was at least marked by good behaviour. It also brought the defending champions back to within a point of Celtic.

Quo Vadunt? This afternoon only Celtic of the leaders have the important advantage of playing in front of their own supporters.

Sean Fallon – "I thought we might have been worth a point at Ibrox for our second half onslaught" – adds one intriguing name to the pool, Steve Murray, who has been training in Dundee, is included and, according to the manager, "will be substitute at least."

Celtic need Murray's drive in that area, especially with Kenny Dalglish's poor patch continuing. They must also hope that Dundee do not mark as tightly as Rangers, for the present Parkhead side seem to have trouble breaking the ties that bind them to opponents.

Rangers, whose stamina, intransigence and big staff all now come into play may contemplate one change. O'Hara – a good substitute in the last quarter of the Celtic match – could replace Hamilton.

Rangers (1) 1	Celtic (0) 0
Johnstone D.	

RANGERS:- KENNEDY; MILLER AND GREIG; FORSYTH, JACKSON AND MACDONALD; MCKEAN AND HAMILTON; HENDERSON; MCLEAN AND JOHNSTONE. SUBSTITUTES – SCOTT AND O'HARA.

CELTIC:- LATCHFORD; MCGRAIN AND LYNCH; EDVALDSSON, MACDONALD AND MCLUSKEY; MCNAMARA AND DALGLISH; DEANS; CALLAGHAN AND LENNOX. SUBSTITUTES – WILSON AND HOOD.

Derek Parlane finds space to head for goal as the Celtic defence look on.

Celtic 0, Rangers 0 – Monday, 26th April, 1976

Old Firm Call a Truce at Parkhead

By Ian Archer

Celtic and Rangers discovered last night at Parkhead that even the combustible chemistry of blue mixed with green cannot be ignited into an explosive charge unless it really matters. The Old Firm bored 51,000 at Parkhead.

To the a list of horrific, ecstatic and controversial matches between these clubs must be added a small footnote about the occasion when they met and declared a truce. The fourth and last Premier League match between them this season ended in a goalless draw with honour barely satisfied.

Rangers will be happy that their long unbeaten run now extends to 25 matches and that they emerged unscathed for Saturday's Scottish Cup Final against Hearts. Celtic will be pleased that they avoided defeat in a season which, particularly over the past weeks, has tested the patience of their fans.

The audience was better than the actors on a mild spring evening. Those wearing blue had rampaged down London Road, wearing triumph boldly. Those in green had come via the Gallowgate and mustered on the terraces determined to show their defiance. All night they sang.

Rangers won decisive victory here. Their profane hymns rang round Parkhead in increasing decibels, and they would not go home at the end. It was 10 minutes after the final, thankful, whistle before they departed, the last chorus sung. They said they would win the Cup – and so they should.

The game of course was killed stone dead on Saturday when Rangers ran their lap of honour around Tannadice with the Championship won. They came to Parkhead with Hampden on their minds, and for once Glasgow's bitter divide seemed not to matter much.

Only in the last 10 minutes was there an incident as Celtic began to realise that not only was the title lost but also that a propaganda victory was to be denied them as well. Then they cut up a little rough.

Kenny Dalglish, who had looked out of sorts all night, was booked for the latest in a series of tackles on Derek Johnstone. Pat McCluskey was cautioned for kicking the tiny Tommy McLean some several feet in the air. Those lapses in behaviour at least helped to fill some of the notebook.

Celtic, in fact, were the better side although they were anything but really good. Tommy Burns, the youngster with a career to carve, was busy and perceptible in midfield. Johnny Doyle began to pay the loose change in his £80,000 transfer fee. They at least went forward.

ACTION

Rangers knew their defensive lines but spoke them without passion. In the absence of Tom Forsyth and Colin Jackson, Derek Johnstone moved back to centre half and, ironically, marked Johannes Edvaldsson, who was moved forward.

That little contest was drawn – as were all the other personal confrontations in a match padlocked in man-to-man marking with one side unable to break free and the other largely content to stay in bondage. The big crowd seemed not to mind too much.

A light ball and concrete pitch were no help, with Peter Latchford and Peter McCloy able to kick such huge distances that it seemed they were playing some kind of new ping-pong amongst themselves.

If the action is a long time arriving in this report, so it was in the match itself, although in retrospect it might all have been different if Celtic had taken their first chance of the match.

After only 60 seconds Doyle released Lennox and his shot was only half saved by McCloy. The ball ran loose to Edvaldsson, but his shot was kicked off line by Greig. That was a good start, but led to nothing.

The rest of the first half was memorable only for a Lynch free kick which Edvaldsson headed over the bar at one end, and a McLean shot which flew over the bar at the other.

After 63 minutes Dalglish headed a Burns cross just an inch wide and in that period Celtic deserved victory for effort. McNamara replaced Edvaldsson, and then the bookings brought the game to its end – and allowed the blue fans to do their encore.

So ended an uneventful night without the Celtic recognition of Rangers' championship win which some had anticipated. That reflects no lack of courtesy, just average wisdom. But it might have been more exciting than the slow wait that followed.

Celtic (0) 0	Rangers (0) 0
Attendance	51,000

CELTIC:- LATCHFORD, MCGRAIN, LYNCH, P. MCCLUSKEY, AITKEN, EDVALDSSON, DOYLE, DALGLISH, MCDONALD, BURNS AND LENNOX. SUBSTITUTES – MCNAMARA AND G. MCCLUSKEY.

RANGERS:- MCCLOY, MILLER, GREIG, JARDINE, JOHNSTONE, MACDONALD, MCKEAN, HAMILTON, HENDERSON, MCLEAN AND PARLANE. SUBSTITUTES – STEIN AND DENNY.

1976

Celtic 1, Rangers 3 – Tuesday, 10th August, 1976

Miller Penalty Clinches Cup for Rangers

By Ian Archer

Rangers last night took the Glasgow Cup and so added a small postscript to the end of a last triumphant season. Some 55,000 watched peacefully a stirring Old Firm match, mean, moody and magnificent.

Years come, years go but this ritual continues. Rangers carried back to Ibrox not only a meaningless little trophy but a victory in the propaganda war that precedes every season. They will be well pleased with the goals by Sandy Jardine, Colin Jackson and Alex Miller which gave them another success over Celtic.

Rangers played a clean insistent first half and relaxed in the second. Celtic, though, never stopped trying. With both defences about as secure as an open prison, they abused at least 10 opportunities to score. There was less of a margin of superiority than the scoreline suggests.

There was one odd interesting note about Rangers. The team were playing despite the fact that the majority of them are in dispute with the club over wages. Varying estimates say that between 12 and 16 are unhappy with their conditions of employment for the new season. If so, it did not show on the park. As ever, they wanted to win.

The Final was made by two Rangers goals in the first 10 minutes. It was sustained by the fact that so many attackers could go by their markers like express trains rushing through deserted stations. Uneven goalkeeping added to the excitement and the decibels. The passion of it all was truly Scottish and, thus recharged, the spectators will be back for the routine round of League Cup matches which start the season on Saturday.

Within 60 seconds of the start of the match as loose as an oversize smock, George McCluskey, of Celtic, could have scored at one end, Tommy McLean at the other. That set a pattern of uninterrupted attacking which lasted the night-time through. It made the delayed start – 7.46, with thousands still outside – seem bearable.

Within four minutes Rangers were ahead. Jardine picked up a ball deep and wide with only Lennox there to challenge. He was shrugged aside and Jardine entered the penalty area alone. His shot went under Latchford's body and when the player stumbled as he saluted the crowd, it was his first wrong move.

Six minutes later, there was a second. McCloy's huge kick – that old weapon – found Derek Johnstone. His header was saved under pressure by Latchford, who seemed more surprised than he should have been. A corner followed and much then happened.

McLean took it. Johnstone headed and the goalkeeper palmed out, Jackson volleyed back, the ball struck Lynch and went into orbit over the goal. As it came down everyone watched as if it were a meteor. Then it fell over the line, before being scrambled clear. Referee Foote gave the goal. Dalglish led the protests to the linesman, but after a small seminar the goal stood, rightly. Rangers were triumphant – and clear.

Yet they relaxed. Celtic had much of the rest of the match but could do little with it. McCloy mixed good saves with lucky ones. Yet even he could not stop Celtic's goal three minutes before half-time which brought them back into the match.

An attack was half-cleared, and again players became spectators. Jackson watched out of position and so did the goalkeeper as Glavin lofted the ball back into the penalty area. Edvaldsson, unmarked, eight yards out, simply headed the ball into an inviting net. There was still a contest.

Jackson was hurt and could not come back for the second half. Derek Johnstone dropped back to his best position, centre half, and McKean arrived instead of Henderson, presumably to cover McGrain's overlaps. Rangers contained rather than impressed for the next period. A more experienced Celtic side might have equalised, even won. But Jock Stein took off George McCluskey and then Tommy Burns, replacing them with Pat McCluskey and Paul Wilson. All their possession never quite built up into a sustained rhythm.

With Greig everywhere, Rangers stayed cool and accepted that every ball which spun out of McCloy's hands would drop at the defenders' feet. And then they scored again. Parlane, attacking well on his own, rounded McDonald. The centre half tripped him when he had no need. Miller made the penalty safe, well wide of Latchford.

There was still time for Dalglish to hit the post with a cute cross shot, time too for others to test the goalkeeper. But Rangers were safe, the insurance policy of the first 10 minutes now being cashed in. A dog came on to disturb Celtic's momentum and looked quick in one dash the length of the field.

Thus Greig put another Cup in his hand, after playing so well. Johnstone and Forsyth had done more than their share, as had Parlane. If they are under-paid, it does not show.

Stein's magic failed to give Celtic the draw which, with the right bounce, they might have gained. There is not much to choose between two good sides, at least in Scottish terms, as they enter another season. All the others have much unrewarding work in front of them.

Glasgow Cup Final

Celtic (1) 1	Rangers (2) 3
Edvaldsson	Jardine
	Jackson
	Miller (pen.)
Attendance	55,000

CELTIC:- LATCHFORD, MCGRAIN, LYNCH, GLAVIN, MCDONALD, EDVALDSSON, DALGLISH, DOYLE, MCCLUSKEY, BURNS AND LENNOX. SUBSTITUTES – PAT MCCLUSKEY AND WILSON.

RANGERS :- MCCLOY, MILLER, GREIG, FORSYTH, JACKSON, MACDONALD, MCLEAN, JARDINE, PARLANE, MUNRO AND JOHNSTONE. SUBSTITUTES - MCKEAN AND HENDERSON.

Sandy Jardine and Dixie Deans cannot catch Bobby Lennox's decisive shot in the 1974
Ne'er Day game.

Young embraces Jackson scorer of the winning goal at Parkhead in September 1974.

Tommy McLean curls the ball round the Celtic defence.

Alec MacDonald's header flies into the net.

Celtic 2, Rangers 2 – Saturday, 4th September, 1976
'Great' Old Firm match
By Ian Archer

When the dust had settled and the hail of police car sirens had departed Glasgow's East End, the Old Firm match which started another Premier League season was assessed by Rangers' manager, Jock Wallace – "Great."

Celtic and Rangers again proved the Scottish game's ability to rise above itself in pace, skill, stature and dignity. Some 57,000 watched chilled and thrilled by a stirring match which was almost won by one side and which, if strict justice had worked, ought to have been won by the other. A draw kept everyone – and nobody – happy.

Rangers can reflect that they played poorly, Celtic extraordinarily well, and yet the defending Champions squeezed a point from Parkhead. It is not long ago that they would have been happy with that. Now – after coming within three minutes of a win – they can afford to draw at the dregs of disappointment.

Scottish football wins all round. After those mundane League Cup sections, the infant Championship table puts Dundee and Ayr United at the top, the Old Firm inseparably in the middle, and throughout autumn and winter, and spring, there will be much excitement. But the standard set at Parkhead will rarely be bettered.

Celtic looked as if they just might have the makings of a team again. Pat Stanton's studious start released Ronnie Glavin to play as he first did at Firhill, going forward. Paul Wilson's return to form was as sudden as it was unexpected, for last season he had totally forgotten all his lines. McGrain was something else as usual. Dalglish played one part well instead of several indifferently.

There is still much work ahead for Jock Stein. The first Rangers goal was conceded by marking so close that it was almost united, but at least that problem has been isolated. The eventual promotion of Aitken to the centre half position will give some weight to the defence as well.

Rangers played oddly on the day. Jardine could never get started away from Burns' consistent attention. MacDonald's long runs from deep were spotted and stopped by Celtic. McLean never had enough of the ball and Munro still has to gain confidence to seek it outside the small acre of the left wing. Johnstone came and went.

The scoring was curious. Celtic had four corners in as many minutes and looked the better side before McLean's free kick and MacDonald's header gave Johnstone a present of the first goal. Celtic had hit the bar before Munro's pass to McLean's run gave Parlane a complimentary second.

All the time that lead had looked unjust. Wilson's half-hit goal just after half-time gave some decency to the scoreline, and playing with the bitter dedication that Old Firm occasions produce, Celtic forced McCloy into serious saves for the next 20 minutes.

But the perceptive ones noticed that Celtic were flagging in the last 10 minutes and that Johnstone had abused two chances. Then Burns' pass and Wilson's run and shot gave Celtic their second goal just as the blue choruses were starting after a long silence.

They had deserved no less and it was the green that stayed rooted to the terraces the end. The Old Firm meet again in two months' time.

Celtic (0) 2	Rangers (2) 2
Wilson 2	Johnstone
	Parlane
Attendance	57,000

CELTIC:- LATCHFORD, MCGRAIN, LYNCH, STANTON, MACDONALD, MCCLUSKEY, DOYLE, GLAVIN, WILSON, BURNS AND DALGLISH. SUBSTITUTES – LENNOX AND AITKEN.

RANGERS:- MCCLOY, MILLER, GREIG, FORSYTH, DENNY, MACDONALD, MCLEAN, JARDINE, PARLANE, MUNRO AND JOHNSTONE. SUBSTITUTES – HAMILTON AND MCKEAN

Doyle, Dalglish and McCloy watch Wilson's shot head for goal.

Rangers 0, Celtic 1 – Wednesday, 24th November, 1976

Craig's Clincher

By Ian Archer

Celtic last night ended their bleak spell of more than 1000 days by beating Rangers for the first time since January, 1974 – and so their fans, without transport, floated all the way home from the impassioned terraces of Ibrox.

They played with just enough inspiration, and placed that quality on top of ceaseless effort to take victory over the Champions, who tried just as hard but who were not quite as clever. The scoreline – close – was clearly correct.

It was Joe Craig's goal nine minutes before half-time, that still separated the two teams at the end of a match watched in great good order by a crowd which again showed that an Old Firm occasion must not be missed, even if the buses are locked in the garage.

"I'll walk a million miles for one of your goals, Joe Craig," the green end shouted and maybe corporately they had done just about that.

Curiously, no Celtic player fired on all cylinders for all 90 minutes, but in long patches many were very able. Peter Latchford's second-half saves from a Rangers forward line belatedly recovering their touch, were probably crucial. The defence stood firm, and further forward there were four good performances.

Kenny Dalglish guided most of the good work, while Roy Aitken came of age even as early as his eighteenth birthday, adding forcefulness in midfield. Johnny Doyle ran hard and surprised Rangers occasionally, and Craig, his goal apart, ran to make the space for others. The gradual improvement of this team continues.

Rangers, again, were a puzzle. They could find no insistent rhythm although, as always, their willingness was not in question. Their defence seemed capable of solving most problems; their midfield grafted, but in the forward positions Derek Parlane had far too much work to do.

Latterly, they brought on Colin Stein for his first match in more than a year, but that made no real difference. One will remember most about this match that Jim Steele was booked for his third consecutive match. His tackle on Doyle was as late as a large drink, just as it had been against Hibernian's Edwards on Saturday.

At the end Celtic hugged each other hard. In their long non-winning sequence against the only rivals who ultimately matter, their confidence had been stricken. Last night's match may be a little watershed in the comparative standing of Glasgow's perennial competitors.

There was one other memorable moment in a game which yielded incidents reluctantly. After 12 minutes referee Eddie Thomson decided to give Celtic a penalty and then changed his mind, quite rightly. In real wars one tends to be presented to the Queen and given a gong for such bravery.

The incident was odd. Glavin played a long through ball well into the stride of Bobby Lennox. While the linesman raised the flag John Greig cut the winger in two as he tried to retrieve the situation.

Mr Thomson gave the penalty and, after Rangers protests, spoke to the linesman and turned the decision, correctly, into a free kick. The Celtic crowd, which in other times might have been less than gruntled, merely passed the remark to the official in unison, "Spot the looney."

Lennox went off, sadly, with a broken ankle, and thence to hospital. But that did not deter Celtic, with Wilson coming on, from playing in the next period their best football of the match. Steele was booked for Rangers after 27 minutes and a small segment later Celtic scored their good goal.

Dalglish started the move with a forward pass. Aitken sustained it with a gentle nudge sideways to Craig. The move looked promising and no more, until the centre forward struck a vicious curling shot from 20 yards which flew high into the net, well wide of Kennedy.

Rangers' best chance came after 55 minutes when Parlane's cross tempted Latchford off his line, only to miss the ball. McLean tapped and shot, only for the goalkeeper to flight himself sideways to make a thrilling save. That, possibly, was the best opportunity missed.

Ten minutes later, when a McLean free kick was only half cleared, Latchford again made an instinctive save from MacDonald's volley, pushing the ball wide with a mixture of his hand and foot. At that moment the Celtic people began singing their anthem because they realised the challenge had been received and repulsed.

Rangers (0) 0	Celtic (1) 1
	Craig

RANGERS:- KENNEDY, JARDINE, GREIG, STEELE, JACKSON, WATSON, MCLEAN, HAMILTON, PARLANE, MACDONALD AND MCKEAN. SUBSTITUTES – STEIN AND MILLER.

CELTIC:- LATCHFORD, MCGRAIN, LYNCH, STANTON, MCDONALD, AITKEN, DOYLE, GLAVIN, CRAIG, DALGLISH AND LENNOX. SUBSTITUTES – WILSON AND P. MCCLUSKEY.

Celtic 1, Rangers 0 – Tuesday, 11th January, 1977

Jackson Seals it for Celtic

By Ian Archer

Celtic last night took the points that placed them back on the top of the Premier League from an Old Firm match that left Rangers to wonder whether the Fates had deserted them in their bid to retain the Championship. Some 52,000 watched impeccably.

On a pitch surrounded by straw which was in turns white, brown and green in texture – looking, in fact, like a circus ring – they could not serve their own cause. The victory came from an unlucky own goal by Colin Jackson.

As the Rangers fans departed down the London Road they were neither in sour nor surly mood. They had watched their team play with more finesse than many thought they possessed, battle with some courage, and been robbed by one of these interventions that occasionally make football a cruel game.

All about the goal was messy. Alex O'Hara conceded a corner awkwardly. Rangers were slow to react when Johnny Doyle and Andy Lynch worked the ball short and only Tommy McLean, sprinting 60 yards, realised the danger, but too late.

Lynch crossed adequately on to the head of Roddy MacDonald and he struck the ball firmly, if not decisively. Rangers' goalkeeper, Stewart Kennedy, had it covered until the deflection by Jackson carried it snugly into the net. By such margins titles are won and lost and prove that justice is not always served when men play this game.

That is not to say that Rangers clearly deserved to win, but patently they had contrived in a full-blooded match not to deserve to find themselves in the difficult League position which is theirs this morning. To their credit in the 15 minutes that remained, they struck terror into the Celtic hearts as they pushed for the equaliser.

That might even have been theirs two minutes from the end when McLean lobbed a header from the edge of the penalty area over the arms of Celtic's goalkeeper, Peter Latchford, who was off his line. Somehow Roy Aitken managed to get back to scramble the ball away from under the shadow of the goalpost, and so defeat was doubly hard to take.

An Old Firm draw would have been no bad result after the heroics Celtic had performed just to give the customers a match and after the assured approach of Rangers for much of the first half. But it now leaves one club with the Championship very much in its sights, and another who must now rely on mistakes by others.

There was much action even before the match started. A party of 30 volunteers, under the command of Celtic's coach John Clark, worked furiously to make the ground fit for football. The tons of straw were removed, the snow cleared, the sand spread, and the lines marked even while the crowd stood waiting patiently for a game which started 10 minutes late. The referee inspected with overcoat worn above his uniform.

As it was, the pitch looked worse than it played, at least until the final minutes, and there was no lack of resolution and skill throughout the game. Again the Old Firm habit of man-to-man marking almost to the extent of wearing handcuffs, cut down the number of sweeping attacks.

Aitken's attentions to Derek Johnstone were matched by O'Hara's shackling of Kenny Dalglish.

Kenny Watson controlled much for Rangers while in the first half, Celtic tried to be a little too clever and a little too fast. Commitment was total, incident sporadic.

The goalkeeping was of the highest order with Latchford firm in his handling of the crossball and Kennedy agile at both posts. They both made saves which kept the early play level and in the 20th minute, when Latchford saved a fine Watson drive, he had already earned his money.

Rangers then became a little harsh. If the tackling was not malicious, it was certainly indiscriminate. McLean was booked for a foul on Doyle, no worse than some that had gone before, as Mr Foote exerted his authority. Two minutes later, when Tom Forsyth piled into Joe Craig in the centre circle, the Celtic end cried, "Off! Off!" and it was certainly a possibility. He, too, was cautioned.

SET PIECES

In the second half Celtic released Aitken more often and that tactic made a difference, although most of their action was fashioned from set pieces. They had the ball in the net from Craig after 57 minutes, but a foul on Kennedy silenced the premature jubilation.

Latchford saved an awkward Bobby McKean shot and Kennedy coped adequately when Dalglish flicked on a Glavin shot as genuine excitement came to the contest. But it seemed that we would have to settle for an evening of splendid commitment until, in the 76th minute, Celtic scored one of the most crucial of all the Old Firm crucial goals – by courtesy of Jackson.

In the vast scheme of things Aberdeen may remind us all that the Premier League is not a two-club contest by regaining the lead tonight. But few Glaswegians would place hard cash on the title leaving the city and after last night Celtic look more likely to keep the trophy in these parts. There may never have been a more important own goal ever conceded.

Celtic (0) 1	Rangers (0) 0
Jackson (o.g.)	
Attendance	52,000

CELTIC:- LATCHFORD, MCGRAIN, LYNCH, STANTON, MACDONALD, AITKEN, DOYLE, GLAVIN, CRAIG, DALGLISH AND WILSON. SUBSTITUTES – P. MCCLUSKEY AND GIBSON.

RANGERS:- KENNEDY, JARDINE, MILLER, FORSYTH, JACKSON, WATSON, MCLEAN, O'HARA, PARLANE, MCKEAN AND JOHNSTONE. SUBSTITUTES – MACDONALD AND HENDERSON.

Rangers 2, Celtic 2 – Saturday, March 19th, 1977
Celts Have Title in their Grasp
By Jim Reynolds

Rangers and Celtic showed on Saturday that Scottish football at its best is still the best 70 pence worth in the sporting world. The two Glasgow rivals served up the best Old Firm match in years . . . a game that sent the pulses racing and left everyone limp from excitement at the end.

It was a match Rangers had to win to keep their Championship hopes alive, and, although they narrowly failed, all the signs are there that Jock Wallace's men are moving into top gear at just the right time for the other big domestic honour, the Scottish Cup.

Of the two sides, Celtic were obviously the better pleased with the Ibrox draw.

Both Wallace and Stein agreed that the latest Old Firm confrontation was a classic – and, not surprisingly, both thought their respective sides just about deserved to win. But if either side had lost it would have been a travesty of justice and taken away much from a great occasion that was marred only by a minicrowd invasion from the Celtic end after Rangers had scored their second goal.

MORONS

The mindless morons who showered bottles and cans from the terracing would have done well to take an example from the players on the pitch, who behaved impeccably and set the mood for a relaxed match from which the football flowed like water from a mountain stream.

In the first 20 minutes Celtic's performance was almost brilliant. They scored through Roy Aitken in 12 minutes and should have had a couple more. Just one goal was scant reward for some of the best football they have played this season.

I am sure more than a few Rangers fans had turned towards the exits after 15 minutes when Alfie Conn jinked his way inside the penalty area and curled a shot round Stewart Kennedy towards the net. Even Alfie turned round to receive the congratulations, but the ball came back off the post and Rangers took over.

Derek Parlane equalised with a great drive from the edge of the penalty area in 21 minutes and the Ibrox men continued to dominate right through most of the second half. Kenny Watson had another fine match. Bobby McKean was everywhere trying to push his team mates

on, and little Tommy McLean did everything with the ball, except make it talk.

It was no great surprise when Parlane grabbed his second goal eleven minutes from time. A neat dummy from Derek Johnstone, a slide rule pass from McLean, and there was the Rangers striker in a perfect position to hammer the ball past Peter Latchford. It was a goal worthy of winning almost any game . . . but not this one.

DELAYED

The match was held up for about five minutes as the police and Jock Stein moved the fans back on to the terracing and Neil Mochan attended to Latchford, badly injured in attempting to prevent the goal. After order was restored and Latchford staggered back to his line in agony, Celtic hit back in champion fashion.

Watson fouled Doyle out on the right wing and when the winger's free kick came over, Aitken met it in mid air and sent a tremendous drive high into the Rangers net.

Everyone would have settled for that to signal the end of the excitement, but there was more to come in the closing minutes.

Alex MacDonald scored what he thought was the winner, but after signalling the goal, referee Paterson spotted his linesman with his flag in the air and the score was chalked off.

Rangers still claim that the goal should have stood, but it must be said that the lineman had flagged even before the ball reached MacDonald. Johnstone, in fact, was the man in the offside position when McLean crossed, so the decision was a correct one.

Then the game finished with two wonder saves from the respective keepers . . . the crippled Latchford touching a John Greig pile-driver round the post, and Kennedy throwing himself full length to palm away a Joe Craig shot.

Rangers (1) 2	Celtic (1) 2
Parlane 2	Aitken 2

RANGERS:- KENNEDY, JARDINE, GREIG, FORSYTH, JACKSON, WATSON, MCLEAN, MCKEAN, PARLANE, MACDONALD, JOHNSTONE, SUBSTITUTES – ROBERTSON, MILLER.

CELTIC – LATCHFORD, MCGRAIN, BURNS, STANTON, EDVALDSSON, AITKEN, DOYLE, GLAVIN, CRAIG, DALGLISH, CONN. SUBSTITUTES – WILSON, GIBSON.

Celtic 1, Rangers 0 – Saturday, May 7th, 1977
Drawing Board Victory
By Jim Reynolds

As controversy still raged around Saturday's Cup-winning goal at Hampden Park, a steady stream of wellwishers from places such as Swansea, Blackpool, Birmingham and Luton moved through the corridors of Parkhead yesterday. They had to check themselves from bowing at the feet of Jock Stein as the Celtic manager emerged from his office to conduct his Sunday press conference.

"There is always a controversy when a match is won in such a fashion," said Stein, "but we are all convinced that it was a penalty. Andy Lynch scored and the prize is in there," added Stein, pointing towards the trophy room where the Scottish Cup joined the Premier League Championship trophy for the first time.

The 1977 Final will not go down in history as one of the classics, there was too much tension for that, but it provided high excitement for the lowest post-war attendance for such an occasion – a crowd cut to 54,252 because of lashing rain and live television coverage.

FINEST HOUR

If ever a match was won on the drawing board it was this one, and once again Stein proved that he is the master architect in football planning.

Johannes Edvaldsson, the Icelandic internationalist, who had never previously played in a winning side against Rangers, was brought in to mark Derek Johnstone. He had his finest hour in a Celtic jersey, making Johnstone as ineffective as I have seen him.

Roddy McDonald was given the job of taking care of Derek Parlane, Rangers' other danger in the air. McDonald emerged as the man of the match with a brilliant display and, like Edvaldsson, put the Rangers defence under severe pressure when he moved forward.

Danny McGrain had one of his quieter matches, but this was because Alex MacDonald did such a good job in blocking off the full back's route down the right. Ironically this also suited Celtic, for MacDonald has scored some vital goals in Old Firm matches. On Saturday he was too busy taking care of McGrain to make much positive contribution.

Stein's surprise move in bringing back Paul Wilson was also a winner. Wilson is so unpredictable that he must be watched at all times and it is a tribute to his contribution that Tom Forsyth emerged as Rangers' man of the match. Forsyth, for me, can join McGrain and Kenny Dalglish as Scots who are true world-class players.

Sandy Jardine and Alfie Conn, who has made history by gaining a winners' medal with both Rangers and Celtic, practically cancelled out one another, and so a match which

should have been bursting with flair took on a chessboard look.

HANDLED

With 20 minutes gone Conn swung over a corner from the left. McDonald headed back across goal and the ball was only partially cleared by Stewart Kennedy. Edvaldsson charged in and his shot beat the goalkeeper, but was handled on the line by Johnstone.

Referee Valentine had no hesitation in pointing to the penalty spot, and despite Rangers' furious protests, I feel that the referee was correct.

While the protests were going on, the Celtic players were holding hurried consultations. Their regular penalty expert, Glavin, was absent and it was expected that Dalglish, the captain, would take on the responsibility.

Andy Lynch, who volunteered to take the kick, had taken only two penalties in his career. Both of them were for Hearts, his previous club – and he missed them. It was third time lucky, however, for Lynch, who showed no sign of nerves as he cracked the ball past Kennedy.

Rangers changed their tactics after the interval, moving John Greig in front of the central defenders, but that left a gap at his back, which Celtic quickly spotted. Instead of attacking down the wings, they pumped long balls through the middle and on at least two occasions should have scored.

With 19 minutes left Rangers produced a substitution, a last effort to save the game. Young Chris Robertson came on for Kenny Watson, and he almost gave the Ibrox club a draw, which they thought they deserved. Robertson's header, which cannoned back off the bar in the closing stages, was one of the few highlights.

With Celtic seemingly on course for another era of glory, the big question is: Where do Rangers go from here? At least one new face is needed before Rangers go trophy-hunting at home and in Europe next season. Class players are hard to find at a reasonable cost – but Celtic, buying wisely, are again at the top of the heap, and Rangers must try something similar.

Scottish Cup Final

Celtic (1) 1	Rangers (0) 0
Lynch (pen.)	
(at Hampden Park)	
Attendance	54,252

CELTIC:- LATCHFORD, MCGRAIN, LYNCH, STANTON, MCDONALD, AITKEN, DALGLISH, EDVALDSSON, CRAIG, WILSON AND CONN. SUBSTITUTES – DOYLE AND BURNS.

RANGERS:- KENNEDY, JARDINE, GREIG, FORSYTH, JACKSON, WATSON, MCLEAN, HAMILTON, PARLANE, MACDONALD AND JOHNSTONE. SUBSTITUTES – ROBERTSON AND MILLER.

Rangers 3, Celtic 2 – Saturday, 10th September, 1977
Rangers on Verge of Great Things
By Jim Reynolds

The tale of the latest Old Firm confrontation is one that will be handed down from generation to generation. It will be talked about for years. "This team is on the verge of great things," said Jock Wallace yesterday. And on Saturday's form he could be right.

Saturday also proved that the Ibrox club could have the bargain buy of the decade in Gordon Smith, a £65,000 signing from Kilmarnock. Smith scored twice, bringing his total to six in the last four games.

Spitz Kohn, the coach of Twente Enschede, was also impressed with Smith. Afterwards he told Jock Wallace: "Smith, he is like an auto . . . a Mercedes." Wallace, the patriot, growled back: "You mean a Rolls Royce."

In analysing Rangers' victory it is ironical that the game was perhaps won in the very first minute, when Derek Parlane went down with a very bad knock on the face and looked in some distress. Parlane played out the rest of the first half, but was kept inside at the interval when it was discovered that he had fractured a cheek bone.

Rangers, two goals down by that time, had to reorganise. Derek Johnstone, who had been missing when Edvaldsson grabbed both of Celtic's goals, was moved up to take Parlane's role and John Greig, a substitute for the day, moved into the back four.

The change was dramatically effective. Rangers had started the game playing confidently but it was confidence without any real aggression, and an Old Firm game is never won without the latter quality. While the Ibrox men were weaving pretty patterns, Edvaldsson, in the eighteenth and thirty-first minutes, took magnificent passes from Burns to put Celtic into what seemed a winning position.

Then came the half-time break, an Ibrox re-shuffle and some gentle words of persuasion from Jock Wallace.

Within eight minutes, the lead was cut to one when Johnstone flicked the ball inside to Smith and he blasted it past Latchford. Johnstone himself scored the equaliser in 65 minutes after a tremendous move involving Smith and Davie Cooper. Then with nine minutes left, Rangers grabbed the winner. Young Bobby Russell chipped a ball across from the byeline. Peter Latchford appeared to have it covered, but let it slip through his fingers, and Smith was waiting on the goal-line to prod it home.

Rangers (0) 3	Celtic (2) 2
Smith 2	Edvaldsson 2
Johnstone	

RANGERS:- MCCLOY, JARDINE, MILLER, FORSYTH, JOHNSTONE, MACDONALD, MCKEAN, RUSSELL, PARLANE, SMITH, COOPER. SUBSTITUTES – GREIG, MCLEAN.

CELTIC:- LATCHFORD, MCGRAIN, LYNCH, EDVALDSSON, MCDONALD, CASEY, DOYLE, DOWNIE, GLAVIN, BURNS, WILSON. – LENNOX, MCADAM.

Celtic 1, Rangers 1 – Saturday, 12th November, 1977
Stein not Happy – but Draw Right
By Jim Reynolds

Moral victories never won anyone any prizes, but in recording one at Parkhead on Saturday Celtic look as if they are at long last going to emerge from a long dark tunnel which they entered at the start of the season and managed to lose themselves in.

But a measure of the new-found confidence at Parkhead can be taken from Stein's comment yesterday. "I am certainly not happy with the result," he said. "I think we should have taken more from the match . . . we certainly deserved to, taking everything into consideration."

Although Stein acknowledges SFA rules by not talking about controversial issues, it was clear he was not entirely satisfied with referee Eddie Thomson's handling of the match and I am sure most Celtic fans will feel the same.

After Tom McAdam had given Celtic what looked like the lead in 54 minutes, the referee pulled the play away back into Celtic's half and awarded them a free kick. The referee indicated a free kick some seconds before the ball reached McAdam.

Twelve minutes later, however, I feel the referee boobed and may have cost Celtic both points. Joe Craig rounded Tom Forsyth in the penalty area and was sent sprawling . . . a glaring penalty, but as the ball had broken to McAdam, the referee decided to play the advantage rule.

Rangers were the much better side in the first half as Celtic fought to overcome obvious nerves – and in that spell Derek Johnstone, Alex MacDonald, and Tommy McLean turned on their own particular brand of magic.

But for all their pressure, Rangers went in at the interval only one goal ahead – thanks to the efforts of Roddy McDonald and Johannes Edvaldsson. Ironically, Rangers scored by hitting on the break. Stewart Kennedy punted a long ball towards the Celtic goal, Davie Cooper collected it and ran round Joe Filippi before crossing for Johnstone to sweep it past Peter Latchford.

But it was a different Celtic after the interval. They equalised in 50 minutes when Filippi crossed and Craig headed down to McAdam, who clipped it past Kennedy.

From that point until the final 10 minutes, the Parkhead side looked the more likely team. They won the midfield battle and forced Rangers back on their heels, but the goal that would have put the seal on the fightback just did not come.

Celtic (0) 1	Rangers (1) 1
McAdam	Johnstone
Attendance	56,000

CELTIC:- LATCHFORD, FILIPPI, LYNCH, EDVALDSSON, MCDONALD, AITKEN, DOYLE, GLAVIN, CRAIG, MCADAM AND CONN. SUBSTITUTES – WILSON AND MACKIE.

RANGERS:- KENNEDY, JARDINE, GREIG, FORSYTH, JACKSON, MACDONALD, MCLEAN, RUSSELL, JOHNSTONE, SMITH AND COOPER. SUBSTITUTES – PARLANE AND MILLER.

Rangers 3, Celtic 1 – Saturday, 7th January, 1978

Five Questions for Old Firm Referee

By Jim Reynolds

Two minutes of mayhem at Ibrox on Saturday ruined what could have been one of the best Old Firm matches for a long time, and John Gordon, the referee from Newport-on-Tay must shoulder some of the blame for the extraordinary scene which almost sparked off a riot.

Celtic were trailing to a brilliant Gordon Smith goal and were pressing hard for the equaliser when Joe Craig was pushed in the back by Colin Jackson as he tried to head the ball in at the far post. It looked a clear penalty, but the referee said "no" and was immediately besieged by Celtic players.

While the protests were going on, Rangers took a quick goal-kick, and with only Frank Munro and Peter Latchford against a five man attack, John Greig finished off the move by tapping the ball into the net to make it 2-0.

The fans came over the wall from the Celtic end, the Parkhead players refused to restart the game, and only the appearance of trainer Neil Mochan in the centre circle prompted them to play on.

But five questions surrounding the incident remain unanswered.

Why was what looked like a legitimate penalty claim turned down in the first place?

Why did the referee give everyone the impression he was running to the touchline to consult the linesman, then change his mind when he saw Rangers breaking towards the Celtic goal?

Why did he allow the goal kick to be taken with several Celtic players still inside the penalty area?

Why, if he was convinced he had made the right decision, did he not send off the Celtic players who pushed and jostled him and refused to restart the game?

Why did he not caution Neil Mochan, who had no right to be on the field without permission?

Celtic had an even better-looking penalty turned down in the second half when Alex MacDonald scooped a Roy Aitken shot off the line with his arm, but Johannes Edvaldsson then set the game alight again with a goal in 64 minutes, shooting past Stewart Kennedy from 12 yards after Aitken had touched on a Ronnie Glavin free kick.

But there was more bad luck for the Parkhead side when an Aitken shot cannoned off a post with Kennedy beaten, and from that point Rangers began to put things together again, threatening to score a third goal. And that goal came just three minutes from time with both Rangers substitutes involved. Alex Miller, who replaced Tommy McLean, took a throw on the right to Sandy Jardine, whose shot was fumbled by Peter Latchford. Derek Parlane, who had come on for Davie Cooper, had an easy job of scoring.

Rangers (2) 3	Celtic (0) 1
Smith	Edvaldsson
Greig	
Cooper	

RANGERS:- KENNEDY, JARDINE, GREIG, FORSYTH, JACKSON, MACDONALD, MCLEAN, RUSSELL, JOHNSTONE, SMITH AND COOPER. SUBSTITUTES – PARLANE AND MILLER.

CELTIC:- LATCHFORD, FILIPPI, LYNCH, AITKEN, MCDONALD, MUNRO, GLAVIN, EDVALDSSON, CRAIG, MCADAM AND WILSON. SUBSTITUTES – G. MCCLUSKEY AND DOWIE.

Rangers 2, Celtic 1 – Saturday, 18th March, 1978

Rangers Negotiate First Hurdle

By Jim Reynolds

Rangers took the first positive step towards this season's Grand Slam when they carried the League Cup from Hampden to Ibrox on Saturday afternoon after beating Celtic in one of the most undistinguished Finals in the history of the competition.

My first reaction when referee David Syme signalled the end of the 90 minutes with the score at 1-1 was that an extra half-hour of mediocrity was the last thing we needed.

It was a Hampden bore – tense, tight and untidy. Experienced players looked like nervous Cup Final debutantes. It was left to the Cup Final first-timers to provide the few highlights: Rangers' Davie Cooper who scored a brilliant first goal; Gordon Smith, who grabbed the winner; and young Alan Sneddon, Celtic's right back who gave a tremendous display of skill and composure just a month after making his senior debut.

Celtic, the underdogs, had settled themselves nicely until an error of judgement led to Rangers' opening goal in 38 minutes. Ronnie Glavin and Gordon Smith chased a ball to the bye-line. Smith, managed to get in a foot and whipped the ball across the goal for Cooper to send a tremendous drive high into the net.

Celtic matched Rangers all the way in the second half, which wasn't too difficult, and five minutes from time Johannes Edvaldsson headed in a Sneddon cross to sent the match into extra time.

Celtic had made use of their two substitutes, Paul Williams and Johnny Doyle – for Andy Lynch and Ronnie Glavin – and Jock Wallace decided to push on his two substitutes for extra time. Alex Miller and Derek Parlane replaced Hamilton and Cooper, and it was the drive and pace of Miller which brought the winning goal.

Three minutes from the end, he crossed into the Celtic goalmouth. Alex MacDonald and Peter Latchford both went for the ball. The Celtic 'keeper could only palm it out, and Smith nodded it straight back into the net.

Scottish League Cup Final

Rangers (1) 2	Celtic (0) 1
Cooper	Edvaldsson
Smith	

[after extra time; 90 mins 1-1]
(at Hampden Park)

CELTIC:- LATCHFORD, SNEDDON, LYNCH, MUNRO, MACDONALD, DOWIE, GLAVIN, EDVALDSSON, MCCLUSKEY, AITKEN, BURNS. SUBSTITUTES – DOYLE AND WILSON.

RANGERS:- KENNEDY, JARDINE, GREIG, FORSYTH, JACKSON, MACDONALD, MCLEAN, HAMILTON, JOHNSTONE, SMITH, COOPER. SUBSTITUTES – PARLANE, MILLER.

Celtic 2, Rangers 0 – Saturday, 25th March, 1978

Celtic Turn the Tables

By Jim Reynolds

As one metaphorical curtain came down at Parkhead on Saturday, another was raised. Celtic won the final Old Firm clash of the season in a canter. And at the same time, set the stage for a blistering finish in the Premier League Championship.

Rangers, for so long hot favourites to regain the title, now find themselves faced with a nail-biting run-in, just one point ahead of Aberdeen.

Celtic salvaged a lot of pride in Saturday's match, and in the first half turned on some of their best football of the season. As a spectacle the game was a vast improvement on the League Cup Final of the previous week, but as a contest it fell far short.

NO COMPLAINTS

Rangers were two down at the interval, but it could have been four or five. The first goal came along in 32 minutes after some amazing Celtic misses. Glavin hit a shot from 25 yards. Stewart Kennedy seemed to have it covered, but the ball dropped though his arms and landed in the net. "It was probably my worst effort of the match," said Glavin afterwards. "But I'm not complaining."

Glavin also had a hand in the second goal seven minutes later. He sent a low free kick into the heart of the Rangers goalmouth. Johannes Edvaldsson laid it off with a cheeky back-heel pass, and Roddy McDonald steered the ball high past Kennedy. When the fact is recorded that the sweeper and the centre half worked a 1–2 inside the box to produce a goal, enough has been said about the opposing defence.

The half-time break, and no doubt some sharp talking by Jock Wallace, made a difference after the interval. Rangers at last began to show some urgency and drive. And when Derek Parlane and Alex Miller replaced Davie Cooper and young Russell, they began to get through. But it was Celtic's day and some fine saves by Peter Latchford – one in particular from Parlane late on – prevented any chance of a Rangers fightback.

Both captains, Lynch and John Greig, were booked. But the game was comparatively free from the ugly needling which has spoiled so many Old Firm matches.

Celtic (2) 2	Rangers (0) 0
Glavin	
McDonald	

CELTIC:- LATCHFORD, SNEDDON, LYNCH, AITKEN, MCDONALD, DOWNIE, GLAVIN, EDVALDSSON, MCADAM, BURNS AND DOYLE. SUBSTITUTES – CRAIG AND WILSON.

RANGERS:- KENNEDY, JARDINE, GREIG, FORSYTH, JACKSON, MACDONALD, MCLEAN, RUSSELL, JOHNSTONE, SMITH AND COOPER. SUBSTITUTES – PARLANE AND MILLER.

Rangers 1, Celtic 1 – Saturday, 11th November, 1978

Lunchtime Treat by the Old Firm

By Jim Reynolds

The Old Firm provided a pleasant change at Hampden on Saturday, a complete change from the 100 mph football which often in the past has marred this great Glasgow derby. The usual effort was there, of course, but, with the accent on skill, Rangers and Celtic gave 52,000 paying customers a lunchtime treat.

Celtic used two orthodox wingers to provide a welcome change in this sardine tin of a Premier League. Rangers countered by playing their very effective European game, with patience, discipline and exhilarating breaks from defence.

In many ways it was the perfect match. Celtic had the edge in attack, Rangers were much better organised at the back. Both sides created a similar amount of genuine chances, and at the end of the day, neither deserved to lose.

Rangers sprang a couple of surprises at the start. They had Derek Johnstone up front with Alex Miller at right back and Sandy Jardine sweeping behind Tom Forsyth. Johnstone had his best match of the season in this particular role, and Jardine once again showed he is a defender of the highest class.

Likewise, there was much for Celtic fans to enthuse over. They had three Old Firm debutantes – Murdo MacLeod, Davie Provan and Tom McAdam were having their first match at Hampden. Every one of them played well, and so too did Johnny Doyle, out of the first team for so long.

The best football was played in the first half, but it was not until after the interval that the goals came along. Celtic opened the scoring with a brilliant effort involving MacLeod and Andy Lynch. The former Dumbarton player split the Ibrox defence with a perfect pass inside the box, and there was Lynch in the open space to steer the ball past Peter McCloy.

Rangers hit back furiously, and four minutes later they were level from the penalty spot. Johannes Edvaldsson handled a Johnstone header, and Alex Forsyth stepped up to score his fourth penalty goal of the season.

Rangers (0) 1	Celtic (0) 1
A. Forsyth (pen.)	Lynch
(at Hampden Park)	
Attendance	52,000

RANGERS:- MCCLOY, JARDINE, A. FORSYTH, T. FORSYTH, JOHNSTONE, MCDONALD, MCLEAN, RUSSELL, SMITH, WATSON, MILLER. SUBSTITUTES – PARLANE, COOPER.

CELTIC:- BAINES, ELLIOTT, LYNCH, AITKEN, MCDONALD, EDVALDSSON, PROVAN, MACLEOD, MCADAM, BURNS, DOYLE. SUBSTITUTES – LENNOX, CASEY.

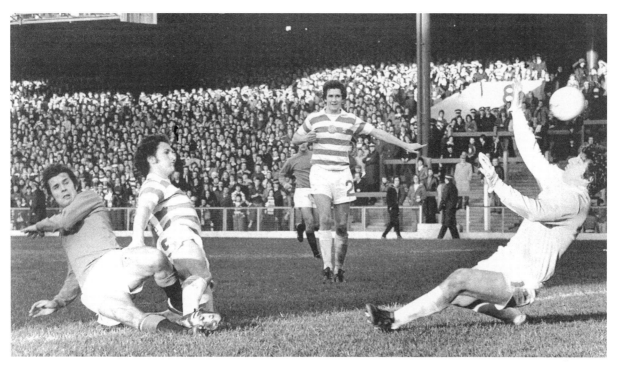

Roddy MacDonald's tackle prevents Johnstone from scoring.

Roy Aitken celebrates the first of two against Rangers at Ibrox in March 1977.

Edvaldsson's header takes the 1978 League Cup Final into extra time.

Peter Latchford saves from John Greig in the 1978 League Cup final but
cannot stop Rangers winning 2-1 in extra time.

Rangers 3, Celtic 2 – Wednesday, 13th December, 1978

Old Firm Thriller

By Jim Reynolds

TWO SENT OFF AS CASEY OWN GOAL ENDS CELTS' RUN

Celtic's world record League Cup run came to an abrupt and controversial end in this Semi-final at Hampden last night as the holders, Rangers, swept them out after 120 minutes of nerve-jangling action.

But what a tragic night for the young Celtic substitute, Jim Casey, who put through his own goal just six minutes from the end of extra-time to end his club's glorious record which has seen them take part in the last 14 finals of this competition.

It was a night of high drama and passion with Rangers twice coming from behind to win on the post and qualify for a Final meeting with Aberdeen back at Hampden on a date still to be decided.

Two players, Celtic's Tommy Burns and Rangers' Alex Miller were sent off and three more were booked as referee Hugh Alexander let the game get away from him for a spell.

The ordering-off affected Celtic more than Rangers, for it was Burns who stamped his class on the game for the 26 minutes he was on the field. He set up Celtic's first goal and looked in the mood to cause unlimited damage to Rangers' defence, and when he left Celtic were robbed of their potential match-winner.

It was a match which at one point looked like being wrecked because of nasty tempers and indecisive refereeing, but which eventually turned out to be a classic for the crowd of almost 50,000.

At the end of the night it was a pity that someone had to lose, for both sides gave everything they had and a little more. Celtic deserved at least another chance.

Rangers left out Gordon Smith and Alex Forsyth at the start, and in just nine minutes Celtic caught them on the break to score what must rank as the goal of the season. Burns picked up a bad Alex MacDonald pass deep in his own half and ran 50 yards before splitting the Ibrox defence with a brilliant pass to John Doyle, who turned and beat Peter McCloy with a low shot.

Miller was then booked for a foul on Mike Conroy, and in 26 minutes the game erupted in a storm of controversy as Rangers hit back to equalise with a doubtful penalty. Davie Cooper went down in the box when challenged by Johannes Edvaldsson, and despite angry protests the referee awarded the spot kick.

Doyle was booked and before the kick could be taken, the stand-side linesman complained to the referee. Burns was called over and sent off, presumably for saying something out of turn.

Again we had angry scenes but when order was restored, Sandy Jardine scored the equaliser and 10-man Celtic were up against it.

Aitken was then booked and with tempers running high, the interval came as a welcome break. But it did nothing to cool things. A minute into the second half Rangers were also reduced to 10 men when Miller clashed with Doyle and was sent inside – again, I felt the decision harsh.

Only after that, however, did the sides begin to concentrate on football, and at last we had a game worthy of the occasion.

McCloy saved brilliantly from Provan, and when Rangers brought on Smith for Cooper in 61 minutes, Celtic surged back into the lead. Doyle, a brilliant player on the night, left Roy Aitken with a chance. McCloy could only parry the ball to McAdam, who knocked it into the empty net.

But how Rangers fought, and with just 10 minutes left they equalised again. Johnstone won a ball in the air, and when Russell pushed it back across goal Colin Jackson hit a shot which was deflected past Roy Baines.

Johnstone should have tied it up for Rangers shortly afterwards – he hit the side netting when it seemed easier to score. And so to extra-time and Rangers' winning goal – another which was bitterly disputed by the Celtic players.

This time Johnstone could have been offside, but was allowed to carry on towards Baines. The Celtic keeper blocked the shot but Casey, who had come on in place of Conroy, could not get out of the way and the ball cannoned off him and into the net.

It was an unsatisfactory ending to an Old Firm encounter, but you won't find any Rangers fans complaining.

Scottish League Cup Semi-Final

Rangers (1) 3	Celtic (1) 2
Jardine (pen.)	Doyle
Jackson	McAdam
Casey (o.g.)	
[after extra time; 90 mins 2-2]	
(at Hampden Park)	
Attendance	50,000

RANGERS:- MCCLOY, MILLER, DAVIDSON, JARDINE, JACKSON, MACDONALD, MCLEAN, RUSSELL, JOHNSTONE, WALLACE, COOPER. SUBSTITUTES – SMITH, PARLANE.

CELTIC:- BAINES, FILIPPI, LYNCH, AITKEN, MCDONALD, EDVALDSSON, PROVAN, CONROY, MCADAM, BURNS, DOYLE. SUBSTITUTES – CONN, CASEY.

Rangers 1, Celtic 0 – Saturday, 7th May, 1979

An Old Firm Triumph for Davie Cooper

By Jim Reynolds

Hampden at the weekend housed one of the most pleasant Old Firm matches of recent years – a lot of skillful football, the proper result at the end of 90 minutes, very few bad fouls and not one shred of controversy.

We even had BOTH managers raising a smile for the after-match talk-in, albeit the one on Billy McNeill's face was rather rueful. Both clubs are to be congratulated on the way they handled a match of such importance, and although it has been agreed that nothing has yet been decided, the events on Saturday should go a long way to deciding the destination of the Premier League Championship.

Rangers now have a one-point advantage over their Old Firm rivals, and, with just four games to go, are firmly in the driving seat.

CONSISTENT

The game was yet another triumph for Davie Cooper, the man who at last is beginning to show consistency along with his amazing skills.

It was the Cooper attitude early on which pointed the way for Rangers and caused a tremor of apprehension throughout the Celtic defence. Davie was in the mood and gave Danny McGrain more trouble than he has had in any game since his return to the first team. If any winger gets the better of McGrain, then it can hardly fail to impress the rest of his team-mates.

Celtic had too many "passengers" on the day and were fortunate to go in at half-time on level terms. But for two bad misses from Bobby Russell and some outstanding work from Peter Latchford and Johannes Edvaldsson, who played for most of the match with a badly damaged ankle following a kick from Derek Parlane – perhaps the only really nasty incident in the entire game – Rangers would have been comfortably ahead.

INVALUABLE

The Rangers pressure had to tell and it did, in 57 minutes, when little Alex MacDonald scored the only goal of the match. Tommy McLean sent over a low cross, Russell dummied, and MacDonald scooped the ball into the net . . . not one of the best goals the midfield man had scored, but one which might prove to be among the most valuable.

Only then did Celtic begin to play to something like their form. With Lynch and McAdam on for Burns and Davidson, they found more power and were desperately unlucky to see a Johnny Doyle shot come off the post.

But had Celtic equalised, it would have been an injustice. Rangers created many more chances and were undoubtedly the more positive side throughout. They seemed determined to win, whereas Celtic merely hoped.

Five men were booked – Burns, McCluskey and Conroy of Celtic, and Parlane and Dawson of Rangers.

Rangers (0 1   Celtic (0) 0
MacDonald
(at Hampden Park)

RANGERS:- MCCLOY, JARDINE, DAWSON, JOHNSTONE, JACKSON, MACDONALD, MCLEAN, RUSSELL, PARLANE, SMITH, COOPER. SUBSTITUTES – URQUHART, DENNY.

CELTIC:- LATCHFORD, MCGRAIN, MACLEOD, AITKEN, EDVALDSSON, CONROY, PROVAN, DAVIDSON, MCCLUSKEY, BURNS, DOYLE. SUBSTITUTES – MCADAM, LYNCH.

Rangers 3, Celtic 1 – Wednesday, 16th May, 1979

Rangers' Colts Show the Lethal Touch

Celtic could not quibble at their defeat from Rangers at this Glasgow Cup Final at Ibrox last night, for the Parkhead colts could not match their Ibrox counterparts when it came to showing the lethal touch.

Rangers were, in fact, two up after only four minutes' play. McDonald headed the first when Morris nodded a Forsyth centre into his path, and Forsyth himself scored number two from a penalty kick, awarded when Young pulled down Strickland.

Casey revived Celtic with a splendidly taken goal in the twenty-sixth minute. He rounded Richardson and beat Kennedy with a 20-yard piledriver.

Rangers, who had Dalziel on for Denny at the start of the second half, and had Forsyth booked for a tackle on Mackie, clinched the tie with a well-taken third goal in 61 minutes by Strickland. He left the Celtic defence standing as he closed in on Bonnar and gave the keeper no chance with a cracking drive.

Celtic used both their substitutes in the last twenty minutes, Reid taking over from Lumsden and Halpern replacing Weir, but it was to no avail.

Glasgow Cup Final

Rangers (2) 3   Celtic (1) 1
McDonald   Casey
A. Forsyth (pen.)
Strickland

RANGERS:- KENNEDY, MCLAREN, A. FORSYTH, DENNY, RICHARDSON, WATSON, MCKAY, STRICKLAND, MORRIS, ARMOUR, J. MCDONALD. SUBSTITUTES – DALZIEL, C. ROBERTSON.

CELTIC:- BONNAR, FILIPPI, SNEDDON, LUMSDEN, YOUNG, DUFFY, MACKIE, WEST, GLAVIN, CASEY, LENNOX. SUBSTITUTES – REID, HALPERN.

Celtic 4, Rangers 2 – Monday, 21st May, 1979
10-man Celtic win the league
By Ian Paul

DOYLE DISMISSAL SPARKS FOUR-GOAL BLITZ

Celtic are the champions – and they did it in champion style coming off the ropes not once, not twice, but three times to clinch a victory every bit as memorable as anything achieved on the domestic scene by the Lisbon Lions or anyone else.

Needing a victory to snatch the prize from Rangers, Celtic, a goal down at half-time, were reduced to 10 men when Johnny Doyle was sent off 10 minutes later, and despite having caught and passed Rangers by the seventy-fifth minute, were knocked flat on their backs again by an Ibrox equaliser.

No wonder thousands of Celtic supporters stayed behind to cheer their bedraggled but triumphant favourites. They barely had the breath to do so, having seen their 10-man team score four goals, a feat which must be something of a record. They had also seen a performance by Roy Aitken which must rank amongst the finest by any Celtic player in a 90-minute spell.

Within nine minutes they were taught the lesson in simple goalscoring by the clever Davie Cooper who went on a sweet run on the left, beat two men, and cut over a perfect cross for Alex MacDonald to knock the ball past Latchford.

By half-time Celtic, despite almost incessant pressure, were still lagging by that choice goal. Ten minutes later Johnny Doyle foolishly aimed a kick at the prone figure of MacDonald, who had been fouled by Mike Conroy. Referee Eddie Pringle, busy admonishing Conroy did not see the incident but the far-side linesman did, and after consultation Doyle was sent off.

That was that, or so we thought. But Celtic, if anything, improved, and their equaliser came in 67 minutes. A cute flick from Provan was turned into the net by Aitken, and the din was deafening. Celtic sent on Lennox for Conroy and Rangers answered by pushing on Miller for McLean. Within a minute Miller very nearly scored, but in 75 minutes the seemingly unbelievable happened – Celtic took the lead.

An Aitken drive was blocked, the ball broke to McCluskey and he simply hammered it into the net. The Parkhead faithful were still trying to touch the clear evening sky when they were hauled back to Earth with a cruel thump. Inside two minutes Rangers had equalised and were looking good for the title yet again in a glorious see-saw game. A Cooper corner broke to Russell, who smashed a low drive through a posse of players and into the net.

Jackson became the fourth man to be booked – Jardine, Aitken and Parlane were the others – but with five minutes left the big centre half involuntarily headed the ball into his own net after a McCluskey cross was pushed out by McCloy.

Celtic were in front again and this time there was no way back for Rangers. Murdo MacLeod emphasised that when he slammed in the fourth goal right on time.

What a way to win a League, never mind a game.

Celtic (0) 4	Rangers (1) 2
Aitken	McDonald
McCluskey	Russell
Jackson (o.g.)	
MacLeod	

CELTIC:- LATCHFORD, MCLEAN, LYNCH, AITKEN, MCADAM, EDVALDSSON, PROVAN, CONROY, MCCLUSKEY, MACLEOD, DOYLE. SUBSTITUTES – DAVIDSON, LENNOX.

RANGERS:- MCCLOY, JARDINE, DAVIDSON, JOHNSTONE, JACKSON, MACDONALD, MCLEAN, RUSSELL, PARLANE, SMITH, COOPER. SUBSTITUTES – MILLER, WATSON.

The Celtic team celebrate winning the 1979 League Championship.

Rangers 2, Celtic 2 – Saturday, 18th August, 1979

Rangers Failed to Learn Their Lesson

By Jim Reynolds

There were two turning points at Ibrox on Saturday which led to one of the most dramatic finishes in the history of Old Firm matches – a finish which saw Celtic grab two goals in the last six minutes to gain a point which at one stage looked as far away as the Sea of Tranquility.

One was when Rangers unwisely decided they had done enough and relaxed their concentration. The other came when Celtic's manager, Billy McNeill, elected to make a double substitution midway in the second half with the side already reduced to 10 men following the thirty-sixth minute sending-off of Roy Aitken.

It was a brave move which inspired bravery among the 10 surviving Celts, and which was rewarded with a breathtaking finale in which the pace and sharpness of both substitutes, Doyle and Lennox, played a major part.

Until then Rangers were comfortably in control with the cushion of a two-goal lead given them by a brilliant header by young John MacDonald in 49 minutes and a blistering drive from Robert Russell five minutes later. Rangers should have added to that tally as they carved holes in the depleted Celtic ranks, but having failed in several attempts, they seemed to decide they already had a big enough lead.

How wrong they were, for Celtic, inspired by a brilliant Danny McGrain, roared back for Alan Sneddon to score with a diving header in 84 minutes and for Tom McAdam to hammer in the equaliser three minutes later. Rangers had clearly failed to learn the lesson of the final match of last season when a 10-man Celtic outfit came from behind to win the Championship.

And that must cause Rangers' manager, John Greig, some concern this morning when he leads a squad of 17 players down the coast to Troon to prepare for tomorrow's European Cup-Winners Cup tie against Lillestrom.

Greig said, "We should have been four or five ahead; instead we lost the place and threw away a point. In the end we didn't come out of the game with credit."

Rangers (0) 2	Celtic (0) 2
J. MacDonald	Sneddon
Russel	McAdam

RANGERS:- MCCLOY, MILLER, DAWSON, JARDINE, JACKSON, WATSON, COOPER, RUSSELL, JOHNSTONE. A. MACDONALD, J. MACDONALD. SUBSTITUTES – SMITH, MCLEAN.

CELTIC:- LATCHFORD, SNEDDON, MCGRAIN, AITKEN, MCDONALD, EDVALDSSON, PROVAN, CONROY, MCCLUSKEY, MACLEOD, MCADAM. SUBSTITUTES – DOYLE, LENNOX.

Tom McAdam scores for Celtic.

Celtic 3, Rangers 1 – Saturday, 9th September, 1979

Rangers Stunner on the Eve of Europe

By Jim Reynolds

As far as Celtic-Rangers games go, it seemed like just another Old Firm Saturday at the weekend . . . great goals, jet-paced action, bookings galore, a missed penalty and the Glasgow constabulary ending the day with almost 200 miscreants in the bag.

But for both sides, the early afternoon happenings at Parkhead could, in the coming weeks, prove to be of special significance.

Celtic's victory must give them a tremendous boost, and the confidence which has been apparent in their play this season should now be running over. It was their tenth straight competitive win under Billy McNeill, and by far the most important.

BIGGEST TEST

It is true that the reward (two points) is the same as they gain for League victory over any other side, but this would be the big test for McNeill's men, and they passed with honours. Only now, after 10 games and 32 goals, can we say that Celtic are again a team to be feared by all.

Playing with such as Danny McGrain, Roddy McDonald and Alfie Conn, they took on the reigning Champions and won with style and courage. The spin-off should be there for all to see in the matches ahead.

For Rangers, the weekend's events must call for a re-think. They have struggled to find their form, especially up front, and now that they trail their great rivals by six points, time becomes the bitter enemy.

Of course, the season is still in its infancy, but such a gap at any stage is a rather frightening one for those in pursuit, and any further slips in the matches ahead could be catastrophic as far as Rangers' chances of retaining the Championship are concerned.

The latest setback could not have come at a worse time for Rangers, who set off for Turin this morning for Wednesday's European Cup-tie against Juventus. John Greig, of course, will be channelling all thoughts towards that one, but immediately it is over, he must sort out some problems.

Is it time to abandon – at least temporarily – the plan of playing Derek Johnstone in defence? The big fellow has not looked comfortable there this season and he even looked out of place in the midfield in the first half against Celtic. Only when he moved up front did he look like the player he was last season.

He is a proven scorer, and that is what Rangers need above all else at the moment.

Rangers were caught cold at Parkhead. Celtic stormed into attack straight from the kick-off and had the Rangers defence running in circles. After McCloy let a Johnny Doyle shot squirm out of his hands within seconds, Celtic scored in a minute. Ronnie Glavin hit a free kick into the penalty area, Johannes Edvaldsson tapped it back to Tom McAdam, and the big striker fired a great shot into the net.

But one thing Rangers do not need to improve is their fighting qualities and they battled back, with Derek Parlane scoring their first Premier League goal of the season in 49 minutes. That signalled their best spell but, just when it seemed that an equaliser must come, Celtic struck again.

With 14 minutes left, substitute Joe Craig set up the clincher with a tenacious run down the right and towards the penalty area. McAdam backed up well and was on the spot to steer the ball past McCloy when Craig released the pass.

Rangers still continued to fight, but seven minutes from time they lost their final lifeline when Peter Latchford, a magnificent keeper, brilliantly saved an Alex Miller penalty.

Five players were booked in a match which Celtic thoroughly deserved to win: Tommy McLean, Alex Forsyth, and Alex MacDonald of Rangers, and Celtic's Johannes Edvaldsson and Ronnie Glavin.

John Greig summed up the match from Rangers' viewpoint when he said afterwards, "In a match like this, you can't give away a two-goal start, miss a penalty and expect to win."

Celtic (2) 3	Rangers (0) 1
Doyle	Parlane
McAdam 2	

CELTIC:- LATCHFORD, FILIPPI, AITKEN, EDVALDSSON, GLAVIN, DOYLE, CONROY, MCADAM, BURNS AND MCCLUSKEY. SUBSTITUTES – CRAIG AND CASEY.

RANGERS:- MCCLOY, JARDINE, ALEX FORSYTH, TOM FORSYTH, JACKSON, MACDONALD, MCLEAN, RUSSELL, PARLANE, JOHNSTONE AND SMITH. SUBSTITUTES – MILLER AND COOPER.

1979

Celtic 1, Rangers 0 – Saturday, 7th October, 1979
McDonald Goal Breaks Celts' October Jinx
By Jim Reynolds

Roddy McDonald's winning goal in the latest Old Firm confrontation at the weekend pushed Celtic six points clear of their rivals in the Premier League table and helped to break an October jinx for manager Billy McNeill.

In his short spell as manager, McNeill has come to dread this particular month, and with good reason. Last season Celtic failed to win a league match during October, dropping seven points out of a possible eight, but despite that they went on to win the Championship.

Events during the past few weeks did nothing to ease Billy's apprehension, but MacDonald's goal on Saturday raised Celtic's points total to five out of eight for the month, and that has brought smiles to the faces at Parkhead.

Alan Sneddon was restored at right back with Danny McGrain moving to the left, and McGrain looked much more comfortable there. Roy Aitken went into central defence, which McNeill considers his best position, and was outstanding; new signing Dom Sullivan brought a smooth, silky touch to the midfield, and Tom McAdam got through a mountain of work up front.

Admittedly Rangers have been hard hit by injuries lately, but they still managed to field a side packed with experience. Their European style, however, in which they conceded territorial advantage, suited Celtic. It made for long spells of boredom but you will not find any Celtic fan complaining this morning.

It might all have been different if Rangers had shown the same commitment all through as they did after McDonald's goal, for they gave the Celtic defence more problems in the final 10 minutes than in the other 80. But they did not, and therefore did not deserve to win.

Celtic, with Davie Provan in the mood, spent most of the afternoon in the Rangers half, but due to fine work in the Ibrox defence they were allowed to create only a few chances in the first half.

But after an hour they began to find the gaps more easily and it became apparent that if any side would break the deadlock it would be Celtic. And with 14 minutes left, they did just that. Provan, that immaculate crosser of a ball, flighted over a perfect corner kick, and there was McDonald soaring high over everyone to head.

Celtic (0) 1   **Rangers (0) 0**
McDonald

CELTIC:- LATCHFORD, SNEDDON, MCGRAIN, AITKEN, MCDONALD, MACLEOD, PROVAN, SULLIVAN, MCCLUSKEY, BURNS, MCADAM. SUBSTITUTES – EDVALDSSON, CONROY.

RANGERS:- MCCLOY, MILLER, A. FORSYTH, JARDINE, STEVENS, WATSON, MCLEAN, A. MACDONALD, JOHNSTONE, URQUHART, COOPER. SUBSTITUTES – SMITH, J. MACDONALD.

Rangers 1, Celtic 1 – Saturday, 29th December, 1979
'Celtic Stole that Point', says Greig.
By Jim Reynolds

The quietest and one of the most enjoyable of Old Firm fixtures in recent years ended all square at Ibrox at the weekend, but the after-match reactions from both camps were poles apart. From Rangers it was bitter disappointment, while all connected with Celtic displayed a quiet satisfaction.

Rangers had to win this one to begin to pin back Celtic's massive lead in the Premier League, but they failed despite having the edge for the 90 minutes. They showed more commitment, which was not surprising considering their desperate need of the two points, and created many more chances.

When they did take the lead late on, they let Celtic off the hook within a minute. Like all good Champions, the Parkhead side took their chance and left with a point.

"They stole a point," said Rangers manager, John Greig, afterwards. "My players thought the Celtic equaliser was offside, so I'm really disappointed at losing a point in such a controversial way."

Bobby Lennox's equaliser was certainly a borderline case, but Celtic could claim that they were denied a second-half penalty when a Roy Aitken shot hit Stevens' arm.

For me, the most pleasant aspect of the game was the behaviour of the players. While all the traditional excitement and effort was there, the match was completely free from the nastiness and petty feuds which have marred many of the recent matches between the clubs.

Rangers produced their best performance for some time and should have been in front at half-time. They would have been had it not been for Latchford who, according to McNeill, is having his best spell ever for the club.

The Englishman denied Rangers three times in that first half, with a wonderful save from a Jackson header and two great interceptions as Johnstone looked set to score.

Latchford was out of luck when Rangers took the lead in 73 minutes. When Tommy McLean crossed from the right, the 'keeper slipped and had no chance with Johnstone's header.

Celtic's reply was immediate and deadly. A Roy Aitken free kick was headed forward and Lennox ended the decade as he started – in scoring mood. And now, with only one more Old Firm match left in the season, Rangers must rely on others to help them close the gap.

Rangers (0) 1   **Celtic (0) 1**
Johnstone   Lennox

RANGERS:- MCCLOY, JARDINE, DAWSON, FORSYTH, JACKSON, STEVENS, MCLEAN, RUSSELL, JOHNSTONE, A. MACDONALD, J. MACDONALD. SUBSTITUTES – COOPER, MILLER.

CELTIC:- LATCHFORD, SNEDDON, MCGRAIN, AITKEN, MCDONALD, MCADAM, PROVAN, SULLIVAN, LENNOX, MACLEOD, DOYLE. SUBSTITUTES – EDVALDSSON, MCCLUSKEY.

The Eighties

Despite the refreshing challenge from Aberdeen and Dundee United, who both won their share of the major honours, the spotlight was never away from the Old Firm, and on May 10, 1980, when Celtic and Rangers clashed in the Scottish Cup Final, the day ended in chaos and shame.

In extra time, George McCluskey diverted a Danny McGrain shot past peter McCloy to give Celtic a 1-0 win, and, at the final whistle, when the Parkhead players moved towards their fans at one end of the ground to celebrate the crowd spilled over to join in. That sparked a violent reaction from the other end as the Rangers fans also took to the field. The result was a riot which was widely reported throughout Europe and brought disgrace to the two great clubs. In fact, the Old Firm were then scheduled to meet in a Glasgow Cup Final, but it was cancelled because of the riot.

There were, however, other memories of a classical nature during the decade. Who among Rangers fans will ever forget Ally McCoist's hat trick against Celtic in the League Cup Final which was played on March 25, 1984? - or two years later Davie Cooper's winning goal from the penalty spot in the Final of the Skol Cup?

For Celtic, there were the goals from Charlie Nicholas and Murdo MacLeod which beat Rangers in the Final of the League Cup in December, 1982, and, for both sets of fans, there was the magnificent 4-4 draw in a Premier Division match at Ibrox in March, 1986.

There was another managerial shuffle during the eighties with Jock Wallace going back to Ibrox for a second spell and Davie Hay taking over at Parkhead from Billy McNeill. But the most significant move of all came during the summer of 1986 when Rangers appointed Graeme Souness as player-manager, with Walter Smith as his assistant.

In his first season at Ibrox Souness led the club to the League Cup and the Championship - their first title since 1978. The 1987-88 season saw Celtic win the double in their centenary year - with Billy McNeill back in charge - and it also saw another nasty Old Firm clash when the sides drew 2-2 at Ibrox in a league match in October. Chris Woods, Terry Butcher and Frank McAvennie were sent off, and in a sensational aftermath all three, along with Graham Roberts were charged. At the trial McAvennie was found not guilty, the charge against Roberts was not proven, but Woods and Butcher were found guilty of breach of the peace.

In the 1989 Scottish Cup Final, a goal from Joe Miller prevented Rangers from winning the Treble, and as we moved towards the nineties the Ibrox club had once again become the dominant force in Scottish football.

1980

Celtic 1, Rangers 0 – Wednesday, 2nd April, 1980

McGarvey's Late Goal Breaks the Deadlock

By Jim Reynolds

Celtic moved a step nearer the League Championship at Parkhead last night with a last-gasp win over arch-rivals, Rangers, who are still without a Premier League win in the east end of the city after five years of trying.

What a magic night it was for Frank McGarvey, Scotland's most expensive footballer, who headed in the only goal of the match with just four minutes left.

It looked long odds on a no-scoring draw and the 52,000 crowd seemed to have settled for that when McGarvey, playing in his first Old Firm match, pounced on a Roy Aitken cross at the far post and knocked it past Peter McCloy.

It may sound like rough justice on Rangers, losing so late on, but the Champions looked the better side over the 90 minutes and deserved their victory. It is a win which further closes the door on nearest challengers, Aberdeen, who come to Parkhead on Saturday but now lie seven points behind Celtic.

The match was untidy and bad-tempered, but also thrilling. Four men were booked, both sides had penalty claims turned down, and both goals had narrow escapes. It was a typical Old Firm clash played at jet pace.

If skills were at a premium, then there was effort in abundance from both sides. And there were heroes. Peter McCloy had a marvellous night in the Rangers goal and Gordon Smith was outstanding in midfield.

Danny McGrain was once again a magnificent captain for Celtic, McGarvey a wasp-like leader, and Murdo MacLeod, probably the best of them all, covering every inch of the pitch and going just as strong at the end as he was in the early stages.

The pace was hot and the tackling hot in the early stages, but a great move in four minutes gave Celtic a chance. Doyle set McGarvey free, and when his low cross flew across goal, Provan hit the ball first time, but past a post.

Then in eight minutes, with the Rangers defence in disarray, Doyle poked the ball towards the net, but Jardine booted it off the line.

McGarvey was next to cause trouble in the Rangers' defence with a fine run which took him past three players. He passed to Provan, but the winger was crowded out and the danger cleared.

But Rangers, who had been out of it, came so close in 15 minutes. A Cooper free kick curled over the Celtic defence, and Johnstone sent a powerful header over the crossbar.

In 21 minutes Forsyth was warned for a foul on Provan, and from the free kick McCloy held an Aitken header under the bar. Minutes later, the referee had to lecture a group of players in the Rangers penalty area.

Cooper should have put Rangers in front in 26 minutes when Johnstone got his head to a Jardine free kick and knocked it down to the winger in front of goal. Cooper's shot was weak, however, and Latchford got a hand to it.

Seconds later, Provan had an equally bad miss when he only had McCloy to beat, but shot weakly at the keeper.

Then controversy in 34 minutes when Rangers broke down the right and Miller sent Smith clear. As the Rangers man turned inside MacDonald, he was sent tumbling down. It looked like a clear penalty, but referee Anderson waved play on, and a minute later booked Smith, who was still protesting.

Miller became the second Ranger to be booked for a foul on Lennox a minute from the interval.

Three minutes into the second half, and a third Rangers name went into the book – that of Ian Redford for a foul on Roy Aitken. Seconds afterwards Aitken had the ball in the net from a Cooper cross, but was clearly offside.

Then McCloy had a magnificent diving save when MacDonald met a Lennox corner with his head, and an even better one when he touched over a McGarvey header from point-blank range.

It was an untidy match, but exciting nevertheless with both sides in with a chance.

McGrain was booked for a foul on MacDonald in 72 minutes and, from the free kick, Latchford was almost caught out.

But in 86 minutes Celtic finally broke the deadlock. Aitken chased a lost ball to the bye-line, stopped it, and sent a cross to the far post for McGarvey to head into the net.

Celtic (0) 1	Rangers (0) 0
McGarvey	
Attendance	52,000

CELTIC:- LATCHFORD, SNEDDON, MCGRAIN, AITKEN, MCDONALD, MCADAM, PROVAN, LENNOX, MCGARVEY, MACLEOD, DOYLE. SUBSTITUTES – MCCLUSKEY AND BURNS.

RANGERS:- MCCLOY, JARDINE, DAWSON, FORSYTH, JACKSON, SMITH, COOPER, MILLER JOHNSTONE, REDFORD, J. MCDONALD. SUBSTITUTES – MCLEAN, RUSSELL

Celtic 1, Rangers 0 – Saturday, 10th May, 1980
Praise for Celtic's Patchwork Heroes
By Jim Reynolds

Celtic will carry Scotland's banner in next season's European Cup-Winners' Cup by virtue of McCluskey's extra-time goal in the Scottish Cup final at Hampden – and it is fitting that Billy McNeill's men ended the season with that particular piece of silverware.

Little went right in the Cup Final build-up. With central defenders Tom McAdam and Roddy McDonald out because of suspension, McNeill had to replan and when he did, those plans were fractured when stand-in Jim Casey had to be ruled out on Thursday because of injury.

As was expected, Rangers were the better side in the early stages. With Davie Cooper in the mood, the makeshift Celtic defence looked in danger of being swept aside with ease. But when Latchford produced a magnificent save from Cooper, that did more than anything else to settle Celtic.

We then saw an enthralling match with both sides playing open football and creating a number of chances, the best of which fell to Derek Johnstone and Frank McGarvey.

The longer the game went on, the better it appeared for Celtic, however. Their frontrunners caused the Rangers defence all sorts of problems, and Provan and Murdo MacLeod were immense in the middle of the park.

Seventeen minutes into extra time, Ally Dawson headed out a corner from the right and Danny McGrain met the clearance first time to send it back towards goal. Peter McCloy had the ball covered, but McCluskey stuck out his left foot and deflected it towards the other corner. Poor McCloy had to change direction but, despite a magnificent effort, he discovered that his arm was about an inch too short.

It was a pity that one of the sides had to lose, but Celtic looked the hungrier side, (eight of their team were chasing their first winners' medal), and at the end of the day that was enough to tilt things in their favour.

Scottish Cup Final

Celtic (0) 1	Rangers (0) 0
McCluskey	

[after extra time; 90 mins 0-0]
(at Hampden Park)

CELTIC:- LATCHFORD, SNEDDON, MCGRAIN, AITKEN, CONROY, MACLEOD, PROVAN, DOYLE, MCCLUSKEY, BURNS, MCGARVEY. SUBSTITUTES – DAVIDSON, LENNOX.

RANGERS:- MCCLOY, JARDINE, DAWSON, FORSYTH, JACKSON, STEVENS, COOPER, RUSSELL, JOHNSTONE, SMITH, MACDONALD. SUBSTITUTES – MCLEAN, MILLER.

From the front page of the Glasgow Herald, Monday, 12th May, 1980
Hampden Riot Sparked off by Players' Actions says Harkness
By Andrew Mccallum, Allan Laing And Charles Gilles

SFA president Willie Harkness yesterday blamed some Celtic players for helping to spark off the invasion of the pitch at Hampden Park which ended in a riot at the Old Firm Scottish Cup Final on Saturday.

If the jubilant Cup winners had not run towards the terracing to seek the acclaim of their supporters, the trouble might never have occurred, he said. Now players could face disciplinary action if they can be identified.

The violence on the pitch from young hooligan supporters from both sides in the crowd of 70,000 led to a casualty list of 100, including four policemen. Fifty fans were taken to hospital and there were 210 arrests, 160 of them inside the ground.

In the aftermath of the unprecedented riot, alarmed senior police officers asked the Chief Constable, Mr Patrick Hamill, to ban Old Firm matches in the public interest and save the risk of serious injury to their men.

For two hours yesterday the Chief Constable and his top aides met to discuss the riot. Later it was stated that the possibility of a ban on all future Old Firm games had been discussed, but that would be up to the regional council.

Already tonight's Glasgow Cup Final between Rangers and Celtic has been abandoned because of Saturday's violence, and both clubs are enquiring into what happened.

The thin blue line of policemen found themselves overwhelmed on Saturday as fans descended upon them from the terracing, scaling the much-vaunted safety fences with ease as the first waves of scarf-waving Celtic fans swept towards the Rangers end. Shouting and taunting the jeering opposition, Rangers fans counter-charged.

In the middle a handful of policemen fought to keep separate the battling fans. The mounted police drew their long riot batons for the first time in Glasgow since the 1926 General Strike. Only when they charged did the warring fans retreat.

A total of 298 policemen and women were involved in the policing of Hampden Park and its approaches.

Sergeant Joe Black, secretary of the Police Federation, said they would ask for police in Glasgow to be the first force in Britain to wear steel helmets and carry riot shields at matches.

Rangers Supporters Association secretary Mr David Miller said yesterday: "The blame must lie with the Chief Constable for allowing the invasion of the park."

A spokesman for Celtic Supporters' Association said that the police were "conspicuous by their absence."

Celtic 1, Rangers 2 – Saturday, 23rd August, 1980
Rangers Wake up to Parkhead Pay-Off
By Jim Reynolds

Celtic may feel they were robbed in the first Old Firm confrontation of the season at Parkhead on Saturday, but they were beaten because Rangers have again found a quality lost during last season's campaign which ended with the Ibrox trophy room bare.

No one could argue that Celtic had most of the pressure, or that Rangers were just a bit fortunate to be level, going into the last 15 minutes of the match. But that is when John Greig's men dug into the past and came up with the quality which typifies the manager.

They refused to settle for a draw and kept going at Celtic right until the final whistle. Their reward was a magnificent goal from Alex Miller 30 seconds from time, and their first-ever Premier League victory at Parkhead.

Greig, as a captain, never allowed Rangers to let up or give up – even when the position seemed hopeless – but when he took over as manager, what he missed most was a player like himself, someone who would coax, cajole and drive the side to their limit.

Now, at last, he seems to have filled that void in his line-up. New boys like Colin McAdam and Jim Bett played their first Old Firm match without any signs of nerves and showed a grim determination to succeed, even when the odds were against them.

Willie Johnston, back at Ibrox for a second spell, is also hungry for success second time round, and this determination and enthusiasm is contagious.

Just two minutes after half-time Celtic took a deserved lead when Sandy Jardine hesitated in trying to clear. Burns was on to the chance in a flash, and sent a powerful drive high into the net.

After an hour Rangers made a double substitution, bringing in Davie Cooper and Derek Johnstone for Robert Russell and John MacDonald, and a minute later a run by Cooper brought the equaliser. He was brought down just outside the box by MacLeod, and fired the free kick into the defensive wall. The ball spun behind the defence and Bett was first to it, hammering it past Pat Bonnar.

Then, just when it looked as if the points would be shared, Rangers made one last charge forward, winning a throw in, out on the left. Willie Johnston prepared for a long throw but changed his mind and threw the ball towards the unmarked Miller on the edge of the box. One bounce and a tremendous left foot shot provided one of the most dramatic finishes.

Celtic (0) 1	Rangers (0) 2
Burns	Bett
	Miller

CELTIC:- BONNAR, SNEDDON, MCGRAIN, AITKEN, MCADAM, MACLEOD, PROVAN, SULLIVAN, MCGARVEY, BURNS, MCCLUSKEY. SUBSTITUTES – MCDONALD, NICHOLAS.

RANGERS:- MCCLOY, JARDINE, MILLER, T. FORSYTH, JACKSON, BETT, W. JOHNSTON, RUSSELL, MCADAM, REDFORD, MACDONALD. SUBSTITUTES – COOPER, D. JOHNSTONE.

Rangers 3, Celtic 0 – Saturday, November 1st, 1980
Emphatic Win Lifts Gloom for Rangers
By Jim Reynolds

Rangers won the battle of the super strikers at Ibrox on Saturday to record their second win of the season over Celtic, and chase away the Chesterfield blues which have been hanging heavily over John Greig's men since last mid-week's defeat by the English Third Division side.

Saturday produced the most emphatic Old Firm victory of recent years, and I doubt if even the most fervent Celtic fan could complain.

For Rangers it was a performance which must give them a massive boost as they chase Aberdeen for the League Championship. After weeks of stuttering, everything clicked back into place. The return of Ally Dawson seemed to stabilise the defence. Ian Redford had one of his best games in a Rangers jersey, and the veteran Willie Johnston turned back the clock to produce some vintage stuff on the left.

For Celtic, who played only in spasms, it was bitter disappointment. They recovered from the first Old Firm defeat earlier in the season to head Rangers in the table, but Saturday's anaemic display means that they are again trailing their rivals.

Celtic began well and created two chances in the opening 10 minutes. But Dom Sullivan missed them both,

hitting Peter McCloy on the legs with his first shot, and sending the second past the post.

Rangers took control after that, and after a period of sustained pressure, they deservedly took the lead when McAdam shot from 20 yards and the ball slipped through past Pat Bonner.

The Ibrox side went two ahead in 37 minutes when the ball spun off Sullivan's head and McDonald, quickly on to it, outpaced Tom McAdam and left the Celtic 'keeper helpless.

Celtic almost got back into the game after an hour when a McAdam effort was booted off the line by Dawson, but Rangers finished the contest 13 minutes from the end when McAdam headed in the third after a brilliant run and cross from Johnston.

Rangers (2) 3	Celtic (0) 0
McAdam 2	
McDonald	

RANGERS:- MCCLOY, JARDINE, DAWSON, D. JOHNSTONE, JACKSON, BETT, MCLEAN, MCDONALD, C. MCADAM, REDFORD, W. JOHNSTON. SUBSTITUTES – T. FORSYTH, RUSSELL.

CELTIC:- BONNER, SNEDDON, MCGRAIN, AITKEN, MCDONALD, T. MCADAM, PROVAN, SULLIVAN, MCGARVEY, BURNS, NICHOLAS. SUBSTITUTES – MCCLUSKEY, DOYLE.

Top: McCloy saves as Burns
and Jardine look on.
Left: Colin McAdam rises
above Dom Sullivan.

157

Frank McGarvey holds off McClelland and Prytz.

McAdam follows up McGavey's shot, April 1980.

Celtic 3, Rangers 1 – Saturday, 21st February, 1981

Charlie is their Darling

By Jim Reynolds

Don't be surprised if Celtic fans change their Saturday anthem from "You'll Never Walk Alone" to "Charlie is My Darling" following Saturday's victory over Rangers at Parkhead, a result which consolidates their position at the top of the Premier League and which virtually kills off Rangers' Championship ambitions for the season.

Said McNeill, "The world is going to hear a lot more about Charlie. I was pleased for him this afternoon, because it's a big thing to score your first goal in an Old Firm match. He's done it now and that should remove any block."

While Celtic must be delighted with a good professional performance from everyone, Davie Provan was outstanding, Nicholas a clinical assassin in front of goal and Frank McGarvey a constant menace with his darts into the penalty area. Colin Jackson, Sandy Jardine and company were run ragged.

Yet Rangers could not have asked for a better start – a goal in just eleven minutes. Davie Cooper foxed the Celtic defence with a curling free kick from the right and with Pat Bonner slow to come off his line, Derek Johnstone glided in to head into the net.

In the second half, the Parkhead men proved they wanted to win the match more than their old rivals. After those early misses, Nicholas equalised in 57 minutes after a shot had been blocked.

Then, in 74 minutes, Nicholas struck again. Jackson misjudged a high ball through the middle, as did the rest of the defence which converged on the young Celtic striker, who controlled the ball and sent a drive past Peter McCloy.

With three minutes left, and Rangers pushing everyone forward to try to save the game, Roy Aitken caught them on the break with a powerful run from the halfway line. He tried to cut the ball across to McGarvey, but when it struck Jackson on the foot, the big Celtic defender hammered the rebound high into the net.

Now Rangers would seem to have only the Scottish Cup left for them this season, but to succeed in that competition manager John Greig has much to do to restore confidence in a side which cannot seem to shrug off the shadow of inconsistency.

Celtic (0) 3	Rangers (1) 1
Nicholas 2	Johnstone
Aitken	

CELTIC:- BONNER, MCGRAIN, REID, SULLIVAN, MCADAM, AITKEN, PROVAN, CONROY, MCGARVEY, BURNS, NICHOLAS. SUBSTITUTES – MCCLUSKEY, DOYLE.

RANGERS:- MCCLOY, JARDINE, DAWSON, D. JOHNSTONE, JACKSON, BETT, COOPER, MILLER, MCADAM, REDFORD, W. JOHNSTON. SUBSTITUTES – MCDONALD, RUSSELL.

Rangers 0, Celtic 1 – Saturday, 20th April, 1981

Celtic in Full Control of Quiet Old Firm Game

By Jim Reynolds

One of the quietest Old Firm matches in my experience ended with a tremendous roar from the Celtic fans which threatened to lift the roof off the stand. Billy McNeil's men had virtually clinched the Premier League title.

Celtic won the first battle of the day in the dressing room. McNeill, quite rightly, decided that it was more important not to lose the game, and announced that Tom McAdam and Roddy McDonald would form the central defence with Roy Aitken sweeping behind them.

That line-up must have thrown Rangers and it worked a treat with the Ibrox front men looking and feeling as if they were playing in a telephone kiosk.

The return of Danny McGrain had a stabilising effect on Celtic. They just did not look like losing the game at any stage.

Manager McNeill agreed afterwards that he never had any cause to worry.

"I thought we played very well and were always in control of the situation," he said. "I felt it was a one-off situation and that's why I made the changes I did. It paid off and we deservedly won the game with a great goal."

Celtic always looked comfortable and when it needed a bit of class to win the points, they provided it in 56 minutes. Provan and Frank McGarvey worked a neat one-two, as Charlie Nicholas ran intelligently into position. When Provan pushed the ball through, the young striker clipped a glorious shot past Jim Stewart.

Celtic were in trouble only once after that when Rangers should have equalised in 65 minutes. Pat Bonner made his only mistake of the game in failing to cut out a high ball, Colin McAdam's effort was knocked off the line by Aitken, and, with the goal wide open, Bett headed against the bar.

Rangers' chance had gone and Celtic virtually cruised though for a win which was well deserved. On a day when it mattered, they had composure and aggression.

Rangers (0) 0	Celtic (0) 1
	Nicholas

RANGERS:- STEWART, MILLER, DAWSON, D. JOHNSTONE, JACKSON, BETT, MCLEAN, RUSSELL, MCADAM, REDFORD, W. JOHNSTON. SUBSTITUTES – JARDINE, MACDONALD.

CELTIC:- BONNER, MCGRAIN, MACLEOD, MCDONALD, MCADAM, AITKEN, PROVAN, CONROY, MCGARVEY, BURNS, NICHOLAS. SUBSTITUTES – DOYLE, REID.

Rangers 0, Celtic 2 – Saturday, 19th September, 1981

Rangers Prove No Threat to Old Rivals

By Jim Reynolds

Paddy Crerand, the former Celtic, Manchester United and Scotland wing half, was asked for his view of the first Old Firm clash of the season at Ibrox on Saturday. "I'll bet Tom McAdam and Roy Aitken didn't need to have a bath after that game." It was Crerand's way of saying that Rangers never threatened any danger on a day which should have been a gala occasion for them with the opening of their new £4m stand, and he was right.

A grim John Greig claimed that Rangers should have had a penalty in the second half when substitute John MacDonald was tackled by Danny McGrain. He pointed to Celtic's opening goal in 11 minutes as a terrible blow.

He said: "Loose marking caused that goal, and it was an uphill fight for us after that, but it's early days yet. This, after all, was only our first defeat by a Scottish side this season."

After the customary hectic opening, Celtic settled first and began probing for weaknesses in the Rangers defence, which they quickly found. When Tom McAdam put Celtic ahead Rangers' "sin" was unforgivable – for they had been warned only seconds before.

McAdam came forward for a corner kick. He was not picked up, and Peter McCloy had a magnificent fingertip save from the header. When Rangers failed to clear that corner, Provan flighted another ball to the far post and, amazingly, McAdam was left on his own again. This time his header went in off the post.

Celtic, in fact, should have had the game won by half-time, but let Rangers off the hook, and while looking comfortable throughout, they had to wait until four minutes from the end to clinch the points.

The goal came when Tom Forsyth fouled McGrain on the edge of the box. Dom Sullivan touched the free kick forward and Murdo MacLeod came up to drive a spectacular shot just inside McCloy's left hand post.

As usual, it was a tough, bruising encounter, and if John Greig was not pleased at the tone of the match, then he must also be angry with four of his players who were booked – Derek Johnstone, Willie Johnston, Gregor Stevens and Tom Forsyth.

Rangers (0) 0	Celtic (1) 2
	McAdam
	MacLeod

RANGERS:- MCCLOY, JARDINE, DAWSON, FORSYTH, STEVENS, MILLER, COOPER, BETT, D. JOHNSTONE, REDFORD, W. JOHNSTON. SUBSTITUTES – MACDONALD, MCADAM.

CELTIC;- BONNER, MCGRAIN, REID, AITKEN, MCADAM, MACLEOD, PROVAN, SULLIVAN, MCGARVEY, BURNS, MCCLUSKEY. SUBSTITUTES – MOYES, NICHOLAS.

Celtic 3, Rangers 3 – Saturday, 21st November, 1981

Fireworks – with not a Damp Squib in Sight

By Jim Reynolds

A more appropriate date for this match would have been November 5, but had the Old Firm served up such a feast on Guy Fawkes Night, it would have put the most elaborate and colourful fireworks display in the shade.

We had hardly time to settle in our seats before news of the first goal was being flashed around the country. A clever move by Celtic ended with Peter McCloy making a tremendous diving save from Dom Sullivan in three minutes, but from the resultant Provan corner Davie Moyes headed towards McCloy, the ball was deflected, and Tom McAdam provided the final touch.

The Celtic fans were still celebrating two minutes later when Rangers came up with the equaliser. Again the build-up was good, with John MacDonald catching out the defence with a long cross from the left. Derek Johnstone headed it down and young Gordon Dalziel, playing in his first Old Firm match, went on his hands and knees to guide the ball past Pat Bonner with his head.

As if that were not good enough for starters, Celtic came up with another great move in 11 minutes and they were back in the lead. Provan sent Moyes down the right on the overlap, and the young full back sent in a precision cross which Frank McGarvey sent high over McCloy.

Rangers kindly gave us nine minutes in which to catch our breath, then had us all gasping again as they swept into the lead with two goals inside three minutes.

First, Dalziel took a pass from MacDonald and jinked his way to the byeline before crossing to the far post for Jim Bett to head home. Then in 23 minutes, when another Dalziel cross had the Celtic defence in all sorts of trouble, MacDonald stepped in to put Rangers in front.

With just six minutes of the second half gone, Celtic were level. Moyes again leaped high to knock down a Provan corner, and Murdo MacLeod thundered a tremendous drive past McCloy.

Two players were booked – Derek Johnstone and Colin Jackson – but the match was played in sporting terms, indeed, in terms befitting the label "the greatest club game in the world."

Celtic (2) 3	Rangers (3) 3
McAdam	Dalziel
McGarvey	Bett
MacLeod	MacDonald

CELTIC:- BONNER, MOYES, REID, AITKEN, MCADAM, MACLEOD, PROVAN, SULLIVAN, MCGARVEY, CONROY, MCCLUSKEY. SUBSTITUTES – NICHOLAS, WEIR.

RANGERS:- MCCLOY, JARDINE, MILLER, STEVENS, JACKSON, BETT, COOPER, RUSSELL, JOHNSTONE, DALZIEL, MACDONALD. SUBSTITUTES – MCKAY, REDFORD.

Rangers 1, Celtic 0 – Saturday, 9th January, 1982
Rangers Open the Doors for Title Changes
By Jim Reynolds

When Celtic's George McCluskey kicked off the Old Firm match at Ibrox on Saturday and played the ball back to Charlie Nicholas, we should, perhaps, have taken that as an omen. Referee Brian McGinlay signalled a false start, and the game never really got going after that.

The magnificent new Ibrox stands and heated pitch provided the perfect platform to give football a great advert; instead, 42,000 fans saw only brief flashes of the good things in the game.

The fact that most of those flashes came from Rangers is adequate proof that they were deserved winners. They were positive, more convincing and made more chances. The fact that they won by a Jim Bett penalty kick 19 minutes from time did not do them justice.

For me, the performances of Jim Bett in midfield and Gregor Stevens in defence contributed more to a victory which prises open the door to the Premier League Championship. They were the best players on the field and it was fitting that Bett should get the goal.

It came from nothing in 71 minutes when the Celtic defence hesitated in going for a long through-ball. Davie Cooper raced inside the box, and, just when he looked as if he might lose control, he was sent sprawling by Pat Bonner. No doubt about the decision – a penalty, and Bett slotted home his fifth spot-kick since being given the job last October.

Only in the hectic last five minutes did Celtic, who looked rusty after their long lay-off, come near to equalising, but it was a match which was all too bitter for this correspondent.

The teams did share the bookings – three from each side: Bett, Jim Stewart and Robert Russell for Rangers, and Celtic's Danny McGrain, Tommy Burns and Roy Aitken.

Now Celtic have allowed Rangers to come back into the title race, and just as the Ibrox club had their undersoil heating on full blast for 48 hours before kick off, Greig promised that it is going to be full blast from his players until the end of the season.

Rangers (0) 1	Celtic (0) 0
Bett (pen.)	

RANGERS:- STEWART, JARDINE, DAWSON, STEVENS, JACKSON, BETT, COOPER, RUSSELL, JOHNSTONE, DALZIEL, MACDONALD. SUBSTITUTES – MCLEAN, MCADAM .

CELTIC:- BONNER, MCGRAIN, AITKEN, MCADAM, MACLEOD, PROVAN, CONROY, NICHOLAS, BURNS, MCCLUSKEY. SUBSTITUTES – MOYES, MCGARVEY.

Crainie scores in the first minute in the April 1982 game.

Celtic 2, Rangers 1 – Saturday, 18th April, 1982

McAdam Puts his Best Foot Forward for Celtic

By Jim Reynolds

While few would deny the fact that a rejuvenated Derek Johnstone was the best player on the field in the final Old Firm confrontation of the season, for me the real hero of a scrappy encounter was Celtic's Tom McAdam.

With Charlie Nicholas, Frank McGarvey and George McCluskey, who have hit 38 goals among them this season, all out through injuries, Celtic were left without an experienced striker for their most vital match against their old rivals this season.

McAdam was asked to move from defence to team up with teenager Danny Crainie up front, and, apart from heading what proved to be the winning goal, he gave a stirring display of commitment and tenacity.

And how Rangers must be sick at the sight of the big fellow. Tom has scored only four times this season – and three of them have been against the men from Ibrox, each one coming at a vital stage.

Over the whole 90 minutes, Rangers frankly did not deserve to lose, but they were not in the same class as Celtic when it came to snapping up the chances. Crainie got Celtic got off to a tremendous start when he scored with just over a minute on the clock. If the goal itself was a bit of a scramble, the move leading up to it was a classic. Tommy Burns set it up with a tremendous pass inside Ally Dawson, and when Jim Stewart could only touch away Dom Sullivan's shot, Crainie nipped in behind Colin Jackson to squeeze the ball over the line.

But the game was won and lost within 60 seconds shortly after half-time. Rangers looked to have equalised when Johnstone got his head to a Davie Cooper free kick, but the ball smacked back off the bar and Celtic raced to the other end to increase their lead.

This time McClelland fouled Crainie on the left side, and when Burns curled his free kick to the far post, McAdam was on the spot to head past Stewart. That left Rangers with a lot to do, and to their credit they never stopped fighting.

But their only reward was a great goal from Johnstone with 15 minutes left. The big striker took advantage of slackness in the Celtic defence to chest down a Bobby Russell cross and fire a full-blooded drive past Pat Bonner.

Having nominated McAdam my man of the match, I must mention the return to form of Derek Johnstone, who is looking sharper than ever. Said Greig: "At the moment he is the best centre forward in Scotland, but he may have left it too late for a World Cup place."

Celtic (1) 2	Rangers (0) 1
Crainie	Johnstone
McAdam	

CELTIC:- BONNER, MCGRAIN, REID, AITKEN, MOYES, MACLEOD, PROVAN, SULLIVAN, MCADAM, CRAINIE, BURNS. SUBSTITUTES – CONROY, MCSTAY.

RANGERS:- STEWART, JARDINE, DAWSON, MCCLELLAND, JACKSON, BETT, COOPER, RUSSELL, JOHNSTONE, REDFORD, MACDONALD. SUBSTITUTES – DALZIEL, MCKAY.

Rangers 1, Celtic 2 – Thursday, 13th May, 1982

Glasgow Cup for Celtic

Celtic are Glasgow Cup winners – but only after a fierce contest last night against Rangers at Ibrox.

Celtic created most of the clear-cut chances and deservedly took the lead in 28 minutes when the pace of John Halpin carried him from the halfway line deep into the Rangers defence.

His shot from 20 yards looked to be well covered by Peter McCloy, who unaccountably allowed the ball to slip under his diving body.

But the game really came to life when in 68 minutes Scottish international Davie Cooper, surprisingly named as substitute when both clubs had sent out their reserve sides, came on to replace Tommy McLean. At the same time Celtic's Jim Dobbin limped off to be replaced by Paul McGuigan.

Rangers equalised four minutes later when in a defensive mix-up, Willie Garner put the ball into his own net.

But Celtic came back and McGuigan got a touch to a Halpin shot to deflect the ball past McCloy.

Glasgow Cup final

Rangers (0) 1	Celtic (1) 2
Garner (o.g.)	Halpin
	McGuigan

RANGERS:- MCCLOY, MCINTYRE, FORSYTH, DAVIES, MCPHERSON, MILLER, MCLEAN, LYLE, FERGUSON, WATSON, BLACK. SUBSTITUTES – COOPER, CLARK.

CELTIC:- LATCHFORD, MCGOLDRICK, MCINALLY, COYLE, GARNER, WEIR, BUCKLEY, MCSTAY, SNEDDON, DOBBIN, HALPIN. SUBSTITUTES – MCGUIGAN, CHALMERS.

Celtic 3, Rangers 2 – Saturday, 30th October, 1982

Old Firm Fortune Favours the Determined

By Jim Reynolds

Scottish Football owes the Old Firm a huge vote of thanks following Saturday's epic during which 22 footballers defied the elements and a gluepot at Parkhead to serve up a feast of all that is good in the game. 60,408 fans – Britain's biggest crowd of the day – will surely agree that there is nothing wrong with Scottish football when it can produce something as good as this.

Rangers will claim they were robbed by losing so late in the match. They will say that they did not deserve to lose after putting so much into the 90 minutes and if I do not agree, then I can certainly understand their way of thinking.

The truth, however, is that Celtic seemed to want to win the match more than their great rivals. Near the point of exhaustion, most other teams would have been content to settle for the draw, but not this Celtic outfit. They called on reserves of strength even they did not know they had and gained a fitting reward in the next couple of minutes.

Rangers, on the other hand, were clearly dejected at twice losing the lead. They let it affect them and when the crunch came – those strength-sapping final 10 minutes when lungs were close to bursting, and feet behaved as if they were cased in lead – they did not have as much left as Celtic.

Yet the day began so brightly for the Ibrox men with a gift of a goal in 15 minutes. Robert Prytz, who was outstanding in the first half, took a corner on the left and when the ball curled towards the near post, the normally reliable Pat Bonner could only punch it into the top of the net.

Celtic for the next couple of minutes looked in desperate trouble, but that is when the youngest man on the field, 17-year-old Paul McStay, took over. With 18 minutes gone he won a tackle in his own half of the field and seconds later was placed two yards from the Rangers goal to tap in an equaliser after a Murdo MacLeod shot had spun off Jim Stewart.

More experienced men would have been content simply to win the tackle, but not this exceptional young man. He went on to stamp himself as man of the match. No wonder Billy McNeill shook his head in wonder at the mention of McStay's name afterwards. He said, 'The boy's a lighthouse. You know, I'm beginning to run out of things to say about him."

Rangers, however, had regained the lead by half-time when, in 40 minutes, Jim Bett chipped a beautiful free kick into the box where it was knocked on by Derek Johnstone, and Davie Cooper headed past Bonner. The Ibrox men deserved to be in front at that point, although Frank McGarvey had a shocking miss just after the second goal when Stewart completely missed his kick and left an open goal. The Celtic striker shot weakly, however, and George Stevens was able to get back and clear off the line.

Another piece of McStay magic in 67 minutes set up the equaliser. Again the youngster won a tackle just outside the box, and catching the Rangers defence square – not for the first time – found McGarvey with a precision pass. Making up for his earlier lapse, the striker easily beat Stewart.

In the closing minutes Celtic mounted fierce pressure, forcing a series of corner kicks, but, ironically, it was on the break that they snatched the winner. McGarvey got the ball after a Rangers attack had broken down three minutes from the end and, with the blue jerseys frantically trying to get back, the ball was pushed on to Charlie Nicholas who in turn put Murdo MacLeod clear for the midfielder to run and hammer a great drive past Stewart.

Celtic (1) 3	Rangers (2) 2
McStay	Bonner (o.g.)
McGarvey	Cooper
MacLeod	
Attendance	**60,480**

CELTIC:- BONNER, MCGRAIN, REID, AITKEN, MCADAM, SINCLAIR, PROVAN, MCSTAY, MCGARVEY, MACLEOD, NICHOLAS. SUBSTITUTES – MOYES AND CRAINIE.

RANGERS:- STEWART, MCKINNON, DAWSON, MCCLELLAND, STEVENS, BETT, COOPER, PRYTZ, JOHNSTONE, RUSSELL, REDFORD. SUBSTITUTES – MACDONALD, MCADAM.

Davie Provan in full stride starts the move which leads to Celtic's opener in the 1982 Scottish league Cup final.

1982

Celtic 2, Rangers 1 – Saturday, 4th December, 1982

Cup Final goes by Form Book

By Jim Reynolds

Hampden, that grey old lady undergoing cosmetic surgery at the moment, saw the thirty-seventh League Cup settled according to the form book. Celtic, that team of all the talents, survived a few self-inflicted wounds to gain their first victory in the tournament for eight years – and deservedly so.

Beforehand, very few had given Rangers a chance of repeating last season's triumph. Their form had slumped alarmingly in recent weeks. There were too many questions surrounding the fitness of key players, and they had the psychological disadvantage of having already lost in the League to their great rivals this season.

But if Rangers lost a trophy on Saturday, they also recovered much of their pride. Their players have recently been heavily criticised, in this column among others, for lack of commitment when the going got tough. It got very tough in this particular Final, but, with the outlook as grey as the skies over Hampden, they pulled themselves together in the nick of time to make a real fight of it.

Had they not done so, then Celtic looked in the mood to inflict a defeat of embarrassing proportions, just as their predecessors did on a similar occasion in 1957.

There is a knack of playing Cup Finals. It is all about getting hold of the nerves and gaining early control, and that is how Celtic went about their business. Rangers' nerves were apparent in the opening two minutes when goalkeeper Jim Stewart collected five pass backs from defenders who were under little pressure.

Meanwhile, Celtic were getting into top gear. Davie Provan, who was later voted man of the match and now collects a holiday for two in America courtesy of the sponsors, Telejector, gave a hint of things to come with a couple of runs to the byeline. Teenager Paul McStay spread his elegance across the pitch with football as neat and tidy as a short back and sides, and one could sense the menace of Charlie Nicholas hovering outside the Rangers penalty area.

Ironically, Rangers looked as if they had weathered the early storm and were beginning to make a positive contribution when they fell behind to a classic goal in 22 minutes.

Provan set it up with another jinking run which took him inside the box and, just when it looked as if he had lost the ball, he poked out a toe and pushed it inside to Charlie Nicholas. The young striker seemed surrounded by blue jerseys and the obvious move would have been for him to pass to Frank McGarvey, who was backing up. The buck stops here, seemed to be Charlie's motto, however, and without breaking stride, he fired the ball low inside Jim Stewart's left-hand post. It was opportunism at its best.

The second goal came in the thirty-first minute, and again Provan had a hand in it. This time Provan sent over a cross from near the right-hand touchline. McAdam knocked it. McKinnon headed it back out to the edge of the box, and MacLeod hit it first-time into the net.

Rangers' only chance in the firsthalf came in 42 minutes when Derek Johnstone forced his way past the Celtic defence and hit a low shot, which was well anticipated and held by Pat Bonner.

It was a transformed Rangers after the interval, however. The measure of skill had not increased, then certainly there was much more fight and conviction about them – all sparked off by a beautiful goal in the opening minutes of the half.

The Celtic defence gifted the chance by dithering on the edge of their own box, and when the slack pass was made, McAdam had to foul Gordon Smith to stop him. Davie Cooper lined up to take the free kick but stepped over the ball and Jim Bett, coming in behind him, chipped the ball delicately over the wall and into the top right-hand corner of the net.

That single act drained much of Celtic's composure, and when young McStay had to limp off in 64 minutes to be replaced by Mark Reid, another of their valuable assets had gone. Rangers too made substitutions – Ally Dawson and John MacDonald, for Robert Prytz and Robert Russell – but while they spent much of the time in Celtic territory, they failed to create genuine chances.

Scottish League Cup Final

Celtic (2) 2	Rangers (0) 1
Nicholas	Bett
MacLeod	

CELTIC:- BONNER, MCGRAIN, SINCLAIR, AITKEN, MCADAM, MACLEOD, PROVAN, MCSTAY, MCGARVEY, BURNS, NICHOLAS. SUBSTITUTES – MCCLUSKEY, REID.

RANGERS:- STEWART, MCKINNON, REDFORD, MCCLELLAND, PATERSON, BETT, COOPER, PRYTZ, JOHNSTONE, RUSSELL, SMITH. SUBSTITUTES – DAWSON, MACDONALD.

Nicholas in his prime: here he squeezes past Paterson and Dawson.

So close, McCloy narrowly fails to save a penalty from Nicholas to make it a
4-2 win in May 1983.

Burns slots home the winner in Celtic's 2-1 victory over Rangers in November 1983.

Dave McPherson and Tom McAdam
reach for the skies.

Bonner rises above McGrain and
Cooper to fist clear.

Celtic 0, Rangers 0 – Wednesday, 24th March, 1983

Close Encounters as Celtic go Top

By Jim Reynolds

Celtic climbed back to the top of the Premier Division last night, taking the point needed to overtake Aberdeen on goal difference, and despite the blank score sheet, more than 51,000 fans were thoroughly entertained.

There was a tremendous display by Rangers goalkeeper Peter McCloy, who was equal to the task of keeping out those swerving shots of Charlie Nicholas and the thunderbolts from Murdo MacLeod.

Celtic had a definite edge in the play, but all credit to a fighting display by Rangers. They have been struggling for much of the season and were clear outsiders last night. Now they are fighting with pride and gearing themselves up for an effort in the Scottish Cup.

It was end-to-end stuff with the tackles fierce and uncompromising, and when Dawson won one of them on the edge of the Celtic penalty area, he then fired in a cracking drive which Bonner did well to hold.

But in 16 minutes Celtic missed a great chance of going ahead. Sullivan robbed Redford in midfield and sent McGarvey galloping down the left. When his low cross reached the near post Nicholas was first to it but shot against McCloy. It was an uncharacteristic miss by Scotland's top scorer.

As the first half ended the match was finely balanced in every aspect, and seconds before the whistle Bonner had a tremendous save when he palmed away a flashing drive from McKinnon, then leapt to cover the rebound.

Seconds after the restart it was McCloy who had to leap to pick a drive from McStay out of the air. Then Rangers' keeper made it a double when he blocked another shot when McStay had made some good space for himself.

In 73 minutes McCloy had a marvellous save when Nicholas created space. This time the shot was low and swerving away from the keeper, but one of those telescopic arms reached out to turn the ball away.

With nine minutes left Prytz replaced Redford and two minutes later McCloy had another magnificent save from a MacLeod thunderbolt. Immediately Celtic sent on McCluskey for Provan.

Celtic (0) 0	Rangers (0) 0
Attendance	51,000

CELTIC:- BONNER, MCGRAIN, REID, AITKEN, MCADAM, SULLIVAN, PROVAN, MCSTAY, NICHOLAS, MACLEOD, MCGARVEY. SUBSTITUTES – MCCLUSKEY, MOYES.

RANGERS:- MCCLOY, DAWSON, MCCLELLAND, MCPHERSON, PATTERSON, BETT, COOPER, MCKINNON, CLARK, REDFORD, MACDONALD. SUBSTITUTES – PRYTZ, DALZIEL.

Rangers 2, Celtic 4 – Saturday, 14th May, 1983

Old Firm Matches Bring out the Best in Celtic Players

By Ian Paul

If Celtic had been able to find the self-motivation in other games that they have displayed against Rangers this season, there would probably not have been such a close finish to the Premier Division.

Neither the Parkhead players nor their fans accepted the legitimacy of the half-time scoreline (2-0 for Rangers) and, with Rangers apparently content to hold what they had, the comeback was not entirely unpredictable.

Although Rangers had snatched two goals, one a fine free kick from Cooper which probably took a slight deflection, and another by Clark whose head deflected a wayward McKinnon shot, they were not really convincing, even in the first half.

Nevertheless, with that two goal cushion, it was surprising how they capitulated, admittedly to some fine Celtic play.

Rangers may have been unfortunate to lose two penalty goals (I felt the second was certainly soft) but in truth, they were so outplayed that the final scoreline was accurate enough.

Celtic, simply took complete charge of the midfield area and, valiantly though Peter McCloy, Ally Davidson and Craig Paterson performed, the tide was too much to stem indefinitely.

For Celtic, MacLeod had perhaps his best game of the season and Burns and McStay were only marginally behind. Even then they were all runners-up to Davie Provan as the most effective player on the field.

With all that going for them there was little doubt that Celtic would triumph in the end. In fact it was only when they went 3-2 up with a neat McGarvey header that the opposition found some aggression of their own. With Russell on for McKinnon, and Dalziel for MacDonald, Rangers almost resurrected their chances, Cooper hitting the post and Bonner saving well from Russell.

When Nicholas scored his second penalty four minutes from the end, however, there was no road back for an Ibrox team which will need to show a great deal more midfield commitment if they are to succeed against Aberdeen in the Scottish Cup Final on Saturday.

Rangers (2) 2	Celtic (0) 4
Cooper	
Clark	

RANGERS:- MCCLOY, DAWSON, MCCLELLAND, MCPHERSON, PATTERSON, BETT, COOPER, MCKINNON, CLARK, REDFORD, MACDONALD. SUBSTITUTES – RUSSELL, DALZIEL.

CELTIC:- BONNER, MCGRAIN, SINCLAIR, AITKEN, MCADAM, MACLEOD, PROVAN, MCSTAY, NICHOLAS, BURNS, MCGARVEY. SUBSTITUTES – MCCLUSKEY, REID.

Rangers 1, Celtic 0 – Saturday, 13th August, 1983

Prytz Works Hard to Give Rangers the Cup

By Jim Reynolds

The prize was only a Glasgow Cup, but success was so sweet for Rangers at Hampden on Saturday, when a Sandy Clark goal gave the Ibrox side only their second win in the last dozen Old Firm clashes. It was a win they deserved.

New Parkhead manager Davie Hay almost admitted as much afterwards when he said: "We didn't give that little bit extra which is needed, especially against Rangers."

On the whole what should have been a showpiece to celebrate the centenary of the Glasgow Association, ended with a directive from the authorities that the winning team could not parade the trophy in front of the fans.

Rangers manager John Greig said: "I wanted the players to go back out but we were forbidden to do so, and I must apologise to our fans. After all, they have stood by us in two losing Finals on the same ground in the last year."

Rangers played a 4-4-2 with Clark and new signing Ally McCoist up front, but I feel that McCoist is at his best when coming forward from a midfield position and I am sure that is where he will be used eventually, with, perhaps, John MacDonald moving forward.

Rangers' big success was the Swedish internationalist Robert Prytz, who not so long ago seemed set to leave Ibrox. He showed a tremendous appetite for the game and must have covered every blade of Hampden grass.

Celtic, having lost Charlie Nicholas and George McCluskey in the transfer market and Frank McGarvey through injury, looked to be struggling up front, but it would be unfair to be too critical while new signings like Brian McClair and Jim Melrose have still to settle in.

It is essential that they find their scoring touch quickly, for Celtic learned a painful lesson at the weekend. They missed early chances and lost the Cup to a beautiful fiftieth minute goal set up by Ally Dawson, who trailed the ball to the byeline and then cut it back to the post for Clark to sweep it into the net.

Glasgow Cup Final

Rangers (0) 1	Celtic (0) 0
Clark	
(at Hampden Park)	

RANGERS:- MCCLOY, DAWSON, MCCLELLAND, MCPHERSON, PATERSON, REDFORD, PRYTZ, MCCOIST, CLARK, RUSSELL, MCDONALD. SUBSTITUTES – COOPER, MCKINNON.

CELTIC:- BONNER, MCGRAIN, REID, AITKEN, MCADAM, MACLEOD, PROVAN, P. MCSTAY, MCCLAIR, BURNS, CRAINIE.

Celtic 2, Rangers 1 – Saturday, 3rd September, 1983

McGarvey Winner another Damning Ibrox Statistic

By Jim Reynolds

Frank McGarvey's late goal at Parkhead on Saturday did more than snatch a point from Rangers (and one could not argue that John Greig's men deserved a share); it added another damning statistic to the Ibrox club's Premier Division record in matches against their old rivals.

Saturday's was the thirty-third meeting between the clubs since League reconstruction in 1975, and Rangers have won only 6 to Celtic's 16. Of the last 21, they have won only 2 and, since 1975, they have only won one match on Celtic territory.

That must make sad reading for Rangers fans, and with the emergence of Aberdeen and Dundee United at the top of the pile, the winning of the Championship looks like a gigantic task for a club which is desperate for success in the League.

Ally McCoist did everyone a favour when he scored a tremendous goal with around just 30 seconds on the clock.

Rangers could not have dreamed of a better start. Roy Aitken fouled Sandy Clark, and Robert Prytz caught Celtic on the hop with a quickly-taken free kick to Davie McKinnon on the overlap. When the full back cut his cross into the penalty area, McCoist hit it first time from 15 yards and it whizzed through Pat Bonner's legs.

It was a blow struck with all the force of a Marvin Hagler hook, but Celtic merely brushed it off as nothing more than an irritant, and stormed forward for the equaliser. They had to wait only eight minutes.

Again the goal came from a free kick, this time Ally Dawson committing a foul on Jim Melrose. Davie Provan took the kick, McGarvey knocked it down, and Aitken, up with the attack, shot home from close range. Unfortunately for Peter McCloy, there was a deflection.

It was frantic stuff, with the tackling fierce, but class did shine through on occasions, particularly from Celtic's young Paul McStay and Rangers' young Australian striker, David Mitchell, who looks like a real prospect.

Then, with the match seemingly destined for a draw, Celtic hit on the break. Tommy Burns shot against McCloy, Provan did the same, but, even while on the ground, the little winger showed marvellous reflexes to push the ball back for McGarvey to shoot into the net for the winner and Celtic's 50th Premier Division goal against their oldest rivals.

Celtic (1) 2	Rangers (1) 1
Aitken	McCoist
McGarvey	

CELTIC:- BONNER, MCGRAIN, WHITTAKER, AITKEN, W. MCSTAY, MACLEOD, PROVAN, P. MCSTAY, MCGARVEY, BURNS, MELROSE. SUBSTITUTES – REID, MCCLAIR.

RANGERS:- MCCLOY, MCKINNON, DAWSON, MCPHERSON, MCCLELLAND, REDFORD, PRYTZ, MCCOIST, CLARK, RUSSELL, MITCHELL. SUBSTITUTES – COOPER, MCDONALD.

Rangers 1, Celtic 2 – Saturday, 5th November, 1983
Class Tells in the End
By Jim Reynolds

One would have thought that former Rangers player Alex Willoughby had been given a preview of the latest Old Firm confrontation. Either that, or the man could be psychic. His quotes in Saturday's match programme were bang-on.

Talking about Old Firm matches, Willoughby said: "As an event, it's tremendous, but as a football spectacle it tends to be over-rated. There is so much tension, so much pace, and, at times, so little cool thinking."

That was exactly how this one was played, and although the almost-capacity crowd roared their heads off for 90 minutes, there was little for the football purist. They have been playing this particular fixture for almost 100 years and this must surely rank as one of the poorest.

Rangers had the slight edge in the first half, but even at that, the only time they troubled Pat Bonner was when Ian Redford sent in a free kick which the goalkeeper saved brilliantly.

However, at the end of the day, Celtic did deserve their victory for the simple reason that this game is called football and they played more of it than Rangers.

When the pace of the game dropped midway in the second half, creative players like Paul McStay and Tommy Burns emerged to win the match. To be fair to Rangers, they never stopped trying, but they did not have anyone in the same class as the Celtic pair.

It was McStay who set up the first goal in 54 minutes, when he held the ball, then released it at the right time into the path of Frank McGarvey, who drove low inside

Peter McCloy's left-hand post.

That gave Celtic the confidence they needed and they went on to clinch the match in 76 minutes with a magnificent goal from Burns, who tried a one-two with McGarvey, changed his mind, and took the ball back off the striker and shot past McCloy.

Sandy Clark managed a consolation goal for Rangers with four minutes left – deserved for their afternoon's effort – but Celtic comfortably played out time to record the second victory of the season over their old rivals.

Rangers, with only three League wins this season – incidentally, their next two Premier Division matches are against Aberdeen and Dundee United – are struggling with just seven points. The taunts of "relegation . . . relegation" must have been more embarrassing than hurtful.

The fact is that this is a club without confidence, and just when it looked as if it might be returning on Saturday, McGarvey put them back to square one. The first job when the new manager arrives at Ibrox is to restore confidence – the rest will follow.

Rangers (0) 1	Celtic (0) 2
Clark	McGarvey
	Burns

RANGERS:- MCCLOY, NICHOLL, DAWSON, MCCLELLAND, PATERSON, MCPHERSON, MCCOIST, MCKINNON, CLARK, REDFORD, MITCHELL. SUBSTITUTES – COOPER, MACDONALD.

CELTIC:- BONNER, MCGRAIN, WHITTAKER, W. MCSTAY, MCADAM, MACLEOD, PROVAN, P. MCSTAY, MCGARVIE, BURNS, MCCLAIR. SUBSTITUTES:- MELROSE, SINCLAIR.

Rangers celebrate their 1984 Scottish League Cup victory.

Rangers 3, Celtic 2 – Sunday, 25th March, 1984

Rangers Meet Wallace's Final Demands

By Jim Reynolds

McCOIST HAT-TRICK HERO AS CELTIC FIGHT BACK IN VAIN.

Rangers yesterday reached the heights demanded of them by Jock Wallace. Just four months after taking over at Ibrox for the second time, Wallace sent out a patchwork side at Hampden to win the League Cup in dramatic style – the only honour left to them this season.

But what an amazing Final, with Celtic looking down and out, only to come battling back from two down to equalise with a last-gasp Mark Reid penalty, which sent the game into extra time.

It was a victory against the odds, but Wallace's conviction that the side he had built at the last minute would be good enough on the day was well-founded. Rangers, with their tremendous commitment, fought harder and longer than their Old Firm rivals and took the silverware back to Ibrox, their first major trophy in two seasons.

Ally McCoist, their 21-year-old striker, was the goal hero with a hat-trick – two of them from the penalty spot – but for me, the main man was midfield player Bobby Russell, who was head and shoulders above anyone else on the field. Having lost two midfield men because of suspension, it was thought Rangers might be vulnerable there; there was no chance of that with Russell in this kind of form.

There must be praise, too, for Celtic, for a fightback as dramatic as any seen at Hampden. And they did score the best goal of the game through Brian McClair. It was of the quality which should have won a Cup but failed to win this one.

So Jock Wallace, in a short space of time, has done the job Rangers brought him back to do. No wonder he leapt from the dug-out at the end, a huge fist waved in the air, to salute a famous victory.

The match was too tense and fierce to come anywhere near being a classic in terms of finer skills and referee Bob Valentine had his busiest afternoon in a long time, but he did well in a difficult situation.

Rangers settled first and in seven minutes they almost opened the scoring with a tremendous move sparked off by Russell, who put McCoist clear on the right. When his low cross came over, Clark completely missed it right in front of goal, and it carried to MacDonald whose first-time shot was blocked on the line by McAdam.

The game badly needed someone to slow it down. It was all too hectic, with little football being played. McStay was certainly trying but several openings which he created were squandered.

But there was joy for Rangers a minute from half-time when they took the lead from the penalty spot. Russell, having a tremendous match, sped inside the box and when he went down after a MacLeod tackle, the referee had no hesitation in pointing to the spot.

McCoist was given the job and he performed perfectly, slamming the ball inside Bonner's left-hand post. The goal

had come against the run of play, but it was a tribute to Rangers' determination that they had hit the front at the half way mark after absorbing so much pressure.

Two minutes after half-time, Celtic were almost level when McClair took a brilliant pass from Burns and fired in a low shot which McCloy blocked.

In 55 minutes Rangers made a substitution, bringing on Burns for MacDonald, and three minutes later Russell was to be booked after he had fouled Burns.

That disappointment was forgotten in 60 seconds as Rangers scored again. It came by chance from a massive clearance by McCloy which had Aitken and Clark chasing the ball inside the Celtic Penalty area. It broke from Clark to the unmarked McCoist, who beat Bonner from a couple of yards.

McClelland was then booked for fouling Burns on the edge of the box in 67 minutes. It was a costly tackle, as from the free kick Celtic scored a magnificent goal which started their fightback.

Burns took the kick himself, putting his toe under the ball and bobbing it over the defence to McClair, who met it on the volley and beat McCloy.

With 14 minutes left both sides made substitutions. Melrose took over from McGarvey and McAdam came on for Clark. McPherson was then booked for a foul on Provan.

Substitute Melrose was the sixth player to be booked as Celtic mounted a last-gasp effort to hold on to the trophy, and as the game swept into injury time, the Parkhead side came up with as dramatic an equaliser as Hampden has ever seen.

MacLeod looked certain to score as he had only McCloy to beat from a few yards, but he was pulled down by McCoist and the penalty was given. Reid showed no signs of the pressure he must have felt as he hammered the ball high into the net.

Sinclair took over from a tiring Provan 10 minutes into extra time, but in 14 minutes Rangers came up with the winner. Again it was from the penalty spot after McCoist had been sent crashing by Aitken. This time Bonner blocked McCoist's spot kick, but the Ranger followed up to score.

Aitken and McCoist brought the bookings total to eight for a little bit of nastiness near the end.

Scottish League Cup Final

Rangers (1) 3	Celtic (0) 2
McCoist 3 (2 pen.)	McClair
	Reid

[after extra time; 90 mins 2-2]
(at Hampden Park)

RANGERS:- MCCLOY, NICHOLL, DAWSON, MCCLELLAND, PATERSON, MCPHERSON, RUSSELL, MCCOIST, CLARK, MCDONALD, COOPER. SUBSTITUTES – MCADAM, BURNS.

CELTIC:- BONNER, MCGRAIN, REID, AITKEN, MCADAM, MCLEOD, PROVAN, MCSTAY, MCGARVEY, BURNS, MCCLAIR. SUBSTITUTES – SINCLAIR AND MELROSE.

Celtic 3, Rangers 0 – Monday, 2nd April, 1984'

McStays Team up to Deflate Rangers

By Jim Reynolds

Oh, brother did Celtic gain revenge over their Old Firm rivals in this rearranged Premier Division match before a crowd of 53,229 at Parkhead last night, when Paul and Willie McStay led the way in keeping Davie Hay's men in with a slim chance of the title.

Just eight days after having lost to Rangers in the League Cup Final Celtic produced some devastating form to run Rangers ragged and leave them completely bewildered before the end.

Paul McStay, who flies out to Yugoslavia with the Under-21 squad this morning, was the outstanding man afield. He opened the scoring with a magnificent solo goal in the first half and Celtic never looked back.

Brother Willie grabbed No. 2 with a goal that will haunt Rangers' goalkeeper Peter McCloy for many a day, and substitute Davie Provan finished it off with a third goal five minutes from the end.

In 22 minutes Celtic produced a move which almost paid off, Burns swinging in a cross from the right and McClair's header hitting the side netting. Celtic were certainly having the better of it at that stage, but could not break the deadlock.

McCloy then held a McLeod header. McPherson headed behind his own posts, and Rangers were rocking. Then in 31 minutes Celtic took the lead with a quite magnificent goal from Paul McStay.

The youngster collected the ball midway inside the opposition's half and set off with a tremendous run which carried him right through the entire Rangers defence to the byeline where he somehow managed to squeeze the ball past McCloy, perhaps with the help of a deflection. It was no more than Celtic deserved.

Rangers again almost produced an equaliser in 68 minutes when Paterson rose to meet a Cooper corner. It looked like going in, but Bonner pulled off a brilliant save, touching the ball over the bar.

Ten minutes later we saw the other side of goalkeeping when McCloy was badly at fault as Celtic took a two-goal lead. This time Willie McStay ran on to a loose ball 25 yards out and hit a first-time drive which the 'keeper looked to have covered. He missed it, however, and the ball shot in off a post.

In 85 minutes Celtic completed a comprehensive drubbing of their old rivals when they scored a brilliant third goal. Two back-heelers from Paul McStay and McGarvey set it up and Provan scored with a left foot drive just inside the left hand post.

Celtic (1) 3	Rangers (0) 0
P. McStay	
W. McStay	
Provan	
Attendance	**53,229**

CELTIC:- BONNER, MCGRAIN, REID, AITKEN, MCADAM, W. MCSTAY, MCCLAIR, P. MCSTAY, MELROSE, MACLEOD, T. BURNS. SUBSTITUTES – PROVAN, MCGARVEY.

RANGERS:- MCCLOY, NICHOLL, DAWSON, MCCLELLAND, PATERSON, MCPHERSON, RUSSELL, MCCOIST, CLARK, WILLIAMSON, COOPER. SUBSTITUTES – REDFORD, BURNS.

Rangers 1, Celtic 0 – Saturday, 21st April, 1984

Williamson is Quick to Make Amends

By Jim Reynolds

Rangers finished this season's series of Old Firm matches on a high note, beating their rivals at Ibrox in only the second time in four years, and there was no happier man on Saturday than Bobby Williamson, signed from Clydebank just four months ago.

It was a spectacular goal from Williamson early on which eventually separated the sides who, incidentally, put on a more entertaining performance than is the norm for these tension-packed episodes. I do not think that either side would have complained if the match had ended all square, but Williamson's opportunism gave Rangers the edge, and his goal was worthy of winning any match.

The reason that Rangers had to play for almost half an hour with 10 men was that full back Jimmy Nicholl, playing his last game for the club before returning to Toronto Blizzard, was sent off by referee Hugh Alexander for retaliation against Brian McClair. The Irishman had been booked in the first half, and had to go.

The defeat means that it is now almost impossible for Celtic to win the Championship, although manager Davie Hay says they will just have to keep plugging away. He said: "It was a very tight game with few chances, but Rangers stuck away a half chance, and that was it."

With both goalkeepers, Peter McCloy and Pat Bonner, in excellent form, there was never a chance that we would see many goals, but the one we did see was a bit special, although the Celtic defence made a real mess of things. It came in 55 minutes when Davie Cooper sent over a corner from the right. Danny McGrain failed to head clear, Murdo MacLeod mishit the clearance, and Williamson, facing his own goal, scored with a spectacular overhead kick.

Celtic came storming back, especially after Nicholl had been sent off, but, although they had much more of the ball, the Rangers defence stood firm, with Craig Paterson immense and John McClelland organising brilliantly.

Rangers (0) 1	Celtic (0) 0
Williamson	

RANGERS:- MCCLOY, NICHOLL, MCCLELLAND, MCPHERSON, PATERSON, REDFORD, RUSSELL, PRYTZ, WILLIAMSON, MCCOIST, COOPER. SUBSTITUTES – MCDONALD, MCKINNON.

CELTIC:- BONNER, MCGRAIN, REID, GRANT, MCADAM, W. MCSTAY, MCCLAIR, P. MCSTAY, MCGARVEY, MACLEOD, BURNS. SUBSTITUTES – MELROSE, PROVAN.

1984

Rangers 0, Celtic 0 – Saturday, 25th August, 1984
Paterson Putting Troubles Behind Him
By Jim Reynolds

In these days when footballers seem to be making constant demands on clubs, it is quite refreshing to hear the opposite. The fortunate club in this instance if Rangers, and manager Jock Wallace can be certain that is any of his players come knocking on the door with a complaint, it will not be centre half Craig Paterson.

Paterson signed from Hibernian two years ago, and has never quite managed to establish himself because of a series of injuries, but against Celtic at the weekend he showed just what he can do when he is fully fit. Paterson was quite magnificent, and one second-half tackle on Brian McClair ranks as one of the best I have ever seen at any level.

It is amazing that in his two years at Ibrox Paterson's longest first team run is 13 matches and that was when he first arrived. Last season, his longest run was a mere 11 games and the stop-start career has had the player near to despair.

Saturday's match was one of the tamer Old Firm confrontations, with both sides having their moments, but Rangers must be regretting a few missed chances when they were clearly on top early in the second half. Iain

Redford should have scored instead of blasting high over after getting the break of the ball off Roy Aitken, and Iain Ferguson should have done better than send a header against Pat Bonner.

However, a draw was perhaps the proper result, for Celtic were the better side in the first half and also finished strongly, although they did not create as many chances as Rangers. Where they did fall down was in midfield, when Rangers stepped things up at the start of the second half.

Paul McStay did as well as could be expected for someone who is obviously not 100% fit and the young Peter Grant is certainly a bright prospect, but Celtic are sadly missing the drive of Murdo MacLeod, and he could be out for two or three weeks yet.

Rangers (0) 0   Celtic (0) 0

RANGERS:- WALKER, MCKINNON, DAWSON, MCCLELLAND, PATERSON, REDFORD, RUSSELL, C. FRASER, I. FERGUSON, CLARK, COOPER. SUBSTITUTES – BURNS, MCCOIST.

CELTIC:- BONNER, MCGRAIN, SINCLAIR, AITKEN, MCADAM, GRANT, COLQUHOUN, P. MCSTAY, MCCLAIR, BURNS, MCINALLY. SUBSTITUTES – MCGARVEY, W. MCSTAY.

Celtic 1, Rangers 1 – Saturday, 22nd December, 1984
Costly Error by Bonner but Rangers Worth Their Point
By Jim Reynolds

What is it every goalkeeper has and wishes he hadn't? It is one mad moment he would rather forget but will, in fact, remember for the rest of his life. Ray Clemence, Peter Shilton, Alan Rough, and Pat Jennings have had a few. Even Gordon Banks would admit to having at least one.

At Parkhead on Saturday Pat Bonner made one mistake which will haunt him for the rest of his career, a mistake that deprived Celtic of victory.

With just five minutes left of one of the most enthralling Old Firm matches of recent seasons, the big Irishman came off his line to cut out a Ted McMinn cross. He could only palm it weakly down, and Davie Cooper rifled in for the equaliser.

It would be wrong, however, to lay the whole blame for the loss of the point on Bonner, because for the rest of the match he was quite magnificent in his handling of the ball. He had immaculately cut out every cross, made a wonderful penalty save from Cammy Fraser, and another instinctive save from John MacDonald.

The real problems for Celtic were further forward when, after having controlled the game for most of the first half, they began to give the ball away too easily. Even the reliable Paul McStay was wayward with his passes, and with Rangers totally committed to their job, they staged a great second half comeback in which 17-year-old Derek

Ferguson showed all the touches to suggest he is one of the best young Scottish players to emerge for years.

At the end of the day, Celtic have no excuses. Rangers' reshuffled side did enough to earn a point and they came out of the game with most credit. Celtic got off to a fine start with a goal after only nine minutes. Brian McClair cleverly set up a chance for Mo Johnston, and when the striker's shot came off the legs of Peter McCloy, McClair was first to the rebound to score. Thereafter Celtic had several chances to go further ahead, but by half-time they only had that goal to show for their efforts and each side had one chalked off for offside.

They should have equalised in 51 minutes when Mark Reid fouled Davie Cooper in the box but, although Fraser hit the penalty well, Bonner made a magnificent diving save. Sadly for him that was overshadowed by his late lapse which brought the game level.

Celtic (1) 1   Rangers (0) 1
McClair   Cooper

CELTIC:- BONNER, MCGRAIN, REID, MCCLAIR, AITKEN, MACLEOD, COLQUHOUN, MCSTAY, JOHNSTON, BURNS, MCGARVEY. SUBSTITUTES – SINCLAIR, PROVAN.

RANGERS:- MCCLOY, BURNS, MUNRO, MCPHERSON, MCKINNON, REDFORD, MACDONALD, FRASER, MITCHELL, D. FERGUSON, COOPER. SUBSTITUTES – MCMINN, PRYTZ.

Rangers 1, Celtic 2 – Tuesday, 1st January, 1985

Hay's Resolution – to Reshape Celtic Team

By Ian Paul

[EXTRACTED FROM A ROUNDUP OF THE NE'ERDAY MATCHES ON THURSDAY 3RD JANUARY]

Happy though he was with Celtic's 2-1 win over Rangers at Ibrox on Tuesday, manager David Hay is sticking to his resolution made before the game to begin reshaping the Parkhead team.

Hay explained his views to his players before they went to Ibrox, and even though the warnings clearly had the desired effect he remains convinced that a gradual redevelopment of the side is necessary.

While Tuesday's win kept Celtic very much in the race for the Premier Division Championship, Rangers, who had begun to harbur title ambitions themselves, have to start the chase again. They had looked in good shape when they went ahead through a splendid Davie Cooper goal, especially as Celtic missed a penalty, but when Maurice Johnston, the spot kick sinner, made amends with a headed goal inside the first minute of the second half, Rangers lost all their discipline and were outplayed. The winning goal, a Brian McClair shot which was deflected past McCloy, summed up a generally scrappy contest.

Rangers manager Jock Wallace was entitled to be upset at his side's inept second-half display. "They let themselves down, not to mention the fans and me. If you don't pass the ball, you are defending," he said.

Rangers (1) 1	Celtic (0) 2
Cooper	Johnston
	McClair

RANGERS:- MCCLOY; BURNS AND MUNRO; MCPHERSON, MCKINNON AND REDFORD; MCMINN AND D. FERGUSON; I. FERGUSON; PRYTZ AND COOPER. SUBSTITUTES - MACDONALD AND DAWSON.

CELTIC:- BONNER; MCGRAIN AND REID; MCCLAIR, AITKEN AND MACLEOD; COLQUHOUN AND MCSTAY; JOHNSTON; BURNS AND MCGARVEY.

Murdo MacLeod is congratulated by Peter Grant and Paul McStay.

Celtic 1, Rangers 1 – Wednesday, 1st May, 1985

Nine-Man Rangers Draw after Cooper and Dawson Sent Off

By Ian Paul

You can always trust the Old Firm to end their season of confrontation in dramatic style, and no one can deny that they did so in extraordinary fashion at Parkhead last night.

Two Rangers players, Davie Cooper and Ally Dawson, were sent off in the second half, five other players were booked, and yet the nine-man Ibrox team finished up sharing the points with Celtic.

Even the dramatic missed penalty by Celtic's Roy Aitken, who had scored with his previous three, was reduced to the ordinary in a game of unrelenting action, ferocious tackling and breakneck football.

The consequences of it all (and in itself a cameo of the season) is that Aberdeen are now officially Premier Division Champions. Not that this entered the thoughts of the 40,079 who stayed enthralled to the end, even if the Celtic throngs were stunned by the fact that their team failed to win.

Certainly Celtic had most of the play and when Alan McInally, deputising for surprise absentee Frank McGarvey, put them in front in nine minutes after Cooper had been ordered off, they seemed set fair. But it was after Dawson's dismissal, 18 minutes from time, that Rangers, remarkably, had their best spell and in 78 minutes Ally McCoist smacked the equaliser from the penalty spot.

If anyone in the large crowd imagined there would be an end-of-season touch about the proceedings, it took a mere two minutes to dispel such nonsense. Davie McPherson quite blatantly whipped the legs from Maurice Johnston inside the area, leaving referee Bob Valentine with only one choice, a penalty kick.

The drama only began then when Roy Aitken had two or three tries at getting the ball to remain static on the spot. When he did finally smack it into the net, Mr Valentine correctly ordered a retake. Even Aitken's nerve must have been jangling by this time, and it was no surprise when the second effort crashed off the legs of McCloy to safety.

McPherson, whose foul, therefore, was not properly punished by Celtic was not so fortunate soon afterwards when he fouled Johnston again. This time the referee took his name.

Paul McStay and Brian McClair looked sharp from the start for Celtic and one piece of play by McStay ended with a low cross in front of the goal which eluded everyone. McClair also had two well-struck long-distance shots, one wide and one stopped by McCloy.

Russell gave the Rangers end some encouragement with a good effort, but a few minutes later the same player missed completely when a Durrant cross landed in his path.

But the best yet came at McCloy's goal when Willie McStay, after having worked a 1-2 with McInally, fairly belted a shot towards the net, only to see McCloy pull off a magnificent save. Then Mo Johnston, who would know he was in a game, almost broke the deadlock with a drive that went across the face of the goal.

The Scotland internationalist then got a foot to a Paul McStay attempt and nearly diverted it out of the goalkeeper's reach. A few minutes later Davie Cooper was booked for a wild tackle on Willie McStay, and Derek Johnstone could count himself fortunate to escape censure after he downed McInally, further evidence that Celtic's pressure was having its effect on the Ibrox side.

Nerves were evident among the Celtic players too, however, and young Paul McGuigan, playing in his first Old Firm Game, had his name taken after a foul on Eric Ferguson. McKinnon had the first serious effort of the second half, a dipping shot which dropped just over the bar. Before that Peter Grant was booked for a foul on Cooper, and after it Cooper foolishly returned some of the same to Grant in full view of the referee. Having already been booked he was sent off, and this just seven minutes after the break.

Almost immediately McClair missed a glorious chance to put Celtic ahead, heading over from close range.

But 10-man Rangers had plenty of spirit left, as illustrated by Eric Ferguson, whose shot was brilliantly touched over the top by Latchford.

Then Celtic had claims for another penalty but the referee had spotted handball by a Celtic man. Paul McStay was next to worry McCloy with a drive, but he was just off target.

In 61 minutes, however, Celtic did get a breakthrough. Johnston, put clear on the right, hit a hard shot which McCloy did well to halt, but could not quite grasp. The ball bounced before McInally managed to touch it past a couple of despairing defenders, and it went slowly over the line.

Soon after Rangers brought on Iain Ferguson for his namesake, Eric.

In 71 minutes, there was further sensation as Ally Dawson was sent off after an off-the-ball fracas with Mo Johnston. Referee Valentine, having booked Johnston, consulted his linesman and then ordered off Dawson.

The "fun" was not over. In 78 minutes Rangers were awarded a penalty, the referee indicating that Aitken had handled the ball as he was challenged by Ferguson. Ally McCoist made a good job of the kick and levelled the score.

Shortly afterwards Derek Johnstone was booked for fouling Grant.

Celtic (0) 1	Rangers (0) 1
McInally	McCoist (pen.)
Attendance	40,079

CELTIC;- LATCHFORD, W. MCSTAY, MCLEOD, AITKEN, MCGUIGAN, GRANT, PROVAN, P. MCSTAY, JOHNSTON, MCCLAIR, MCINALLY. SUBSTITUTES – MCKECHNIE, COLQUHOUN.

RANGERS;- MCCLOY, DAWSON, MUNRO, MCPHERSON, JOHNSTONE, DURRANT, RUSSELL, MCKINNON, E. FERGUSON, MCCOIST, COOPER. SUBSTITUTES – I. FERGUSON, BURNS.

Danny McGrain

A schoolboy internationalist, McGrain, born in Glasgow in 1950, joined Celtic as a full professional in 1967, and when he played for Scotland in the World Cup Finals in West Germany in 1974, he was widely regarded as the best full-back in the world.

He could play either on the right or the left, had perfect timing in the tackle, and blistering pace. Throughout his career, Danny defied the odds. He fractured his skull in a match against Falkirk at Brockville in 1972, he was diagnosed as a diabetic four years later, and he missed a full year because of a serious foot injury, sustained in 1977. He came through all that to become Scottish Player of the Year, and he was awarded the MBE.

As a player, McGrain played 57 times for Scotland and won five Championship medals, four in the Scottish Cup and one in the League Cup. He was another of the club's inspirational captains. He left Celtic in 1987 and joined Hamilton. Was coach at Clydebank and had a short spell as manager at Arbroath.

Tommy Burns

Now manager of the club he supported as a boy, Burns is one of the best left–sided players to have represented the club since the war. Many will say that Tully was the best, but Burns has the medals to back up his claim.

A gifted player and a caring, honest person, he had a special rapport with the fans which still exists today.

Burns joined the club from Maryhill Juniors in 1975 and, despite earlier disciplinary problems – he was sent off three times – he emerged as a mature, intelligent midfielder – he also filled in at left back with success – who made more than 400 appearances for the club. He won six Championships, four Scottish Cups and a League Cup.

Burns made his last appearance for the club against Ajax in 1989 before moving on to Kilmarnock, where he helped them gain promotion to the First Division. Was appointed manager at Rugby Park and took them into the Premier Division before returning to Parkhead as boss in 1994. In his first season Celtic won their first trophy in six years by beating Airdrie 1-0 in the Final of the Tennents Scottish Cup.

Charlie Nicholas

Held in the same esteem by Celtic fans as Tully and Johnstone – an extrovert character, who has a love of the club that is found in very few modern day players. "The Cannonball Kid" and "Champagne Charlie" were just two of the nicknames he picked up early in his career. Nicholas was a superb striker, who probably made a mistake when he left Parkhead for Arsenal for a fee of £750,000 in 1983. He was just 21 and many shrewd footballing people felt he would have been better to have spent another couple of seasons at Parkhead.

Charlie's impact on the Scottish football scene was immediate and spectacular. First time around at Celtic he scored 79 goals in less than 100 appearances, won two Championship medals and scored in the 1982-83 League Cup Final when Celtic beat Rangers.

Although a favourite with the Highbury fans – he scored both goals in a 2-1 win over Liverpool in a Littlewoods Cup Final at Wembley – he was not an outstanding success, and returned north of the border to Aberdeen for £500,000 in 1988. At Pittodrie he won Scottish and League Cup medals before returning to Celtic for £450,000 in 1990. He played for Scotland on 20 occasions, including the World Cup Finals in Mexico in 1986.

Paul McStay

Has represented Scotland at every level from schoolboy, and undoubtedly one of the finest players this country has produced since the war. Born in Lanarkshire in 1964, McStay made his full debut for Celtic in January 1982 and has seldom been out of their first team since, except in the case of injury.

His vision in midfield is quite remarkable and he is one of those players it would be hard to imagine at any other club.

He has played for Scotland on 72 occasions, and was a member of the World Cup Finals squads in Mexico in 1986 and in Italy four years later. If McStay has one fault, it is that he is too nice a person, lacking a touch of arrogance or a bit of the swagger.

He took over as club captain when Roy Aitken was transferred to Newcastle, and before then he had won three Championships, three Scottish Cups and one League Cup. For a spell, it looked as if Paul would go down in history as one of the few Celtic captains never to lift a major trophy, but that all changed with the 1995 Tennents Scottish Cup win over Airdrie.

Celtic 1, Rangers 1 – Saturday, 31st August, 1985

Celtic are Unable to Topple Rangers from the Top Perch

By Jim Reynolds

Celtic should be perched on top of the Premiere Division this morning after the first Old Firm confrontation of the season. They outplayed Rangers for most of an intriguing Parkhead match, conducted brilliantly by Paul McStay, yet had to settle for a point which leaves them looking up at their old rivals, who lead the race for the Championship.

Still, the Parkhead men should not feel sorry for themselves. It is true that they faced a magnificent display of goalkeeping by Nicky Walker, but they still managed to miss enough genuine chances to have won two or three matches.

Manager David Hay said afterwards: "I'm disappointed because, apart from 15 minutes at the end of the first half, we played well enough to have won. We needed the extra break or bit of sharpness in front of goal."

As it was, the breaks went Rangers' way, and it was a relieved, though angry, Jock Wallace at the end of the game. Said the Rangers manager: "I'm angry because we only played for 20 minutes. Getting a draw at Parkhead is always acceptable and the result was the best thing about the game. Celtic kept running and did their business."

Celtic certainly did their business – up to a point, which was the Rangers penalty area. It was almost 20 minutes before the Ibrox men mounted a serious attack, and by that time Celtic had seen a Tom McAdam "goal" disallowed, Walker save brilliantly from Murdo MacLeod, and Brian McClair send a header just over.

Celtic had complete control in midfield and it seemed only a matter of time before they would score. But as so often happens in such a situation, the team on the receiving end suddenly burst forward to take the lead, and when Rangers' goal did come in 34 minutes, it was a gem.

Hugh Burns, quickly developing into one of the best attacking full-backs in the country, set it up with a gallop up the right. Faced by namesake Tommy, the Ranger cheekily pushed the ball through the Celtic man's legs and sent over a low cross which was swept into the net by Ally McCoist.

From then until half-time Rangers had their purple patch, but Celtic were soon back in charge after the interval, and it was fitting that McStay should get the equaliser. It came in 52 minutes and there appeared to be little danger when Celtic won a free kick (one of 29 they received during the match) well away from the penalty area. Murdo MacLeod pushed the ball to McStay, who strode forward to crack a great drive past Walker from 22 yards.

Incidentally, I thought that referee Bob Valentine's early booking of Roy Aitken a harsh decision. Aitken was cautioned for a bodycheck on McCoist. It was his first foul of the match. Two others, Hugh Burns and Dougie Bell, were also yellow-carded.

Perhaps the most pleasing aspect of the whole day however, was that the huge crowd of almost 60,000 gained top marks. I think Hay summed it up best when he said; "I'm really pleased by the behaviour of both sets of fans, and that was important."

Celtic (0) 1	Rangers (1) 1
McStay	McCoist
Attendance	60,000

CELTIC:- BONNER, MCGRAIN, BURNS, AITKEN, MCADAM, GRANT, PROVAN, P. MCSTAY, JOHNSTON, MACLEOD, MCCLAIR. SUBSTITUTES – MCINALLY, O'LEARY.

RANGERS:- WALKER, BURNS, MUNRO, MCPHERSON, PATERSON, BELL, MCCOIST, RUSSELL, WILLIAMSON, MCKINNON, COOPER. SUBSTITUTES – FLECK, DAWSON.

Ian Durrant's goal decides the first Old Firm match of the 1986/7 season.

Brian McClair pokes the ball past Woods into the net.

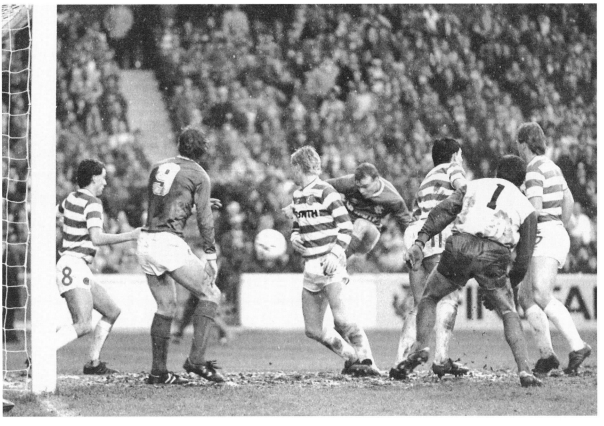

Robert Fleck finds a way through the crowd.

Butcher is the second Rangers player
sent off in the infamous 2-2 draw in
October 1987.

Right : Woods and McAvennie are both
sent off after trading blows.

Below : Stand-in goalie Graham
Roberts is helpless as Celtic score.

Rangers 3, Celtic 0 – Saturday, 9th November, 1985

Celtic Made to Suffer as Ibrox Babes Finally Get Their Act Together

By Jim Reynolds

Jock Wallace's faith in his young brigade paid off at the weekend as techniques previously only seen on the training ground were paraded before a packed Ibrox, and used to torment and finally obliterate a Celtic side experiencing their worst form slump for years.

It was Rangers' most emphatic win over their rivals since 1980 and quite frankly, the scoreline does not flatter them. Rangers, who managed just two wins in their 19 previous matches, were far too good for a poor Celtic. They were ahead in every aspect of the game – more determined, more adaptable and certainly much more competent in the basics of stringing together passes.

Weeks of misery for the Ibrox fans were blown away in a 90-minute spell in which Rangers, at long last, looked like genuine Championship contenders. "We were brilliant . . . out of this world," said manager Wallace afterwards, and no one could argue with him, even allowing for the fact that Celtic were a mere shadow of their normal selves. Much of that was because Rangers made them look that way.

Wallace also has to be admired for taking the opportunity for making soap-box speeches. For weeks now he has had to face the media, putting on brave face as disaster followed disaster. Saturday was his chance for a bit of drum-beating, but he declined.

"I don't gloat at times like this, and I don't cry when things are not going so well," he said.

For vastly different reasons Celtic manager, Davie Hay, was just as short with his summing-up of the afternoon's events. He said, "The better team won – they wanted to win more than we did, and that's all I can say."

The day belonged to Rangers from the moment referee David Syme started the proceedings and Wallace's boys – whose average age is just 23 – gave as good a performance as I have seen from any Rangers outfit in recent years. The only question mark about their showing is that it took them a long time to clinch the match. Mind you, from the early stages it was evident that they were not going to lose it.

Head and shoulders above anyone else on the field was 19-year-old midfielder Iain Durrant. He pointed the way towards victory with the opening goal after 30 minutes, his first goal at top level for the club, but his overall contribution was tremendous. This lad does not just play when he has the ball. His work off the ball was a revelation, and he certainly has a bright future in the game.

Derek Ferguson, at 18, was also outstanding in midfield until he had to be taken off injured. His was a refreshing performance which showed maturity way beyond his years.

At the back, 21-year-old Davie McPherson was commanding, both in the air and on the ground. He even had the confidence to gallop forward with the attack on occasion, and was given tremendous backing in the middle of the defence by one of the older hands, Davie McKinnon,

a man who seldom grabs the limelight but who goes about his job in a completely professional way.

Another "quiet man" is 23-year-old leftback Stuart Munro, the only outfield player to have played in all of Celtic's matches this season. He kept a tight rein on Rangers' Davie Provan, who normally sparkles in this type of match, and, like Dougie Bell, had probably his best game since coming into the first team.

Certainly one good win does not mean that Rangers' troubles are over, but this victory should go a long way towards restoring confidence. They are tucked in just three points behind Aberdeen.

Celtic's experiment of playing three central defenders was a failure and the display of the entire defence emphasised just where Hay's problems are, although everyone at Parkhead has surely been aware of that for some years. It is absolutely vital that Hay is given the go-ahead and the cash to hire one top-class defender.

The Parkhead men have now lost 10 goals in their last three matches and it does not need someone of super-intelligence to realise that if the trend continues, there will be no title for Celtic this season.

New striker Mark McGhee had a fiery baptism and admits that while he was with Hamburg, he had forgotten how tough the tackling could be in the Premier Division, but the former Aberdeen man battled well and will certainly be an asset to the club once he has a few matches under his belt.

But Rangers never looked back after they had taken the lead in half an hour. Davie Cooper set the goal up with a jinking run into the box and a shot that bounced off Pat Bonner's foot. The ball fell to young Durrant and, although he had his back to goal, he quickly wheeled and shot into the net.

With 10 minutes left, Cooper himself clinched the points when he shot home after a shot from substitute Bobby Russell had come off a defender, and a couple of minutes later Rangers added a third, with Ted McMinn pushing the ball over the line after a chip from Ally McCoist bounced off the bar.

McCoist, however, is claiming the goal. He said: "I spoke to the linesman after the match and he told me that when the ball came down off the bar, it bounced down behind the goal line. So, as far as I'm concerned, it's my goal."

Rangers (1) 3	Celtic (0) 0
Durrant	
Cooper	
McMinn	

RANGERS:- WALKER, DAWSON, MUNRO, MCPHERSON, MCKINNON, BELL, MCCOIST, D. FERGUSON, WILLIAMSON, DURRANT, COOPER. SUBSTITUTES, RUSSELL, MCMINN.

CELTIC:- BONNER, W. MCSTAY, BURNS, AITKEN, MCGUIGAN, MCADAM, PROVAN, P. MCSTAY, MCGHEE, GRANT, MCCLAIR. SUBSTITUTES – MCGRAIN, JOHNSTON.

Celtic 2, Rangers 0 – Wednesday, 1st January, 1986

Celtic Left to Count the Cost of Old Firm Victory

By Jim Reynolds

Celtic may have had cause to celebrate the New Year because of their convincing 2-0 win over Rangers at Parkhead on Wednesday, but as they head towards two crucial matches in the race for the Premier Division Championship, manager Davie Hay finds that his problems are piling up, and that the quality and strength of the Celtic squad is going to be tested to the full.

Wednesday saw one of the better Old Firm clashes and Rangers, although beaten, can take some consolation in the fact that they played well enough in spells. In fact, I thought they were rather unfortunate to be behind to that Paul McGuigan goal at half-time, because they had more of the play and set up several chances which should have been put away.

Celtic then wrapped up the points four minutes after half time when hesitation in the Rangers defence allowed Brian McClair to head home a cross from Paul McStay. It left the Ibrox men with too much to do, and long before the end Celtic looked comfortable in front of a crowd of almost 50,000.

While McGuigan and McClair were applauded as the scoring heroes, my man of the match was the veteran Danny McGrain, who, at 35, seems to relish making nonsense of those who keep writing him off. "He typifies what Celtic is all about," said Davie Hay. "Every time he is left out of a side people think they have seen the last of Danny, but I would never write him off. He is a magnificent professional."

For Rangers, these are desperate times. They have won only two of their last dozen games. And while youngsters such as Iain Durrant and Derek Ferguson are fulfilling their promise, the more experienced men are struggling, as was illustrated when, for the second time in five days, international winger Davie Cooper was substituted.

Celtic (1) 2	Rangers (0) 0
McGuigan	
McClair	
Attendance	50,000

CELTIC:- BONNER, W. MCSTAY, MCGRAIN, AITKEN, MCGUIGAN, GRANT, MCCLAIR, P. MCSTAY, MCGHEE, BURNS, ARCHDEACON.

RANGERS:- WALKER, DAWSON, MUNRO, MCPHERSON, PATERSON, DURRANT, MCCOIST, RUSSELL, WILLIAMSON, D. FERGUSON, COOPER.

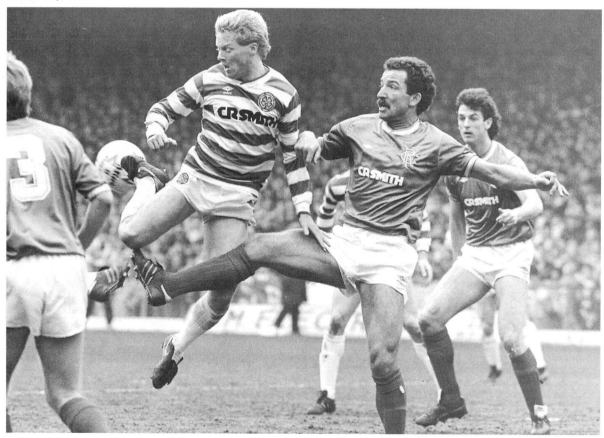

Graeme Souness shows no quarter to Maurice Johnston.

Davie Coopper

The Moody Blue was quite simply a born genius and probably the most exciting, entertaining Rangers player of all time. He was born in Hamilton in 1956 and joined Clydebank in 1974. Four years later he signed for Rangers in a £100,000 deal and that coincided with his first call-up to the Scotland International squad, a summer tour of Chile, Argentina and Brazil.

Although a natural left-sided player, Davie often operated successfully on the right. He was outstanding in many Old Firm matches before moving on to Motherwell in 1989. At the time it was thought he was merely playing out time until retirement, but the Cooper influence on the Fir Park club was enormous and he was an inspiration in their run to a Scottish Cup Final win over Dundee United in 1991.

He played for Scotland on 22 occasions, and his honours with Rangers included three Championships, three Scottish Cups and seven League Cups. After leaving Motherwell, Cooper returned to his first senior side, Clydebank, and he collapsed and died at Broadwood Stadium, Cumbernauld in 1995 while coaching kids.

Maurice Johnston

The most controversial signing in the history of the club, simply because he was the first major Catholic signing made by Rangers – and for the fact that shortly beforehand he had been paraded at Parkhead, wearing a Celtic jersey and indicating he was joining the club for a second spell. That was in 1991. Began his professional career at Partick Thistle in 1980 and was transferred to Watford for £200,000 three years later.

In November, 1984, Johnston returned north to sign for Celtic for £400,000 and often caused Rangers problems before departing for Nantes in France, believing that a move abroad would help keep him out of the glare of publicity at home. His return, however, made him a more controversial figure than ever, and one can imagine how the Celtic support felt when Mo banged in a goal for Rangers at Parkhead in November 1991 on the way to a 2-1 win.

Since leaving Ibrox he has had spells with Everton and Hearts, and is now playing for Falkirk. Capped by Scotland 38 times, he also won two Championship medals with Rangers.

Graeme Souness

One of the finest midfield players to have played for Scotland, and the man who sparked the Ibrox "revolution" by agreeing to become player-manager of the club in the summer of 1986. Although he brought many big money transfers to the club, perhaps his shrewdest move was to persuade Walter Smith to move from Dundee United as his assistant for his knowledge of the Scottish scene.

Graeme played for Tottenham and Middlesbrough before joining Liverpool for £350,000 in 1978. He won every honour with the Anfield club, including the European Cup, and was eventually transferred to Sampdoria for £650,000 in 1984. He was a totally uncompromising player and nobody could doubt his commitment to football or the club which paid his wages.

It is enough of a commendation that the great Jock Stein made him captain of Scotland, despite the fact that he was often the subject of controversy. In his first match for Rangers, he was sent off against Hibs at Easter Road. He played for his country on 54 occasions and won a Championship badge with Rangers. After leaving Ibrox, he managed Liverpool, but that didn't work out and after a break from the game he is now managing in Turkey.

Terry Butcher

He and goalkeeper Chris Woods were Rangers' first major signings under the Souness regime. Butcher, an established English internationalist and a star during the 1986 World Cup Finals in Mexico, joined Rangers from Ipswich Town that same summer and was captain at Ibrox. That proved to be a master stroke as the big central defender was a born organiser. He was brilliant in the air, and his skill on the ground enabled Rangers to build many attacks from the back.

Butcher was a great influence on those around him, and Rangers fans were sad to see him go when he joined Coventry City as player-manager. That didn't quite work out, and nor did a spell as manager of Sunderland. But Butcher will always be remembered as another of those great Rangers captains.

He is now back in Scotland where he runs a restaurant in the Stirling area and also does sports broadcasting. He remains a hugely popular figure with the Rangers fans. His medal collection in Scotland was three League Championships and two League Cups.

Rangers 4, Celtic 4 – Saturday, 22nd March, 1986

No Game this, More of a Happening

By Ian Paul

Sometimes, rarely, the People's Game transcends its own confines and becomes an experience, rather than mere entertainment. This was one of those occasions, when the normal criteria had to be discarded, insignificances like winners and losers, and neither being important. The match itself was the complete entity, the result a mere addendum for those desperate for statistical evidence.

It included all the wonderful frustrating facets that, when the chemistry is correct, combine to make the most satisfying and exhilarating spectator sport. The faults were plentiful, most of them patently obvious in the two defensive zones. Had Britain a defence like either of these two, we would be laughed out of NATO.

Equally, it could be pointed out that the almost constant supply of attacking skills was illustration of a naivety which might be one reason for the slide of both teams from their ruling pedestals, but no one among the 44,000 who watched will want to indulge in such fanciful analysis. As one of them put it succinctly enough at the end: "That wiz a bleedin' belter" (the use of an uncharacteristic adjective is mine, not his, in deference to the needs of the Glasgow Herald).

Not many Old Firm contests leave the participants and the watchers glowing. Even the managers were happy. Jock Wallace, so clearly exhilarated by it all, praised McCoist's goal and then showered even greater praise on MacLeod for his score for Celtic.

If this was not enough to demonstrate that, like the game, everyone present had gone slightly potty, David Hay compounded matters when, as well as actually looking a little excited, he praised the referee, David Syme, and his officials. For a moment I thought they were going to thank us all for being there. But there are limits.

Hay's reference to the referee was fully justified, and all the more to his credit considering that Mr Syme had sent off one of his players, Willie McStay, in 33 minutes when Celtic were leading 2-0.

That was perhaps the one depressing moment of the afternoon but I imagine it was most depressing for McStay, who was quite foolish enough to deserve his early exit. After being warned for a foul on McMinn, then booked for a foul on McMinn, he was inevitably sent off after another madcap foul on McMinn. If Celtic were unhappy to see him leave, McMinn must have been relieved.

What effect this had on the outcome, not to mention the marvellous drama to come, is impossible to gauge, but what is undeniable is that Celtic were not worthy of a two goal lead at that time.

Rangers had been much the better side in the opening 20 minutes during which they could reasonably have been a goal or two ahead, but, as often happens at Old Firm meetings, it was the team under pressure that produced the goal. Maurice Johnston, who had an excellent game, was alert and accurate when Brian McClair mis-hit his shot following a great Paul McStay run and Owen Archdeacon cross.

Archdeacon was again heavily involved when Celtic went two up, his cross from the left being pushed on by MacLeod for McClair to steer it wide of Walker.

So, as Rangers soldiered on, scarcely able to believe the situation, Willie McStay came to their aid by getting himself sent off. Celtic were still regrouping when Rangers reduced the gap, Cammy Fraser heading home following a good move on the left.

By halftime, with three goals, one sending off, and enough incident to fill half a season, we would all have settled for an ordinary second half, but there was as much chance of that as picking the Lincoln Handicap winner. Celtic left out Archdeacon for tactical reasons, putting on Peter Grant to cover the gap left by Willie McStay, and before three minutes had passed the 10 men had gone two goals clear again. Johnston waited and waited until he delivered a gorgeous pass into the path of Tommy Burns who popped the ball past Walker.

I do not know how the Rangers players felt at this point but I am sure no one watching believed that even this goal, the fourth of the day, would be decisive. Sure enough they took almost complete command and in a pulsating 12-minute spell scored three times, through McCoist with a magnificent 25-yard shot; Fleck with a swiftly and accurately placed touch from inside the area; and McKinnon or Fraser, both of whom received credit when McKinnon's header after a slack punch-out by Bonner went over everyone on to the line where Fraser headed in. Whoever gets the credit – and Fraser was apparently the stronger claimant – it was a goal which sent the Rangers legions into something approaching apoplexy.

Yet there was more. Celtic, who by any assessment, ought to have been drained physically and mentally, remarkably found the wherewithal to launch themselves at Rangers again and equalised with the most spectacular goal of the lot. Murdo MacLeod, from 30 yards, sent a right-foot drive of exquisite precision flashing into the bottom right hand corner of the net. If there could have been a more fitting climax, it is difficult to envisage.

For Celtic the dropping of a point reduced further their chances of the Premier Division title; for Rangers the loss of a point did not help their hopes of a UEFA Cup place next season; but no one really cared. On an appalling afternoon we had all had a great day out. Thanks.

Rangers (1) 4	Celtic (2) 4
Fraser	Johnston
McCoist	McClair
Fleck	Burns
Fraser	MacLeod
Attendance	44,000

RANGERS:- WALKER, BURNS, MUNRO, MCPHERSON, MCKINNON, DURRANT, MCMINN, RUSSELL, FLECK, FRASER, MCCOIST. SUBSTITUTES – COOPER, D. FERGUSON.

CELTIC:- BONNER, W. MCSTAY, WHYTE, AITKEN, O'LEARY, MACLEOD, MCCLAIR, P. MCSTAY, JOHNSTON, BURNS, ARCHDEACON. SUBSTITUTES – GRANT, MCINALLY.

Kevin Drinkell and Mick McCarthy.

Whyte and Fleck show their
acrobatic skills.

John Spencer finds a way past Traynor and Baillie.

Rangers 3, Celtic 2 – Friday, 9th May, 1986
McCoist Treble Does the Trick
By James Traynor

The Glasgow Cup Final never looked so good. Just under 41,000 squeezed into Ibrox last night to see the Old Firm dispute the ownership of this modest trophy, and each of them was given plenty to shout about as the match spilled over into extra time.

At the end it was the Rangers fans who were sent homewards rejoicing. But no one celebrated better than Ally McCoist. It was he who had supplied the vital touches, all three of them, to give Graeme Souness his first prize as player-manager of Rangers. It was McCoist's second hat-trick against Celtic in a final, his treble at Hampden two years ago winning the Skol Cup.

Twice Celtic had dragged themselves back onto level terms through Brian McClair and Mo Johnston, but when McCoist struck again in extra time there was to be no way back for the Premier Division winners.

Naturally, the Ibrox regulars took great delight in inflicting their old enemy's first defeat in their new role as Champions and it was also a triumphant departure for Dave McKinnon, who has been given a free transfer along with Derek Johnstone, Billy Davies and Andy Bruce.

Souness no doubt is making space for a few new faces, and although it was made clear yesterday that Rangers will not be increasing their £650,000 offer for Dundee United's Richard Gough, they might just return with the same cheque plus a player.

However, in the eyes of the fans every player in a blue jersey last night was awarded the status of superstar. It might only have been the Glasgow Cup, but it will be seen as the dawning of a new era. Time will tell.

Celtic's triumph, and speculation about imminent arrivals at Ibrox had added spice to the occasion, while the Rangers fans saved their loudest singing and voices for the appearance of Graeme Souness, who strolled onto the pitch to regroup his troops before the extra time period kicked off.

It took Rangers only nine minutes to breach the Champions' defence. As the heavens opened up, so too did the Ibrox side, with Burns surging down the right, as is his wont, and McCoist was waiting unmarked in the box to hook the ball into the net. Latchford, it has to be said, was deceived by the fact that the striker mis-hit his shot.

Aitken, who has been Celtic's inspiration on numerous occasions, decided it was time to go to work. His burst through the heart of the Rangers defence produced the equaliser minutes before halftime. He linked with McStay, and the result was a through ball which was slotted into the net by McClair.

Fraser, who was playing in front of his new gaffer for the first time, almost earned himself a goal early in the second half when he took possession deep on the right and slid a teasing ball across the face of the goal. Unfortunately for him and the waiting McCoist, Latchford was alert to the danger and flopped down to knock the ball away.

However, there was to be no stopping Rangers in 76 minutes when they again edged ahead despite Celtic appeals for offside. Fraser materialised on the right, turned the ball inside, and McCoist diverted it to Latchford's right. Although the keeper got a hand to the ball, it trundled over the line.

But Celtic were quick to respond and were on level terms seven minutes later. A MacLeod shot appeared to bounce off Walker's chest and the ever-alert Johnston was on hand to knock the ball in.

McCoist, who looked remarkably sharp despite a long season, completed his hat-trick seven minutes into extra time with a tremendous shot from all of 20 yards. It was his 11th goal in 13 games against Celtic.

Glasgow Cup Final

Rangers (1) 3	Celtic (1) 2
McCoist 3	McClair
	Johnston

[after extra time; 90 mins 2-2]

Attendance	41,000

RANGERS:- WALKER, BURNS, MUNRO, MCKINNON, MCPHERSON, DAWSON, FRASER, DURRANT, MCCOIST, MCMINN, COOPER. SUBSTITUTES – NISBET, D. FERGUSON.

CELTIC:- LATCHFORD, GRANT, MCGRAIN, AITKEN, MCGUIGAN, MACLEOD, MCCLAIR, P. MCSTAY, JOHNSTON, BURNS, MCGHEE. SUBSTITUTES – W. MCSTAY, MCINALLY.

Rangers 1, Celtic 0 – Sunday, 31st August, 1986

Durrant Drives Rangers to Victory

By Jim Reynolds

BUT MCMINN STEALS THE SHOW AS HE RUNS CELTIC RAGGED.

Rangers won this Old Firm derby at a canter at Ibrox yesterday when they threw off their indifferent early season form and put on their Sunday best for live television. The one-goal margin was indeed a paltry reward for the effort put in by Graeme Souness's men.

But in a match which was billed as the battle of the strikers, between Ally McCoist, Mo Johnston and Brian McClair, the stars were to be found elsewhere and nearly all of them were wearing the blue of Rangers.

Iain Durrant, for example, scored the only goal of the match 17 minutes from the end, and it was a magnificent effort. Apart from that, he and his teenage partner, Derek Ferguson, dominated the midfield against a Celtic side who were badly out of touch and did not really compete as they should have done.

But man of the match for me was gangling Ted McMinn, he of the eccentric legs. He ran Celtic ragged wherever he chose to appear, and during the 90 minutes he must have visited every area of the pitch.

Rangers could have been a couple of goals in front at the interval, but Celtic, instead of thanking their luck at being on level terms at halftime and sorting themselves out, continued to allow themselves to be swept out of the match and in the end paid the penalty. They can have no complaints.

The only black spot for Rangers was the booking of captain Terry Butcher for a foul on Willie McStay. It brings him up to eight penalty points and one more two-point caution will see him face an automatic suspension.

That is for the future, however; for the present Rangers have pulled themselves to within a point of their old rivals and this victory can do nothing but boost their confidence as they try to find the right blend.

As usual in this fixture, the opening exchanges were tense, but Rangers were first to get their act together and in four minutes, after some hesitation in the Celtic defence, Bonner had to rush off his line to pluck the ball away from McCoist and Cooper.

McMinn was looking particularly menacing, and when he swept past Whyte and sent a cross to the far post, there was danger for Celtic until Paul McStay stepped in to punt the ball away.

Then, as Rangers came forward again, Davie Cooper sent Durrant free on the left and as the Ranger tried to turn inside Roy Aitken, he was hauled down. It resulted in a free kick for Rangers and a booking for the big Celtic captain.

Rangers were the much more positive side and, again, McMinn had Celtic in trouble as he cut inside the box and tried a low cross. The ball seemed to come off Paul McGuigan's hand but referee Kenny Hope gave a corner despite strong appeals for a penalty.

There was a definite chance for Rangers in 31 minutes when Bonner missed a corner from the right and McGuigan headed the ball straight for Cammy Fraser 15 yards out. He snapped at the shot, however, and it flew harmlessly over the bar.

Six minutes later there was another amazing let-off for Celtic when Ferguson let fly with a drive from outside the box. The ball struck the right-hand post and rebounded straight to McCoist who had only Bonner to beat but the Celtic 'keeper pulled off a tremendous one-handed save to knock the shot away.

It was a first half which gave absolutely no joy to Celtic.

Celtic made a change for the start of the second half, with Willie McStay replacing Tommy Burns. He went to full back with Peter Grant moving to midfield, and in two minutes Celtic made their most positive move when Paul McStay touched the ball to Murdo MacLeod, and it was only a great tackle from Jimmy Nicholl that blocked the Celt as he tried the drive.

It was soon back to the old pattern, however, of Rangers driving forward and in 56 minutes, when Rangers swung over a free kick from the right, Butcher's header was only inches wide.

Three minutes later Celtic committed their second substitute, Alan McInally replacing Owen Archdeacon, and although there certainly was a hint of more urgency from the Parkhead men, Rangers still looked the side more likely to succeed.

After Butcher had been booked for a foul on Willie McStay, the Ibrox men got the reward all their pressure deserved when they took the lead with a superb goal in 73 minutes.

The Celtic defence was caught napping as Cooper made a break through the middle and as Durrant made the run with him, Cooper put the young midfield man clear with a reverse pass. Durrant kept cool as he closed in on Bonner, and as the keeper came off his line, he drove the ball low inside the right hand post.

With six minutes left Nicholl became the third player to be booked for showing dissent when Celtic were awarded a free kick and from the kick McClair should have equalised. He was given a free header four yards out but knocked it over the bar.

Celtic, however, simply did not deserve to take a point from this match.

Rangers (0) 1	Celtic (0) 0
Durrant	

RANGERS:- WOODS, NICHOLL, MUNRO, FERGUSON, MCPHERSON, BUTCHER, FRASER, MCMINN, MCCOIST, DURRANT, COOPER. SUBSTITUTES – NISBET, FLECK.

CELTIC:- BONNER, WHYTE, GRANT, AITKEN, MCGUIGAN, MCLEOD, MCCLAIR, P. MCSTAY, JOHNSTON, BURNS, ARCHDEACON. SUBSTITUTES – W. MCSTAY, MCINALLY.

Celtic 1, Rangers 2 – Sunday, 26th October, 1986
Ten Booked, One Sent Off in Rangers Victory

By Jim Reynolds

BAD ADVERT FOR FOOTBALL MARS A CLASSIC CUP FINAL

Rangers carried off the Skol Cup at Hampden yesterday afternoon in one of the most controversial Finals in the history of the competition. International winger Davie Cooper grabbed the winning goal from the penalty spot six minutes from the end and the match then deteriorated into an utter shambles as confusion and ill-temper reigned.

After the winning goal, Celtic striker, Mo Johnston, booked earlier, was sent off for an incident involving Rangers leftback Stuart Munro, who was also cautioned. That sparked off amazing scenes.

The Celtic players surrounded referee David Syme and his linesman who had spotted the incident, and amid protests, the referee appeared to show young Tony Shepherd the red card, but for some reason the Celtic midfield man stayed on until the end. Such was the confusion that maybe Mr Syme thought that Johnston, who also has blond hair, had refused to go.

Parkhead manager Davie Hay also got himself involved – on one hand ushering his players back onto the field, and then making his own strong protests to the referee. It all marred what had been an exciting and well-fought contest, although the final tally of 10 bookings and the ordering-off cannot be looked on as a good advert for the game.

But a marvellous day it was for Rangers player-manager Graeme Souness, who had to rule himself out of the match because of injury. In his first season he has steered the Ibrox side to their first trophy under his guidance and there is certainly promise of more to come. The Rangers goals may have come from Iain Durrant and Cooper, but the player who deservedly won the man of the match award was teenager Derek Ferguson, playing in Souness's role. With young men like that around, the future looks bright for Rangers.

Both goalkeepers were quickly into the action.

Woods twice got down to hold efforts from Shepherd and McClair, but Rangers came even closer when Roy Aitken fouled Cooper 25 yards out after eight minutes. With everyone expecting Cooper to take the kick himself, Cammy Fraser stepped forward and hit a fierce low drive that Bonner brilliantly touched on to his left hand post. Seconds later another Fraser free kick found the head of Butcher but McCoist, with plenty of time, hurried his shot and sent it straight into the keeper's arms.

Then came two Celtic bookings within a couple of minutes, first Aitken for a tackle on Cooper, and the Alan McInally for a foul on the same player. After that Rangers seemed to take a grip on things and certainly there was more to their build-up than Celtic were showing.

As the first half drew to a close, however, Celtic forced themselves back into the match and in 41 minutes they were unlucky not to be in the lead. Aitken charged forward and released a perfect ball for Johnston to turn past Terry Butcher inside the box. The striker did everything right, including beating Chris Woods with his shot, but the ball came back off the post and Mark McGhee hit the rebound against the goalkeeper.

Johnston became the third Celtic player to be booked in 55 minutes for an off-the-ball incident involving Jimmy Nicholl, and seconds later the Rangers full back had his name taken for a foul on McClair.

At that point Celtic decided to make a substitution, Owen Archdeacon replacing McGhee, but in 62 minutes it was the huge Rangers support who were celebrating as the Ibrox side shot into the lead.

Peter Grant fouled Cooper out on the right and when Fraser pumped the free kick into the box, the ball glided off the head of Butcher. It fell straight to Durrant at the far post and he wasted no time in smacking a low drive past Bonner.

But how Celtic roared back. Their reply to the setback was intense pressure which paid off with an equaliser in 70 minutes. Before that, however, McClair had chipped a free kick against the Rangers bar.

It was, perhaps, fitting that he should get the goal. It began with Aitken pushing the ball inside the box, Johnston touched it to the side, and from 15 yards McClair thundered it into the top left-hand corner of the net.

Three minutes later Davie McFarlane took over from Fraser, and in 77 minutes Derek Whyte became the fifth booking when he crudely hauled down Cooper. Then Grant brought the cautions to half a dozen for a foul on McCoist. It was all getting out of hand.

Then, with just six minutes left, Rangers grabbed the cup in the most dramatic circumstances. Young Ferguson swung a free kick towards the far post and referee Syme judged that Aitken had pushed Butcher in the back. He seemed to take an eternity to point to the spot, and when he did, he was surrounded by Celtic players.

Both Archdeacon and Bonner were booked for protesting, but Cooper kept his cool throughout it all, and when order was restored he made a perfect job of the spot kick.

McCoist was then booked for fouling Whyte, and in a most untidy finish came the Johnston ordering-off, the booking for Rangers' Munro, and all the rest of the nonsense that followed.

Skol Cup Final

Celtic (0) 1	Rangers (0) 2
McClair	Durrant
	Cooper (pen.)

(at Hampden Park)

CELTIC:- BONNER, GRANT, MACLEOD, AITKEN, WHYTE, MCGHEE, MCCLAIR, P. MCSTAY, JOHNSTON, SHEPHERD, MCINALLY. SUBSTITUTES – W. MCSTAY, ARCHDEACON.

RANGERS:- WOODS, NICHOLL, MUNRO, FRASER, DAWSON, BUTCHER, FERGUSON, MCMINN, MCCOIST, DURRANT, COOPER. SUBSTITUTES – MCFARLANE, FLECK.

Celtic 1, Rangers 1 – Saturday, 1st November, 1986
Old Firm Choirboys Hit the Right Note
By Jim Reynolds

The Old Firm never ceases to amaze me. A week ago Celtic and Rangers were involved in the stormiest Skol League Cup Final of all time and Hampden, that old stadium of thousands of glorious memories, was tainted by players who, in turn, behaved like spoiled children, cheats and downright thugs.

On Saturday, just six days afterwards, the same players contested Premier Division points and came out of the situation like choirboys. The mood was set right at the very start when Roy Aitken and Terry Butcher, who were involved in the controversial penalty incident in the Final, embraced prior to the toss-up, and sportsmanship abounded thereafter. It was a pleasure to be there.

Rangers' player-manager, Graeme Souness, who is doing more managing than playing at the moment, was hoarse at the end of it all, but still managed to make himself heard as he enthused over the 90 minutes which kept his side tucked in just behind the leaders in the Championship race.

The first chance of the game came in only 30 seconds when Robert Fleck got himself to the byeline and cut the ball to the near post where Iain Durrant somehow managed to balloon the ball over the bar. Then, after 30 minutes, Fleck himself had a red face when he was left with a free header only a couple of yards out but knocked it wide of the post.

Celtic, however, deserved their interval lead, the goal coming after 25 minutes. Rangers must learn to play to the whistle, for they hesitated as Mark McGhee pushed a ball forward to Brian McClair. The Celtic striker was onside and the hesitation was all that was needed to give him the space and the time to poke the ball past Chris Woods as the goalkeeper came off his line. Rangers drew level just three minutes after halftime when Fleck beautifully slipped past Derek Whyte in the box and whipped over a low cross which Ally McCoist swept past Pat Bonner. From then on, the game could have gone either way but no one really deserved to lose.

A crowd of 60,000 went home well satisfied with the entertainment, and behind the scenes came the sporting touch when Graeme Souness came into Davie Hay's office to say he was leaving. Both men shook hands and wished each other all the best for their European matches this week. What a nice day it was. Why can't it always be like that?

Celtic (1) 1	Rangers (0) 1
McClair	McCoist
Attendance	60,000

CELTIC:- BONNER, MCGRAIN, MACLEOD, AITKEN, WHYTE, GRANT, MCCLAIR. P. MCSTAY, JOHNSTON, SHEPHERD, MCGHEE. SUBSTITUTES – ARCHDEACON, W. MCSTAY.

RANGERS:- WOODS, NICHOLL, MUNRO, FERGUSON, MCPHERSON, BUTCHER, FRASER, FLECK, MCCOIST, DURRANT, COOPER. SUBSTITUTES – MCMINN, BELL.

Rangers 2, Celtic 0 – Thursday, 1st January, 1987
[Extracted from the Glasgow Herald for Saturday, 3rd January, 1987.]
But Souness is Being Sensible
By Jim Reynolds

Rangers player-manager Graeme Souness and his assistant Walter Smith are being sensibly coy when people talk about a Championship flag flying over Ibrox for the first time in nine years, but events on New Year's Day certainly suggest that the smart money will be wagered on them making a rare appearance in the European Champions' Cup next season.

Two first-half goals within the space of two minutes from Robert Fleck and Ally McCoist were enough to clinch victory over Celtic, and now Rangers are just three points behind their rivals with a match in hand. But, more importantly, they now look like a side which takes to the field expecting to win, rather than hoping.

Celtic were sadly inept on the first day of 1987, but let that take nothing away from Rangers, who were magnificent. They won well and with style, and had they not taken the foot off the pedal, the scoreline could have proved embarrassing.

The composure and bite of Terry Butcher and Graham Roberts, the orchestration of Souness in midfield, and the trickery of Davie Cooper, were too much for Celtic. Davie Hay's side gave away bad goals, but one had the feeling that, if they had to, Rangers could have moved up a gear.

Rangers did not look like losing a goal as they completed their eighth match in a row without Chris Woods having to pick the ball out of the net. Celtic goalkeeper Pat Bonner will have nightmares about his gaffe when he dropped a Cooper cross and gave Rangers their second goal. Woods can feel pleased with two second-half saves from Paul McStay and Brian McClair.

Rangers (2) 2	Celtic (0) 0
Fleck	
McCoist	

RANGERS:- WOODS, ROBERTS, MUNRO, SOUNESS, MCPHERSON, BUTCHER, FERGUSON, FLECK, MCCOIST, DURRANT, COOPER.

CELTIC:- BONNER, WHYTE, GRANT, AITKEN, MCGUIGAN, MACLEOD, MCCLAIR, MCSTAY, JOHNSTON, MCKINLAY, ARCHDEACON.

Celtic 3, Rangers 1 – Saturday, 4th April, 1987

Celtic Hustle Rangers Out of Their Stride for Title

By Jim Reynolds

Rangers' relentless march to their first Championship in nine years slid to a halt at the weekend – although I would suggest it merely delays what seems inevitable – when they were outfought and often outplayed at Parkhead by their main rivals, Celtic. It was the first time player-manager Graeme Souness had tasted defeat in an Old Firm match in his first year at Ibrox and, doubtless, there will be some stern talking done this week.

The fact that Celtic's first two goals came from the penalty spot and the third was, in strict terms, not legitimate, should be no consolation to Rangers. Davie Hay's Celtic were the better side and deserved their two-goal winning margin.

That was admitted afterwards by Rangers' assistant manager, Walter Smith, when he was asked if he felt aggrieved by some of referee Bob Valentine's decisions. He said: "We only have to look to our own performance to see how we lost the game. Maybe some decisions didn't go for us in this game, but in others they have gone for us. We have no excuses."

Although Celtic have now narrowed the gap at the top to just two points to give themselves a fighting chance, they know that they must rely on other sides over the five remaining matches to help them out. Said Hay: "Our target is clear – we have to win all five games and hope that Rangers slip up again.

"I thought that we had a very good first half, but then Rangers came back at us, as we knew they would. However, our lads battled away well and, at the end of the day, they got the result they deserved. I've got nothing but praise for their efforts in this match."

I will not dispute that. Celtic had the better players on the day, and there some quite magnificent individual performances. Roy Aitken, playing in the sweeper's role, was outstanding, as were Paul McStay, Peter Grant and Mo Johnston, although he did not manage to get his name on the scoresheet. Murdo MacLeod had his best game for a long time, while young Derek Whyte continues to improve at such a rate that he seems to be destined for a glorious career both at club and international level.

There may be those who say that Rangers are feeling the pressure of being so close to the Championship, but I do not think that is the case. On Saturday they kept to the same patient pattern that has served them so well in earlier matches, but it was clearly the wrong approach for this sort of game.

Rangers were simply hustled out of the game in the first half and forced to concede two penalty kicks, neither of which referee Valentine could possibly have turned down. The first came when Chris Woods punched a ball straight to Brian McClair, whose scoring shot was handled on the line by Stuart Munro. McClair himself took the spot kick and sent the Rangers keeper in the wrong direction.

Three minutes later, Johnston skipped past Terry Butcher, but did not appear to be causing much danger until the Rangers captain brought him down. Although Woods guessed correctly on that occasion, McClair's shot was too powerful.

Before the goals Rangers had the ball in the net from a Davie Cooper corner, and, although I could see nothing wrong, the referee chalked it off and pointed an accusing finger at Robert Fleck at the near post. Presumably the Rangers striker had committed a foul.

Eight minutes after the interval, Rangers got themselves back into the game when an otherwise subdued Davie Cooper swung over a low cross and Ally McCoist scored from close range. For a spell it looked as if the Ibrox men were going to save the game, but gradually Celtic got themselves back in control and clinched the points five minutes from the end with perhaps the silliest goal of the season.

Rangers were given a free kick in their own penalty area and when Woods played the ball to Jimmy Nicholl, the full back's return pass was short. In nipped Celtic substitute Owen Archdeacon and toe-poked the ball into the empty net. Woods protested strongly that the Celtic man was not the regulation 10 yards away when the free kick was taken, but he should perhaps ask himself why he took the kick himself when he thought Archdeacon's positioning would cause a danger.

Celtic (2) 3	Rangers (0) 1
McClair 2 (2 pen.)	McCoist
Archdeacon	

CELTIC:- BONNER, GRANT, MCGRAIN, AITKEN, MCGUIGAN, WHYTE, MCCLAIR, MCSTAY, JOHNSTON, MACLEOD, MCINALLY. SUBSTITUTES – ARCHDEACON, BURNS.

RANGERS:- WOODS, ROBERTS, MUNRO, SOUNESS, MCPHERSON, BUTCHER, FERGUSON, FLECK, MCCOIST, DURRANT, COOPER. SUBSTITUTES – NICHOLL, PHILLIPS.

Celtic 0, Rangers 1 – Thursday, 7th May, 1987
Late Own Goal Gives Trophy to Rangers
By James Traynor

Rangers' supporters, still in a party mood after last Saturday's Premier-Division Championship clincher at Pittodrie, accounted for more than half of the 15,000 or so who manned the Parkhead terracings for last night's Glasgow Cup Final.

It mattered little that the Rangers goal was scored by one of the enemy, the unfortunate Lex Baillie, son of former Rangers centre half, Doug Baillie, who allowed a Kirkwood cross to ricochet off a leg and into the net in 75 minutes.

But really, the quality of the match, or the result for that matter, was not of great significance. Rangers' supporters had come to taunt while those in green were more concerned with demonstrating that they are not about to hide indoors because their team has been toppled.

All of this was just as well, since the game was largely a prosaic affair. Excitement was rationed strictly and there was little from either side to suggest an abundance of fresh talent waiting for a call-up to the big teams.

As a consequence of the general inability to make the telling pass or run in to space, both 'keepers were allowed to depart the Old Firm scene quietly. Celtic have, of course,

given Peter Latchford a free transfer, and it is extremely likely that Nicky Walker, who has become surplus to Ibrox requirements, will be moving on also.

Perhaps the major disappointment was the anonymity of John Spencer, the 16-year-old Rangers player. His progress in his first season has been charted with increasing euphoria, but he showed little perhaps because of a failure to supply him often enough or well enough. Perhaps also, his teammates did not notice him. After all, he is of impish proportions.

The evening ended with Rangers fans beginning their celebrations all over again, while Celtic's faithful trudged off into the night, wondering when their time will come again.

Celtic (0) 0   Rangers (0) 1
                       Baillie (o.g.)

CELTIC:- LATCHFORD, TRAYNOR, ROGAN, SHEPHERD, BAILLIE, O'LEARY, SMITH, MCGEE, MCGHEE, MCINALLY, BURNS. SUBSTITUTES – ARCHDEACON, FRASER.

RANGERS:- WALKER, MCPHERSON, PHILLIPS, MCFARLANE, DAWSON, THOMSON, KIRKWOOD, NISBET, MCSWAGAN, WEST, SPENCER. SUBSTITUTES – MCEWAN, NICHOLL.

Rangers 0, Celtic 1 – Saturday, 29th August, 1987
'Magnificent' New Men Impress McNeill
By Jim Reynolds

Celtic manager Billy McNeill started where he left off in the rather unique world of Old Firm matches. Before leaving for a four-year spell in England, McNeill guided the Parkhead club to a 4-2 win over Rangers, and, on Saturday, he marked his return to the Scottish scene with another victory in the fixture, which lifts his club back to the top of the Premier Division.

There is little doubt that Celtic were the more determined side, but the real deciding factor was that their good players played, whereas Rangers' did not. And there was no better player on the pitch than Billy Stark – not just because of his winning goal, magnificent though it was.

At 30, it is as if he has been reborn. Towards the end of last season, he had lost his place in the Aberdeen side and his career seemed to be heading downwards. Then Celtic stepped in and the result has been quite remarkable. Stark already has six goals this season, and on Saturday showed just how good a player he is. He seems to thrive on responsibility, and the positions he takes up in the opposition's penalty box are quite uncanny.

After only five minutes on Saturday, he again showed that happy knack when Tommy Burns and sent Mark McGhee free on the left. As the whole Rangers defence moved to their right, Stark stole in behind them and met McGhee's low cross first time with his left foot to power a

drive inside the right-hand post.

Celtic then tormented Rangers with football of the highest quality, with everyone in the midfield making a telling contribution, and McGhee and Andy Walker continually putting the pressure on Rangers' back four.

Then in 54 minutes, Rangers' task was made all the more difficult when player-manager Souness was sent off for a bad tackle on Stark. He had earlier been booked for dissent. He had not made a great contribution to the game, but while he was on the field there was always the chance that he could get his side going. When he left there was no-one capable of lifting them.

Apart from Chris Woods and the hard-working Ally McCoist, Rangers did not have a player who played true to his form. With Souness and captain Terry Butcher both out of Wednesday's Skol Cup against Hearts, Rangers now are on dangerous ground.

Rangers (0) 0   Celtic (1) 1
                       Stark

CELTIC:- MCKNIGHT, MORRIS, ROGAN, AITKEN, WHYTE, GRANT, STARK, MCSTAY, MCGHEE, WALKER, BURNS. SUBSTITUTES – MCGUGAN, ARCHDEACON.

RANGERS:- WOODS, NICHOLL, MUNRO, ROBERTS, SOUNESS, MCGREGOR, FERGUSON, FALCO, MCCOIST, DURRANT, COOPER. SUBSTITUTES – COHEN, MCCALL.

Rangers 2, Celtic 2 – Saturday, 17th October, 1987

Celtic Stand Accused of the Cardinal Sin

By Jim Reynolds

In praising eight Rangers heroes – stand-in goalkeeper Graham Roberts was not pressurised enough to come into the heroic category – who came back from the dead to snatch a draw with Celtic's 10 men, one must accuse the Parkhead side of a lack of professionalism which, come the end of the season, could cost them the Premier Division Championship.

Playing against a side who had their goalkeeper sent off after 17 minutes, Celtic threw away a chance to inflict a severe drubbing on their oldest rivals. The fact that they had a striker sent off at the same time cannot serve as an excuse. The huge psychological advantage lay with Celtic, and they made a mess of what should have been a simple enough job.

Immediately after Chris Woods and Frank McAvennie were sent packing for swapping blows, Celtic quickly seized the advantage. Peter Grant missed an easy chance before, with 33 minutes gone, Derek Whyte hit a long ball into Rangers territory and Andy Walker outpaced Terry Butcher to smack the ball under Roberts and put his side ahead.

Two minutes later, another long ball had Rangers in trouble again. This time Walker touched the ball inside and, with Roberts off his line, Butcher, under pressure from Grant, toe-poked the ball into his own net. At that point even the most optimistic Rangers fan must have feared a trouncing, but Celtic then made the cardinal error of thinking they had done enough.

The second half was a nightmare for them. Instead of sending a stream of shots, lobs and crosses towards Roberts, they dithered around in midfield, sending passes astray and giving the advantage back to Rangers. The Ibrox men sensed something wrong in the opposing camp, and after Butcher had been sent off after a foul on Celtic goalkeeper Allen McKnight after 62 minutes, they still looked the more dangerous side.

Even although their starting line up of 4-4-2 had been reduced to 3-3-2, Rangers were the team going forward. A change of tactics took £1.5 million defender Richard Gough up front to partner Ally McCoist and now that move paid off, because within three minutes of Butcher's sending off, Rangers were back in the match with a real chance.

Young Derek Ferguson began the move with a fine run and pass to Gough, who touched the ball on to the unmarked McCoist, who strode forward and sent a shot in off the post. Amazingly Celtic still failed to pressure Roberts, apart from a header from Billy Stark which came off the crossbar, and they paid the penalty in the last minute when Rangers equalised.

Iain Durrant, who had practically run himself to a standstill, found one last burst of energy to speed past substitute Anton Rogan. He made straight for the byeline and fired a low cross which completely baffled McKnight, Mick McCarthy and Chris Morris. As they lay on the ground, along with Gough, it was the big Ranger who reacted first. He stuck out a foot and knocked the ball over the line to give Rangers a draw which will grow into legendary proportions in coming years.

Celtic manager Billy McNeill, who earlier this season also saw his side throw away a two-goal lead to Aberdeen, said: "At half-time I told my players they could only toss the game away. I didn't anticipate they would actually do just that."

Rangers manager Graeme Souness was a much happier man. He refused to comment on the unsavoury incidents which led to the orderings-off, but said, "It was an eventful game and I'm glad we got something from it."

In a match which did nothing to promote the game of football, the men who emerged with most credit were Gough, Durrant and Ferguson for Rangers and Celtic's McCarthy, Roy Aitken and Paul McStay. There should also be much praise for the fans who declined to follow the hooliganism attitude displayed by certain of the players.

Rangers (0) 2	Celtic (2) 2
McCoist	Walker
Gough	Butcher (o.g.)

RANGERS:- WOOD, GOUGH, PHILLIPS, ROBERTS, FERGUSON, BUTCHER, FRANCIS, FALCO, MCCOIST, DURRANT, MCGREGOR. SUBSTITUTES – COOPER, COHEN.

CELTIC:- MCKNIGHT, MORRIS, WHYTE, AITKEN, MCCARTHY, GRANT, STARK, MCSTAY, MCAVENNIE, WALKER, BURNS. SUBSTITUTES – ROGAN, ARCHDEACON.

Celtic 2, Rangers 0 – Saturday, 2nd January, 1988

Magical McStay is the Winning Card in Parkhead pack

By Jim Reynolds

Celtic could not have begun their 100th birthday celebrations in a more spectacular fashion than they did at Parkhead on Saturday. It would have been enough for the fans in the crowd of 60,800 just to have beaten their Old Firm rivals, but to do so in such a comprehensive fashion, with pace, passion, flair and style, really put the icing on the cake.

"This should do wonders for our confidence, as well as giving our Championship chances a huge boost," said a highly satisfied Billy McNeill afterwards.

The victory was achieved without first team regulars Pat Bonner – his deputy Allen McKnight hardly had to use his hands throughout the 90 minutes – Mick McCarthy and Peter Grant, but the men who did wear the hoops were so far ahead in almost every aspect of the game, that had it been a boxing match, the referee would have called an early halt.

While applauding Celtic for a performance of the highest quality, I must also commend Rangers for their dignity in defeat. They are sorely missing the influence of captain Terry Butcher, their midfield was the poorer without the youthful exuberance of the injured Derek Ferguson, while goalkeeper Chris Woods had to be taken off near the end with what later was diagnosed as a broken rib, which will keep him out of action for around six weeks.

Still, there were no excuses from Rangers' assistant manager, Walter Smith. He said: "The result was just about right because at no stage did we put any real pressure on Celtic.

We pulled back a big deficit to win the Championship last season but to come back this time will be very difficult, because the other teams are stronger than they were last season. It's time for everyone at Ibrox to pull together again."

Saturday certainly belonged to Celtic, and to Paul McStay in particular. Frank McAvennie was the man who grabbed both the goals, but for my money, McStay was head and shoulders above everyone else on the field. His was a performance to match the balance and grace of Nureyev, the gentle arrogance of Beckenbauer and the chilling accuracy of a hired assassin.

He carved out Celtic's first goal in a moment of sheer brilliance just as the referee was about to blow for half time. Confronted by a couple of Rangers players inside the centre circle, Paul "Daniels" McStay sent one of them in the wrong direction with an intricate little turn, then conjured a glorious pass to Chris Morris, who had made up so much ground on the right. In those couple of seconds the Rangers defence had been ripped apart, and when Morris sent in a low cross, McAvennie slid in to knock the ball past the helpless Woods. It was no more than Celtic deserved at that point, for they had completely dominated the first half.

Celtic, however, continued to miss a mass of chances while McKnight earned his money with his only real save of the game from Rangers' new boy Mark Walters, who, for the most part, must have wondered if he had moved to a different planet, never mind country. The former Aston Villa winger will be a good player for Rangers, but this was certainly not the game to give him his first taste of Premier Division football.

Celtic had to wait until eight minutes from the end to put a more fitting look to the scoreline. A minute earlier Woods had to be taken off following a clash with Lex Baillie, and Graham Roberts took over in goal. His first touch was to pick the ball out of the net. Morris swung in a free kick from the right and McAvennie rose to send a marvellous header inside the right hand post. I doubt if even Woods would have got to it. The game, which had always looked like going Celtic's way, officially was over and all that was left was for Billy McNeill to take on the difficult task of singling out individuals in his team.

"Paul McStay's performances this season have been of such a consistently high standard that he is now doing what he has been threatening to do for the past couple of years. Both he and Roy Aitken were magnificent."

The final words were for goal hero McAvennie, who must now be pushing very hard for an international recall.

Celtic (1) 2	Rangers (0) 0
McAvennie 2	
Attendance	60,8000

CELTIC:- MCKNIGHT, MORRIS, ROGAN, AITKEN, BAILLIE, WHYTE, MILLER, MCSTAY, MCAVENNIE, WALKER, STARK. SUBSTITUTES – MCGHEE, BURNS.

RANGERS:- WOODS, NISBET, MUNRO, ROBERTS, WILKINS, GOUGH, COOPER, SOUNESS, MCCOIST, DURRANT, WALTERS. SUBSTITUTES – FRANCIS, MCGREGOR.

Rangers 1, Celtic 2 – Sunday, 20th March, 1988

McStay's Super Show Devastates Rangers

By Jim Reynolds

IBROX VICTORY PUTS CELTIC SIX POINTS CLEAR AT
THE TOP

Celtic yesterday took a giant step towards the Premier Division Championship by beating their Old Firm rivals for the third time this season, leaving them trailing six points behind in second place. Rangers now have only seven games left to play, with Celtic having one more.

It was by no means a Sunday spectacular, rather a tame end-of-season affair – until the elegant Paul McStay put Celtic ahead with a wonder goal after 67 minutes.

Ibrox suddenly came to life; we at last had a real game on our hands and 43,650 fans were treated to a classic finish.

First of all, Rangers' Danish full back Jan Bartram hit a magnificent equaliser, then with just 11 minutes left, Andy Walker knocked in his 26th goal of the season to hand Celtic the victory which gives them a comfortable cushion. They can only throw the title away now.

Not unexpectedly the opening was packed with tension, yet there was composure about both sets of midfield men, especially McStay, Tommy Burns and Ray Wilkins. Chances, however, were at a premium in that early spell.

Celtic looked to have a genuine penalty claim in four minutes when Nisbet pulled Billy Stark by the jersey as the lanky Celt was going to meet a free kick from Chris Morris. Referee Bob Valentine stared stonily at the claimants and waved them away.

Then, after 10 minutes, Rangers got a good break when Derek Whyte was too casual and Derek Ferguson took the ball from him. Ferguson had acres of space and raced down the right before cutting the ball back to Walters, whose shot from the edge of the box sailed past Pat Bonner's right hand post.

Four minutes later Celtic came close when Morris hit another free kick. This time he sent it towards the back post, and Frank McAvennie rose high to send it right over.

Then came a spell when nothing much happened – unusual enough for an Old Firm match – although Morris raised Celtic's hopes with a neat turn near the byeline, but his only reward was a corner.

After 33 minutes Rangers took a quick corner, and had the Celtic defence in trouble as the ball carried to the far post. Ian Ferguson brought it down, but the shot hit the side net.

At the other end Burns set McStay off and with everyone expecting a pass, the Celtic man let fly a tremendous drive from 30 yards which was brilliantly turned over the bar by Woods. It was by far the highlight of the match thus far.

With three minutes of the first half left, Whyte had his name taken for a crunching tackle on Mark Walters, who had switched to the right wing. All in all, however, it was a tame first half by Old Firm standards.

Bonner was called on to make his first genuine save two minutes into the second half when Wilkins sent a long ball into the box. Ian Ferguson was on it quickly and hammered in a low drive which the keeper dived to turn round the post.

A minute later Rangers came even closer when Wilkins brought down a ball 25 yards out and sent in a shot that Bonner palmed on to the top of the bar. The keeper thought it was going over and stopped, but when it dropped back into play, he had to make a desperate dive to save.

This was a good spell for Rangers, but in 57 minutes Scott Nisbet became the second player to be booked, for a crude tackle on McAvennie, and a few minutes later the Celtic striker had his name taken for dissent when Rangers were awarded a free kick just outside the box.

With 64 minutes gone Celtic sent on Anton Rogan for the out-of-touch Miller, and almost immediately Woods and Nisbet got themselves in a tangle over a cross from Morris. Luckily for them they repaired the damage before McAvennie could react. But in 67 minutes Ibrox erupted in an explosion of green and white as Celtic took the lead with a quite magnificent goal from McStay.

When Rogan headed a ball into the box, Graham Roberts was under pressure from McAvennie and when the striker touched the ball to McStay, the international midfield man hit a blistering drive from 18 yards that flashed inside Woods' left-hand post, giving the keeper no chance.

Rangers, however, did not waste any time in setting about a salvage job, and in 73 minutes they grabbed the equaliser. Again it was a classic strike. Celtic gave away a free kick on the edge of the box and when it was only partially cleared, Bartram stepped in to power a 20-yard drive low past Bonner.

The game had suddenly come to life, and now it was Celtic doing the chasing. In 79 minutes they again shot ahead. This time Rogan – what a good substitute he had been – headed a Burns corner towards goal. It looked as if it might go in anyway, but just to make sure, the razor-sharp Walker supplied the finishing touch.

There was no way back for Rangers after that, because, although they did not stop trying, Celtic were playing with confidence, inspired, of course, by that man McStay.

Rangers (0) 1	Celtic (0) 2
Bartram	McStay
	Walker
Attendance	43,650

RANGERS:- WOODS, NISBET, BARTRAM, ROBERTS, WILKINS, GOUGH, D. FERGUSON, I. FERGUSON, MCCOIST, DURRANT, WALTERS. SUBSTITUTES – MUNRO, SOUNESS.

CELTIC:- BONNER, MORRIS, WHYTE, AITKEN, BAILLIE, BURNS, STARK, MCSTAY, MCAVENNIE, WALKER, MILLER. SUBSTITUTES – MCGHEE, ROGAN.

Rangers 5, Celtic 1 – Saturday, 27th August, 1988

Celtic Defensive Frailties are Exposed by Rangers

By Ian Paul

Even when the pain of humiliation eventually eases, Celtic will not listen kindly to any suggestion that, in trouncing them so comprehensively, their old rivals did them a great service in the opening session of the derby season.

For those involved with the Parkhead side, that suggestion can be put alongside the notion that decapitation is a cure for migraine. Perhaps it is not outlandish to say that the 90 minutes of Saturday could prove a watershed for both sides.

In Rangers' case, the growing conviction within the stadium that they are approaching the jackpot payout window after massive investment, was given a significant boost. Celtic may one day look back and accept that the lesson was better learned early than late.

The defence, which has not suffered public criticism from manager Billy McNeill in his year-long spell back in charge, fully earned his ire this time. "I cannot believe we could have defended so badly," was his unambiguous summing-up, one with which few Celtic or even Rangers fans would disagree. It is true that the defence was placed under great strain by the fact that Rangers established clear superiority in midfield from an early stage, but good back divisions are supposed to be able to cope with severe pressure at times.

The indecision and uncertainty around him did not assist the new goalkeeper, Ian Andrews, as he attempted to understand the mysteries of the great occasion, but the £300,000 signing from Leicester did seem to be caught man-watching when he allowed McCoist's speculative header to beat him a minute after the interval.

That was a crucial moment, for if Celtic had emerged with ambitions of overtaking the one-goal deficit from half-time, their confidence was immediately drained. Even so, as McNeill said, they had been second best until that point, and from then on slid further and further behind.

Rangers, whose manager Graeme Souness has maintained all along that a settled side would bring the desired result, looked a thoroughly professional team with sprinklings of excellence in every area. Ray Wilkins was the dominant factor in midfield, indeed in the game. After a couple of wild tackles early on when the adrenalin was clearly pumping too fast, he staked his claim as the leader and ended up without a challenger.

Paul McStay, upon whom Celtic lean so heavily, was overwhelmed by a posse of players, Wilkins, Durrant and Ferguson all playing their part. With his influence erased, these three were then able to create openings for their front line troops, among whom McCoist was brilliant. Unlike the previous week against Hibs when the Ibrox midfield seemed short on ideas in the areas where it mattered, they were full of imaginative support of McCoist, Drinkell and Walters.

Only in the first 10 minutes was there any indication that Celtic, winner of seven out of eight points against Rangers last season, were in the form needed to subdue their rivals again. When Frank McAvennie, who looked sharp and tried all day, grabbed a snap chance after Grant hit a post, the Celtic fans blissfully were unconcerned by the rainstorm that swept across the stadium.

But when the rain was turned off, Rangers were turned on. McCoist intelligently steered the ball away from Andrews after a Brown shot had been parried by the defence . . . and Rangers were on their way.

Wilkins scored one of the season's great goals when he crashed in an unsaveable shot from 20 yards. Just after the break, McCoist back-headed the ball into the air and Andrews, with one eye on the attendant Drinkell, fluffed his attempt at touching it over the bar.

Mark Walters then added his contribution, sending over a sweet cross for Drinkell to head in for the fourth, and shooting in the fifth after Aitken had been caught loitering by McCoist.

Rangers might have made more if McCoist's couple of close things in the first half are recalled and two borderline penalties had been allowed.

The defeat has come early enough in the season for Celtic to effect repairs. Their chances of going far in Europe will depend largely on whether a solid back can be established. Maybe the European Championship exertions of Mick McCarthy and Chris Morris are taking their toll. Neither looked comfortable. Perhaps a dominant central figure is still a requirement.

Finally, some praise for the referee, Kenny Hope, who stayed alert and firm throughout.

Rangers (2) 5	Celtic (1) 1
McCoist 2	McAvennie
Wilkins	
Drinkell	
Walters	

RANGERS:- WOODS, STEVENS, BROWN, GOUGH, WILKINS, BUTCHER, DRINKELL, I. FERGUSON, MCCOIST, DURRANT, WALTERS. SUBSTITUTES – SOUNESS, COOPER.

CELTIC:- ANDREWS, MORRIS, ROGAN, AITKEN, MCCARTHY, GRANT, STARK, MCSTAY, MCAVENNIE, WALKER, BURNS. SUBSTITUTES – WHYTE, MILLER.

Celtic 3, Rangers 1 – Saturday, 12th November, 1988

Celtic Have the Title Glow Again

By James Traynor

All right, so it was not 5-1. It was vengeance with a sweetness for Celtic and their followers, all the same.

The Parkhead side still are a long way back, but at least they now know the quest is not impossible. More important than any basic desire to take retribution for the hurt inflicted upon them at Ibrox a couple of months back, is the warming hope in which the faithful were able to wrap themselves during homeward journeys, which probably were long and winding. For them, Saturday was a night for spirited indulgence.

Even if most neutrals – looked upon as heretics at Old Firm games – remain convinced Rangers should win the Premier Division Championship, Celtic have served notice that they are still around and still a formidable obstacle on a landscape barren of genuine challengers.

Their form has been improving steadily, and Saturday's match was their last stand. Had they lost, they could have gift-wrapped the Championship trophy and handed it to Rangers in time for Christmas.

It would appear, however, that Celtic have grown weary of giving things away, even if Mick McCarthy did present Rangers with a penalty early in the match. These were fraught minutes during which there were a few frightful signs that the Parkhead defence again was about to self-destruct.

However, apart from McCarthy's handball, these were false alarms, although few believed them to be so when Mark Walters skipped forward to stroke the ball off the spot and into the net. It was a splendid beginning from which Rangers were never able to build.

They proceeded to run around without obvious direction, and when Celtic had wound themselves up and were sweeping forward in that often breathtaking manner of theirs, they discovered that the Rangers defence – regarded as the strongest part of the team – were in a fragile state. It was alarming the way Terry Butcher and his colleagues in the back division were turned and twisted, particularly by Mark McGhee, who had a marvellous productive afternoon.

"Back four did not perform," muttered Graeme Souness in a fleeting visit to the press room. He would have more to say downstairs behind closed doors.

No-one capable of following the bouncing ball needed managerial pearls to realise that Butcher, in particular, was always struggling to find his confidence, which totally deserted him the moment he scored an own goal. It was a spectacular diving header from a Tommy Burns cross, driven in fiercely from the left. Frank McAvennie could not have done better himself.

Naturally, the Celtic support made the most of the Englishman's dreadful misfortune. He lay on the damp grass for a few seconds, which probably seemed to him like an eternity. But there is no hiding place in an Old Firm match, and he had no choice but to get up and carry on as his name was revered in song by the massive choir draped in green and white.

It surprised no-one when he was booked later in the day for a foul on McAvennie. It was not Butcher's day.

He was not alone in this discomfort. Many other Rangers players were struggling to produce their best moves while trying to cope with Celtic's advances. As the scoreline suggests – and it could have been an even greater embarrassment – they failed miserably to play.

Prompted by the ferocious desire of Roy Aitken and the more subtle contributions of Paul McStay, the Parkhead team took command of a game which had started off at dangerously high speed. The importance of the occasion was stifling the flair and talent upon which several of the players on both sides can call.

It was almost possible to reach out and touch the tension and generally the match was a scrappy, fragmented contest. But Celtic in particular were able to piece together several sweet, flowing movements and had they been able to give these manoeuvres the finishing touches they deserved, the margin of the victory could have been ridiculous.

However they were content enough to chaperon the half-time scoreline through to the end. They and Rangers knew the game had been won and lost by the interval, as Souness admitted afterwards, "We had a mad 15-minute spell before half-time that cost us everything."

It was during this depressing period that disaster befell them. Butcher scored, then McGhee, who was allowed to turn inside the box, shot through flailing limbs and, a minute from the break, that same player supplied Billy Stark, who struck the ball low and beyond the reach of Chris Woods.

Celtic are now able to roll up their sleeves and look ahead to the winter with great confidence, but doubt begins to gnaw at Rangers, although they remain in a strong position.

Without Ally McCoist, who has missed the last few games because of injury, there is a distinct lack of potency up front. This is a worry which will have to be addressed, and perhaps enough already has been said about a defence, assembled at great expense, which was alarmingly insecure.

Those who would be Champions will be required to display more composure, greater understanding and more awareness at seething, noisy places like Parkhead, where tension has to be beaten before attention can be turned towards the opposition.

Celtic (3) 3	Rangers (1) 1
Butcher (o.g.)	Walters (pen.)
McGhee	
Stark	

CELTIC:- BONNER, ROGAN, MORRIS, AITKEN, MCCARTHY, WHYTE, STARK, MCSTAY, MCAVENNIE, MCGHEE, BURNS. SUBSTITUTES – BAILLIE, MILLER.

RANGERS:- WOODS, STEVENS, BROWN, GOUGH, WILKINS, BUTCHER, DRINKELL, I. FERGUSON, D. FERGUSON, COOPER, WALTERS.

Mark Walters scores the fifth in Ranger's 5-1 win at the beginning of the 1988/9 season.

Ferguson and Gough make it tough for McAvennie.

Ally McCoist and Roy Aitken try out a Cossack dance .

Joe Miller scores the winner in the 1989 Scottish Cup final.

Rangers 4, Celtic 1 – Tuesday, 1st January, 1989

Rangers Bounce Back in Style: Celtic Flag Hopes Now Lie in Tatters

By James Traynor

None of those who had scampered around the Ibrox grass during an Old Firm match which only threatened to enthral, despite the regularity with which the ball hit the nets, was willing to concede the Premier Division Championship had been wrenched away from Celtic. Players and managers remained cautious and defiant after 90 minutes of prosaic work.

The manner in which Celtic had been led towards defeat was a shock to the system. Even those who had avoided the usual excesses at this time of the year left Ibrox with hangovers.

How could Celtic have been so meek? Injuries denied them Derek Whyte and Paul McStay, and Frank McAvennie departed deep into the first half, nursing a broken left arm. But there was more to it than that, even if the last two named are the most gifted Parkhead players. This was a game crucial to Celtic's prospects of retaining the Championship. They failed miserably.

They had won an immediate initiative with a goal in 85 seconds, yet they ended up playing second best to opponents who were not all that exhilarating themselves, despite their four goals. Celtic were unable to do much about their predicament after Rangers had been stung into more positive action.

The Old Firm again are separated by a gap of seven points and few of Celtic's supporters who watched in horror yesterday believe their team possess the resources to recover.

Rangers' manager Graeme Souness and two of his players, Mark Walters and Terry Butcher, had all appeared, stated the obvious – they were delighted – and gone away again before McNeill arrived to offer his reflections. He was a man wrestling with anger.

He was unwilling to make allowances for the psychological bashes his players had received in losing two players before the kick-off, and one shortly afterwards. "I have to question the character of my team," he said. "They accepted too readily the fact that things turned against them."

He will ask his questions this morning and several egos could be carted off to intensive care. In particular the manager will deliver home truths to his defence, at the heart of which Mick McCarthy and Lex Baillie struggled to contain Kevin Drinkell.

Walters also teased and scored twice, the first from the penalty spot after Anton Rogan had suffered an aberration. The full back galloped in pursuit of Drinkell, who had possession inside the box but was not threatening havoc, and lunged. Rogan's clumsy challenge was an act of sheer folly and when Walters swept the ball into the net, the defender had paid a cruel price. Rangers were in front, and they never looked back. They didn't have to. There was no one in pursuit.

Celtic, without McAvennie, injured in a tackle with Butcher after six minutes and who struggled on for another twenty-five before Andy Walker took over, were unable to trouble the Rangers keeper, who had little to do after he had retrieved the ball from his net. Ray Wilkins fouled McAvennie just outside the box, and from the free kick, Chris Morris's right foot placed the ball in the left-hand corner of Nicky Walker's net with pinpoint accuracy.

It was a splendid beginning and few in the crowd of 42,515 were thinking back to the last Old Firm game at Ibrox when Celtic had taken the lead but ended up losing 5-1. However, with Derek Ferguson enjoying himself in midfield, Rangers took control.

It was as though they drew strength from the pain of McAvennie, who was playing with his left arm useless and dangling by his side. It was obvious he would have to retire, and when he did go, he took with him many of Rangers' fears.

Their equaliser arrived in 16 minutes, a Wilkins free kick nudged on by Ferguson to Butcher, who got the jump on Baillie and glanced the ball into the net. Walters' penalty followed, and just when the referee was fumbling for his whistle to signal half time, Ian Ferguson shot from 20 yards and the ball, which took a wicked deflection, ended up in the net with Bonner wrong-footed.

Celtic's supporters could only pray another humiliation would not be visited upon them. They had not been forsaken completely since Rangers scored only once more when, 12 minutes from time, Ferguson slipped a delightful ball to Walters, who ran 10 yards or so before directing his shot into the left-hand corner of Bonner's net.

Four players were booked, Rangers' Richard Gough and Ian Ferguson, and Aitken and McCarthy of Celtic. Morris's goal apart, the bookings of his team-mates were just about the only noteworthy aspects of Celtic's play.

Rangers (3) 4	Celtic (1) 1
Butcher	Morris
Walters 2 (1 pen.)	
I. Ferguson	
Attendance	42,515

RANGERS:- WALKER, STEVENS, MUNRO, GOUGH, WILKINS, BUTCHER, DRINKELL, I FERGUSON, D FERGUSON, BROWN, WALTERS. SUBSTITUTES – N. COOPER, MCCALL.

CELTIC:- BONNER, MORRIS, ROGAN, AITKEN, MCCARTHY, BAILLIE, STARK, GRANT, MCAVENNIE, MCGHEE, BURNS. SUBSTITUTES – WALKER, ARCHDEACON.

Celtic 1, Rangers 2 – Saturday, 1st April, 1989
Old Firm Serve up Another Mixed Dish
By Ian Paul

There is nothing quite like an Old Firm game to remind those who think they know something about the game that they know nothing about the game.

By halftime it was quite clear to the experts, all 60,171 of them, that Celtic, who had been completely outplayed, would be hard-pushed to finish second. By full time, Celtic were genuinely unlucky to have lost.

Rangers would contend, with justification, that they were so far ahead in the first half that a two-goal lead did not properly reflect the gap and, therefore, when the overall picture is taken, they fully deserved their victory. Celtic, on the other hand, are perfectly entitled to cite a missed penalty and a disallowed goal as evidence of the misfortune which prevented them from at least sharing the points.

Certainly, Rangers played with such command and professional awareness during the opening period that they did look like a team heading for great things, at last revealing teamwork which will be necessary if all these European dreams are to be realised. Only the amazing Paul McStay, who was outstanding, looked in the same league during that spell.

Ray Wilkins, upon whom so much depends, was also marvellous, the ideal link between a solid, comfortable defence and the dashing, eager front-liners. Among them Mark Walters was tremendous, torturing Anton Rogan with dazzling skills and infuriating changes of direction.

With his brilliance and the added assistance of Ian Ferguson operating in his most effective role, just behind the front men, Rangers looked a side of some class, bearing in mind that they were giving this show amid the manic atmosphere that prevails on these occasions.

They were helped to their interval lead by the uncertainty of their opponents, who seemed taken aback by the controlled mastery of Rangers. The warnings of their manager about conceding free kicks, and thus giving Rangers opportunities to throw in their aerial division clearly did not sink in, because in no time at all, less than a minute in fact, they had given one away. However, it was the one taken by Wilkins in just four minutes, after Rogan had fouled Walters, that brought about the first setback to their hopes. He flighted in a neat cross which reached an unhindered, unchallenged Kevin Drinkell, whose powerful header was diverted past Pat Bonner by the head of Steve McCahill.

As Billy McNeill was to indicate later, that left his team with a mammoth chase, and when the second goal was scored in 32 minutes, Celtic looked as if they might have to work hard to avoid a thrashing. Bonner did try magnificently to prevent that goal, which came from another free kick. This time Ferguson hit the hardest dead ball shot I have seen this season, and the fact that Bonner managed even to halt its progress was remarkable.

It bounced from his hand, and was chased by the ever-alert Ally McCoist as well as the despairing keeper, who seemed to get a hand to it on or just over the line. Ally, too, got his head to it and, as is his wont, claimed the goal for his own. We will accept his word, of course, even if we know that his thirst for scoring recognition is such that he is already claiming any scored next week.

Rangers might well have been awarded a penalty when Walters went down after a Rogan challenge, but when they went in for their break, they no doubt felt confident that two goals in their present mood would be a sound cushion for the next half.

They were to revise that view very quickly, as Celtic, within two minutes, were chasing only a single goal deficit. Andy Walker had reminded his fans of his great manoeuvrability, turning speedily on a Morris cross and beating Chris Woods off the post.

Now it was, indeed, a different ball game as Celtic, urged on by supporters who sensed a famous recovery, pushed Rangers into retreat. The Ibrox defence had to stand firm and disciplined as Joe Miller, who had replaced Billy Stark 10 minutes before half time, began to use his skill and pace to torment Rangers as Walters had done to Celtic on the same wing earlier.

It was from one of his crosses that Gough, who had been outstanding, was unlucky to concede a penalty seven minutes from the end. As he tried to control the ball it bounced on to his arm and referee Douglas Hope immediately gave the penalty.

Miller, clearly on a high, grasped the ball from his captain, Roy Aitken, who had scored from the spot the two weeks previously, strode forward confidently, but hit a weak shot which Woods, after having chosen the correct side, parried. Even then Miller was odds-on to score as he lined up the bouncing rebound. Challenged by Gary Stevens, the unfortunate Celtic man hit the ball high over the bar.

That and the goal they had disallowed convinced Celtic it was not their day. The one that got away came when Morris stretched to reach the ball on the goal-line near the corner flag. He put over a marvellous cross which sailed over the head of Woods, who was clearly claiming that the ball had been over the line, and landed in the net. Referee Hope signalled a goal, but after talking to his linesman, gave a goal kick.

Celtic (0) 1	Rangers (2) 2
Walker	McCahill (o.g.)
	McCoist
Attendance	60,171

CELTIC:- BONNER, MORRIS, ROGAN, AITKEN, MCCAHILL, GRANT, STARK, MCSTAY, WALKER, MCGHEE, BURNS. SUBSTITUTES – COYNE, MILLER.

RANGERS:- WOODS, STEVENS, MUNRO, GOUGH, WILKINS, BUTCHER, DRINKELL, FERGUSON, MCCOIST, BROWN, WALTERS. SUBSTITUTES – STERLAND, D COOPER.

Celtic 1, Rangers 0 – Saturday, 20th May, 1989

Tension and Fear Spoil Show-Piece: Miller Steps in as Referee and Stevens Blunder

By James Traynor

Tommy Burns and Tommy Craig hugged one another as though they would never let go. Other Celtic players and officials skipped around the Hampden turf like children who had escaped after months of detention. Celtic, in fact, had just been liberated from a season of depression.

They held on to the Scottish Cup, and a campaign which had until Saturday offered them nothing but heartache ended in unfettered joy. On the final day of the season they emerged from an ominous shadow cast by Rangers and basked in the warming glow of the summer sun, not to mention football glory.

While green-and-white hooped jerseys darted around and winners' baubles glinted in the sunlight, the picture downfield was a stark and morose contrast. It looked like the aftermath of a battle. Rangers players, as though mortally wounded, lay in the dirt, none of them able to bear the weight of defeat.

As Ian Ferguson trudged towards the tunnel he took off his boots and tossed them away. Probably at that time and long into Saturday night he would be of the opinion that this business is too cruel and that he could never play again. He was inconsolable. And still we will say it is only a game.

Ian Durrant, his damaged limb again encased in plaster, laboured on to the pitch and offered words of comfort to his team-mates, as did Ray Wilkins, another denied a game in the Final because of injury. The elder statesman of the Ibrox midfield sought out those hurting most, putting an arm around shoulders and ruffling hair. There will be other Finals, he would have been telling them, yet for himself, who can say.

It is reasonable to assume that the 90 minutes could have unfolded in a different manner had Wilkins and Durrant been healthy, since without them Rangers failed miserably to command the midfield area. They did not have a visionary and rarely put together any passing sequences worthy of note.

The few flashes of inspiration shown in that particular zone came from the mind of Paul McStay, who took a couple of heavy knocks, including a particularly sore one from Mel Sterland, the extent of which might not be known until today when he and the rest of Celtic's players return from euphoria.

The poignant display of contrasting emotions made it easy to forget the Final had been a colourless contest between two teams who found it impossible to break free of the shackles fastened around legs by a stultifying tension. Players lived in fear of making the error which could win and lose the prize. After 42 minutes fate singled out Gary Stevens.

Butcher could not clear a ball delivered by Peter Grant to the edge of the penalty area, and Stevens stepped forward. He took control and directed the ball back towards the embrace of Chris Woods. The pass was short, and Joe Miller intercepted.

It was one of those moments for the 72,069 crowd when time seems to drag its heels. The Celtic striker didn't and in a flash he was clear and stroking the ball with a sweet accuracy.

Miller's finish was perfect, and considering the pressure on players in Old Firm Finals the little one, whose recently improved diet has helped him regain an immense appetite for the game, deserves to have praise heaped upon him. Nevertheless, it seemed to me that Rangers had suffered as much from a refereeing error as Stevens' aberration or Miller's exquisite touch.

Roy Aitken, tussling with an opponent, appeared to have dragged the ball out of play on the right, and although the linesman and Bob Valentine, refereeing his last game before retiring, looked unsure, the Celtic captain was not of a mind to stop and ask questions, and he quickly took the throw-in. The ball ended at Grant's feet and we have already dealt with what happened next.

Souness, who had taken off Stuart Munro and sent himself on 20 minutes from the end, later suggested that a couple of his players had run out of position thinking it was their throw-in, but he was unwilling to elaborate, knowing anything he says can be taken down and used against him.

Rangers may also feel aggrieved that a goal scored by Butcher was disallowed three minutes from time, Valentine saw Pat Bonner being impeded in the scramble, but the bottom line still is that the Cup fell into the hands of the players who deserved it more.

Derek Whyte stood tall at the centre of their much-maligned defence, which survived a period of pressure in the second half. "We lived dangerously then," their manager, Billy McNeill, was honest enough to concede. Naturally, he was delighted by the way they coped.

"There has been a lot of criticism about our defence and it had been suggested they would collapse under pressure. But they didn't," he added.

However, there were a few occasions when his back division made his heart miss a beat. They did get themselves in the odd fankle and Bonner found himself in no man's land on more than one occasion and could have been punished severely, particularly towards the end after Souness had ordered Richard Gough and Butcher forward.

Still, the Cup remains in their possession and that is a grand success on which McNeill can build.

Scottish Cup Final

Celtic (1) 1 Miller	Rangers (0) 0
Attendance	72,069

CELTIC:- BONNER, MORRIS, ROGAN, AITKEN, MCCARTHY, WHYTE, GRANT, MCSTAY, MILLER, MCGHEE, BURNS. SUBSTITUTES – STARK, FULTON.

RANGERS:- WOODS, STEVENS, MUNRO, GOUGH, STERLAND, BUTCHER, DRINKELL, I FERGUSON, MCCOIST, BROWN, WALTERS. SUBSTITUTES – SOUNESS, D. COOPER.

Celtic 1, Rangers 1 – Saturday, 26th August, 1989
Players overtaken by Hysteria

By James Traynor

It will not matter much to the supporters of either side, as they look back this morning on a raucous afternoon in the east end of Glasgow, that the season's first Old Firm gathering produced little in the way of fluent, smooth football. This match was much more important than that.

Besides, since when have Celtic and Rangers games been delightful spectacles? These encounters, usually tasteless celebrations of ancient instincts, had been brought bubbling to Glasgow's surface because of Maurice Johnston's change of heart. The fans of both clubs wanted to be there to lambast and support.

In the end, most retreated breathlessly from Celtic Park, content that nothing had been lost. Celtic's legions were delighted Johnston had done little of any consequence, and applauded his two missed second-half opportunities (under normal circumstances he would have bulged the net) with the same degree of gusto which used to greet his contributions when he wore the green and the white. They revelled in his acute embarrassment.

On the other hand, or on another part of the terracings, Rangers followers, if still not ecstatic about his presence, did their best to offer him support, but they, too, went away happy. After all, they had avoided defeat. Rangers now have their first goal and their first point in the Championship race.

However, now that the shouting and screaming has subsided and the players have lapsed back into a slower, more civilised pace of life, the ugly reality of what had gone on at Parkhead begins to emerge. Watching Celtic and Rangers set about one another was like spectating at a pile-up on a motorway.

Sitting in the stand, it was almost impossible to resist the urge to feel for a seat belt as players appeared determined to collide at high speeds. Sometimes the ball bounced loose from a tangle of limbs as if it were of no significance to the proceedings. Too many of the players appeared driven by the hysteria whipped up on the surrounding terracings by 53,000 throats.

The referee, David Syme, himself guilty of eccentricities on several occasions, scribbled in his book the names of six culprits, Aitken, Grant, and McStay of Celtic and Rangers' Ginzburg, who dragged Jacki Dziekanowski to the floor on the edge of the box and was fortunate not to have given away a penalty.

Richard Gough, who hobbled from the pitch at the end, will be in hospital. He had been due to have minor surgery on a foot complaint last midweek.

Word that he would play at Parkhead was being carried on the grapevine on Friday afternoon, but his appearance still came as a surprise. It was another piece of Ibrox one-upmanship, although it might also have been testimony to Rangers' wariness of Dziekanowski.

The Polish striker had shown signs that he was capable of upsetting the centre of Rangers' back line, which would have been weakened without Gough. However, Dziekanowski, while proving that he has a big-game temperament, held on to the ball too long, thus allowing defenders opportunities to dispossess him. Still, it was his first Old Firm experience, and he did find the net.

Terry Butcher's powerful header from a Steven corner on the right had given Rangers the lead in five minutes, but Celtic, knocking the ball around with greater assurance, deserved their equaliser in 20 minutes. Hewitt's corner found Coyne, and his downward header was directed across the line by Dziekanowski.

The finest opportunities after this fell to Johnston, but his composure deserted him and twice he clipped the ball wide of Bonner's right hand post. Johnston scanned the slate-grey sky and then hung his head. It was not to be his day.

Celtic (1) 1	Rangers (1) 1
Dziekanowski	Butcher
Attendance	53,000

CELTIC:- BONNER, MORRIS, BURNS, AITKEN, WHYTE, GRANT, GALLOWAY, MCSTAY, DZIEKANOWSKI, COYNE, HEWITT. SUBSTITUTES – ROGAN, WALKER.

RANGERS:- GINZBURG, STEVENS, MUNRO, GOUGH, WILKINS, BUTCHER, STEVEN, FERGUSON, DRINKELL, JOHNSTON, BROWN. SUBSTITUTES – WALTERS, MCCOIST.

Rangers 1, Celtic 0 – Saturday, 4th November, 1989

It Had to Happen but Johnston Goal was a Killer Blow

By James Traynor

Maurice Johnston, always mindful never to leave home without his bodyguard, might now have to remember his balaclava, designer, of course, worn back to front next time he steps out to the shops. His first goal for Rangers against Celtic finally has ingratiated him with one half, but has distanced him further from the other.

Everyone knew it would have to happen, that some day the striker would score against his old team, but the timing of his goal was hard to take for the reduced number of Celtic supporters (7500) who were confined to the Broomloan Road stand. It was a killing blow.

Johnston's goal, a crisp and clean finish from 15 yards two minutes from the end of what would otherwise have been an easily forgettable match, allowed Rangers to vault over Celtic and assume the Premier Division lead. They are ahead of Aberdeen because of a superior goal difference.

Although Billy McNeill and his players, who improved their play considerably in the second half, will be aggrieved at having been sent back empty-handed to their end of the city, it is fair to say they were fortunate to have reached the interval with their goal intact. Rangers dominated that period, although their lack of menace around goal was alarming.

Celtic played with the captain, Roy Aitken, at the back, looking after Derek Whyte and Paul Elliott, a wise tactical move given the fragile condition of the defence which had been exploited by Dunfermline the previous Saturday. The intention was to have Chris Morris and Tommy Burns driving forward in support of Mike Galloway and Paul McStay in midfield.

The intentions were laudable, but Rangers' four-man middle line assumed control. Morris, who can be such a potent force in supplementing Celtic attacks, was too busy wondering what Mark Walters was going to do next, to think of overlapping.

Walters was in the mood, and after only a short period it was easy to see why Rangers' manager Graeme Souness had been fulsome in his praise of the winger prior to the match. Walters teased and tormented Morris, and any other Celtic defender who tried to stop him, including Paul Elliott, whose second-half challenge on the winger inside the box appeared worthy of a penalty.

There was a point late in the game when Morris actually offered the Englishman, who had fallen over, a helping hand. It was not exactly a gesture of defeat by the Celtic player, but it was enough to suggest that he recognised his opponent had won their individual contest.

Perhaps if he had known genuine misery was rushing towards him as the seconds ticked away, Morris might have been less accommodating. It was his mistimed clearance from Gary Stevens' over-hit cross which presented Johnston with his opportunity around the time the fans were thinking of heading off up the road. The ball rolled in front of the striker, who steadied it and then swung his right leg. Pat Bonner dived to his right, but the ball was placed perfectly and entered the bottom corner.

What happened next will live for a long time in the memories of the people whose bigotries charge the atmosphere during these matches. Johnston celebrated with his new chums – he was booked for having gone too far, off the pitch, in fact – while his former subjects sat slumped in their seats. The roar from the wildly animated Rangers support was deafening, but the fans in the Broomloan Road stand were still and silent.

They heard nothing. They were in a state of shock. The unspeakable had happened. One of their own had done for them, and after they had tried to dissuade him from doing anything so ridiculous when, in the first half as he ran before them to retrieve the ball, he was pelted with objects.

Yet, while Rangers deserved their triumph, Celtic could have escaped from Ibrox with both points. If only Dariusz Dziekanowski had been given a proper supply. Unfortunately for Celtic, just after they had started to come to grips in midfield, their striker emerged lame from a tackle by John Brown and was taken off in 66 minutes to be replaced by Andy Walker.

Before then, however, Celtic had been presented with a gift. Terry Butcher swished like a windmill at Burns's long ball from defence and Joe Miller was clear and in front of Chris Woods. The shot was too straight, but the ball squirmed away from the keeper to Tommy Coyne, who clipped it against a post.

Rangers (0) 1	Celtic (0) 0
Johnston	

RANGERS:- WOODS, STEVENS, MUNRO, BROWN, WILKINS, BUTCHER, STEVEN, FERGUSON, MCCOIST, JOHNSTON, WALTERS. SUBSTITUTES – DODDS, NISBET.

CELTIC:- BONNER, MORRIS, BURNS, AITKEN, ELLIOTT, WHYTE, GALLOWAY, MCSTAY, DZIEKANOWSKI, COYNE, MILLER. SUBSTITUTES – GRANT, WALKER.

Johnston and Whyte keep their eyes on the ball.

Paul McStay involved in the action.

The Nineties

Rangers had already won the first of their seven-in-a-row Championships when the new decade began, and there were to be more managerial changes. Walter Smith took over from Graeme Souness as the No. 1 at Ibrox. Souness rocked the whole of Scottish football when he suddenly announced, with another title on the horizon, that he would be moving to Anfield to take on the job as manager of Liverpool. He was willing to hold on until the end of the season, but Rangers chairman David Murray, quite rightly, decided that if the man had made up his mind to move, he should do so immediately. The chairman's confidence that Smith could clinch the title was well founded.

As Celtic struggled and failed to make up the ground on Rangers, former Republic of Ireland midfield player Liam Brady moved into the hot seat, only to be replaced by the former Celtic striker Lou Macari.

Then Celtic were almost torn apart by board room struggles and it was alleged that the great club was only days away from bankruptcy when Fergus McCann bought control. It was all change in the board room and another new manager was put in place, former favourite with the fans Tommy Burns, who had served his managerial apprenticeship with great distinction at Kilmarnock. He brought with him as his assistant another former player Billy Stark. Now, with a magnificent new stand in place as the first phase of the rebuilding of Celtic Park, new star players and money to spend hopes are high among the Parkhead faithful.

But the Old Firm is all about the actual matches, and while Rangers dominance in the championship has been massive, Celtic have not been without their moments in the nineties. For example, they pulled off two emphatic victories over their old rivals in eight days in March, 1991. First in a Scottish Cup quarter final tie at Celtic Park which they won 2-0 and then a Premier Division match at the same venue which they won 3-0.

That same season, however, Rangers came from behind to beat Celtic 2-1 in the League Cup Final with goals from Mark Walters and Richard Gough. And in season 1992-93, on their way to another title, there were two vital 1-0 wins for Rangers over Celtic in the Championship, with Ian Durrant scoring at Celtic Park and Trevor Steven at Ibrox.

Whether we are being just a wee bit parochial in calling it the greatest club match on earth is open to debate. There are passionate club matches in cities such as Milan, Madrid, Turin, Rio and Buenos Aires, but there is certainly no doubt that Rangers versus Celtic IS a bit special, and will continue to be so.

Celtic 0, Rangers 1 – Tuesday, 2nd January, 1990

Cheers for Rangers, Despair for Celtic: Spackman Spoils any Chance of a Parkhead Revival

By James Traynor

The new decade began at Parkhead the way the last one had ended. Celtic's supporters trudged out of the place they call Paradise yesterday with darkness and despair closing in rapidly.

Rangers remain at the top of the Premier Division, but they are able now to look back across a six-point chasm at their oldest rivals, and although Celtic will refuse to give up the struggle, it is doubtful if they have the necessary quality to pick themselves up and reclaim the Championship.

In their own backyard they tackled Rangers in a most slovenly manner. They surrendered possession regularly, the tackling was untidy, and there was no direction to their play.

Paul McStay ran hard, but rarely was able to shake off opponents such as Nigel Spackman, who marked his first Old Firm encounter by scoring his first goal for Rangers. Spackman, in fact, was one of the best players on the pitch and handled the occasion as though he were an Old Firm veteran.

It was always going to be a game for his type as Trevor Steven, like McStay, also had a quiet afternoon. Genuine players, those with breathtaking skills, that is, should have been kept away from Celtic Park on an afternoon when there was no need for them.

The game was all about fierce tackles and strong running, and Celtic's tactics of three up front, Mike Galloway, Joe Miller and Tommy Coyne, never worked. They didn't look like scoring, and it was no coincidence that Celtic's best opportunity was a header from Paul Elliott.

There were looks of disbelief when Billy McNeill released his team from their dressing room and Dariusz Dziekanowski took up a seat in the dug-out along with Andy Walker. The manager had been concerned about his team's lack of punch, but it was only after the Pole had been sent on as a second half substitute that Celtic began to pin Rangers back.

However, they were never able to produce enough creative flair to break down Rangers' defence. Peter Grant enjoyed a decent amount of ball in the first half, but he lacks the ingenuity to make threatening use of it.

The only time McStay showed, 24 minutes into the second half, he split Rangers' defence with calm precision and two players, Coyne and Roy Aitken, raced clear. Aitken got to the ball first, but his first touch was woeful, and Chris Woods was able to flop down and smother the danger.

The Celtic captain stabbed out a foot in a forlorn gesture and he was booked as Woods lay on the ground. Aitken's team-mates, Elliott and Galloway, also were booked, as was Rangers' Mark Walters, but although a lot of snarling

had gone on, the game was not a particularly foul one.

It was fast, sometimes furiously so, and hard on the eyes of Celtic's supporters in particular. They were frustrated by the number of high balls played up to the front line which was overshadowed by Richard Gough and Terry Butcher, players who thrive on aerial contests.

The balls which dropped were usually picked off by John Brown and Stuart Munro, who was taken off eight minutes from time, allowing Chris Vinnicombe to sample the unique flavour of an Old Firm match. Apart from bringing on Dziekanowski, Celtic also sent on Walker in place of Galloway, but Rangers always looked as though they were moving towards victory.

Their goal, scored in 14 minutes, was a result of the best move of the game. Spackman took the ball on the halfway line and played it to Johnston, out on the left. The striker, oblivious to the wrath of Celtic's supporters, pushed the ball on to Ally McCoist, and when his cross, which may have been a shot gone astray, broke between a defender's legs, Spackman had a clear sight of goal.

Pat Bonner was already moving across his line in track of the ball when Spackman prodded it in the opposite direction and into the net. It was a slick and swift move which had Graeme Souness and his assistant, Walter Smith, on their feet in the directors' box.

Thereafter, Rangers were required only to remain calm and rebuff Celtic's few attempts at goal. Despite their second half pressure – there was a period when they won six corners in rapid succession – Celtic were unable to create clear chances.

Neither goalkeeper, in fact, had been troubled regularly and Celtic are now left to pick up the pieces and set off on the long pursuit of Rangers, who face another daunting challenge on Saturday when they play Aberdeen. The Dons could win at Ibrox, but noone who has watched Celtic's last three games can be sure they can beat St Mirren at Love Street.

A great deal of rehabilitation work will have to be done at Parkhead, but if Celtic are to emerge from this dark period and sustain a genuine challenge, McNeill might be required to spend money, and lots of it. McStay and Dziekanowski need a better hand.

| Celtic (0) 0 | Rangers (1) 1 |
| | Spackman |

CELTIC:– BONNER, MORRIS, WDOWCZYK, AITKEN, ELLIOTT, WHYTE, GRANT, MCSTAY, COYNE, GALLOWAY, MILLER. SUBSTITUTES – DZIEKANOWSKI, WALKER.

RANGERS:– WOODS, STEVENS, MUNRO, GOUGH, SPACKMAN, BUTCHER, STEVEN, WALTERS, MCCOIST, JOHNSTON, BROWN. SUBSTITUTES – DODDS, VINNICOMBE.

Rangers 3, Celtic 0 – Sunday, 1st April, 1990

Rangers in Champion Form: Celtic are Completely Outplayed as Rogan Decides to Take a Hand

By Ian Paul

From the moment the unfortunate Anton Rogan went into what he might call his 'Hand of Satan' performance, giving away the zaniest of penalty kicks, Celtic took the huff and never came out to play again. They were utterly outplayed, scarcely mounted a serious attack, and generally compiled as inept a display as the sparkling stadium in Govan has seen from the rivals across the city.

Inexplicably, for this first live satellite TV broadcast, Celtic played like a team from a different planet . . . not over the moon, either.

Rangers, on the other hand, once they had settled and tucked that opening penalty kick into the net, grew more and more confident, eventually establishing a superiority that was as embarrassing for the Parkhead team as their manager declared he felt afterwards.

Trevor Steven took control of the sway of play, covering the width of the midfield in intelligent and effective style, and as the Ibrox defence soon shrugged aside puny efforts at counter-attack, the only real doubt was when and who would add to the score. The penalty had been despatched firmly by Mark Walters, another good contributor to the Rangers cause, even though Pat Bonner made a superb attempt to halt it, and when Maurice Johnston made it two by half time, it was patently clear that the final Old Firm fling of the season was done with.

Celtic made little headway after the break and the loss of the second penalty kick and the goal that followed, scored by record breaker Ally McCoist, could hardly have been said to be unjustified on the overall play.

They were a champion side, at least in comparison to the team who most years would be expected to give them their hardest challenge. As well as Steven and Walters, the entire defence, especially Richard Gough, was excellent, while the energy and eagerness of Johnston and McCoist always bothered the Celtic defence which, without Chris Morris, had a tough time in coping.

It was difficult not to feel sorry for their central defender, Paul Elliott, even if he had used unparliamentary language to referee Jim McCluskey. Elliott was booked for the fifteenth time this season after some loud dissent following a claim for a penalty. He believed Terry Butcher had impeded him as he went to reach a cross from the right. He looked to have an arguable case, but was cautioned for giving vent to his feelings.

Rangers, who had needed this win almost as much as Celtic had required to beat them in the Scottish Cup tie on the last occasion they met, rediscovered the desire that had been missing then and, indeed since, as they struggled through six League games without a win. Perhaps the fear of their manager's wrath proved as motivating a force as the urgency of their title challenge.

In any case, they were as good as they have been for a long time, never looking like surrendering their superiority once the opening goal was scored. That came in 28 minutes

when poor Anton Rogan had what can only be called an aberration. He was under some pressure as Gough challenged him for a high ball sent into the penalty area by Butcher but seemed odds-on favourite to get there first. No-one was more astonished than Gough when the Irish internationalist flashed his arm over his head and knocked the ball away. His Celtic team-mates looked around in dismay.

And when the entire 41,926 of us regained our breath, Mark Walters stepped up (after going through the nervous ordeal of having to replace the ball on the spot on the referee's instructions) to hit the spot-kick low and hard.

Before that turning point Celtic had had their best spell, especially early on when Paul McStay went close with a splendid left-foot shot that was just too high. A Mike Galloway drive that went past a post was to be the only other serious attempt at goal by the visitors in the 90 minutes.

After the loss of the Walters goal Celtic went into retreat, but within 10 minutes their effort to hold the fort collapsed. Gough just beat McStay to the ball, it was knocked on to McCoist, and he cleverly squared it across the field for Johnston to knock it forward before hitting it from knee height past the diving Bonner and into the net.

Rangers concentrated on making sure there were no foolish errors to let Celtic back into the action and even though the Parkhead side was switched, Steve Fulton replacing Rogan in 55 minutes and Andy Walker taking over from Dziekanowski 12 minutes later, they achieved that comfortably.

Any ambitions Celtic may have harboured (difficult though they were to spot) were dismissed 12 minutes from the end when they conceded a second penalty. A Walters cross caused some consternation before, Peter Grant pushed Johnston in the back. The referee had no hesitation in awarding the spot kick and this time McCoist, who had been chasing his record-breaking goal – his 133rd – for some time, smacked the penalty past Bonner.

Little else happened, other than Coyne having his name taken for shouting at a linesman and the crowd baying their respective cries of defiance. The two lots will now go their separate ways for the rest of the season. Hostilities will be resumed in due course.

Rangers (2) 3	Celtic (0) 0
Walters (pen.)	
Johnston	
McCoist	
Attendance	41,926

RANGERS:– WOODS, STEVENS, MUNRO, GOUGH, SPACKMAN, BUTCHER, STEVEN, FERGUSON, MCCOIST, JOHNSTON, WALTERS. SUBSTITUTES – DODDS, BROWN.

CELTIC:– BONNER, GRANT, WDOWCZYK, ROGAN, ELLIOTT, WHYTE, GALLOWAY, MCSTAY, DZIEKANOWSKI, COYNE, MILLER. SUBSTITUTES – FULTON, WALKER.

1990

Bonner Shuts Door on Rangers
By James Traynor

Endeavour seems to be fashionable these days. We saw it drag Scotland away from defeat and on to victory against Romania last midweek, and then Celtic used it to good effect at Ibrox, where they refused to be subdued and almost won a game which should have been beyond their reach after 45 minutes.

Again the worth of down-to-earth honest toil was highlighted in a world dominated by high finance and bloated salaries. Sometimes the basic, simple values surface and upset the game's modern playing patterns and strategies.

Celtic, under pressure in the first tribal gathering of the season because of an appalling start to their campaign, started off on Saturday unable to do even the simple things properly. At times in the first half, their struggles formed the impression that all of their concentration was having to be centred on running without falling over.

The game's other fundamentals, passing and shooting, were beyond the Celtic players and Rangers quickly discovered that they could cut through the opposition's lines at will. Another of those high-scoring encounters, which have become the norm in the past couple of seasons, seemed likely.

However, a combination of erratic finishing and the brilliance of Pat Bonner bought Celtic time and when they retreated to the sanctuary of their dressing room at half-time, they were entitled to harbour notions of causing an upset, although they were more than happy to settle for the 1-1 draw. Throughout the first period they had taken a beating and the tortured expressions on the faces of most of Celtic's players reflected the harrowing tale.

One or two of them may have had to step into the toilet at the thought of going back out, but manager Billy McNeill must have talked a splendid half-time game, because soon after the interval, Celtic began to let everyone know they were there. They made tackles they had mistimed earlier, and the ball no longer was the exclusive property of Rangers.

The game's complexion altered dramatically from the moment Chris Woods saw his net billow. While everyone else in the stadium was stunned, eight minutes into the second period, at the sight of Derek Whyte jumping to nod a John Collins free kick beyond the keeper's grasp, Celtic began to believe an afternoon which had opened in such dismal fashion could be concluded in unbridled joy.

They knocked the ball around with more precision, and suddenly Rangers were playing off the back foot. A remarkable turnaround was taking shape until Terry Hurlock, whose tenacity overshadows a healthy degree of skill, ran forward just as the ball was being cleared from Celtic's goal area.

This latest import from the land beyond The Wall thumped the bag of wind from 20 yards and it whistled into the net low at Bonner's right-hand corner. The Celtic keeper clenched his teeth in frustration. He was not invincible after all.

Until this moment, recorded 12 minutes after Celtic's goal, Bonner had stopped everything hurled his way. Despite being such a tall and burly man he was able to throw himself across his goal area with an agility normally associated with circus acts.

He emerged beaming after the game to say he had just played his best 90 minutes in the traditional enemy's stronghold, and if he can reach such breathtaking heights of excellence regularly, Celtic's defence, which continues to be weakened by uncertainty, might be given time to tighten up. It must become more assured if the Parkhead side are to mount a genuine challenge for Rangers' title.

One of the central components, Paul Elliott, was missing on Saturday because it was felt his damaged ankle would not stand up to the strain, and Whyte and Lex Baillie, who has only recently returned from a nasty leg break, were positioned at the heart of the defence. Although erratic at times, they coped well enough with Maurice Johnston and Mark Hateley, but it was Ally McCoist, playing in his deeper role just off the front two, who escaped attention.

He is revelling in the freedom his new role allows, and he went into the game on a high, having scored Scotland's winner against Romania. The ball has been running kindly for him, and he was so full of confidence that he may have thought he could score from anywhere. After only 16 minutes, he was disabused of that notion.

Nigel Spackman played a sweet pass through the middle to McCoist, whose run carried him just inside Celtic's box, and although Johnston and Pieter Huistra were through in support, he decided to go it alone. He shot, and the ball sailed wide of Bonner's right-hand post.

It was a rather sheepish McCoist who trotted back into position with the glares of Johnston and Huistra burning into the back of his skull. The striker missed another opportunity on the stroke of half-time when, standing in front of goal, he swiped at Huistra's cross and did nothing but displace some air.

McCoist being what he is, incorrigible, will have forgotten all about Saturday already and will be convinced he'll score a hat-trick against Valetta on Wednesday night. The crazy thing is, he will probably do it. But, then, he won't be playing against Bonner.

Rangers (0) 1	Celtic (0) 1
Hurlock	Whyte

RANGERS:- WOODS, STEVENS, HURLOCK, GOUGH, SPACKMAN, BUTCHER, STEVEN, MCCOIST, HATELEY, JOHNSTON, HUISTRA

CELTIC:- BONNER, MORRIS, ROGAN, GRANT, BAILLIE, WHYTE, MILLER, MCSTAY, DZIEKANOWSKI, WALKER, COLLINS

Stevens adopts the Highland Fling approach to tackling Paul McStay.

Walker sweeps the ball away from Hurlock.

The midfield generals: Ray Wilkins and John Collins.

Tommy Coyne eludes Munro and Spackman.

Celtic 1, Rangers 2 – Sunday, 28th October, 1990

Gough Books Another Europe Ticket: Extra-Time Strike Gives Rangers Skol Cup Again

By James Traynor

An astonishing run of success in the Skol Cup competition continued on a bleak Sunday afternoon at Hampden as Rangers won the trophy yesterday for the fourth time in the last five Finals they have contested with Graeme Souness as manager. As the Ibrox side appear to be heading towards the exit of this season's European Cup, they already have forced entry at least into next year's UEFA Cup.

Celtic desperately wanted the comfort of being guaranteed a European passage, which was the additional prize on offer yesterday, but despite a sterling effort, they will have to wait and hope for better luck in the League and Scottish Cup campaigns.

However, as their fans shuffled out into a bitterly cold night, they looked as though all hope had been drained for ever. They had watched their heroes take the lead when Paul Elliott, who had a marvellous match, scored a remarkable goal, and still they had to settle for second best.

Souness stood by the back four which had served him well before the Red Star game, and again they coped admirably, although it has to be said Dariusz Dziekanowski was unable to cause them any lasting problems. There must be doubts about the Celtic striker's temperament, since he fails too often when it really matters.

He, and all the 62,817 supporters inside Hampden, will remember for a long time the opportunity he squandered just after the game had entered overtime. Anton Rogan's powerful run and pass had put the Polish internationalist clear, but he hit the ball straight at Chris Woods.

Dziekanowski held his head in his hands. Perhaps he knew then the Final had slipped away from his team, and Richard Gough's goal in 104 minutes was merely confirmation. Gough, therefore, was able to collect his first piece of silverware as Rangers' captain, and already he has designs on the treble.

The first Rangers goal, the equaliser, was scored by Mark Walters who was merciless in his torment of Rogan, an honest, willing, but inferior player. Indeed, there were other Celtic players on the pitch who looked anything but good enough.

Billy McNeill's team, who had played the better football in the first half because the likes of Paul McStay, Steve Fulton, and Gerry Creaney refused to be subdued or intimidated by the marauding Terry Hurlock – who was eventually booked before his gaffers decided to take him off – lack a cutting edge up front.

McStay is still seeking his first trophy as a captain, and he sank to his knees at the end. Some of his moves and touches had the mark of genius, but without proper assistance from Collins, who failed to do himself justice, it was never going to be enough. Celtic survived a few threatening manoeuvres before they managed to work the ball downfield, and it was Creaney and McStay who were first to demonstrate a degree of subtlety in midfield.

The Final quickly developed into a thrilling encounter, and Hateley was allowed a free header at a Spackmann cross before Fulton and Dzienkanowski combined to put Creaney clear in the box. His shot was saved only because Woods dived full length to his left.

Bonner had an aberration when, after he seemed to have gathered a Rogan pass back, the ball squirmed from his grasp. McCoist, as you would expect, was there immediately, but by the time he had worked his way clear, Celtic's defence had galloped back into position.

Celtic's keeper appeared unsure of himself yesterday and he was fortunate not to have given away a penalty after meeting McCoist just inside the box. The striker went down, but the referee indicated he had taken a dive.

Celtic's end of the stadium housed the first celebration of the day after a corner had been won on Rangers' left in 52 minutes. Collins delivered the ball deep beyond the far post where Miller was waiting to roll the ball back to Wdowczyk. His shot appeared to be going wide when Elliott, remarkably alert, dived and headed the ball in.

The Rangers support found their voices in time to howl disagreement at the referee, Jim McCluskey, who finally caught Hurlock in the act of fouling Fulton. The official was not having a good game because he was missing too many illegal challenges and off-the-ball incidents, but he was correct to book Hurlock, and also Hateley and Dziekanowski.

Celtic made a tactical switch by taking off the anonymous Miller and sending on Chris Morris, who went into the back four, where presumably his presence would help to slow down Walters. Peter Grant stepped forward into midfield, but Rangers would not be denied.

Gough's long pass from defence after 66 minutes was nodded down by Hateley to McCoist, and his touch left Walters free to beat Bonner at his right hand corner.

The game surged into extra time and after Dziekanowski's appalling miss, Gough was in position to pounce on the loose ball, after Bonner and Morris collided in the box in trying to cut out out a Gary Stevens' free kick.

Skol Cup Final

Celtic (0) 1	Rangers (0) 2
Elliott	Walters
	Gough

[after extra time; 90 mins 1-1]
(at Hampden Park)

Attendance   62,817

CELTIC:– BONNER, GRANT, WDOWCZYK, FULTON, ELLIOTT, ROGAN, MILLER, MCSTAY, DZIEKANOWSKI, CREANEY, COLLINS. SUBSTITUTES – MORRIS, HEWITT.

RANGERS:– WOODS, STEVENS, MUNRO, GOUGH, SPACKMAN, BROWN, STEVEN, HURLOCK, MCCOIST, HATELEY, WALTERS. SUBSTITUTES – FERGUSON, HUISTRA.

Celtic 1, Rangers 2 – Sunday, 25th November, 1990

Controversial Old Firm Victory Puts Rangers Top of the League

By James Traynor

Rangers arrived in the east of the city yesterday afternoon still with a makeshift team because of injuries, but it was the sight of Paul McStay taking up a position in the centre stand which ought to have alerted everyone to what was about to unfold on a rain-soaked pitch.

Without the captain Celtic's midfield does not function smoothly, and long before the end of another tense Old Firm encounter, Rangers had assumed control.

Their victory, secured in the most controversial of circumstances, has put them on top of the Premier Division, and the way they have been chiselling out victories lately suggests they will be difficult to dislodge.

Yesterday's defeat has left Celtic six points behind the leaders and it is doubtful if they will be able to bridge such a gap. They needed to do something against Rangers, but without McStay their midfield lacked the creativity required to overcome the tenacity of Terry Hurlock and Nigel Spackman, who were operating on either side of the promising Sandy Robertson.

Hurlock, in fact, had a splendid match, particularly his second half. He prevented Celtic's play from flowing in midfield, and he was involved in the incident which has left a sour taste among those who lean towards the Parkhead side. The players, management, and fans of that club probably believe they were robbed of a point.

The score was tied at 1-1 when, early in the second half, Hurlock and Steve Fulton contested possession of a ball which was chest-high. Each player had a foot up, but it was Fulton who was left lying on the turf.

Hurlock stopped momentarily as though expecting a foul to be called, but there was no whistle, and he scampered forward before pushing a pass through to Ally McCoist, who had taken over from Maurice Johnston at the interval. Celtic's defence, presumably believing a foul had been committed, was caught off-balance and square while McCoist, who had been a fraction away from being offside, sprinted away and rounded Bonner before scoring in an empty net.

Celtic were furious and Fulton, who felt a great injustice had been perpetrated, complained vociferously and was booked by the referee, Brian McGinlay. The Parkhead people looked at McCoist celebrating and could not believe what was happening to them.

As long as the English midfield player, who was eventually booked along with Robertson, Mark Walters, Ally McCoist, and Dariusz Wdowczyk, continues to tramp pitches, there will always be heated debate, because he is an extremely untidy tackler, although that does not make him dirty. He is all action and hard, but generally his tackles are fair.

Having said that, most referees would have considered his challenge on Fulton illegal and they would have been right. Rangers were fortunate to maintain possession, although there was nothing lucky about McCoist's exemplary finish.

After their second goal Hurlock and his team-mates dealt with Celtic in a most professional manner. Their job was made easier when Gerry Creaney was sent out to the right wing to accommodate Tommy Coyne, who was a second-half substitute for the ineffectual Joe Miller. Creaney had a splendid first half, and was Celtic's most dangerous player. The edge was taken from his game when he moved wide.

Much had been expected of Charlie Nicholas, but again he appeared sluggish, although he still retains a repertoire of touches. Indeed, if his shot just after the interval had gone in instead of hitting the base of Chris Woods' left-hand post, Celtic might have gone on to win the game.

Rangers reshuffled their back four to compensate for their injuries. Gary Stevens and John Brown were the central defenders with Scott Nisbet and Stuart Munro the full backs. It was a combination which appeared sound enough in the early part of the first half, but which began to crack as Celtic, particularly Creaney, stepped up the level of their performance.

But by then they were a goal behind, and few in the capacity crowd of 52,265 could believe the generosity of Lex Baillie, whose attempt to head back to Pat Bonner was weak and left Johnston to lob over the keeper.

Only eight minutes had been played and Celtic were already in desperate trouble. It is to their credit that they fought back, and they were entitled to consider themselves unlucky to have scored only once before half-time. The equaliser went to Paul Elliott, who rose above everyone else to head in Collins' free kick, awarded after Nisbet had fouled Fulton.

Hopes of a triumph rose among the Celtic faithful when Rangers resumed without Johnston, who had been suffering from a stomach complaint. However, his replacement, McCoist, would soon disabuse them of notions of victory.

Celtic (1) 1	Rangers (1) 2
Elliott	Johnston
	McCoist
Attendance	**52,265**

CELTIC:– BONNER, MCNALLY, WDOWCZYK, FULTON, ELLIOTT, BAILLIE, MILLER, GRANT, NICHOLAS, CREANEY, COLLINS. SUBSTITUTES – ROGAN, COYNE.

RANGERS:– WOODS, STEVENS, MUNRO, NISBET, SPACKMAN, BROWN, HURLOCK, ROBERTSON, HATELEY, JOHNSTON, WALTERS. SUBSTITUTES – HUISTRA, MCCOIST.

Rangers 2, Celtic 0 – Wednesday, 2nd January, 1991

Rangers Rub Salt into the Wounds

By James Traynor

The New Year started as the old one finished for Celtic and their supporters who, despite their defiant chants and songs at the end of another miserable afternoon, must be wondering how much longer they will be asked to suffer. Some might even be questioning the wisdom of continuing to look out the colours every week.

They are paying to watch one of the most ineffectual Celtic teams ever, which is bad enough, but the fact that their club's slump coincides with Rangers in better shape than ever before, heightens the pain and the anguish.

Celtic have become a depressing sight. They are disjointed, uninspired, and short on genuine talent.

Gone are the days when they played this game in the most thrilling of attacking styles, and unless better players arrive Celtic will never recapture old glories. The players ran around trying hard on the slippery turf, but they are a team without direction and belief.

They rarely came close to scoring in a match so untidy that more than meteorological changes were to blame. Celtic don't seem to have the appetite for the big challenges any more.

The opposite is true of Rangers, and their manager, Graeme Souness, will hardly be bothering too much about the poor standard of play because his team are five points clear of Aberdeen, who stay in second place despite their defeat by Dundee United, and Rangers are 14 in front of Celtic.

Even though current circumstances would suggest Celtic's need was greater, it was the Ibrox side who appeared the more determined. Generally they were first to the ball and more committed in the tackle, and although their goals were the results of appalling defensive lapses, they deserved to win.

The first was scored after 35 minutes when Derek Whyte gave away a corner on the right. Mark Walters hit the ball with the outside of his right boot, and Celtic's fans were stunned into silence at the sight of Pat Bonner's net bulging.

Paul McStay had been at the near post, but neither he nor his keeper could prevent the ball from going in, and their embarrassment will not be eased, even though Walters described his thirteenth goal of the season as a "complete fluke." He explained that as he took the corner his studs caught in the grass and he didn't make proper contact.

"The wind caught the ball and made it fade in a little. It was harder then for Pat Bonner," he said.

Celtic tried to have more of an influence on the march thereafter, but they didn't cause too many problems for a Rangers defence kept in line by the captain, Richard Gough, who strolled through yesterday's game as though it were a bounce match in the public park, and his calming influence was not lost on the manager.

"I think he has been outstanding, given the injuries he has had," said Souness. "He has had a season during which he was in and out of the team, and when some other players might not have, he played through a lot of pain."

A different kind of suffering was registered clearly on the face of Billy McNeill when he finally left his team's dressing-room. "There's a lot of disappointed players in there who feel they don't deserve to be leaving Ibrox with nothing," said the Celtic manager. "We were always in the game at 1-0, but we committed the cardinal sin of stopping in anticipation of a penalty."

McNeill was referring to an incident inside Rangers' penalty box in 77 minutes when Tommy Coyne went down, and it must be assumed Celtic believed their striker to have been pushed by Mark Hateley. The referee allowed play to proceed, and while Coyne ran to register his disapproval, Hateley ran back upfield in support of a Rangers attack.

The ball eventually was taken by Peter Grant, but he made a terrible mess of trying to roll the ball back to Bonner. Sandy Robertson, who had been sent on to replace Pieter Huistra, stepped in, rounded Bonner, and squared the ball into the middle where Hateley was waiting to score.

Despite the atrocious weather, 38,399 people squeezed into Ibrox and the police were pleased to report that there had been only six arrests before, during, and after the match. On a dismal afternoon for those who prefer smooth, thoughtful football, this statistic was ample consolation.

Where exactly Celtic will find consolation is anyone's guess, but it is clear they can't blunder on much longer and, as has been said before, their fans deserve much better. To be so many points away from the top end of the League is an affront to the supporters, and if they start deserting, Celtic will be left with absolutely nothing.

The club has reached a critical point in its history and if the right moves are not made soon, Celtic will be finished as a force. The great sadness, of course, is that few people believe the people running the club possess the necessary foresight and acumen to reverse the downward spiral.

Rangers (1) 2	Celtic (0) 0
Walters	
Hateley	
Attendance	38,399

RANGERS:– WOODS, STEVENS, MUNRO, GOUGH, SPACKMAN, BROWN, WALTERS, HURLOCK, HATELEY, JOHNSTON, HUISTRA. SUBSTITUTES – ROBERTSON, MCCOIST.

CELTIC:– BONNER, MORRIS, ROGAN, GRANT, ELLIOTT, WHYTE, CREANEY, MCSTAY, COYNE, WALKER, COLLINS. SUBSTITUTES – NICHOLAS, MILLER.

Celtic 2, Rangers 0 – Sunday, 17th March, 1991

Old Firm in St Patrick's Day Parade: Four Ordered off as Celtic Reach Semis

By Ian Paul

Celtic still have something to play for after having manoeuvred their way comfortably into the semi-finals of the Tennents Scottish Cup on a Sabbath afternoon when there seemed a real danger that they would be left to play among themselves.

The St Patrick's Day parade of Rangers players leaving the field had become so alarming that it seemed sensible to count the blue shirts as the final whistle went just in case one or two others had gone while we were taking notes of the mayhem.

Celtic, too, lost a player, Peter Grant, as a result of a red card, but the really depressing casualty was the Ibrox midfield man, Trevor Steven, who had to go off after 11 minutes, suffering from knee-ligament damage which will put him out for the rest of the season.

When the body count had been completed – four orderings off and six bookings – the tempers soothed, and the consequences assessed, Celtic were entitled to feel pleased with themselves. They had deservedly and comprehensively won the quarter-final contest which, had they lost, would have left them with a season in tatters, however much they would have claimed that the chase for a high placing in the Premier Division mattered.

They were fired with a confidence and belief which catapulted them into their most important game of the season in such a fashion that Rangers managed their first corner only after 20 minutes' play. By then they were a goal down and struggling to make any kind of impact.

Celtic's spirits had been sent soaring by a splendid opening goal in six minutes. Hateley had fouled Whyte, although he protested vigorously against the award, and Celtic defender Darius Wdowczyk made the first of two especially telling intrusions on the game. He sent a deep free kick into the Rangers penalty area, where Richard Gough was just beaten to the touch by Tommy Coyne. The ball bounced in front of Gerry Creaney, and he whisked it past Chris Woods in superb style.

Before half-time Rangers had lost Steven, who twisted his knee as he stretched to tackle Miller, and brought on Pieter Huistra, but still made very few incursions into the Parkhead defensive area, where Paul Elliott was a commanding and outstanding figure. And when Celtic went two ahead in 37 minutes, the chances were that the League leaders and were en route for a hiding.

This time Wdowczyk took a free kick, awarded when Terry Hurlock fouled Creaney, and hit it with such venom from 40 yards out that, after it was deflected by the outstretched foot of Hurlock (it was not his day), the ball hurtled past a stranded Woods.

Mark Walters was booked for a foul on Coyne, then Maurice Johnston's name went into the book for dissent, but as the players trooped off to their dressing-rooms at the the interval, there was nothing to suggest the madness that was to follow in the second half.

Andrew Waddell, the Edinburgh referee handling his first Old Firm match, was to spend much of the time raising his arm with one of those coloured cards at the end of the extension.

First, he booked Grant of Celtic for pulling the jersey of Johnston as he raced in on a terrific through ball from Scott Nisbet. Then the Celtic man achieved something of a record, a second booking within seconds of his first, after he moved out of the 'wall' as Ian Ferguson smashed the free kick. Mr Waddell decided he had broken ranks before the ball was kicked and, as Grant offered his opinion on that verdict, the red card was hoisted aloft.

For a spell afterwards, Celtic seemed distinctly unsettled and Rangers, for the first time in the match, looked capable of staging a revival. In fact, it was as manager Graeme Souness and his assistant Walter Smith were involved in a lengthy discussion, no doubt about their next tactical move, that Terry Hurlock reduced their deliberations to the irrelevant.

The Cockney midfielder had a wee elbow at Coyne, was spotted by the referee, and then made the inevitable walk up the gangway. That, effectively, killed off Rangers' chances. The initiative was lost, the revival doused, and the Cup exit door shut behind them.

Elliott had to come off, too, but only to change his blood-spattered jersey, which was the result of a full blow in the mouth from a ferocious Ferguson free kick.

Hateley was then booked for a foul on his fellow-Englishman before Walters decided it was his turn to go doolally. Twice he tried to foul Coyne, and after the ball had gone he made it, elbowing the striker in full view of the referee. Maybe he felt it was time for a wash before the rush hour. At any rate he, too, had the red card hoisted above his head.

Next for the big hook was Hateley, who lunged recklessly at Anton Rogan. After the two had a wee set-to on the touchline, Rogan was booked and the Rangers man sent off to try to find some space in the bath.

Nisbet was booked near the end for doing a wee dance of dissent, but there was not enough time for anybody else to get in on the act.

That was probably just as well. By then, we had all had enough.

Tennents Scottish Cup Quarter-Final

Celtic (2) 2	Rangers (0) 0
Creaney	
Hurlock (o.g.)	

CELTIC:– BONNER, WDOWCZYK, ROGAN, GRANT, ELLIOTT, WHYTE, MILLER, MCSTAY, COYNE, CREANEY, COLLINS. SUBSTITUTES – MCNALLY, WALKER.

RANGERS:– WOODS, STEVENS, MUNRO, GOUGH, NISBET, HURLOCK, STEVEN, FERGUSON, HATELEY, JOHNSTON, WALTERS. SUBSTITUTES – COWAN, HUISTRA.

Celtic 3, Rangers 0 – Sunday, 24th March, 1991

Celtic Spring Double adds some Spice to the Title Race

By Ian Paul

Celtic completed a remarkable Spring Double over their oldest rivals with a victory that was not quite as comprehensive as the scoreline suggests, but was clear enough to confirm their own confident emergence from the doldrums.

If a week is a long time in politics, it is a short, sharp shock in football. Suddenly, as a consequence of Celtic's two victories – they beat Rangers 2-0 in the Tennents Scottish Cup quarter final last Sunday – the prospect of a trophy-winning season has been re-opened for the Parkhead team.

They were nowhere near as positive in the first half yesterday as they had been the previous Sunday but they defended well, took the chances that came their way, and in the end were worthy enough winners. So, too, was referee George Smith, who might have been inclined to be a wee bit schoolmasterly, but after the nonsense of last week, he can be forgiven a touch of over-vigilance.

There were five bookings, some of them for relatively minor offences, and one sending-off. That came 12 minutes after the interval when Scott Nisbet took a flying tackle at the back of Paul McStay and really had little cause for complaint when the red card was displayed.

Otherwise, there was little of the vindictiveness of the previous contest, but there was no exchange of pleasantries, either. Oddly, two men who invariably retain their composure, Richard Gough and Paul Elliott, became involved in angry skirmishes which ended in their being booked, but Davie Dodds and Mark McNally, for fouls, and Tommy Coyne, for dissent, did nothing villainous.

Perhaps the happiest man around was Anton Rogan, who has had his share of miserable Old Firm occasions, after scoring his first goal in these contests and, indeed, his first goal of the season. It was his opening score, in eight minutes, which put Celtic en route to victory, and it was his long ball through the middle which set up the move for Joe Miller to score his team's second goal. By the time Tommy Coyne scored the third five minutes from time, there was no doubt in anybody's mind whose team busload would be celebrating.

Yet if Rangers, particularly young John Spencer, had been half as lethal near goal, the story might have been very different. Ironically, Spencer outshone his two Scottish international partners, Ally McCoist and Maurice Johnston, but he missed the two best chances of the afternoon.

Nonetheless, the team that Graeme Souness described as 'makeshift' had never quite showed the authority to win such a derby.

Celtic, on the other hand, while not as decisive as the previous Sunday, were always threatening on the forward run, especially on the right, where wee Joe Miller has recaptured the form that enticed Billy McNeill to pay £650,000 for him.

McNeill would be content with his contribution and equally so with that of his £1m man, John Collins, who, as well as being specially gifted, does an enormous amount of less obvious work in defence as well as attack.

He and McStay once again won the midfield contest, although it was closer than last time, but it was in defence that Celtic were more solid-looking than their rivals.

Rangers elected to switch Scott Nisbet from defence to midfield, where he didn't do too badly in the first half, and called in 32-year-old Davie Dodds into the back four alongside Gough. It was not a success.

Rogan's goal was the result of a free kick flighted into the danger area by Miller. Gough managed to get his head to it, but only nodded it up in the air where Chris Woods rose along with Gerry Creaney and Cowan. The English internationalist was not quite positive enough to clutch the ball, however, and when it dropped, there was Rogan sweeping it over the line.

McCoist who, hard though he tried, rarely got involved in the action, took a sore-looking knock when Elliott inadvertently caught him with his boot as the Rangers player met a Nisbet cross. Johnston, who had a similar afternoon, did get a head to another Nisbet cross, knocking it on to Spencer, whose header was saved.

Those efforts and a fine Bonner save from Gough illustrated Rangers' recovery from the set-back of that goal, but soon after the break Celtic scored their second. Rogan punted the ball through the middle, where Coyne cleverly held off Dodds, but the chance seemed to have been lost when Woods raced out and forced the Celtic striker to go too far left. However, Coyne stopped the ball on the bye-line, sent it across the face of goal and there, racing in on a full tank, was Miller to hammer it past the goalkeeper.

Four minutes later Nisbet lunged at McStay, was sent packing, and with him probably went any hope of a recovery.

Robertson came on for Ferguson and did some intelligent things, and Walker replaced Creaney in the Celtic team. It was the industrious Coyne who was to snatch the third goal nine minutes from the end when, after Miller laid the ball back to McStay, the captain's cross found Tommy free to head comfortably past Woods. Near the end Celtic put on Steve Fulton for Collins.

Celtic (1) 3	Rangers (0) 0
Rogan	
Miller	
Coyne	

CELTIC:– BONNER, WDOWCZYK, ROGAN, MCNALLY, ELLIOTT, WHYTE, MILLER, MCSTAY, COYNE, CREANEY, COLLINS. SUBSTITUTES – FULTON, WALKER.

RANGERS:– WOODS, STEVENS, COWAN, GOUGH, SPACKMAN, NISBET, DODDS, FERGUSON, MCCOIST, JOHNSTON, SPENCER. SUBSTITUTES – ROBERTSON, HUISTRA.

Celtic 0, Rangers 1 – Tuesday, 31st March, 1991

McCoist Goal Sweeps Rangers into the Final

By James Traynor

EARLY BODY BLOW WHEN ROBERTSON IS SENT OFF BUT THEN HAMPDEN IS A BLUE HEAVEN

A foul and treacherous night out at Hampden Park began with Rangers embroiled in controversy, but ended with the Ibrox side's supporters singing in the rain. Rangers finally overcame Celtic in the Scottish Cup.

Last night, Rangers staggered out of a traumatic and ugly Semi-final tie against their ancient enemy, exhausted but smiling again. They pranced and squelched around the wet turf like children who had just been told the school had burned down, and saluted their fans who hailed the result as though the Cup had just been won.

Rangers had gone a man down after only six minutes when David Robertson was dismissed. The full back fouled Joe Miller and the referee, Andrew Waddell, produced a red card and was immediately surrounded by a posse of furious Rangers players.

Technically, I suppose, Robertson should have walked for having body-checked Miller, but it was not too difficult to understand Rangers' fury. Most referees probably would have cautioned Robertson for his challenge, but Waddell has always been quick to impose himself, and when he did, it seemed as though the Ibrox side, who have not won the Cup since 1981, were destined to wait another year.

Yet Celtic appeared unsure of themselves after Robertson's departure, and did not press home their advantage until the second half, when they had the wind behind them. However, Rangers had reshuffled and closed ranks at the back.

They simply kept gulping in oxygen and battled for every ball inside their own half, something they had failed to do a week past last Saturday when Celtic cruised to a 2-0 win in the final Old Firm League match of the season at Ibrox. There was nothing fancy about their work, but it was effective on a night when football was the last thing anyone should have been thinking about.

Ally McCoist, a lonely worker up front, had his reward on the stroke of half-time when he broke clear and on to a delivery by Stuart McCall, who had dispossesed Brian O'Neil. McCoist then did the two things he does best. He placed the ball in the net for his 30th club goal of the season, and then turned to the crowd and beamed that wide smile of his.

Celtic resumed the match in much more determined fashion and pinned Rangers back in their own half. Even though the Parkhead side hit the woodwork three times – Paul McStay's shot from 20 yards was struck with venom and seemed destined for the net, before smacking the the face of the bar – the impression that they were not making the most of their greater numbers persisted.

Bad luck and an opposing defence held together by Richard Gough and Nigel Spackman continued to deny them, and now Rangers can relax and watch the second Semi-final on Saturday when Hearts and Airdrie meet at the national stadium.

Liam Brady's players trudged out of view at the end, unable to come to terms with harsh reality. They had been playing so well in recent months and, in fact, it is no exaggeration to say they were the form team in the country.

Also, they had restored to their team those players left out at the weekend, and even Miller, who was doubtful because of a leg knock, was on the right wing, no doubt anxious to start where he had left off before his injury.

That was in the previous Old Firm match in which he had given Robertson such a hard time, and when his marker departed the scene early last night, the Celtic winger must have thought he was about to have a wonderful night. It didn't work out for him or his colleagues.

The evening belonged to Rangers, who will not be concerned about the lack of football. When they had to produce more basic qualities, like fighting spirit, they came through and so, too, did Ian Durrant.

The midfield player displayed some subtle touches and his recent form suggests that maybe, just maybe, he will recover fully from that horrendous knee injury suffered two-and-a-half years ago at Pittodrie.

By way of contrast, Celtic's O'Neil, a 19-year-old who will surely blossom into a potent midfield operator, never looked comfortable in the slippery conditions and was withdrawn.

His place was taken by Mike Galloway. It had always been a match for the workhorse rather than the thoroughbred, although Galloway had a couple of shots which were struck superbly well and would have beaten a goalkeeper other than Andy Goram.

The Parkhead side made their second substitution when they took off Charlie Nicholas, another who could not function with his usual artistry in the conditions midway in the half, and sent on Tommy Coyne. They continued to push forward, and just after Rangers had taken off Dale Gordon and sent on Paul Rideout, the Celtic players and fans were appealing for a penalty.

John Collins had gone down inside the box, but the referee waved play on, ignoring the Celtic players who claimed John Brown had taken the legs away from their man.

Scottish Cup Semi-Final

Celtic (0) 0	Rangers (1) 1
	McCoist
(at Hampden Park)	

CELTIC:– MARSHALL, MORRIS, BOYD, O'NEIL, MOWBRAY, WHYTE, MILLER, MCSTAY, CREANEY, NICHOLAS, COLLINS. SUBSTITUTES – COYNE, GALLOWAY.

RANGERS:– GORAM, STEVENS, ROBERTSON, GOUGH, SPACKMAN, BROWN, GORDON, MCCALL, MCCOIST, DURRANT, HUISTRA. SUBSTITUTES – RIDEOUT, SPENCER.

Celtic 0, Rangers 2 – Saturday, 31st August, 1991

Referee Deserves a Red Card for Failing to Follow the Guidelines

By James Traynor

The vast majority of people inside Celtic Park on Saturday believed that Pieter Huistra should have walked. Since most of the customers were Celtic supporters, no-one will convince them that the referee, Jim McCluskey, was correct to allow the Dutchman to continue playing after a foul on Tommy Coyne, who was bearing down on Rangers' goal.

The incident, which had Celtic's people on their feet and howling in protest, occurred midway through the first half, when a beautifully-struck ball from Steve Fulton sent Coyne galloping in the direction of Andy Goram. Coyne must have thought his moment had arrived.

However, he was halted just on the edge of the penalty box as Huistra lunged from the back and pulled him down. Huistra's head sagged onto his chest, as the realisation that it could be time to go, dawned.

The referee arrived and, instead of the expected red card, waved a yellow one. Celtic and their fans could not believe their eyes.

McCluskey, were he not gagged by the SFA's rejection of free speech for all, would tell us he felt it was not exactly a one-on-one incident, because Gary Stevens was arriving like a train on Coyne's left and could well have managed a saving tackle. Huistra's attempt was a forward's tackle, in that it was badly timed and clumsy.

Nevertheless, the fact is that Coyne was bearing down on goal, and Huistra did foul him. He should have gone, if only to make it clear that referees intend to be consistent in their application of the amended law.

There is no point in starting off the season with a spray of red cards and then slackening off just when it seems the players are getting the message. There are reasonable grounds to believe Celtic were denied an obvious scoring opportunity. A free kick, which came to nought, was hardly justice.

It was after this tackle and Huistra's fortunate escape that Rangers got around to some serious work, with their defence tightening up considerably, and Stuart McCall and Nigel Spackman taking a grip in midfield. Then it was over to Mark Hateley, who becomes a more menacing striker as the weeks go by.

McCall played a good ball out of defence, and Gary Gillespie, who had been strolling through the match, moved to intercept but misjudged the pace of the ball, which bounced through to Hateley.

"I just ran and had the legs to keep going," he said afterwards. "From the moment I moved, I made up my mind to go around Pat Bonner, because I knew that he wouldn't pull me down."

Hateley's speed as he surged through was impressive and, as soon as he cut across Bonner's path, it was obvious he would score. From having survived an incident which could have left them a man short, Rangers had gathered themselves and moved into the lead.

Celtic's game began to crumble soon after and, although they had moments in the second half, it is fair to say that Rangers were not in a great deal of trouble. They defended well as the game progressed, and the match was finished as a contest when Hateley scored his second goal in 59 minutes.

The manner in which he and Maurice Johnston fashioned the goal was stunning in its speed and accuracy. The taller and more powerful of the two strikers rose above his marker and headed the ball forward to Johnston on the edge of Celtic's box, and he had the wit to head it back to Hateley.

The Englishman moved away from a defender and, after controlling the return pass, hit the ball towards Bonner's bottom left-hand corner. The keeper seemed slow in going down and, although he managed to get a touch on the ball, he couldn't prevent it from going in.

Hateley was away and celebrating before the Rangers support, who have been won over by his goal-scoring ability. He's not the prettiest player to watch, but he is one of the most powerfully effective.

Both his goals were perfect examples of the finisher's art, but questions have to be asked about Bonner's speed of reaction at the second goal. "If Pat holds up his hands, I'm sure he would admit he could have stopped that second goal," said Liam Brady, Celtic's manager, who had just watched his team fail for the second week in succession.

Too many of his players were unable to change the direction of the game or do much to undermine Rangers' confidence, which grew as the time passed. Brady is absolutely correct when he says his team have a bit to do yet before they can hope to challenge the Ibrox side's supremacy.

Rangers found it a pretty straightforward matter in dealing with Celtic's attacks in the latter stages, and the Parkhead team's lack of spirit seemed to have a dampening effect on the supporters, who lapsed into silence long before the full-time whistle sounded.

Celtic (0) 0	Rangers (1) 2
	Hateley 2

CELTIC:- BONNER, MORRIS, ROGAN, GRANT, WHYTE, GILLESPIE, FULTON, COYNE, CREANEY, NICHOLAS, COLLINS.

RANGERS:- GORAM, STEVENS, ROBERTSON, GOUGH, SPACKMAN, NISBET, MCCALL, FERGUSON, HATELEY, JOHNSTON, HUISTRA

Rangers 1, Celtic 1 – Saturday, 2nd November, 1991

At Last Cascarino Enjoys the Cheers. But Striker Expects to be Back on the Bench Against Swiss

By Ian Paul

Two men with English accents settled the latest get-together of the Old Firm at Ibrox, when a 1-1 draw left no-one depressed, but no-one satisfied either. One of them, Tony Cascarino, is Irish (at least in football terms), while the other, Nigel Spackman, very nearly became a Scot last season. Celtic's £1.1m striker may well have cause to thank the Rangers midfielder for more than just the generosity of presenting him with the equalising score.

The goal might well become the turning point for the Republic of Ireland internationalist, who has made a slow beginning to his career with the Parkhead team. Any man who scores against Rangers is inclined to be given hero status for a while by the Celtic fans, and the sound of his name being chanted must have been thrilling, if unexpected, for the likeable forward signed by manager Liam Brady from Aston Villa.

"If I had missed that chance, I would have gone home and hung myself," said Cascarino with admirable honesty. It is the case, of course, that had he missed he might have found himself well down the queue of those with rope in hand, but struggling careers have been given impetus by less significant incidents, and it may be just the psychological lift that Cascarino needs to get going as an international player should.

Cascarino has not allowed himself to become dumped by his relegation to the substitutes' bench since he came to Glasgow, nor is he too suprised by his failure to produce his best form. "It was the same even when I went to Millwall," he said. "I seem to take time to get adjusted at a new club. I am sure there is much more to come from me yet. I certainly hope so."

He does not imagine that his equaliser will catapult him into the side to face Xamax of Neuchatel on Wednesday in the return leg of the UEFA Cup tie . . . "with Charlie Nicholas and Tommy Coyne playing so well, I will just have to wait for my turn again."

In the meantime, he will no doubt relive that goal at Ibrox many times, as will Spackman, who would probably have been most people's idea of the player least likely to make such an error on Saturday.

A consistently good midfielder, Spackman rarely releases the ball to one of the enemy, but this time he did not see Cascarino lurking behind Richard Gough as he sent the ball back towards Andy Goram. To his obvious consternation, the Celtic man materialised from nowhere to whip the ball through the legs of the goalkeeper and put Celtic on level terms at a time when they looked as if they might be heading for defeat.

Oddly enough, Rangers had gone ahead through a typically sharp piece of Ally McCoist play at a point when Celtic had given the impression that they were the more likely side.

Consequently, a draw probably worked out about right. You can usually say that, anyway, when both managers feel they just about deserved to win. Certainly, the man who would be happier would be Brady, because a point at Ibrox was no bad start to the tough series of matches coming up.

Rangers, on the other hand, have not won any of their last three games, a run which is rare indeed these days. It is a form line which does not augur too well for bottom-of-the-League Dunfermline, who meet the Ibrox lot at East End Park on Saturday.

Yet Rangers began in impressive style against Celtic. In fact, McCoist thought at that point his team were going to "run all over" Celtic, but apart from a superb opening created for himself by Pieter Huistra, whose shot was blocked by a timely Derek Whyte tackle, they did not create too many clear-cut chances.

Nevertheless, their failure to make the most of their superiority at that stage was bound to be paid for later. As McCoist also said, no Old Firm team can expect to dominate all the way through. Celtic, fired by the words of their manager, who was very disappointed with their first-half showing, took over from the start of the second period and were in full flight when Rangers stopped them in their tracks with the opening goal.

Mark Hateley set up the move with a pass to Gary Stevens, whose clever chip to the near post gave McCoist just the space he needed for a diving header which gave keeper Pat Bonner no chance.

Nine minutes later, as Celtic worked hard to try to regain the momentum, Brady took off both Nicholas and Joe Miller, sending on Cascarino and Chris Morris. It was Morris who made the bigger contribution at first, his play on the right side of midfield proving an eye-opener, but in 70 minutes Cascarino was to step in with the goal that mattered for his club.

Despite the disappointment of losing that goal, McCoist was justified in his opinion that Rangers played better than they had done for a while, but so, too, was Brady, who felt that the gap between the clubs, as identified by him after their first meeting, had been closed.

Rangers (0) 1	Celtic (0) 1
McCoist	Cascarino

RANGERS:- GORAM, STEVEN, ROBERTSON, GOUGH, SPACKMAN, NISBET, MCCALL, FERGUSON, MCCOIST, HATELEY, HUISTRA

CELTIC:- BROWN, MCNALLY, WDOWCZYK, GRANT, WHYTE, GILLESPIE, FULTON, COYNE, CASCARINO, NICHOLAS, COLLINS.

Celtic 1, Rangers 3 – Wednesday, 1st January, 1992

Generous Celtic Still Too Good at Bearing Gifts

By Ian Paul

In time-honoured Scottish tradition, Celtic broke their resolution before the New Year had dipped towards its first sunset.

They leapt into the Leap Year in just as startlingly generous a fashion as they had behaved for much of 1991, giving goals away to the opposition, and languishing in the dressing-room afterwards, exhausted and deflated by defeat.

It would also be no coincidence that their scorers included Ally McCoist and Mark Hateley, whose talent for making the most of their chances has been the predominant reason for the fine scoring run of their team over recent weeks.

Yet the best Rangers goal was saved for the last, when substitute John Brown, who had presented Dunfermline with a goal last Saturday, hit a marvellous 20-yard shot in off a post.

Celtic, on the other hand, could point only to a superb bullet of a header by Tony Mowbray as their counting strike, although they also could claim to have by far the best player on the field in the magnificent Paul McStay.

It would be true to say that a bizarre episode involving the Parkhead captain was another major factor in the way the game developed, along with the controversial penalty awarded to Rangers after McCoist had been impeded by Celtic keeper Gordon Marshall. They were the main talking points for the 51,381 who turned up on a foul afternoon.

The McStay pantomime began midway in the second half when he rose from a challenge with a cut just below his eye. He was ordered to the touchline by referee George Smith, and after receiving attention from physiotherapist Brian Scott, tried to return to the field.

Mr Smith sent him off again where he changed his blood-stained shirt and attempted to get back once more. Again he was refused permission and disappeared up the tunnel where he was given a couple of stitches in the gash.

In the six minutes that McStay was going through his cuckoo-clock routine, Celtic seemed almost voluntarily to concede the initiative at a time when they had been putting Rangers under severe pressure.

They then found it difficult to restore their leading role, even with McStay back, and when they lost that second goal, the return journey was too demanding.

Ironically, the goal followed a quick piece of thinking by the Celtic keeper, who had rushed out as McCoist was sent into the area by a splendid pass from Brown.

Marshall dived at the striker's feet, diverting the ball away from goal quite legitimately. But then, as he and McCoist struggled to get to their feet to chase the ball, which was heading for the bye-line, he seemed to catch the leg of the Rangers man, who went back down again.

The crux of the matter was simply whether or not Marshall intended to hamper Ally. In the referee's view he did, and Hateley, taking over from McCoist, took his first penalty kick as a Rangers player.

Celtic had gone behind just before half time when Peter Grant lost possession to Nigel Spackman, when he had seemed well in control of the situation. His lapse was to prove deadly as Spackman rode another couple of tackles and sent Gordon off on the right. When his cross came over, Hateley appeared to mishit the ball, which spun forward to McCoist who popped it past Marshall.

If that was not the prettiest goal these two have conjured, up it at least made amends for the two they had missed early on. Ally had tried a clever chip after Gordon had sent him clear, but it landed just wide of the post; and Hateley had headed over the bar after a McCoist cross had left him with a clear cut chance.

During that early 20 minutes Rangers had looked the part. Assured and controlled, confident at the back and adventurous up front, they threatened to make Celtic look ordinary indeed. McStay and John Collins, however, began to demonstrate their special skills.

Celtic really went at the opposition in admirable style after the break and scored a wonderful equaliser within five minutes. Galloway took a corner on the left, Derek Whyte back-headed towards goal, and Mowbray hurtled forward to smash the ball with his head into the back of the net.

There was every chance then of Celtic going on to win, but when the McStay episode came and went, the penalty followed, and Rangers were on the way to a couple of very valuable points.

With a minute left, Brown, who had replaced Stuart McCall in the second half, meandered forward with Celtic players appearing to take little interest. Eventually, as he approached the penalty area, the defender let fly with his left foot, and the ball snuggled behind Marshall.

The result certainly was rough on Celtic, however, and they find themselves 10 points behind their old rivals in what is surely a forlorn attempt at winning the Championship. Not that Liam Brady would say so. Hardly. "This club and its supporters demand that we keep going right to the end. And we will."

Celtic (0) 1	Rangers (1) 3
Mowbray	McCoist
	Hateley (pen.)
	Brown
Attendance	51,381

CELTIC :– MARSHALL, MORRIS, MCNALLY, GRANT, MOWBRAY, WHYTE, GALLOWAY, MCSTAY, COYNE, CASCARINO, COLLINS. SUBSTITUTES: CREANEY, FULTON.

RANGERS :– GORAM, STEVENS, ROBERTSON, GOUGH, SPACKMAN, KUZNETSOV, GORDON, MCCALL, MCCOIST, HATELEY, MIKHAILICHENKO. SUBSTITUTES: BROWN, HUISTRA.

Rangers 0, Celtic 2, – Saturday, 20th March, 1992

Cup Problems for Rangers as the Celtic Game Plan Proves Decisive

By James Traynor

There are two ways of looking at what happened at Ibrox. On one hand you could say Rangers were so awful they deserved to suffer the bad things which happened to them on Saturday, but that is too simplistic. Celtic's performance, which was intelligent and potent, must be taken into consideration.

Celtic stuck to their game plan. They prevented Rangers from playing in their usual expansive manner and eventually took control of the match. Liam Brady's team performed well, perhaps even exceptionally well given the circumstances, and he was entitled to the smile which he wore when he appeared afterwards to talk about how the 2-0 triumph had been engineered. The manager had opted to deploy Derek Whyte in the heart of defence alongside Tony Mowbray, rather than Gary Gillespie.

Pace was the deciding factor in that decision. Gillespie, Celtic's £1m signing from Liverpool, doesn't have a great deal of it. Whyte does, and he used it to keep Ally McCoist and Mark Hateley in check.

They played well in partnership, and will be used again when the teams meet in the Semi-final of the Tennents Scottish Cup at Hampden Park a week tomorrow. The Ibrox side will have to produce a much higher level of awareness and be more creative if they are to lay hands on the trophy for the first time in more than a decade.

Mowbray is in no doubt the task will be tougher next time around, and believes Rangers could be stung into more positive action because of Saturday's failure. "I have to say it was one of the most comfortable games I have had with Derek Whyte," he began. "In fact, he was very good. His pace, which is essential in the modern game, got him to danger areas and he was able to snuff it out."

In particular he feels Hateley and McCoist will be more threatening at Hampden, and few who were at Ibrox would dispute that notion because Rangers' strikers were pretty ineffective. Their cause was not helped by the failure of others to provide them with a decent supply of ball, but even allowing for that these strikers, who have scored 49 goals between them this season, were expected to contribute more than they did.

"They are good players," Mowbray said, perhaps to remind himself more than any of his audience, "it was just that they didn't have the best of days this time. However, I don't think it would be fair to say that we won because Rangers didn't play particularly well. We kept the ball from them and we played in nice little triangles. We showed what this club is all about."

Mowbray was speaking after his first match at Ibrox, and the fact that he displayed not a sign of nervous tension at all was indicative of Celtic's mood these days. They are on a high, and confidence is coursing throughout the club.

"We seem to have this feeling of invincibility about us just now," he explained, "and if it is still there a week on Tuesday, then we will have a good chance of reaching the Cup Final. I know they will say they can't play as badly again, but we will feel we can do just as well and it will be a battle of wits."

Rangers will have to find ways of bringing their fullbacks, David Robertson and Gary Stevens, into forward positions, a ploy which has served them well throughout the season, but which didn't work against Celtic because of Joe Miller and John Collins.

Miller had a good game and his exuberance kept Robertson occupied. His frustration eventually got the better of him in the second half when he was booked for a foul on the winger. That foul, incidentally, was enough to send Miller hobbling off the field, but the game had been won and lost by the time he left to be replaced by Mike Galloway.

On the opposite flank, Stevens' forward momentum was being blocked successfully by Collins, who had an excellent game in a quiet sort of way. His covering and tackling work was exceptional, while the other midfield players, Paul McStay and Brian O'Neil, concentrated on playing passes.

Rangers might offer the reminder that their defence was weakened significantly by the absence of Richard Gough, who ought to be fit in time to play against St Johnstone on Saturday, but they were so out of touch and Celtic so much in a groove, that it is difficult to believe the Ibrox side's captain could have prevented them from meeting with their first defeat in 20 matches.

No-one could have done anything about the first goal, scored in 34 minutes, when Nicholas, who admitted to having been surprised when selected before Tommy Coyne, struck with precision. His looping shot from just outside the box was a thing of beauty.

The second goal was created by McStay, whose powerful run across Rangers' 18-yard line in 57 minutes took out a couple of defenders before he released Gerry Creaney. The striker veered to his right inside the box, gaining space for himself, and his shot was accurate.

Celtic (1) 2	Rangers (0) 0
Nicholas	
Creaney	

RANGERS:- GORAM, STEVENS, ROBERTSON, NISBET, BROWN, FERGUSON, MCCALL, MCCOIST, HATELEY, MIKHAILICHENKO

CELTIC:- MARSHALL, MORRIS, BOYD, O'NEILL, MOWBRAY, WHYTE, MILLER, MCSTAY, CREANEY, NICHOLAS, COLLINS

Grant and Elliot for Celtic enter into aerial combat with Nisbet and Gough.

Ally McCoist scores with a flying header.

Brown volleys Rangers' third in their 3-1 win in the 1992 Ne'er Day game.

Joe Miller and Peter Huistra battle it out.

Rangers 1, Celtic 1 – Saturday, 22nd August, 1992
McStay and Steven Victims of Stampede
By James Traynor

Old Firm games rarely enhance football's image, and the latest one, conducted at a furious pace inside Ibrox, was no different. There were glimpses of what the game is supposed to be about, but football became a bystander as players clattered into one another.

Those of us who merely watch the Old Firm at work can never fully appreciate the effects on players of the intense pressures which swirl around the pitch and stadium, although an indication of just how damaging these tensions can be is seen when professionals forget to do the things that come naturally to them any other Saturday.

When they do remember, they seem unable to pass or kick the ball properly. It is as if the ball is an intruder which has rolled into the path of of a stampede, so it is hardly surprising McStay and Steven are unable to bring their influences to bear.

Their kind do try to calm everyone around them and slow play down, but most of the time they, too, are overtaken, if not exactly overcome, by the undiluted passion, excitement and hatred which surrounds games between Rangers and Celtic.

These are contests dominated by fear. No-one wants to be the one who loses the ball or makes the mistake which leads to defeat.

For a long time in the first half, Rangers were the team under most pressure, as their midfield was compressed towards the back line, leaving too wide a gap to the front two, Ally McCoist and Mark Hateley, and it was only when Pieter Huistra, an Ibrox enigma, moved further forward on the left that the Ibrox side began to look more menacing. Indeed, they were still pushing forward when Celtic scored in 53 minutes.

Mark McNally, who continues to show signs that he could develop into one of the country's finest defenders, stole forward on the right and on to a flick by Joe Miller. McNally looked up and clipped the ball across, but John Brown's head got in the way – and the trajectory was altered, cruelly so far as Rangers were concerned.

Those at the heart of the Ibrox defence were caught too far forward and Gerry Creaney was allowed to pounce. It was a difficult chance, but he remained calm, watching the ball all the way and was able to thump it into the roof of the net.

However, Ian Durrant, a second-half substitute for Steven, whose legs had grown weary of the rush, was in exactly the correct place when Hateley, who lost the aerial duel with Tony Mowbray, held off a challenge as Huistra's left-wing cross dropped in Celtic's box in 69 minutes. The ball was touched back to Durrant, and he slammed it into the top left-hand corner of Gordon Marshall's goal.

The midfield player's contribution prevented Celtic from opening up a three-point lead over Rangers, but his goal also made sure justice was done, because the Ibrox side, who created more chances, had scored what seemed to me to have been a perfectly good goal after only five minutes.

Steven and Hateley combined well to set up an opportunity for the former, who drove the ball low into the net only to see a linesman flag for offside. The official was wrong, and it was a credit to Rangers that they did not waste time complaining.

Ferguson's wild tackle on Galloway was indicative of a player who is prone to reckless acts and who may be frustrated because he has not met the expectations many had when he arrived at Ibrox just over than four years ago. However, he did display some deft touches and the powerful, surging runs which tempted the then Rangers manager, Graeme Souness, to part with £1m. If he could only harness his abilities and show them with more consistency, perhaps he could still become the genuine article.

The same applies to Huistra, who must be a source of great irritation to manager Walter Smith. The Dutchman can confuse and bewilder defenders by executing a shuffle, the slightest of feints, but he squanders more balls then he delivers, yet on Saturday most of Celtic's troubles came from the few crosses Huistra managed to fire in.

However, Smith's greatest concern must still be the right back position, which is vulnerable without Gary Stevens, a long-term casualty. Dave McPherson was deployed there against Celtic, and the big fellow was not always comfortable.

Of course, Celtic also had to re-arrange their defensive line because of injuries to Gary Gillespie and Dariusz Wdowczyk, and Mowbray had to play even though he had 10 stitches in a head wound sustained last midweek. Nevertheless, the defence coped admirably and Celtic were entitled to leave Ibrox happy with their afternoon's work and reward.

Celtic have now sucessfully negotiated the toughest of opening Premier Division programmes, and they can look forward to European competition in confident mood.

There is a sense of purpose about Brady's team these days and their supporters, who have not seen the team collect a trophy in the past two seasons, are growing optimistic.

Rangers (0) 1	Celtic (0) 1
Durrant	Creaney
Attendance	43,239

RANGERS:- GORAM, FERGUSON, ROBERTSON, GOUGH, MCPHERSON, BROWN, STEVEN, MCCALL, MCCOIST, HATELEY, HUISTRA.

CELTIC:- MARSHALL, BOYD, GALLOWAY, GRANT, MOWBRAY, MCNALLY, MILLER, MCSTAY, CREANEY, PAYNE, COLLINS.

Celtic 0, Rangers 1 – Saturday, 7th November, 1992

Million Reasons why Celtic Could Remain Second Class

By James Traynor

Celtic believe they are not far away from being a Championship-winning side and in the sense that they require only one, perhaps two top-class players, their argument has credence. However, the kind of players required don't come cheaply and considering the club's financial predicament, it becomes apparent that they are at least a million miles, or to be precise, a million pounds away from the glory they crave.

Consider this: Had they been able to call on a striker, a younger Charlie Nicholas or a Frank McAvennie, when he was a player, Celtic probably would have been only two points behind Rangers this morning.

Instead, they are six points off the blistering pace being set by the Ibrox side, who are determined to finish their League business as soon as possible. It is all extremely ominous for the challengers and Scottish football in general because attendances would fall if Rangers shake off their rivals and start cruising towards another title.

Celtic had a chance to remind everyone that there is more than one force in the land, but as has been the case with them throughout this season, they were unable to convert pressure and possession into goals.

Stuart Slater had several good chances but, like Leeds United's Eric Cantona a few days previously, he found Andy Goram still in splendid form, although it can be said the English striker often flatters to deceive.

He is fast and able to take the ball with him when in full flight – a rare talent these days – but too much of his work is done too far away from the opposition's goal.

It is also the case that, too many times, Celtic's midfield players, Paul McStay included, fail to produce the killing pass. You know, the one which wrong-foots defenders as it slices through the back line.

The manager, Liam Brady, has been allowed to spend something like £5m which is more money than any other Celtic manager was given, although inflation, of course, would help make the figure higher, and he is unlikely to be given any more.

The fact is that Celtic, who are faced with the problem of financing the refurbishment of Celtic Park or a completely new stadium, don't have money for new quality players.

Brady will have to make do with the squad he has and once players like Gerry Creaney and Slater run into good fortune, the goals may start to come again. The trouble is, though, that by then Rangers may well have disappeared over the horizon with the silverware.

They have developed the quality of being able to defend for lengthy periods and hold out, knowing that someone will take a chance at the opposite end. On Saturday it was Ian Durrant's turn to put the ball in the net, and again Rangers scored because of intelligent play.

They had been playing for 32 minutes when Mike Galloway allowed a ball played diagonally into the box to pass through. That was the first mistake, as Dale Gordon was waiting to chip the ball across goal to the unmarked Ally McCoist, who normally can't resist such opportunities.

However, this time the striker headed back into the middle of the box where Durrant, also unmarked, was arriving. He scored easily and Celtic's misery became acute.

Rangers were forced to re-arrange their defence during the break when it became obvious that John Brown, who damaged a hamstring, could not continue, and Dave McPherson moved into the heart of the back line with Stuart McCall dropping back from midfield to right full back. Pieter Huistra took over in the midfield.

However, Rangers, who were giving the ball away in midfield too easily, still refused to buckle at the back and remained resilient after Richard Gough, who had tried to continue although injured, went off in 68 minutes. The captain aggravated his groin injury in a clumsy challenge on Slater and was booked before hobbling off the pitch.

Rangers pulled Mark Hateley back into the centre of defence – Alexei Mikhailichenko was sent on to provide support up front for McCoist – alongside McPherson, and they continued to stand firm.

"It's been a good week for us," Smith said afterwards. "I can't praise the players highly enough because everyone had expected them to feel adverse effects after the game against Leeds in midweek."

Brown should not be out too long, but Gough could be sidelined for a few weeks, which means he will miss Scotland's game against Italy next midweek. Smith is hoping the player will be fit in time to play against Marseille.

| Celtic (0) 0 | Rangers (1) 1 |
| | Durrant |

CELTIC:- BONNER, GALLOWAY, WDOWCZYK, GRANT, MOWBRAY, GILLESPIE, BOYD, MCSTAY, SLATER, CREANEY, COLLINS.

RANGERS:- GORAM, MCCALL, ROBERTSON, GOUGH, MCPHERSON, BROWN, GORDON, FERGUSON, MCCOIST, HATELEY, DURRANT.

Rangers 1, Celtic 0 – Saturday, 2nd January, 1993

Celtic's Forwards Again Fail to Supply Winning Punch

By James Traynor

Celtic had dominated the second half of the season's third Old Firm match, but were preparing to go home with nothing. They should have left with both points and some hope, albeit faint, that their Championship challenge could be resurrected.

By way of stark and cruel contrast, Rangers can't help winning, even when they play badly, as they did on Saturday. Their form deserted them, leaving them to give the impression they did not know what it was they were supposed to be doing, yet the League table tells a different story.

They have played two matches fewer than Celtic, yet have a 10-point lead. If there were any real justice Celtic would be only six points behind, and their title credentials would still be intact. But as things stand now, Celtic can chase only the Scottish Cup, the last competition in which they still have a chance of success.

"As regards us and the Championship, I think the challenge is over," said Brady, who, like his players, was desperately disappointed with the 1-0 scoreline.

Indeed, Celtic would have secured the points they needed so badly, had they taken half of their chances. They had three wonderful opportunities to score, but Andy Payton, Gerry Creaney, and John Collins, who also missed another chance, squandered them all, and therein lies the reason for Celtic's downfall.

A team cannot challenge for honours without scoring goals, something Celtic have difficulty doing. There have been times this season when their football was a joy to watch, but without front-line punch, they will be remembered only as failures.

Also, their own fans are growing weary of finishing second best to others who may not have played as well. You know, sometimes it seems as though Celtic are more of an exhibition team, in that they look good, but lack the drive required to win prizes.

Rangers have that in abundance, and it was a combination of their determination, Celtic's slipshod finishing, and Andy Goram's reflexes which took them through a traumatic afternoon. The Ibrox side did not play at all well. In fact, they were dreadful, but they still managed to start the New Year as they had finished the old one.

But they have developed a habit of winning, regardless of how many of their players are having bad days. "It's sort of like a rolling stone thing," says their captain, Richard Gough, "and we are not going to be easily stopped."

Trevor Steven scored the crucial goal in 33 minutes, but he did not look good, although in his defence it should be said he was used out of position. In the absence of the injured Ally McCoist, he had to back up Mark Hateley, and there is no doubt Steven will be relieved to know McCoist should be fit for tomorrow night's match against Dundee United.

Ian Durrant's touch was also off and Dale Gordon struggled to make an impact, as did Ian Ferguson. Also, Rangers' defensive line was not too impressive, and they know they were extremely fortunate to get through the afternoon without losing a goal.

"Once again we had the luck," said Gough. "That's twice we've played Celtic and I'd be lying if I said we deserved to take four points.

"We were well below our usual standard, but you can play only as well as the other team allows. It will be no consolation to them or their fans, but Celtic deserve credit and I thought they played very well. They were the most attack-minded Celtic team I've seen here."

That, of course, is Celtic. They believe in attacking football, and even after their strategy was disrupted when Tony Mowbray tore a thigh muscle only a few minutes into the game, the thought of defending in numbers did not enter their minds.

Peter Grant took over, and Celtic also shrugged off the loss of Payton (hamstring) early in the second half. They always tried to go forward and their play was pretty at times, but it was never sharp enough inside Rangers' box.

It is vital that Celtic and others try to entertain, but their work will be denied proper respect – and may even become meaningless – if they continue to be kept off the podium on prize-giving days.

As for Rangers, their manager, Walter Smith, must be growing alarmed at the number of times his players have enjoyed more than their fair share of good fortune. One of these days that luck will run out.

"We've played better," said Smith, "but the players have been asked to get up for big matches so many times this season that we can't expect them to sparkle in all of them.

"Sometimes it is down to determination, and there is no shortage of that in this squad."

That is true, of course, but Smith knows the score. He knows his team played badly, and he is also aware that had they been playing against a side in possession of a genuine finisher, they would have been punished.

Rangers (1) 1   Celtic (0) 0
Steven

RANGERS:- GORAM, MCCALL, ROBERTSON, GOUGH, MCPHERSON, BROWN, STEVEN, FERGUSON, GORDON, HATELEY, DURRANT.

CELTIC:- BONNER, MCNALLY, BOYD, GALLOWAY, MOWBRAY, COLLINS, MILLER, MCSTAY, PATON, CREANEY, SLATER.

1993

Celtic 2, Rangers 1 – Saturday, 20th March, 1993

Hesitant Rangers Punished by Collins and Payton

By James Traynor

It was exciting while it lasted. But everyone, including Rangers themselves, knew their run of matches without defeat could not go on indefinitely. They reached 44, but the forty-fifth match took them back to Celtic Park.

It had been suspected that Rangers might experience some difficulties in the final Old Firm match of the season because of their heady exploits in the Champions' League, but they were much more out of touch than anyone could have anticipated.

The Ibrox side spent most of the afternoon in forlorn pursuit of the game, and although they had a flourish towards the end after Mark Hateley's goal had injected fresh hope and enthusiasm, Celtic were in control.

In spite of another sterling performance from Stuart McCall, who draws from a limitless reservoir of energy, Celtic commanded the midfield area and deserved their victory.

John Collins was especially effective for Celtic, and his goal in 37 minutes gave his own side greater belief that they could go on and beat Rangers. Until Collins beat Andy Goram with a strong and accurate shot from the edge of the box, Celtic had missed a few opportunites and frustration might have undermined their game.

In the opening seconds of the match John Brown whipped a leg from Andy Payton inside the box and Celtic should have been given a penalty, but referee Douglas Hope decided there had been nothing illegal about the challenge and play rolled on, although Brown was booked minutes later for a crude body-check on Stuart Slater.

The Rangers defender was living dangerously, and it soon become apparent that such erratic play was widespread throughout the side.

Celtic took advantage and might have had another penalty just before the interval, when it appeared as though David Robertson had played Slater's attempted cross with an arm. Again the referee waved play on, but the incident was further evidence of Celtic's dominance and Rangers' hesitancy, a failing which led to the second goal.

Collins hurled the ball over from a corner on the left early in the second half, Goram seemed to watch Neil Murray, who was watching McCall, while Payton watched the ball's free passage across the face of goal, and slid in to make contact.

The scorer went off soon afterwards to have four stitches inserted in a head wound, but he was able to finish the game and celebrate with his team-mates at the end. They and their supporters had waited a long time for a triumph like this, and even though it meant nothing in terms of the title, a win over the arch-rivals is always welcome.

Rangers departed the scene without saying much at all, but then they are unfamiliar with the misery of defeat, although manager Walter Smith hung around long enough

to say a few words about the attitude of his players during the course of their run. They could not, he said, have given any more.

If the injury problems with which Smith has had to cope are taken into consideration, his team really should not have gone on so long without suffering a loss, but it was inevitable the strain would take a toll. Apart from McCall, they ran out of steam at Parkhead.

They had to start the game without players like Richard Gough, Gary Stevens, Pieter Huistra, Dale Gordon and Ally McCoist, who were all injured or ill. In fact, Smith, who was reduced to 14 players, had to ask McCoist to be a substitute, even though he was unfit and suffering from food poisoning.

After half an hour McCoist had to go on because Scott Nisbet injured his groin, and the team had to be reshuffled. All McCoist received for his trouble was a booking after a minor squabble with Mike Galloway, who did not care too much for a tackle by the Rangers striker. The Celtic player was also booked.

Before the end an injury to Ian Durrant, who hobbled off with a sore knee, allowing Alexei Mikhailichenko to run on, sealed a thoroughly miserable afternoon for Rangers, even though the Ukrainian combined well with Hateley to reduce Celtic's lead.

It would have been unjust, however, had Rangers equalised and denied Celtic a rare moment, because they displayed some nice skills. According to their man of the match, Collins, the aim now is to finish the season unbeaten.

They have gone 10 games without defeat, and if they can maintain their form they may be entitled to harbour greater expectations for next season, provided Brady is able to strengthen the team. When they play like this it is obvious they are not too far off the required standard, but they are short of a few quality players and also consistency.

Many of their supporters will be wondering why the team cannot produce performances like Saturday's with increased regularity, but perhaps this win will give them greater self-belief.

"I think we all had something to prove to ourselves and to our fans against Rangers," said Collins. It certainly showed.

Celtic (1) 2	Rangers (0) 1
Collins	Hateley
Payton	

CELTIC:- BONNER, BOYD, WDOWCZYK, GRANT, MCNALLY, GALLOWAY, SLATER, MCSTAY, MCAVENNIE, PAYTON, COLLINS.

RANGERS:- GORAM, NISBET, ROBERTSON, WATSON, MCPHERSON, BROWN, STEVEN, HAGEN, MCCALL, HATELEY, DURRANT.

Ally McCoist

The most prolific scorer in Rangers' history, with 299 competitive goals to his credit before the start of the 1995-96 season. McCoist is idolised by the Ibrox fans, for his playing exploits, his conduct on and off the field, and his courage. The striker, in recent seasons, has had to suffer a series of bad injuries, including a broken leg, but keeps bouncing back.

He turned professional with St. Johnstone in 1978 and, three years later, went to Sunderland for a fee of £350,000. Never really settled down south and signed for Rangers in a £180,000 deal in 1983. The one unhappy spell for him at Ibrox came under the Graeme Souness era when Souness brought in strikers to replace McCoist, but the player refused to get involved in a war of words and eventually won back his place.

He is another who loves playing in Old Firm matches, and Celtic know that to their cost. Probably his most satisfying show against the Parkhead side came in the League Cup Final of season 1983-84 when he scored a hat-trick in Rangers' 3-2 win. He also holds a record number (eleven) of Premier Division hat tricks and has been capped 46 times. Medals won with Rangers are eight Championships, one Scottish Cup and eight League Cups.

Mark Hateley

Another English inter-nationalist, who gained legendary status at Ibrox joining the club from Monaco in the summer of 1990. Until he settled at Ibrox, Hateley was something of a footballing gypsy, playing for clubs in England before heading for Milan, then on to Monaco.

Mark, however, did not have an easy time of it in his first season in Scotland. Injury had kept him out of football for a lengthy spell, and the fans, sensing that he had been brought to the club to replace McCoist, did not exactly give him a rapturous welcome. Hateley, however, is one of the best professionals in the game, and he answered his critics in the best possible way, getting himself razor sharp and scoring many spectacular goals.

Rather than replacing McCoist, Hateley formed an almost telepathic partnership with the Scot. In September 1995, he went to Queens Park Rangers for £1 million, rejoining his former Ibrox colleague, now QPR manager, Ray Wilkins. With Rangers, he won five Championships, two Scottish Cups and two League Cups.

Andy Goram

Those who claim that Andy is perhaps the greatest Rangers goalkeeper of all time will find few who would argue. And now that it would appear he has finally got over a serious knee injury, there will surely be many other great occasions ahead for him. Although on the small side for a keeper, he has tremendous agility and technique, and he is also brave.

Andy took a roundabout route to Ibrox, starting his professional career at Oldham in 1981 after not being offered terms by West Bromwich, who had him as an apprentice. Won the first of his Scottish caps while at Boundary Park, but moved north to Hibs for around £300,000 in 1987. Four years later he joined Rangers for £1 million. Andy has not been the most disciplined of players, but there is no doubting his outstanding talent.

Although he was born in Bury, Lancashire, he has been capped by Scotland on 33 occasions, and has also represented Scotland at cricket. His domestic honours are three League Championships, two Scottish Cups and one League Cup.

Brian Laudrup

Although having spent just one season with Rangers, this Danish internationalist has made such a huge impact on the Scottish scene. So much so, in fact, that at the end of that first season he was voted Scottish Player of the Year by the football writers, and also by his fellow professionals. By far the most exciting player in the country at the moment, he can operate with great effect in a number of roles.

Brian also gets his share of the goals, and Rangers fans are relishing the prospect of him teaming up with Paul Gascoigne in their quest for success in the European Champions' League. Laudrup was a member of the Danish international squad which won the last European Championship. Began his senior career with Brodby and played in Italy with Fiorentina and on loan for AC Milan before joining Rangers for £2.2m. Has one Scottish Championship medal.

Celtic 0, Rangers 0 – Saturday, 21st August, 1993

McGinlay's Tale Gives All a Choicer View of Old Firm

By Ian Paul

We needed somebody to tell us it was a special game. And Pat McGinlay came over the hill to the rescue.

Celtic's new boy was filled with the flush of excitement that comes with taking part in the country's most notorious derby for the first time, and he made it sound a lot better than it looked.

"Everybody tells you what it is like, but until you try it, you can't guess how it feels," McGinlay said later. "The noise just hits you as you come out of the tunnel. You can't hear a thing during the game. Except Peter Grant, but you hear him anywhere."

McGinlay enjoyed his experience and did well into the bargain. The no-scoring draw may not have been the result Celtic wanted, but their performance left the team and the management encouraged. Rangers seemed quite content, too.

Duncan Ferguson, the £4m man, made his first entrance in a blue shirt and lasted 83 minutes, during which he nearly manufactured a couple of goals out of nothing, but like Mark Hateley, he had little decent service and was also accurately marked by the Parkhead defence which, in contrast to so many past occasions, deserved praise. In fact, most of the plaudits go to the defenders.

Richard Gough was outstanding, with Davie McPherson, who returned to the team for the first time this season, and Steven Pressley, only marginally behind. But even they were outshone by the man on trial, Fraser Wishart. The former Falkirk, St Mirren and Motherwell full back looked very much at home among the internationalists on the field, and if Rangers are unwilling to keep him, there should be a queue of eager managers.

It should also be emphasised that the Rangers back four had to put in a hard afternoon's work. Celtic's attacking unit was far more penetrating than the opposition, whose midfielders were too busy coping with the McGinlay-McStay-Collins flair to provide proper ammunition for the twin towers up front.

Charlie Nicholas and Gough had a great old tussle all the way through, a sure indication that Nicholas, who looks far sharper than last season, is a threat again.

Maybe Celtic could use a different, faster foil, like Andy Payton, beside him, but that is not to criticise Frank McAvennie, who did not let anybody down.

The question is whether two strikers of the Nicholas-McAvennie style marry well. The same poser could be put at the sharp end of the Rangers team, where Hateley and Ferguson often seemed to be doing the same job. It was impossible to resist the notion that Ally McCoist would fit perfectly beside either.

Ferguson might learn a great deal from Hateley, however, especially if he watches the way the Englishman floats away from markers.

He didn't manage to cause his usual bother to Celtic, but that was perhaps a testament to Mark McNally and Mike Galloway, who stand a couple of inches shorter than the Ibrox duo, but who attacked the high ball with a gusto and accuracy that won the day most times. With Pat Bonner in confident form and Tommy Boyd and Dariusz Wdowczyk lending their support, the Parkhead defence had its most efficient day for a while.

Celtic had most of the play but, in the circumstances, that was to be expected. Theirs was the more needy cause. For most of the second half, and a good slice of the first half, they had the upper hand territorially and no-one could have complained too loudly (excepting those wearing Rangers favours) if they had collected both points.

John Collins might have done the trick with one particular chance in the second half, while McGinlay admits he might have been better passing to McAvennie, rather than attempting a shot, when he was sent clear earlier on.

McPherson diverted a McAvennie header against a post, Gough made at least two magnificent tackles to halt attackers inside the penalty area, and Ally Maxwell was in splendid form in his first Old Firm battle. For all that has been said about Rangers and their injury problems, they are still so solid at the back that it needs a lot of imagination and good fortune to get ahead of them.

Celtic came close to achieving it, and the midfield combination, boosted by the direct approach of the powerful McGinlay, looks as skilled and efficient as any in the country. If the defence really has got its act together – one clean sheet doesn't make a bed – times may be about to improve.

Their fans went home not too displeased, even if they had been desperate for a win. And Rangers fans went off even more chuffed. It was a funny old day.

Celtic (0) 0   **Rangers (0) 0**

CELTIC:- BONNER, BOYD, WDOWCZYK, GRANT, MCNALLY, GALLOWAY, MCGINLAY, MCSTAY, MCAVENNIE, NICHOLAS, COLLINS.

RANGERS:- MAXWELL, PRESSLEY, WISHART, GOUGH, MCPHERSON, MURRAY, STEVEN, I. FERGUSON, D. FERGUSON, HATELEY, HUISTRA.

Celtic 0, Rangers 1 – Wednesday, 22nd September, 1993

Marksman Hateley is Right on the Target Again

By James Traynor

The spirit of fortitude which dragged Rangers through so many demanding and seemingly impossible assignments last season returned just in time to fuel hearts and legs as the Ibrox club swept into the Final of the Scottish League Cup, where they will meet Hibernian in next month's final.

In fact, both teams will play a Premier Division match at Ibrox on Saturday when it will be interesting to discover if Rangers can use the defeat of Celtic to launch themselves properly into a season which had been fairly mundane until last night's semi-final. With 47,420 of the most committed supporters in the country squeezed into the same ground, excitement was guaranteed.

The standard of football hit acceptable levels only occasionally, but it is the passion and tension of these affairs which makes them compulsive. Often, it is simply the team with the greater desire and determination which wins. Rangers were up for this game much more than Celtic, who took control for only about 10 minutes after Pieter Huistra had been dismissed for violent conduct.

The second half had been underway only four minutes when the Dutchman lost his temper after he had failed to lay off a ball to the inrushing Stuart McCall. Huistra, for reasons known only to himself, swung a leg wildly at Tommy Boyd, who would have suffered serious injury if contact been made.

The intent was enough and Huistra had to walk, leaving his team-mates, who had created more chances than Celtic in the first half, to re-arrange themselves and struggle on. It seemed then that Celtic, whose supporters roared long and loud, would take the initiative and then the match, but after a brief flurry, it became obvious that they did not have the guile to stretch Rangers' depleted resources.

The Ibrox side took heart and in 70 minutes, when Mike Galloway tried to employ finesse deep in his own half while in pursuit of Gary Stevens' forward pass with Ian Durrant, they took full advantage. Durrant's low ball into the heart of the Celtic box was perfect, and Mark Hateley surged in to side-foot his seventh goal of the season.

It was an appalling error by Galloway and Celtic's fans, who had been playing their part, fell into shocked silence while Rangers' hordes rejoiced. Rangers always managed to have enough bodies behind the ball whenever Celtic moved in search of an equaliser, and rarely was there any great danger.

Frustration got the better of Peter Grant and Boyd before the end, and they were booked for crude challenges on Durrant and Hateley respectively, but the Rangers pair had already caused the damage and plunged Celtic deeper into depression. Celtic may never have a better opportunity to beat their traditional rivals, and questions must be asked of all concerned.

Another trophy has escaped their grasp, and one wonders how much longer a lack of silverware can be tolerated. Celtic continue to play some neat football at times, but they lack genuine menace in the opposition's half of the pitch.

Liam Brady was asked afterwards if the result would make him reconsider his own position, and although he replied with a terse "no", the manager must surely be anxious about his team's inability to go the distance.

It could be pointed out that both John Collins and Charlie Nicholas were unfit, but injuries plague Rangers to a greater degree, and only hours before the tie, Duncan Ferguson was sent for an X-ray to a foot. He took a knock, but the medical picture showed no sign of a break.

Andy Goram, John Brown, and Ally McCoist have still to return and if this win provides the lift required, Rangers could embark on another long run of success. Saturday's match will provide further evidence while Celtic, who are at Tynecastle, have to rummage around among their own doubts.

Rangers might have scored early in the match when Hateley thundered after a through ball from Ian Ferguson, who did a marvellous job in midfield, and as the striker prodded the ball beyond Pat Bonner, the keeper appeared to carry on into him. Hateley went down just inside the box, but referee Douglas Hope did not give a penalty.

Had he done so, he would have been obliged to send Bonner off, but it was significant that Rangers players did not pursue the official to express a sense of injustice.

Instead they continued to fashion chances, which must have been encouraging for their manager Walter Smith, who has been dismayed by the lack of creativity in his side, and Ferguson and Hateley both had opportunities before the interval.

Even after Huistra had gone, Celtic failed to pressure Ally Maxwell often enough. "We were going nowhere," Brady lamented. "It was a poor performance."

For him, his players, and their fans it was a depressing end to an evening which had promised much. Brady's side still appears to lack belief, and without that commodity they will all continue to go nowhere.

Scottish League Cup Semi-Final

Celtic (0) 0	Rangers (0) 1
	Hateley
Attendance	47,420

CELTIC:– BONNER, BOYD, WDOWCZYK, GRANT, MCNALLY, GALLOWAY, MCGINLAY, MCSTAY, MCAVENNIE, CREANEY, SLATER. SUBSTITUTES – O'NEIL, MOWBRAY, MARSHALL.

RANGERS:– MAXWELL, STEVENS, ROBERTSON, GOUGH, MCPHERSON, MCCALL, STEVEN, IAN FERGUSON, DURRANT, HATELEY, HUISTRA. SUBSTITUTES – WISHART, MORROW, SCOTT.

1993

Rangers 1, Celtic 2 – Saturday, 30th October, 1993

Maxwell again Fails to Handle the Big Occasion and Celtic Celebrate

By James Traynor

Celtic's supporters, who were stationed behind Ally Maxwell's goal in the second half of Saturday's Old Firm match, sang his praises long into the night. That just about says it all.

The goalkeeper blundered badly and cost Rangers two points, and not for the first time this season. No-one was willing to jab a finger in Maxwell's face, but it was clear the keeper's dreadful handling had caused the defeat, although it would be wrong to foster the impression that Celtic had played no part at all in a triumph which ought to set them up nicely for the away leg of their UEFA Cup match against Sporting Lisbon.

Celtic, in fact, had the better of the first half, and it was in this period that doubts about Maxwell's ability to handle the occasion began to surface. He looked uneasy, and at times petrified, when one of his own players played the ball back to him. His clearances were the work of a desperate man, and it was only a matter of time before his anxiety washed over his defensive line.

As the match progressed the possibility of Maxwell making some kind of mistake increased, especially since Celtic swarm forward at every opportunity.

Even after Ally McCoist, who will require a handful of games before he can shake off the debilitating effects of five months of idleness caused by injury, had bundled Rangers in front in 67 minutes, Celtic simply breathed deeper and surged forward again.

Three minutes after falling behind – and with the Rangers support still celebrating – they were darting towards Maxwell's box. Pat McGinlay lofted the ball over from the right and the Rangers keeper rose easily and gathered the ball in. However, as he landed, the ball slipped free from his grasp and dropped at the feet of John Collins.

The midfield player ran right across the box and away from two defenders before scoring in front of his own supporters. If looks could kill, Maxwell would have suffered almost 40,000 deaths.

After his error it seemed both sides had decided to settle for a share of the points, but in 88 minutes Celtic's new manager, Lou Macari, decided to take off Charlie Nicholas and, as the game ran into injury time, his replacement, Brian O'Neil, scored the winner.

"I was surprised Charlie kept going so long," said Macari. "It was just a case of needing fresh legs, that's all. Inspired substitution? There's no such thing."

Two minutes into injury time Celtic forced a corner on the right, and as Collins' delivery drifted into the centre of the box, Maxwell moved out to intercept, but could only wave at the ball as it eluded him. O'Neil, not knowing a great deal about what was happening, bundled the ball into the net for his first Old Firm goal.

Only seconds remained before it was all over and Celtic had secured a much-needed win in the backyard of their traditional rivals. It was some time before the fans stopped singing and left the premises. They were certainly going to enjoy the rest of their evening, although they will be cautioned by Macari in the days ahead not to think all is suddenly well at the club.

It was a dreadful match, with not a lot of football played, and Macari was not fooled. He knows the breaks went his side's way, but he also knows that if players take full advantage of strokes of good fortune when they present themselves, good things can follow.

While Macari, who was applauded by one lot and derided by the other on his return to Ibrox after 20 years – "Yes, same old abuse," he said – was pleased to have a positive start to his second career with Celtic, he may have been dismayed by the poverty of the play.

A couple of players, Paul McStay and Richard Gough, managed to detach themselves from the sweaty collisions around them, but their unhurried and more cultured contributions were not enough to give the game a polished look. It was poor stuff from players unable to run away from their own fears.

Smith's strategy had to be altered slightly when first Gary Stevens, who was galloping to tidy up a poor clearance from Maxwell, damaged a hamstring and then, just before half-time, Trevor Steven had to leave to have stitches inserted in a long gash on his face. He had been wounded by Tommy Boyd, but it was not deliberate.

Stevens' place was taken by Steven Pressley and Alexei Mikhailichenko stood in for Steven, and although the Ukrainian looked in the mood, he did not see much of the ball, which was being thumped around without obvious method. He has been here for 27 months now, but the madness of these Old Firm occasions is still beyond him.

Rangers (0) 1	Celtic (0) 2
McCoist	Collins
	O'Neil

RANGERS:- MAXWELL, STEVENS, ROBERTSON, GOUGH, MCPHERSON, MCCALL, STEVEN, FERGUSON, MCCOIST, HATELEY, DURRANT.

CELTIC:- BONNER, GILLESPIE, BOYD, GRANT, MOWBRAY, MCGINLAY, BYRNE, MCSTAY, CREANEY, NICHOLAS, COLLINS.

Celtic 2, Rangers 4 – Saturday, 1st January, 1994

Celtic's Back-Line is Found to Have a Weak Heart

By James Traynor

Footballers! If only the game could be played without them, it would be so much easier. Often, it seems as though professional players have the concentration span of an amoeba.

A manager can preach at them, warn constantly of the dangers presented by the next set of opponents, and plead with his players to be vigilant. Sometimes they are taken away to the seaside where they can all be together in tranquil surroundings. The idea is to focus minds.

Like Celtic managers before him, Lou Macari took his squad to Seamill prior to Saturday's Old Firm match, and made it clear what they should expect and how they should react. They were reminded that thousands of people were depending on them producing the correct response.

One or two of them would have nodded, giving the impression of stern listeners, but it turned out that Macari's words had fallen on deaf ears. The work of the management team, the training sessions, and Macari's talk were all wasted, especially on the defenders, who were not at home when Mark Hateley came calling early in the afternoon.

Gary Gillespie and Dariusz Wdowczyk, who formed a particularly weak heart in Celtic's back line, were in the wrong places when Stuart McCall played a good ball through the middle for Hateley to sprint away. The match had been going only a minute and the striker had not yet warmed to his task, but, unlike those who were supposed to be marking, he was sharp and ready.

Hateley took control, surged towards Pat Bonner, who narrowed the angle pretty well, and curled the ball beyond the keeper's right hand and into the net for his twenty-first goal of the season.

Where had these defenders been since the start of the season? They looked as though they were the only people on the planet unaware of Hateley's menace.

Macari must have been mystified. He had been quoted as saying that it would suit his team if the match became a scrap. He must have felt he had the players capable of going the distance with Rangers, but it was difficult to see who they could be.

Rangers went two goals in front, when Hateley touched the ball back to Gordon Durie, and his delightful pass found Murray on his own. His shot was parried by Bonner, but Alexei Mikhailichenko struck the telling blow.

Three minutes gone, and Celtic's cause was undermined beyond repair. Again the heart of the defence was no more than a gaping hole, and even before many of the ticket holders had filed into their places, Rangers had exploited the negligence and flatness of Celtic's defence.

Mikhailichenko scored his second in 28 minutes, and it was when Bonner's net was disturbed for the third time within half an hour that some Celtic fans broke. Violence flared around the ground and in the main stand, where Rangers' directors came under fire, probably because of their close proximity to Celtic's directors.

One Celtic follower, who had been receiving first aid, decided to get up and run at Rangers' keeper Ally Maxwell, but fortunately the interloper was apprehended.

The sporadic violence had its roots in the frustrations which have been mounting since Rangers' revival began more than seven years ago with the arrival of Graeme Souness and then David Murray's money and leadership. The Ibrox side have been collecting trophies, whereas Celtic have been suffering from decades of boardroom negligence.

Saturday saw a small explosion as pain, frustration, bewilderment, and anger boiled and spilled over the terracings. It was made worse, of course, because, until Hateley struck, Celtic had not conceded a goal at home since the arrival of Macari at the end of October and the fans were beginning to believe that something good might happen this season.

After all, their team were up among the leaders and maybe, just maybe, the Premier Division Championship could belong to them. Optimism arrived at Celtic Park with Macari and perhaps it was the realisation on Saturday that recent weeks have been no more than a false dawn which snapped some temperaments.

Behaviour might have deteriorated further, had John Collins not scored at the start of the second half. His goal came from an intelligent free-kick move on the edge of Rangers' box – instigating a much more positive performance from Celtic. The second half largely belonged to them as they pushed Rangers, who probably thought the job had been done, back. Had Charlie Nicholas's long-range shot gone in instead of striking the bar, Macari's side could have gone on and rescued a point.

However, Oleg Kuznetsov, sent on to take over from Murray, who had given his all, took up where his Ukrainian countryman, Mikhailichenko, had left off, and scored a goal which subdued the rebellion. The goal also reminded us all that Kuznetsov might yet have something to offer Rangers.

Alas for Celtic, all evidence that they were on the mend again has been swept away.

Celtic (0) 2	Rangers (3) 4
Collins 2	Hateley
	Mikhailichenko 2
	Kuznetsov
Attendance	48,506

CELTIC:- BONNER, GILLESPIE, BOYD, GRANT, WDOWCZYK, MCGINLAY, BYRNE, MCSTAY, O'NEILL, NICHOLAS, COLLINS.

RANGERS:- MAXWELL, STEVENS, MURRAY, GOUGH, PRESSLEY, BROWN, STEVEN, MCCALL, DURIE, HATELEY, MIKHAILICHENKO

Saturday, 1st January, 1994

Celtic Fans Fear Action Replay of Violence

By Duncan Black

The trouble which marred the Old Firm match on New Year's Day could erupt again unless the beleaguered Celtic board quickly resolves the club's current problems, worried supporters claimed last night.

During Saturday's game at Celtic Park, which Rangers won 4-2, fighting broke out among Celtic fans, missiles were thrown at members of the board in the directors' box, and three supporters invaded the pitch, one of them running towards Rangers' goalkeeper Ally Maxwell before being removed by police officers.

The Scottish Football Association is certain to investigate, and the club is conducting its own inquiry.

Celtic chairman Kevin Kelly last night insisted that Saturday's scenes reflected supporters' dissatisfaction with what was happening on the field of play – Rangers were leading by three goals to nil at one stage, having scored twice in the first four minutes.

But many supporters believe at least part of the explanation for the trouble is a growing frustration with the board.

The chairman last night promised the club would be making an inquiry into Saturday's incidents to establish whether they could have been prevented or alleviated in any way.

He said the club would be prepared to take action against anyone who could be identified as being responsible for the trouble. Options would include banning any such supporters from the ground.

"We are taking this very seriously," said Mr Kelly. "We have had very little trouble over the years at Celtic Park, especially with Rangers games. It is disappointing that this has happened at this stage.

"We will be addressing the problem and doing something about it."

At one stage in the match, a number of missiles were thrown towards the directors' box, apparently aimed at members of the Celtic board. It is understood that one narrowly missed Rangers' chairman David Murray.

Mr Kelly said Mr Murray had later made very light of this incident. "I understand there was a confectionery packet thrown, but I think it missed him," said the Celtic chairman.

He denied suggestions that the trouble reflected supporters' frustration with the board.

But Mr Peter Rafferty, chairman of the Affiliation of Registered Celtic Supporters' Clubs, said: "I think it was a mixture of both – the scoreline at the time and the frustration over what has been happening in the past two or three years.

"It has just all boiled over. In some ways, it was a disaster waiting to happen. People were showing severe frustration at what has been happening. It is like a cancer, and it is growing and spreading."

He feared there could be more trouble. "The board should seriously reflect on its position. The frustration is not going to go away. It is getting uglier. There is more bitterness creeping in."

Mr Rafferty added: "I don't want to see anybody taking the law into their own hands and doing something stupid. We have been very proud of our good behaviour record in recent years.

"The board has to say 'enough is enough', get some talks going, and at least speak to supporters. The board has lost all the goodwill that was there. It has to reflect very quickly on what direction it is taking the club, and on the damage that is being done to the club."

The ARCSC last month decided to ballot its members on a boycott of Celtic home matches as a protest against the board. The ballot results will be announced later this month.

Mr Kelly has described the ARCSC as a breakaway group from the official Supporters' Association, but Mr Rafferty says it is a bona fide organisation representing about 12,000 supporters.

In November, the board survived a takeover challenge from a rebel consortium led by Canadian millionaire Fergus McCann and Glasgow businessman Brian Dempsey, a former Celtic director.

Last night, Mr Dempsey said of the trouble at Saturday's game: "I am really saddened that Celtic should be brought to this point." But he declined to comment further.

Strathclyde Police said 54 people had been arrested inside and outside Celtic Park during the match.

A police spokesman said that, contrary to some press reports, they had not received any complaints of assault from either Celtic or Rangers team members or other representatives.

A Roman Catholic priest was hurt at the match. Father Peter McBride, 36, last night based his sermon at St Martin of Tours church in Renton, Dumbartonshire, on religious bigotry and the need for tolerance. He pointed at a gash on his forehead, caused when he was struck by a coin after Rangers scored their third goal.

Father McBride, who is a Royal Navy chaplain based at Gosport, near Portsmouth, said: "I have been to many Old Firm games in the past, but this is the first time I have seen the ugly side of things."

Rangers 1, Celtic 1 – Saturday, 30th April, 1994

Celtic's Young Striker is One to Watch for the Future

By James Traynor

Lou Macari took Simon Donnelly off the Ibrox pitch nine minutes from the end of the 19-year-old's first Old Firm match. The striker was rewarded with a pat on the head, which seemed paltry thanks for what he had done on Saturday afternoon, when he offered further evidence that he is a player of exciting promise.

He ran across Rangers' defensive line constantly, and was always available to take possession, and then invite challenges which he often escaped. Early in the match, he took the ball on the right flank and David Robertson hurtled in to halt the Celtic player's progress. Even though solid contact was made, Donnelly was perfectly balanced to ride the tackle and move on.

It is precisely this kind of awareness which can make the difference between a good player and an exceptional one, and even this early in his career, Donnelly catches the eye.

Ideally, he would be used sparingly, but Macari is so short of players that he cannot afford to allow Donnelly time out to catch his breath or gather his thoughts. Fortunately, the end of the season is in sight and the player will be able to relax, although at this moment he probably feels as though he could go on for ever. Very often young players have to be protected from themselves and, properly advised and protected, Donnelly could become one of the finest players our game has produced in many years.

Already Gough and Dave McPherson would vouch for his ability, although it has to be said that the teenager was helped by their hesitancy. Rangers' defence was erratic and untidy, and one can only wonder what might have happened if Celtic had been more ambitious. It is doubtful if Gough and those around him will be so unsure of themselves again.

Apart from a tendency to give the ball away, they insisted on running into one another. Gough and McPherson collided in the first half, and in the second, Robertson and Stephen Pressley came together with a dull thud. These were examples of a basic lack of communication, but they summed up Rangers' afternoon. Hardly anything went right for them.

Rangers' equaliser was a strange goal indeed, and even after Alexei Mikhailichenko's shot 11 minutes from time had cannoned off Mark McNally, the ball seemed to hang in the air for a moment which must have passed like an eternity for Rangers fans. Eventually, it looped over Pat Bonner and into the net.

Until then, however, Rangers had been toiling to break down a Celtic side which looked likely to get away from Ibrox with a victory which would have given great delight to the thousands of their fans who were denied access to the final Old Firm match of the season because of the ban imposed by Rangers' chairman, David Murray.

Celtic had taken the lead in 29 minutes and the goal was a thing of wonder. John Collins, captain in the absence of the injured Paul McStay, stepped forward to take a free kick 25 yards out, and his powerful shot curled over a densely populated defensive wall and into the top right-hand corner.

Like Donnelly, 24-year-old Scott was making his Old Firm debut because Ally Maxwell had hurt his back, and collecting the ball from the net was not what the newcomer had planned after having been told on Saturday morning that he would be in goal. However, he reacted well enough to the pressures created by this particular fixture as did other Old Firm freshmen, Celtic's Barry Smith, Lee Martin, and Willie Falconer, although all three were booked.

So, too, were Bonner and Rangers' Gordon Durie, but while the match was frenetic, it was not rough or nasty. In fact, there were times in the match when it looked as though many of Rangers' players simply wanted it all to end. They were leaden-footed and lacked the guile to break through Celtic's defences.

In midfield, John Collins had a more productive time than anyone in blue, and behind him Tony Mowbray played exceptionally well, but then he always rises to the challenge when the opposition resort to the basic tactic of lobbing high balls forward. Again, Mowbray's desire to play on despite his wife's illness had to be admired, and neither Mark Hateley nor Ally McCoist was able to trouble him too much.

Celtic, who were no more than a makeshift eleven because of injury problems, left Ibrox feeling they had won at least a moral victory, and pleased that they had delayed Rangers' progress towards the Premier Division Championship. Of much greater significance is the point, which could help Celtic in their quest to secure a place in next season's UEFA Cup.

Rangers (0) 1	Celtic (1) 1
Mikhailichenko	Collins

RANGERS:- SCOTT, MCCALL, ROBERTSON, GOUGH, MCPHERSON, PRESSLEY, STEVEN, I. FERGUSON, MCCOIST, D. FERGUSON, DURIE.

CELTIC:- BROWN, SMITH, MARTIN, GRANT, MOWBRAY, MCNALLY, WDOWCZYK, MCGINLAY, DONNELLY, FALCONER, CREANEY.

Rangers 0, Celtic 2 – Saturday, 27th August, 1994

Celtic Again Expose the Deficiencies in Rangers' Defence and Midfield

By James Traynor

How quickly they forget. It was only a few months ago that Rangers supporters were hailing the players as heroes. "Championees", I think was how they addressed their team.

Another Premier Division Championship – the sixth in succession – had been won, and all was well in their blue heaven. Now, three weeks into another campaign, Rangers fans have only derision for the players.

Abject failure in Europe, followed quickly by an appalling performance against Celtic, was too much. On Saturday the Ibrox crowd rose from their seats in protest.

They criticised the players, howled at Walter Smith, and one fan stormed towards the directors' box to make sure the chairman, David Murray, knew of his disgust.

Changed days. Dark days. And dangerous times, too, for many of Rangers' players, as well as Smith.

The chances are that the manager will come through the next few months, which will seriously challenge his own abilities and resolve, but in order for him to remain secure, some of his players will have to be discarded. This is one of football's inevitabilities. Besides, Smith has given some players more chances than they were entitled to expect.

After AEK Athens had destroyed Rangers' defence over two legs of a European Cup tie, Celtic went to Ibrox with their fans back in the Broomloan Stand, and they also pulled Smith's team out of shape. In fact, the 2-0 scoreline flatters Rangers.

Their defence is a cause for great concern. Always there is about it a hesitancy which was not evident two years ago, when Rangers enjoyed a Champions' League run, and no matter who Smith plays, the problem remains. He has tried various players in various positions, but the defence is full of holes, and it is not Dave McPherson's fault.

The central defender/full back has long been the fall-guy at Ibrox. If the bath water is too cold he gets the blame, if it rains it's his fault, and in the dressing room players glare at him when their shoe-laces snap.

Even when McPherson is sitting on the bench or in the stand he is to blame for poor defensive performances, but Rangers will have to look much deeper for the answers to their problems. They are erratic no matter who plays in defence, and it appears now that the captain, Richard Gough, is no longer commanding his forces.

Gough spends much of his time looking to see where his team-mates are and trying to pull them back into position. He also appears to be having severe difficulty in forming a solid partnership with Basile Boli, all of which is making him nervous and hesitant.

Another serious Rangers deficiency was also highlighted by Celtic, who ran the midfield with Paul McStay, John Collins, Peter Grant, and Pat McGinlay all enjoying productive afternoons.

Smith's greatest concern as he picks through the wreckage of an extremely costly week must be the lack of flair in his midfield. Without Trevor Steven, who is injured, there is no playmaker, no decent level of creativity.

Ian Ferguson works hard and tries to help his defence and also support attacks, but he does not concentrate enough on playing passes. Much of his work is done in too deep a position, whereas he might be better employed nearer the opposition's area, where his power of shot could be brought into play more often.

In the past Stuart McCall has been one of the most influential figures in the midfield, but while he is still running and trying to tackle, he is not as productive. Both McCall and Ferguson need people around them who can take the ball and use it intelligently, but there is no-one of that nature, although Ian Durrant could yet step forward and accept the responsibility.

Celtic, the team we had all forsaken, had no such problems. They looked vibrant and positive. They believed.

Tommy Burns, who was at Ibrox for the first time as manager of Celtic, has restored confidence among the players, and if they can maintain Saturday's form, they will be serious contenders for the League title.

It was especially pleasing to see McStay and Collins, whose games suffered during the bad old days of boardroom turmoil, play as we know they can. Some of their passes and runs were of the highest quality, and it was fitting that each should score a goal.

Collins claimed his from a free kick 25 yards from goal with only seconds of the first half remaining. His shot curled around the defensive wall and caught Andy Goram stranded.

The second goal was also stunning. Cutting inside from the right, Grant supplied McStay and he ran across the defence before hitting a low shot. The ball beat Goram, hit the base of his right-hand post, and bounced into the net.

Rangers (0) 0	Celtic (1) 2
	Collins
	McStay

RANGERS:- GORAM, MCCALL, PRESSLEY, GOUGH, BOLI, MCPHERSON, DURRANT, I. FERGUSON, DURIE, HATELEY, LAUDRUP. SUBSTITUTES – D. FERGUSON, MOORE.

CELTIC:- MARSHALL, GRANT, BOYD, MCNALLY, MOWBRAY, MCGINLAY, GALLOWAY, MCSTAY, DONNELLY, WALKER, COLLINS. SUBSTITUTES – NICHOLAS AND O'NEIL.

Mark Hateley scores the only goal in the 1993 League Cup Semi-final.

Alexei Mikhailitchenko and Gary Gillespie have a few words to say as the action hots up during the match.

It's Byrne's night for Celtic as the striker equalises in the 1995 Ne'er Day game.

Pierre Van Hooydonk heads past Craig Moore.

Celtic 1, Rangers 3 – Sunday, 30th October, 1994

Rangers' Depth the Telling Factor. Laudrup and Hateley make the Difference

By James Traynor

The second Old Firm match of the season yesterday strengthened several beliefs, but two in particular. Rangers remain the most dominant force in Scotland and Celtic, despite their success in reaching the Coca-Cola Cup final, will require more than talents currently at the manager's disposal if genuine success is to be gained.

Both Rangers and Celtic had to deal with the contest without key players because of injury, but the Ibrox side were able to overcome their difficulties in a much more flamboyant fashion than their opponents, who had no-one like Brian Laudrup or Mark Hateley.

Then again, few managers can call on such special players, but there was a difference also in the level of performance among even the artisans. Until Celtic eventually stepped up the level of their performance, Rangers appeared slightly the more industrious and the hungrier of the two sides.

For long periods in midfield Celtic couldn't cope with the loss of Peter Grant, who was injured, while the industry of Stuart McCall and the running and passing of Charlie Miller were significant in giving a much-maligned Rangers team the advantage.

Rangers had about them a determined air and with Hateley, who scored twice, and Laudrup, scorer of their third goal, it was all too much for Celtic, who had to field players who were not fully fit.

Paul McStay didn't impose himself, but he has been struggling to shake off an injury, and, with John Collins troubled by Fraser Wishart, Celtic's midfield was unable to function efficiently enough. Again, however, it was shown that Celtic still lack a midfield force who can take control of a match. Celtic were beaten 3-1, falling six points behind Rangers, who are still better equipped to deal with injuries and suspensions than any other club.

If anyone on Celtic's board had thought Tommy Burns had the players to go the distance in the Premier Division and win the Championship, they must think again. Burns is short of the raw materials and when he seeks finance to improve his lot, the directors must provide.

"Yes, we did have one or two players not fully fit, but they had to play because we are short of numbers," Burns said after the game. "That's something we will have to look at."

Burns admitted that Laudrup had caused his players various problems, and added: "It's difficult to put someone like him out of the game totally, but there were some good things for us to look at. Again, we saw that Brian O'Neil can play at the centre of the defence, and if Andy Walker's header had gone in, who knows what might have happened. We're not ready to stick our heads in the oven."

Even though O'Neil and Mark McNally continue to form what could eventually be a solid, central defensive partnership, Burns must have been at least slightly envious of his opposite number, Walter Smith, who purchased a player Celtic had wanted. Rangers offered more for Alan McLaren, however, and he played extremely well in blue yesterday.

His was an impressive Old Firm debut, and Rangers' attempt to win their seventh successive Championship will be strengthened greatly when the captain, Richard Gough, recovers from injury and slots back into the defence. Even so, Smith was delighted with the way his defenders performed, especially since the back line was a new one.

"McLaren, Basile Boli, and Wishart hardly knew one another, but they played well," he said. "I saw that Wishart was saying he would probably be on the dole at the end of the season, but he might just find himself in employment for a while yet."

Although back on top of the Division, Smith was unwilling to say that Rangers would go on and win the title because he believes they still lack the consistency required. "We have also lacked the quality of performance I want, but perhaps with us being back on top, the other sides will have to remember that they, too, will need to be more consistent."

Celtic 1	Rangers 3
Byrne	Hateley 2
	Laudrup

CELTIC:- MARSHALL, SMITH, MCNALLY, O'NEIL, BOYD, BYRNE, MCSTAY, O'DONNELL, COLLINS, DONNELLY, WALKER. SUBSTITUTES - NICHOLAS, FALCONER, BONNER.

RANGERS:- GORAM, WISHART, MCLAREN, BOLI, ROBERTSON, MURRAY, MCCALL, MILLER, HUISTRA, HATELEY, LAUDRUP. SUBSTITUTES - MCCOIST, HAGEN, SCOTT.

Rangers 1, Celtic 1 – Wednesday, 4th January, 1995
Celtic make a point on Byrne's night

By James Traynor

Another step towards a seventh successive Premier Division Championship was taken by Rangers last night, but other than that, the Ibrox side had little about which to celebrate. Much was expected of them and, frankly, they failed to deliver while Celtic, patched up and fresh-faced in various positions, stole the show in the second half.

With a shade more good fortune, Tommy Burns' side would have scored more than once, but while a second goal would have given them three points, it might also have taken the shine off Paul Byrne's second-half strike, which was quite stunning.

The Irishman, who scored in his last first team appearance, also against Rangers at Hampden back in October, equalised the goal scored in the first half by Ian Ferguson – his first of the season – who probably believed his team-mates would go on and secure maximum points. But Celtic had other ideas. They resumed with greater zest and skill, and as the second half progressed they grew in confidence.

One Rangers fan in the back of the main stand couldn't stand the pressure, and in his anxiety to shout at his team, he let go of his teeth. His wallies ended up about three rows in front.

Celtic's fans held on to their teeth and their credibility, and were, in fact, the happier of the two sets of supporters. They had probably arrived at Ibrox expecting another defeat, but left for home much more confident about what Burns is trying to achieve.

However, Ferguson's goal was the only notable event of the first half, in which Brian Laudrup played only on the fringes. It was as though he kept looking in and deciding against taking part in what he saw going on.

Celtic's problems were evident as they lined up with Stuart Gray in a defence which also had Tommy Boyd in the centre. Mike Galloway, who had not featured in the first team for a month, was at right full back.

Also Byrne was in, and the tiny figure of Brian McLaughlin was there, but could barely be seen on Celtic's left flank. Even though they were unfamiliar in appearance, Celtic didn't waste any time in introducing themselves to Rangers, and in particular clattering into Gordon Durie and David Robertson.

However, Laudrup demonstrated he can pass defenders almost as though he has a divine right to do so, and after he had skipped away from Galloway, he tried to chip Pat Bonner from an acute angle. The ball sailed narrowly wide, perhaps a reminder that the Dane is, after all, a mortal.

Laudrup should have found the net in 25 minutes, though, after Durie's pass had been deflected by O'Neil, but he slid the ball wide of Bonner's right-hand post.

The keeper was exposed again in 38 minutes when McCall's high ball dropped just inside Celtic's box, and

Miller managed to jab out a leg and touch the ball on. Gray seemed to hesitate as the ball flew to the right of Bonner's goal, but Ferguson was alert and his shot was low and true.

A silence fell over Celtic's supporters, and just before half time when McLaughlin hit his shot from the edge of Rangers' penalty area over the bar and high into the Copland Road stand, their hearts sank. The Ibrox regulars were in full voice, anticipating their team would go for the jugular in the second half.

Miller, who had taken a heavy knock in the first half, didn't re-appear after the break, and Rangers resumed with Ian Durrant in midfield, yet another example of their strength in depth.

Still, it was Celtic who made the running with Phil O'Donnell, a surprising inclusion in their side since he had been labouring because of injury, being denied only by the speed of Robertson, who managed to block a shot after the Celtic player had run through a sparsely populated Rangers defence.

A few minutes later O'Donnell tried again, this time with a header, but the ball carried too far and dropped on to the roof of Colin Scott's net.

Celtic were growing in confidence and pinning Rangers in their own territory, where they were behaving in a most erratic manner, with the ball being swiped at wildly. It was inevitable that Celtic would take advantage, and they did in 59 minutes.

John Collins collected the ball on Celtic's left and saw Byrne arriving at speed towards the far post. Collins' ball was delivered with stunning accuracy, and Byrne's finishing shot from just inside the box was equally brilliant.

Celtic's midfield players were enjoying the freedom, but just when it looked as though they would engineer a second breakthrough, Laudrup burst forward.

The Dane caught Celtic's defence short and picked out Durie running to his left. The ball was played perfectly, but Durie shot straight at Bonner.

At the other end Andy Walker had a go, but knocked the ball into the side netting.

In the closing minutes Rangers almost stole the points when Laudrup weaved his way into the box, but Bonner denied him and also Durrant, who tried to score from the rebound.

Rangers (1) 1	Celtic (0) 1
Ferguson	Byrne

RANGERS:– SCOTT, MCCALL, ROBERTSON, GOUGH, MCLAREN, BOLI, HUISTRA, FERGUSON, DURIE, MILLER, LAUDRUP. SUBSTITUTES – BROWN, DURRANT, THOMSON.

CELTIC:– BONNER, BOYD, GRAY, O'NEIL, GALLOWAY, O'DONNELL, BYRNE, MCSTAY, MCLAUGHLIN, WALKER, COLLINS. SUBSTITUTES – NICHOLAS, HAY, MARSHALL.

Celtic 1, Rangers 3 – Sunday, 30th April, 1995

Rangers' Cup Floweth Over

Rangers secured victory for the fourth year in a row over old rivals Celtic in the Glasgow Cup after having to come from behind, watched by a crowd of 5500.

Winger Steven Boyack had a hand in all three goals and must be considered a star of the future, while first-team regular Craig Moore, whose equaliser brought Rangers level, put his experience to good use in central defence.

It was Celtic who struck first in 27 minutes with a stunning goal from Michael Craig. After Moore had fouled Paul Dalglish, son of Kenny, Craig stepped up and rocketed home the free kick from 25 yards.

Rangers, who had a strong penalty claim turned down when Lee Dair tumbled in the box, struck back in firsthalf injury time, Boyack curling a free kick on to the head of Moore, who despatched it home in great style.

With 17 minutes left, Boyack secured victory when he set up two goals in less than a minute.

First his driving run and pass released Paul McShane, who cut inside his marker before firing home. Less than 60 seconds later he skipped to the bye-line, where his driven cross was turned home by Dair.

Celtic centre half Jim Slaven was sent off in the last minute and promising striker Marc Anthony had three bones in his foot broken, to round off a miserable afternoon for the Parkhead team.

Glasgow Cup Final

Celtic (1) 1	Rangers (1) 3
Craig	Moore
	McShane
	Dair

CELTIC:– MCCONDICHIE, MCCRINDLE, ADAMS, KELLY, SLAVEN, WILSON, WALKER, CARBERRY, CRAIG, ANTHONY, COUGHLIN. SUBSTITUTES – MORRISON, CORR, DALGLISH.

RANGERS:– RAE, SHIELDS, KERR, WILSON, MOORE, NICOLSON, MCSHANE, MCGINTY, MCKNIGHT, DAIR, BOYACK. SUBSTITUTES – FERGUSON, CALDWELL, BROWN.

Brian Laudrup scores in Rangers 3-1 victory in October 1994.

Celtic 3, Rangers 0 – Saturday, 6th May, 1995

Keeper's Red Card is Final Straw for Rangers. Celtic Shine Brightly as Champions Lack Lustre

By James Traynor

Clearly, with their manager Walter Smith out of town most of last week in pursuit of Paul Gascoigne, Rangers' players obviously thought holiday time had arrived and, in fact, they played like tourists in an environment for the first time as they wandered around Hampden Park while Celtic ran away with the points.

Of course, with a seventh consecutive Championship safely back in the Ibrox trophy room, Rangers had no real need of more points, but pride alone should have stirred them to greater effort than they produced yesterday.

Billy Thomson didn't so much give up as capitulate when he was dismissed, after having fouled Brian McLaughlin nine minutes from time. The Celtic winger was about to round the keeper when he was hauled down, leaving referee Les Mottram with only one choice.

Celtic, of course, have much to play for yet and their comfortable triumph in the season's final Old Firm game will strengthen their confidence for the Tennents Scottish Cup Final against Airdrie on May 27, when the atmosphere at Hampden will be much more charged than it was yesterday.

Only 31,025 supporters showed up, which suggested Rangers' fans had also decided the season was over, while a number of Celtic's followers will be conserving energies and money for the Cup Final.

Those who stayed away missed little in the first half with Celtic reserving their best for the second period, during which they scored all of their goals, with Pierre van Hooydonk leading the way. His goal was his seventh for Celtic and he was especially pleased, since he was making his Old Firm debut.

The two other goals came courtesy of an own goal by Craig Moore and a 25-yard free kick from Rudi Vata.

It was a pass from McStay early in the match which first brought Celtic's followers to their feet, and his precise delivery found Simon Donnelly, who touched shoulders with Alan McLaren. The Rangers man went down, leaving the young striker clear inside the box. However, his shot was poor and Thomson had only to drop down and smother the ball.

Pat Bonner's task in grasping Mark Hateley's swerving shot from just outside the penalty box was equally straightforward, but the ease with which the striker had escaped Brian O'Neil was alarming.

Collins might have found the net first after he had intercepted a poorly directed pass by Alex Cleland, but the midfield player, who ran unchallenged to the edge of the box, shot a yard wide.

John Brown, who body-checked McLaughlin and was booked, injured himself in the process and hobbled off, with Neil Murray pressed into action after 27 minutes.

O'Neil became the second player booked after he had tripped Laudrup and then the Dane had to suffer a degree of ridicule after he had tried a back-heel pass which went wrong. Celtic's fans jeered him roundly, but he took it all in good humour, bowing to them almost apologetically. Such banter is unusual in Old Firm matches, but it added to the peculiarity of the atmosphere of this one.

However, it became much more like the real thing five minutes into the second half when Celtic scored a splendid goal, engineered by the diminutive McLaughlin, who had darted through Rangers' defence on the left. The winger looked up and rolled the ball across the edge of the 18-yard line to van Hooydonk, who beat Thomson to his right with a low shot.

Suddenly Celtic's fans were ecstatic, and 10 minutes later they were lifted to even greater heights of joy when Craig Moore hooked the ball into his own net. Simon Donnelly had been released on the right by McStay and when his cross curled into Rangers' box, the unfortunate full back, whose balance was all wrong, tried to clear but turned the ball into Thomson's net.

Five minutes later Donnelly limped off and Willie Falconer took over, and soon afterwards Rangers took off Ian Ferguson and sent on Mikhailichenko. Celtic's second substitution was made 15 minutes from the end when Phil O'Donnell relieved van Hooydonk.

Rangers may have felt two goals was to be the extent of their punishment, but Rudi Vata added to the misery by scoring from a direct free kick 25 yards from goal, nine minutes from the end. Cleland had handled the ball and Vata surprised everyone, including himself, by beating Thomson with a low shot which crept in low at the keeper's left-hand post.

Thomson was probably relieved when the referee sent him off for his foul on McLaughlin.

Celtic (0) 3	Rangers (0) 0
Hooydonk	
Moore (o.g.)	
Vata	
(at Hampden Park)	
Attendance	31,025

CELTIC:- BONNER, BOYD, MCKINLAY, VATA, O'NEIL, GRANT, MCLAUGHLIN, MCSTAY, DONNELLY, HOOYDONK, COLLINS. SUBSTITUTES – FALCONER, O'DONNELL.

RANGERS:- THOMSON, MOORE, CLELAND, BOLI, MCLAREN, BROWN, STEVEN, FERGUSON, DURRANT, HATELEY, LAUDRUP. SUBSTITUTES – MURRAY, MIKHAILICHENKO.

Old Firm League Champions

1892-93	Celtic
1893-94	Celtic
1895-96	Celtic
1897-98	Celtic
1898-99	Rangers
1899-1900	Rangers
1900-01	Rangers
1901-02	Rangers
1904-05	Celtic
1905-06	Celtic
1906-07	Celtic
1907-08	Celtic
1908-09	Celtic
1909-10	Celtic
1910-11	Rangers
1911-12	Rangers
1912-13	Rangers
1913-14	Celtic
1914-15	Celtic
1915-16	Celtic
1916-17	Celtic
1917-18	Rangers
1918-19	Celtic
1919-20	Rangers
1920-21	Rangers
1921-22	Celtic
1922-23	Rangers
1923-24	Rangers
1924-25	Rangers
1925-26	Celtic
1926-27	Rangers
1927-28	Rangers
1929-30	Rangers
1930-31	Rangers
1931-32	Rangers
1933-34	Rangers
1934-35	Rangers
1935-36	Celtic
1936-37	Rangers
1937-38	Celtic
1938-39	Rangers

[League competition suspended]		
1946-47	Rangers	[Celtic 7th]
1948-49	Rangers	[Celtic 12th]
1949-50	Rangers	[Celtic 5th]
1952-53	Rangers	[Celtic 8th]
1953-54	Celtic	[Rangers 4th]
1955-56	Rangers	[Celtic 5th]
1956-57	Rangers	[Celtic 5th]
1958-59	Rangers	[Celtic 3rd]
1960-61	Rangers	[Celtic 4th]
1962-63	Rangers	[Celtic 4th]
1963-64	Rangers	[Celtic 3rd]
1965-66	Celtic	[Rangers 2nd]
1966-67	Celtic	[Rangers 2nd]
1967-68	Celtic	[Rangers 2nd]
1968-69	Celtic	[Rangers 2nd]
1969-70	Celtic	[Rangers 2nd]
1970-71	Celtic	[Rangers 4th]
1971-72	Celtic	[Rangers 3rd]
1972-73	Celtic	[Rangers 2nd]
1973-74	Celtic	[Rangers 3rd]
1974-75	Rangers	[Celtic 3rd]
[Premier League opens]		
1975-76	Rangers	[Celtic 2nd]
1976-77	Celtic	[Rangers 2nd]
1977-78	Rangers	[Celtic 5th]
1978-79	Celtic	[Rangers 2nd]
1980-81	Celtic	[Rangers 3rd]
1981-82	Celtic	[Rangers 3rd]
1985-86	Celtic	[Rangers 5th]
1986-87	Rangers	[Celtic 2nd]
1987-88	Celtic	[Rangers 3rd]
1988-89	Rangers	[Celtic 3rd]
1989-90	Rangers	[Celtic 5th]
1990-91	Rangers	[Celtic 3rd]
1991-92	Rangers	[Celtic 3rd]
1992-93	Rangers	[Celtic 3rd]
1993-94	Rangers	[Celtic 4th]
1994-95	Rangers	[Celtic 4th]

Old Firm Appearances in the Scottish Cup Final

1876-77	Vale of Leven 3, Rangers 2		1948-49	Rangers 4, Clyde 1
1878-79	Vale of Leven 1, Rangers 1		1949-50	Rangers 3, East Fife 0
1888-89	Third Lanark 2 ,Celtic 1		1950-51	Celtic 1, Motherwell 0
1891-92	Celtic 5, Queens Park 1		1952-53	Motherwell 4, Dundee 0
1892-93	Queens Park 2, Celtic 1		1953-54	Celtic 2, Aberdeen 1
1893-94	Rangers 3, Celtic 1		1954-55	Clyde 1, Celtic 0
1896-97	Rangers 5, Dumbarton 1		1955-56	Hearts 3, Celtic 1
1897-98	Rangers 2, Kilmarnock 0		1959-60	Rangers 2, Dumbarton 0
1898-99	Celtic 2, Rangers 0		1960-61	Dunfermline Athletic 2, Celtic 0
1899-1900	Celtic 4, Queens Park 3		1961-62	Rangers 2, St Mirren 0
1900-01	Hearts 4, Celtic 3		1962-63	Rangers 3, Celtic 0
1901-02	Hibernian 1, Celtic 0		1963-64	Rangers 3, Dundee 1
1902-03	Rangers 2, Hearts 0		1964-65	Celtic 3, Dunfermline Athletic 2
1903-04	Celtic 3, Rangers 2		1965-66	Rangers 1, Celtic 0
1904-05	Third Lanark 3, Rangers 1		1966-67	Celtic 2, Aberdeen 0
1906-07	Celtic 3, Hearts 1		1968-69	Celtic 4, Rangers 0
1907-08	Celtic 5, St Mirren 1		1969-70	Aberdeen 3, Celtic 1
1908-09	Celtic 1, Rangers 1		1970-71	Celtic 2, Rangers 1
	[Declared a friendly because of weather]		1971-72	Celtic 6, Hibernian 1
1910-11	Celtic 2, Hamilton Academicals 0		1972-73	Rangers 2, Celtic 1
1911-12	Celtic 2, Clyde 0		1973-74	Celtic 3, Dundee United 0
1913-14	Celtic 4, Hibernian 1		1974-75	Celtic 3, Airdrie 1
1920-21	Partick Thistle 1, Rangers 0		1975-76	Rangers 3, Hearts 1
1921-22	Morton 1, Rangers 0		1976-77	Celtic 1, Hearts 0
1922-23	Celtic 1, Hibernian 0		1977-78	Rangers 2, Aberdeen 1
1924-25	Celtic 2, Dundee 1		1978-79	Rangers 3, Hibernian 2
1925-26	St Mirren 2, Celtic 0		1979-80	Celtic 1, Rangers 0
1926-27	Celtic 3, East Fife 1		1980-81	Rangers 4, Dundee United 1
1927-28	Rangers 4, Celtic 0		1981-82	Aberdeen 4, Rangers 1
1928-29	Kilmarnock 2, Rangers 0		1982-83	Aberdeen 1, Rangers 0
1929-30	Rangers 2, Partick Thistle 1		1983-84	Aberdeen 2, Celtic 1
1930-31	Celtic 4, Motherwell 2		1984-85	Celtic 2, Dundee United 1
1931-32	Rangers 3, Kilmarnock 0		1987-88	Celtic 2, Dundee United 1
1932-33	Celtic 1, Motherwell 1		1988-89	Celtic 1, Rangers 0
1933-34	Rangers 5, St Mirren 0		1989-90	Aberdeen 0, Celtic 0
1934-35	Rangers 2, Hamilton Academicals 1			[Aberdeen won 9-8 on penalty kicks]
1935-36	Rangers 1, Third Lanark 0		1991-92	Rangers 2, Airdrie 1
1936-37	Celtic 2, Aberdeen 1		1992-93	Rangers 2, Aberdeen 1
1947-48	Rangers 1, Morton 1		1994-95	Celtic 1, Airdrie 0

Old Firm Appearances in the Scottish League Cup Final

1946-47	Rangers 4, Aberdeen 0		1975-76	Rangers 1, Celtic 0
1948-49	Rangers 2, Raith Rovers 0		1976-77	Aberdeen 2, Celtic 1
1951-52	Dundee 3, Rangers 2		1977-78	Rangers 2, Celtic 1
1956-57	Celtic 3, Partick Thistle 0		1978-79	Rangers 2, Aberdeen 1
1957-58	Celtic 7, Rangers 1		1981-82	Rangers 2, Dundee United 1
1960-61	Rangers 2, Kilmarnock 0		1982-83	Celtic 2, Rangers 1
1961-62	Rangers 3, Hearts 1		1983-84	Rangers 3, Celtic 2
1963-64	Rangers 5, Morton 0		1984-85	Rangers 1 Dundee United 0
1964-65	Rangers 2, Celtic 1		1986-87	Rangers 2, Celtic 1
1965-66	Celtic 2, Rangers 1		1987-88	Rangers 3, Aberdeen 3
1966-67	Celtic 1, Rangers 0			[Rangers won 5-3 on penalty kicks]
1967-68	Celtic 5, Dundee 3		1988-89	Rangers 3, Aberdeen 2
1968-69	Celtic 6, Hibernian 2		1989-90	Aberdeen 2, Rangers 1
1969-70	Celtic 1, St Johnstone 0		1990-91	Rangers 2, Celtic 1
1970-71	Rangers 1, Celtic 0		1992-93	Rangers 2, Aberdeen 1
1971-72	Partick Thistle 4, Celtic 1		1993-94	Rangers 2, Hibernian 1
1972-73	Hibernian 2, Celtic 1		1994-95	Raith Rovers 2, Celtic 2
1973-74	Dundee 1, Celtic 0			[Raith Rovers won 6-5 on penalty kicks]
1974-75	Celtic 6, Hibernian 3			

Old Firm Player of the Year Awards

[Scottish Football Writers' Association Award]

Billy McNeill	(Celtic)	1965
John Greig	(Rangers)	1966
Ronnie Simpson	(Celtic)	1967
Bobby Murdoch	(Celtic)	1969
Dave Smith	(Rangers)	1972
George Connelly	(Celtic)	1973
Sandy Jardine	(Rangers)	1975
John Greig	(Rangers)	1976
Danny McGrain	(Celtic)	1977
Derek Johnstone	(Rangers)	1978
Charlie Nicholas	(Celtic)	1983
Brian McClair	(Celtic)	1987
Paul McStay	(Celtic)	1988
Richard Gough	(Rangers)	1989
Ally McCoist	(Rangers)	1992
Andy Goram	(Rangers)	1993
Mark Hateley	(Rangers)	1994
Brian Laudrup	(Rangers)	1995

[Scottish Professional Footballers' Association Award]

Derek Johnstone	(Rangers)	1977/78
Davie Provan	(Celtic)	1979/80
Charlie Nicholas	(Celtic)	1982/83
Brian McClair	(Celtic)	1986/87
Paul McStay	(Celtic)	1987/88
Paul Elliott	(Celtic)	1990/91
Ally McCoist	(Rangers)	1991/92
Andy Goram	(Rangers)	1992/93
Mark Hateley	(Rangers)	1993/94
Brian Laudrup	(Rangers)	1994/95

The Old Firm Presence in Europe

1956-57
Rangers: European Cup
1957-58
Rangers: European Cup
1959-60:
Rangers: European Cup
1960-61:
Rangers: Cup Winners' Cup
(beaten 4-1 by Fiorentina in Final on aggregate)
1961-62
Rangers: European Cup
1962-63
Rangers: Cup Winners' Cup
Celtic: Fair Cities Cup
1963-64
Rangers: European Cup
Celtic: Cup Winners' Cup
1964-65
Rangers: European Cup
Celtic: Fair Cities Cup
1965-66
Celtic: Cup Winners' Cup
1966-67
Rangers: Cup Winners' Cup (beaten 1-0 by Bayern Munich in Final)
Celtic: European Cup (beat Inter Milan 2-1 in Final)
1967-68
Rangers: Fair Cities Cup
Celtic: European Cup
1968-69
Rangers: Fair Cities Cup
Celtic: European Cup
1969-70
Rangers: Cup Winners' Cup
Celtic: European Cup (beaten 2–1 by Feyenoord in Final)
1970-71
Rangers: Fair Cities Cup
Celtic: European Cup
1971-72
Rangers: Cup Winners' Cup (beat Moscow Dynamo 3-2 in Final); European Super Cup
Celtic: European Cup
1972-73
Celtic: European Cup
1973-74
Rangers: Cup Winners' Cup
Celtic: European Cup
1974-75
Celtic: European Cup
1975-76
Rangers: European Cup
Celtic: Cup Winners' Cup

1976-77
Rangers: European Cup
Celtic: U.E.F.A. Cup [formerly Fair Cities Cup]
1977-78
Rangers: Cup Winners' Cup
Celtic: European Cup
1978-79
Rangers: European Cup
1979-80
Rangers: Cup Winners' Cup
Celtic: European Cup
1980-81
Celtic: Cup Winners' Cup
1981-82
Rangers: Cup Winners' Cup
Celtic: European Cup
1982-83
Rangers: U.E.F.A. Cup
Celtic: European Cup
1983-84
Rangers: Cup Winners' Cup
Celtic: U.E.F.A Cup
1984-85
Rangers: U.E.F.A. Cup
Celtic: Cup Winners' Cup
1985-86
Rangers: U.E.F.A. Cup
Celtic: Cup Winners' Cup
1986-87
Rangers: U.E.F.A. Cup
Celtic: European Cup
1987-88
Rangers: European Cup
Celtic: U.E.F.A Cup
1988-89
Rangers: U.E.F.A. Cup
Celtic: European Cup
1989-90
Rangers: European Cup
Celtic: Cup Winners' Cup
1990-91
Rangers: European Cup
1991-92
Rangers: European Cup
Celtic: U.E.F.A Cup
1992-93
Rangers: European Cup
Celtic: U.E.F.A Cup
1993-94
Rangers: European Cup
Celtic: U.E.F.A Cup
1994-95
Rangers: European Cup